The Handbook of Equity Market Anomalies

The Handbook of Equity Market Anomalies

Translating Market Inefficiencies into Effective Investment Strategies

Edited by

LEONARD ZACKS

WILEY

John Wiley & Sons, Inc.

Published by John Wiley & Sons, Inc., Hoboken, New Jersey.
Published simultaneously in Canada.

For general information on our other products and services or for technical support, please contact our Customer Care Department within the United States at (800) 762-2974, outside the United States at (317) 572-3993 or fax (317) 572-4002.

Wiley also publishes its books in a variety of electronic formats. Some content that appears in print may not be available in electronic books. For more information about Wiley products, visit our web site at www.wiley.com.

Library of Congress Cataloging-in-Publication Data:

Zacks, Len.
   The handbook of equity market anomalies: translating market inefficiencies into effective investment strategies / Len Zacks.
      p. cm.
   Includes bibliographical references and index.
   ISBN 978-0-470-90590-6 (cloth); ISBN 978-1-118-12776-6 (ebk);
   ISBN 978-1-118-12775-9 (ebk); ISBN 978-1-118-12774-2 (ebk)
   1. Investment analysis–Handbooks, manuals, etc.   2. Stocks–Handbooks, manuals, etc.   3. Portfolio management–Handbooks, manuals, etc.   I. Title.
   HG4529.Z33 2011
   332.63′22–dc22

                          2011015863

Printed in the United States of America

10 9 8 7 6 5 4 3 2 1

Contents

Preface

In the aftermath of the global financial meltdown of 2008, the accuracy of the quant models of Collateralized Debt Obligations (CDOs) was called into question and many of the quants who created these models and worked for the major banks were downsized. At the same time, another type of quant model, the multifactor equity model, and its creators were thriving within the equity management departments at hundreds of buy-side firms and hedge funds.

The basis of the multifactor models is the equity market anomaly research carried out and published by professors of finance and accounting at graduate schools of business throughout the world over the past 20 years. Since 2000, the number of anomaly related academic papers has grown so quickly that it is now almost impossible for any one person to keep up with the full scope of this research. In parallel with this explosion of anomaly research and its use by professional investors, individual investors also began to create their own multifactor quant models to manage their own portfolios.

Consequently, I felt that there was a need for a single volume that summarized the academic research that is the foundation of multifactor models and provided guidance to individual investors interested in creating and using these models in their own portfolios, and so the idea for this book was born.

Although I have followed the anomaly literature for decades, I did not know quite what to expect when I began to ask academics if they were interested in writing a chapter for this book. I was quite lucky to find a number of top academics who have made significant contributions themselves to the anomaly literature and shared my interest in communicating their findings to investors. As you will see as you read the various chapters, the authors have done an exceptional job of explaining the academic research so that each chapter offers a clear understanding of the use and value of an anomaly in quant equity investing.

Readers of this book are expected to have some knowledge of the material covered in a typical MBA course on investing. The book audience includes professional investors interested in a current overview of the anomaly-related academic research and self-directed individual investors considering managing their own quant portfolios using a multifactor model based on these anomalies.

Outline of the Book

To accommodate this broad range of readers, the book begins with a chapter on financial theory, followed by nine chapters, each on a specific anomaly, and ends with a chapter that provides guidance to self-directed individual investors who want to use anomaly research in their own quant portfolios.

Chapter 1, written by Professor Mozaffar Khan, a leading theoretician from MIT and the University of Minnesota, whose research focuses on alternatives to the Fama French 3-factor risk model, defines an anomaly to be a hedge portfolio return that cannot be duplicated by a risk model. Professor Khan clearly explains the financial theory required to understand the concept of a "nonzero risk-adjusted return," which is the statistic used to identify anomalies. Chapter 1 includes an original appendix by Professor Khan that provides an excellent overview of the entire area of academic risk models.

Chapter 2 reviews the extensive research on the accrual anomaly, which has been the subject of hundreds of academic papers. This chapter, written by Professor Richard Sloan, who was the first to identify the accrual anomaly in 1996, along with coauthors, Patricia Dechow, and Natalya Khimich, all from the University of California at Berkeley, clearly explains the concept of accruals, reviews the original 1996 seminal paper on accruals, and discusses later research that further refines the accrual anomaly. The chapter also provides suggestions to individual investors interested in using the accrual anomaly in their portfolios.

Chapter 3, on analyst-related anomalies, was written by George Serafeim, an assistant professor at the Harvard Business School, whose research focus is analyst information. This chapter discusses the performance of broker recommendations and reviews the research on the information anomalies related to estimate revisions and changes in analyst recommendations.

Chapter 4, which provides an overview of the surprise or post-earnings announcement drift (PEAD) anomaly, was written by Daniel Taylor, a professor at the Wharton School of the University of Pennsylvania, whose groundbreaking analysis of trading data led to new insights that clarified the origin of the surprise anomaly. This chapter includes a good overview of the history of the anomaly, an update of performance results, and a clear discussion of the possible causes of the anomaly.

Chapter 5, written by accounting expert Professor Ian Gow, at Harvard Business School, summarizes the research on non-accrual related fundamental anomalies. The chapter provides a concise overview of the anomalies related to financial ratios, investment growth, and distress risk, and discusses the Piotroski and Mohanram stock scoring systems that can be used by individual investors to outperform value or growth indexes.

Chapter 6, written by Professors Dan Cohen, Tom Lys, and Tzachi Zach, reviews the research on stock buybacks, IPO, SEOs, and other stock purchase and stock issuance anomalies, which are referred to in general as net stock anomalies. Tom Lys, a senior professor at the Kellogg School of Business at Northwestern University, who was the first to clarify the relationship between net stock anomalies and the value anomaly, explains why these seemingly unrelated anomalies are in fact closely connected.

Chapter 7 on the insider trading anomaly was written by Ian Dogan PhD, who has managed institutional portfolios using insider data for a number of years. In it, he provides an optimistic view from a professional of the possibility of generating excess returns from insider information, in spite of the many new regulations that some feel have destroyed the opportunity offered by this data set.

Chapter 8, on the momentum anomaly, written by Professor Lee M. Dunham, at Creighton University, who has been investigating technical trading related systems for many years, provides a good overview of how technical trading evolved from a backwater to become a major theme of respected academic anomaly research.

Chapter 9, on seasonal anomalies, was written by Constantine Dzhabarov and Professor William Ziemba, professor emeritus at University of British Columbia, and perhaps the foremost academic researcher who has studied these anomalies. Professor Ziemba brings to this chapter his unique perspective as a partner in an investment firm that manages institutional assets using seasonal anomalies and provides an in-depth overview of the opportunities to earn returns using seasonal anomalies.

Chapter 10, on the value and size anomalies, was written by Professor Oleg Rytchkov, whose PhD thesis at MIT and area of research at Temple University focus on these two types of anomalies. The chapter synthesizes a great deal of research on these two subjects and concludes that value is a real anomaly but that size may not be an anomaly and discusses the basics of tactical asset allocation.

Chapter 11, written by me for the self-directed investor was the acorn from which this book grew. This chapter provides advice to investors who want to build their own multifactor-based quant investment processes. The chapter explains how the market-neutral asset class can increase the expected return of a portfolio at any level of risk, outlines anomaly-based stock scoring systems that can be used to increase the probability that a long portfolio will outperform a specific index, and discusses a number of issues that should be considered by individual investors interested in managing their own quant portfolios.

Finally an appendix at the back of the book provides readers with a top-down overview of the full scope of quant investing. The appendix discusses statistical arbitrage, high-frequency trading, and multifactor models, and outlines the extent to which multifactor models are employed today by professional investors managing hedge funds, separate accounts, and mutual funds.

Can Anyone Beat the Market?

Underlying the widespread interest in anomaly research is always the unasked question "Can anyone consistently beat the market?" Harry Roberts and then Eugene Fama, the famed fathers of the efficient market hypothesis, first formally asked this question when they classified market efficiency into three forms based on sets of information: a weak form where the history of prices cannot be used to generate positive risk adjusted returns; a semi strong form where public information cannot be used to outperform the market; and a strong form where private information cannot be used to outperform the market.

Looking back over the last few decades, one can argue that none of these forms of efficiency are correct. The growth of the hedge fund industry has shown that the market is not strongly efficient while the continued existence of anomalies described in this book and the many billions of dollars managed in the quant investment processes show that public information can be used to outperform the market and the success of statistical arbitrage proves that even historical price and volume patterns can generate positive alphas.

However, not everyone has abandoned the efficient market paradigm. Most academics and professional investors still believe that the market is very efficient. Some believe that index funds are the only rational investment choice, whereas others believe that an investor can earn higher returns but only by bearing higher risk. Your editor's position is that the market is not terribly efficient and that multifactor models based on the anomaly research will continue to produce positive risk adjusted returns.

My hope is that by organizing and summarizing the anomaly research underlying multifactor models, this book will move us one small step forward towards better understanding the extent of market efficiency.

What's on the Web Site?

This book was not written to be a stand alone reference work, but rather to form the core of an ongoing discussion of anomaly research and quant investing. Consequently a web site for the book was created at **http://hema.zacks.com** where readers can provide feedback on the book and ask questions of the authors. The site has a page dedicated to each chapter of the book, and at the bottom of each page is a live discussion group where the authors of the chapter will respond to posts from readers.

The book's bibliography was also expanded on the web site to include abstracts of and links to the papers. Readers who would like to read any of the 650 papers referenced in this book can click on the bibliography on the web site, read an abstract of the paper, and click on the link to view the full paper.

All errors in the book are mine. As you find them, please let us know by posting a comment on the web site. You may win the prize we will give to the reader who finds the most errors.

Read and enjoy. I wish you all the success in your investing.

Len Zacks, Editor
CEO, Zacks Investment Research

Acknowledgments

A book like this is a labor of love. I would like to thank the authors of each of the chapters who were kind enough to explain their areas of research for a nonacademic audience, Dan Taylor and Bill Ziemba for clarifying my understanding of a number of issues, and Kevin Li and, Jon Mensing, and the other research assistants who labored long and hard summarizing academic articles and preparing bibliographies. I also would like to thank the editors at John Wiley & Sons for keeping me on track and, most importantly, my wife for sharing her computer with me during the creation of this book.

CHAPTER 1

Conceptual Foundations of Capital Market Anomalies

Mozaffar Khan

This book describes unexpected price behavior in equity markets, termed Anomalies, that can potentially be exploited by investors to earn abnormal returns. In capital markets, an anomaly is a deviation from the prediction of the efficient markets theory. The purpose of this chapter is to provide a conceptual framework for understanding the academic research on anomalies and to evaluate whether certain anomalies can be profitably exploited. The chapter begins with a discussion of efficient markets theory, which specifies how assets (specifically stocks) are expected to be priced under a set of ideal or theoretical conditions. The discussion then moves on to anomalies, or price behavior, that is unexpected if markets are efficient. The chapter defines anomalies, discusses explanations for anomalies that have been examined in the academic literature, and concludes by weighing the evidence for these different explanations. Since anomalies yield predictable positive risk-adjusted returns, proper risk measurement is critical to the identification of anomalies. Hence, the appendix to this chapter provides a detailed review of risk measurement and expected return models.[1]

---

[1]This chapter was conceived while the author was an assistant professor at the Massachusetts Institute of Technology. He wishes to express his gratitude to the MIT Sloan School of Management and the Carlson School of the University of Minnesota for support. Also Zhaoyang Gu, Prem Jain, Leonid Kogan, Stephannie Larocque, John Douglas Lyon, Hai Lu, Thomas Lys, Stepphen Penman, Konstantin Rozanov and Pervin Shroff for valuable comments.

No specific anomaly is discussed in this chapter, because the discussion here is intended to be applicable to all anomalies. It is hoped that, at the end of this chapter, investors will have the conceptual tools necessary to evaluate and understand observed price behavior in general, and the anomalies discussed in the subsequent chapters in particular.

Efficient Markets

The efficient markets theory is usually credited to Fama (1965, 1970), and also has theoretical roots in Samuelson (1965) and Mandelbrot (1966). A market is informationally efficient if prices are, on average, correct, given the publicly available information. Prices react rapidly to new events, and, on average, correctly impound the new information. This characterizes an equilibrium in a competitive market if the following conditions, among others, hold:

- *Structural Knowledge.* Investors are assumed to have complete information about the underlying structure of the return-generating process. For example, investors know the parameters and functional form of the model that governs the stock's returns. Consider what happens when this information is not known for a given stock S. An event may change the risk or expected cash flows of S, but if there is preexisting uncertainty about the parameters of the pricing equation for S, it is difficult to revise the price so that it correctly impounds the new information.
- *Rational Information Processing.* Investors, on average, are assumed to process information in a cognitively unbiased, Bayesian fashion. They are not subject to psychological biases that cause them to over- or underreact to information. Although there may be some investors who are not rational, their trades are unlikely to be correlated, so their irrational trades essentially cancel each other out (noise trading).
- *No Limits to Arbitrage.* Even if the trades of irrational investors are correlated and result in mispricing, rational investors will quickly step in and arbitrage away the mispricing. Absent frictions, arbitrage facilitates market efficiency by quickly eliminating deviations from fundamental values. Frictions that limit arbitrage include transaction costs, short-sale constraints, a limited number of arbitrageurs combined with specialization among arbitrageurs, the absence of close substitutes for the mispriced stock, lingering heterogeneity of investor opinion about the "correct" price for the stock, and bounded investment scalability.

It is useful to keep the preceding assumptions in mind because, when they are violated, they become potential explanations for observed mispricing. A stock may be mispriced if any combination of these assumptions does not hold. The efficient markets theory is perhaps the single most pervasive organizing principle in finance. Its power lies in:

- The range of phenomena it is capable of explaining and predicting. The average stock at a random point in time is likely fairly priced. If mispricing were rampant and easily identifiable by the average investor, paid investment professionals might be obsolete. Paid investment professionals are more likely needed when mispricing has to be ferreted out of dark corners, than when mispricing exists out in the open.
- The discipline it forces on our thinking. When an ostensibly mispriced stock is identified, it forces us to understand why it is mispriced, or in other words, it forces us to ask why the mispricing signal is expected to be reliable. Investment decisions attempt to anticipate future outcomes, and these outcomes are difficult to predict absent understanding of the reasons for the mispricing.
- The guide it provides to understanding why a stock may be mispriced. This guide is the set of assumptions of the theory outlined previously. The theory then, in essence, tells us which explanations (i.e., assumptions) to explore in attempting to understand why a given stock may be mispriced.

Respect for the efficient markets theory, and an acknowledgement that it sometimes fails (i.e., that mispriced stocks can be identified), can coexist. One need not disdain the theory in the pursuit of anomalies, to which we turn next.

Identifying Anomalies in Capital Markets

Capital market anomalies are deviations from the prediction of efficient markets theory. Such anomalies manifest in predictable nonzero risk-adjusted returns (RAR). A stock with zero risk-adjusted returns provides a fair return for its risk. A stock with positive (negative) risk-adjusted returns provides a more-than-fair (less-than-fair) return for its risk. Investors would like to be long the former and short the latter.

A theory is an approximation of reality. Zero approximation errors are unheard of in practice. According to Kuhn (1962), anomalies are common and expected in every field, and they are an integral part of the routine "puzzle-solving" process of science. Scientists are reluctant to discard a broad theory or paradigm upon discovery of some instances of its falsification (i.e., significant approximation errors). To discard a paradigm, a replacement candidate that better explains at least as wide a range of phenomena is needed. This burden of competition is necessary for robust strains of theory to emerge. Therefore, subjecting anomalies to healthy skepticism should be seen as part of the normal discovery process of science in which the objective is to develop robust theories (Kuhn 1962), in our case, a robust theory of asset pricing.

There are essentially two steps in identifying anomalies. The first step is identifying a mispricing signal. An example of a mispricing and, hence, an investment signal is the magnitude of a firm's earnings surprise. Firms with extreme positive (negative) quarterly earnings surprise have predictably higher (lower) future returns, so the investment strategy is to go long (short) on stocks of firms with an extreme positive (negative) earnings surprise in order to earn positive returns. This is known as the post-earnings announcement drift (PEAD) anomaly. In subsequent chapters, a number of different mispricing signals (or anomalies) are described.

The second step is evaluating the economic significance and statistical reliability of the mispricing signal. The typical approach is to sort the cross-section of firms into, for example, deciles based on a mispricing signal. For example, firms would be sorted into deciles of earnings surprise in the PEAD strategy, with the top (bottom) decile containing firms with the highest positive (most negative) earnings surprise. The magnitude of the average risk-adjusted return, or alpha, on a portfolio that is long on stocks in one extreme decile, and short stocks in the other extreme decile, is a measure of the economic significance of the mispricing signal. The alpha is the raw return on the portfolio minus the expected return based on the risk of the portfolio.[2] A long-short portfolio is not necessarily risk-neutral, and, therefore, it is more common to examine alphas, rather than raw returns, to the long-short portfolio. Many anomalies described in the subsequent chapters typically yield alphas of about 10% per year. The costs, such as information, search, and trading costs of the strategy are also typically subtracted from the alpha in practice to arrive at an estimate of the economic significance of an implementable trading strategy based on the mispricing signal.

The statistical reliability of the mispricing signal is measured by how reliably different the trading strategy's alpha is from zero. Consider a strategy that is implemented annually and can be back-tested on 40 years of data. In this case, we would have 40 separate risk-adjusted returns, one for each year the strategy is implemented. We would expect some variation in risk-adjusted returns across the 40 years. If the variation is low relative to the mean risk-adjusted return, the strategy would be considered statistically reliable. In particular, a t-statistic with a p-value less than 5% is the typical criterion for statistical reliability of an alpha.

---

[2]Risk adjustment and expected return models are reviewed in detail in the appendix to this chapter.

Explaining Anomalies

The academic literature has pursued several potential explanations for capital markets anomalies.

- One subset of the literature explores whether the anomaly in question is real. The ostensible anomaly may be: an artifact of mismeasured risk; a result of mismeasured statistical reliability; or a result of data snooping.
- Another subset of the literature explores whether anomalies can be explained by rational structural uncertainty, whereby mispricing is a result of uncertainty about the underlying return-generating process (a violation of the first assumption of efficient markets identified in the previous section).
- A third subset of the literature explores whether investors' psychological biases are responsible for mispricing (a violation of the second assumption of efficient markets identified in the previous section).
- A fourth subset of the literature explores whether limits to arbitrage can explain the persistence of mispricing (a violation of the third assumption of efficient markets identified in the previous section).

These explanations are discussed in the following section.

Is the Anomaly Real?

A real anomaly is one that can be profitably exploited by investors to earn statistically reliable and positive risk-adjusted returns. Identifying a real anomaly, therefore, requires ensuring that the risk of the investment strategy is correctly measured (for proper risk adjustment), and that the RARs are statistically reliable and expected to persist out of sample, as discussed in the next section.

RISK MISMEASUREMENT　　The expected return on a stock is determined in theory by its risk, so if the theory holds, a stock is not expected to have predictably nonzero alphas. Alpha is the difference between the realized return and a model-implied expected return or benchmark. If the benchmark is too low (high), the alpha can appear positive (negative). This is known as the joint hypothesis problem: any test of market efficiency (the proposition that risk-adjusted returns are zero on average) is also jointly a test of the assumed equilibrium model for expected returns. Therefore, a failure of the joint hypothesis could be due to a misspecification of the expected return model, rather than to failure of market efficiency (Fama 1970). For example, a researcher may find a 5% alpha using the CAPM, but the alpha may be insignificantly different from zero when the Fama and French (1993) model is used. In the appendix to this chapter, risk measurement and expected return models are reviewed in detail.

This literature has a long tradition and continues to be fertile. Researchers develop new expected return models to better explain anomalies. Examples include Fama and French (1993), Lettau and Ludvigson (2001), Campbell and Vuolteenaho (2004), Khan (2008), and Chen, Novy-Marx, and Zhang (2010), among many others. New expected return models have demonstrated success in explaining away some anomalies. Investors are clearly better served by being cognizant of the need for proper risk measurement. If the wrong model is used, a stock considered an attractive buy (i.e., considered to be undervalued) may actually be a poor buy (it may not be undervalued).

STATISTICAL RELIABILITY   Some deviations from market efficiency have been debated on the grounds that the abnormal return is not statistically reliable if alternative statistical methods are used. Measuring long-horizon abnormal stock-return performance after corporate events, such as seasoned equity offerings and mergers, among other events, is particularly challenging. This is because of such problems as survival and selection bias, positive skewness in long-horizon returns and cross-correlation of event-firm returns, among others. Papers such as Barber and Lyon (1997), Kothari and Warner (1997), Fama (1998), Lyon, Barber, and Tsai (1999), and Mitchell and Stafford (2000) have suggested that previously reported abnormal stock returns following corporate events may not be abnormal (i.e., that the stock returns are fair compensation for risk once appropriate statistical issues are addressed). Essentially, these papers point out a statistical Type I error: The null hypothesis of zero abnormal returns is falsely rejected. In response, some authors point out a potential statistical Type II problem: The null hypothesis of zero abnormal returns after corporate events is false, but existing models and tests suffer from low statistical power to detect abnormal stock return performance (Loughran and Ritter 2000; Nekrasov, Singh, and Shroff 2010).

DATA-SNOOPING   Lo and MacKinlay (1990) reiterate the inferential hazard that results from empirically overexploring, or mining, a given dataset such as the return history of all traded stocks. This data-snooping problem is also statistical in nature, but it relates to the manner in which the community of scientists collectively discovers knowledge. In contrast, the statistical issues described in the previous paragraph relate more to one particular researcher's choice of test methodology. In a sense, data snooping is a metastatistical problem.

The problem essentially is that researchers using a dataset might find an accidental pattern in the data; that is, they find an accidental pattern, as opposed to accidentally finding a real pattern. A real pattern is one for which there exists an economic rationale or theory, and a real pattern is expected to persist out of sample. An accidental pattern should be ignored, but given the difficulty in distinguishing an accidental from a real pattern, subsequent researchers may be attracted to the unusual finding or anomaly and will select the sample to be studied based on the previous empirical finding (Lo and MacKinlay 1990). This results in a selection bias that can lead to spurious inferences (see also Leamer 1978). A number of specific anomalies have turned out in subsequent research to be more apparent than real, consistent with data-snooping biases (Schwert 2003).

In summary, a large stream of the literature has studied whether numerous specific anomalies are, in fact, anomalies or whether they are consistent with efficient markets. Several anomalies have been explained away once appropriate risk and statistical corrections are made. However, many anomalies have yet to be explained by these methods. Useful surveys of efficient market explanations for anomalies include Fama (1998), Schwert (2003), and Ross (2005).

Rational Structural Uncertainty

Efficient markets theory assumes investors have complete knowledge of the underlying statistical processes that generate returns; that is, it assumes they know the parameters of the pricing equation for each security. All investors also have homogenous opinions about these parameters. In practice, this assumption is unlikely to hold for young firms with a short history and few assets in place. Empirically, such firms are exactly the ones whose stock returns are generally considered anomalous (e.g., Fama and French 1993). Therefore, such firms may be mispriced if investors have incomplete information about valuation parameters (e.g., Merton 1987) or uncertainty about these parameters (Brav and Heaton 2002). Mispricing generated by such rational structural uncertainty can be hard to distinguish empirically from mispricing generated by behavioral or cognitive biases, since rational structural uncertainty and behavioral theories generate similar testable predictions (Brav and Heaton 2002).

It is important to note that anomalous stock returns are not necessarily due to cognitively biased investors. In this section, we take as given that a specific anomaly is real rather than apparent; that is, that the anomaly is not subject to the problems previously identified. The question is what generates the real anomaly. Rational structural uncertainty theories highlight that it is possible for investors to process information rationally, and yet to misprice stocks if they have incomplete information or uncertainty about valuation parameters.

Behavioral Finance and Limits to Arbitrage

Efficient markets theory assumes that investors process information rationally, without any cognitive biases. Behavioral finance refers to the class of theories that relax the rationality assumption and propose that the behavior of security prices is better explained by investors' behavioral or cognitive biases. Biases such as sentiment, overconfidence, biased self-attribution, conservatism, and a representativeness heuristic generate underreaction and overreaction to information, which manifests in underpricing and overpricing (DeBondt and Thaler 1985; Lee, Shleifer, and Thaler 1991; Lakonishok, Shleifer, and Vishny 1994; Barberis, Shleifer, and Vishny 1998; Daniel, Hirshleifer, and Subrahmanyam 1998; Hong and Stein 1999). Other biases, such as loss aversion (Kahneman and Tversky 1979) generate a reluctance to sell losing stocks, as documented in Odean (1998) for example.

Efficient markets theory also assumes that, even if some investors are irrational and generate mispricing, rational investors will quickly arbitrage the mispricing away. Behavioral finance, in response, highlights numerous limits to arbitrage, such as the following, which allow a wedge between fundamental and observed values to persist.

- *Transaction Costs.* Arbitrageurs evaluate profits after trading costs, so trading costs of X% can sustain mispricing of the same magnitude. In practice, trading costs for large investors are too small to explain the substantial magnitudes (10% to 30% per year) reported for some anomalies.
- *Short Sale Constraints.* These include the cost of borrowing and locating the stock from securities lenders. The direct borrowing costs are negligible (e.g., D'Avolio 2002), but locating the stock can be a substantial barrier. Another impediment is the risk that a borrowed stock may be recalled by the lender when the stock price has gone up, before the borrower has had a chance to earn a profit. Small, young, and illiquid stocks are difficult to locate, and these are the stocks for which mispricing is typically observed empirically. Short sale constraints have the potential to explain sustained overpricing but not underpricing of certain stocks.

  These constraints apply to investors who are permitted to short sell. Many large institutional investors, such as mutual funds, are barred by charter from short selling. Although this may limit the number and type of investors who can bring adverse information to the market through

short selling, it is unlikely a significant constraint, given that there are
many other large investors, such as hedge funds, which do not face
short selling restrictions.

- *Arbitrageur Presence.* Professional arbitrageurs specialize in certain
  stocks that they follow closely based on their expertise and profit opportunities. Combined with a limited numbers of arbitrageurs, this implies
  there are many stocks with limited or no arbitrageur presence.
- *Absence of Close Substitutes.* Arbitrageurs hedge their position in a mispriced stock by simultaneously taking an offsetting position in a close
  substitute. Many stocks or portfolios of securities do not have close
  substitutes, which makes arbitrage risky.
- *Lingering Differences in Investor Opinion.* Even if a stock has a per-
  fect substitute, the arbitrageur faces the risk that the mispricing does
  not correct within his investment horizon. If differences in investor
  opinion about the fundamental value of the stock linger or worsen,
  the arbitrageur may be unable to profitably close his position within
  his investment horizon. As John Maynard Keynes pithily observed, the
  market can stay irrational longer than one can stay solvent (as cited in
  Lowenstein 2001). This risk further limits arbitrage.
- *Unscalable Opportunity.* The mispriced stock may not be available in
  sufficient numbers to allow the arbitrageur to recover fixed costs. This
  is related to arbitrageur presence previously described.

Combining cognitive biases with limits to arbitrage, behavioral finance
theories have sought to explain numerous efficient markets anomalies.

Irrational behavior also motivates reaction to noninformation, as inferred from both the first and second moment of returns (average and
volatility). For example, Shiller (1981) and Roll (1988) suggest returns are
too volatile to be explained by economy-wide, industry, or firm-specific
fundamental news. Shleifer (1986), Greenwood (2005), Coval and Stafford
(2007), and Khan, Kogan, and Serafeim (2011) suggest average returns to
individual stocks change in response to uninformed demand shocks. In the
latter literature, the price movements are not driven by individual investors'
behavioral biases but, rather, by institutional constraints that lead to large
uninformed stock purchases or sales. Therefore, this evidence is not so
much for behavioral biases as it is against efficient markets, but it does rely
on limited arbitrage for the sustained mispricing.

The volume of the behavioral finance literature and the academic repu-
tation of many of its proponents suggest it is the most popular challenger to
efficient markets as an explanation for stock price behavior. Useful surveys
of behavioral explanations for anomalies can be found in Thaler (1993) and
Shleifer (2000).

Anomalies: Weighing the Evidence

The weight of the evidence in the literature both for and against efficient markets is impressive. This makes it difficult to draw unqualified conclusions about which theory best describes stock price behavior. The difficulty stems from the fact that, for many anomalies, the evidence is consistent with both rational and behavioral explanations. It is perhaps safe to say that, currently, no one theory completely describes all price behavior.[3] This need not be unduly distressing, for a few reasons. First, other fields face similar conflicts. In physics, for example, there is one theory for the very large (relativity) and a different theory for the very small (quantum mechanics). In a sense there are two theories of stock price behavior, but the challenge is to discriminate between, and predict, instances when each theory is expected to hold. Ultimately, of course, the Holy Grail, as in physics, is to develop one unified theory. Second, there is a sense of order imparted by markets that are, on average, efficient, yet a sense of hope for investors imparted by occasional deviations from efficiency. Deviations from efficiency stimulate private information search (Grossman and Stiglitz 1980) and competition among investment professionals, activities that make the market more efficient.

Fortunately there is a less controversial answer to the question of whether anomalies are real or apparent. Real anomalies exist, in the sense that they are resistant to efficient market explanations and present opportunities for abnormal profits. However, not all anomalies are real: In some cases the profits are not abnormal but are simply appropriate compensation for risk. The purpose of this book is to describe the state of the academic literature in selected anomalies. The purpose of this chapter is to provide investors and investment professionals the conceptual tools needed to discriminate between real and apparent anomalies. Hopefully, the reader is thus armed as the journey begins in the next chapter.

Appendix 1.1: Risk and Expected-Return Models

In this appendix, models of expected returns are reviewed, in which the expected return is based on the risk of the asset (or the risk in its future cash flows). Proper risk adjustment is critical in identifying anomalies because, for example, a portfolio that really has zero RARs may appear to have positive

---

[3]Another theory of price behavior besides those discussed here is proposed in Lo (2004, 2005), and is known as the Adaptive Markets Hypothesis.

RARs if an inappropriate expected return model is used. In general, risk and expected return models are important for the following reasons.

- Portfolio Selection – Value: Because the expected return, r, is an input in all valuation models, investors need an accurate assessment of risk and expected return to determine whether a stock is fairly priced or fairly valued. Investors will buy (sell) stocks that are undervalued (overvalued) by the rest of the market.
- Portfolio Selection – Risk: Investment managers need accurate portfolio risk assessments, to ensure that it meets the risk tolerance of their clients.
- Performance Evaluation: Investors need accurate portfolio risk assessments, to evaluate the performance of their investment managers. Given the risk-return trade-off, investors evaluate return performance relative to the assumed risk, or, in other words, investors care about risk-adjusted returns rather than raw returns. Consider two investment managers who both earn a 10% raw return on their respective portfolios. However, if one portfolio is riskier than the other, investors will require higher returns on the riskier portfolio. Using risk-adjusted returns to evaluate their performance would yield the correct conclusion that the manager of the less risky portfolio outperformed the manager of the riskier portfolio. Investors are expected to reward managers who produce positive risk-adjusted returns, and punish those who produce negative risk-adjusted returns.

The expected return on any asset is the sum of the risk-free rate and the asset's risk premium. The risk premium on any asset can be thought of as the price of risk multiplied by the quantity of risk. The price of risk is more precisely the required return per unit of risk, while the quantity of risk is the asset's number of units of risk. For example, the unit of risk (or the quantity of risk) could be the asset's CAPM beta,[4] and the price of risk would be the required return on a unit beta asset. The risk premium on a riskier asset, which has a beta of 2 for example, would be 2 times the price of risk. The price of risk is the same for all assets, whereas the quantity of risk varies across assets. This suggests that, to calculate expected returns, we need to start by thinking about how to measure the risk of a stock.

Investors prefer a smooth consumption stream. Stocks that smooth out their consumption stream (e.g., stocks that are negatively correlated with consumption) are less risky than stocks that amplify the volatility of their consumption stream (e.g., stocks that are highly positively correlated with

---

[4]A stock's CAPM beta is the coefficient from a regression of the stock's excess returns on the market excess return. Excess return is the return in excess of the risk-free rate.

consumption). Hence, the fundamental measure of risk is covariance with consumption. This is formally derived by setting up a utility maximization program. Solving for the first-order conditions yields a general expression for the expected return on any asset (Cochrane 2001):

$$E(r - R_f) = -R_f \text{Cov}(\text{SDF}, r) \qquad (1.1)$$

In equation (1.1), SDF is the stochastic discount factor or pricing kernel, and it is approximately equal to consumption growth. Equation (1.1) says that the expected risk premium on any asset is a function of its return covariance with the SDF. A riskless asset is one whose return is known ex ante with certainty, and since its covariance with the SDF is zero, the expected return on the riskless asset is the risk-free rate R_f. A risky asset is negatively correlated with the SDF, and, hence, has a positive risk premium. A hedge is positively correlated with the SDF, and, hence, has a negative risk premium (i.e., an expected return lower than the risk-free rate).

Equation (1.1) is not empirically estimable as is, because it tells us neither the empirical proxies to use for the SDF nor the functional form of the relation between the SDF and these proxies. This task is left to economic models such as the capital asset pricing model (CAPM), the consumption-based capital asset pricing model (CCAPM), the intertemporal capital asset pricing model (ICAPM), and others. These models tell us where the SDF comes from (i.e., what risk factors proxy for the SDF), and also propose a linear relation between the SDF and these risk factors. Hence, expected return models such as the CAPM, ICAPM, APT, Fama-French, and others differ basically in terms of the number and identity of risk factors they propose.

Given a set of risk factors, and a linear relation between the SDF and these risk factors, equation (1.1) is rewritten in most academic work as:

$$E(r - R_f) = \sum (\beta_j \lambda_j) \qquad (1.2)$$

In equation (1.2), j is the number of risk factors, β_j is the beta of a given stock with respect to the jth risk factor, and λ_j is the price of the jth risk factor (i.e., the expected risk premium on a stock with $\beta_j = 1$). Equation (1.2) is one representation of equation (1.1). The Mean-Variance frontier is another representation of the same.[5] In other words, equations (1.1) and (1.2) and the Mean-Variance frontier are equivalent. This is useful to know because it emphasizes the common root of all asset pricing models: These are not different models, but simply different representations of a

---

[5]Portfolios on the upper part of the Mean-Variance frontier are negatively correlated with the SDF, whereas portfolios on the lower frontier are positively correlated with the SDF. An investor may wish to place a portion of her savings in portfolios on the lower frontier, for hedging purposes.

common underlying model (Cochrane 2001). The links between them were first developed in Roll (1977), Ross (1978), and Hansen and Richard (1987). Cochrane (2001) presents an accessible and comprehensive development.

Capital Asset Pricing Model

The CAPM of Sharpe (1964) and Lintner (1965) is the most widely known asset pricing model. It can be derived as a 2-period model (i.e., assuming investors liquidate the investment in the second period) under certain assumptions, but also as an infinite period model (i.e., the stock is held to infinity) assuming that the investment opportunity set (IOS) is nonstochastic. A nonstochastic IOS means that, for example, expected returns and return volatilities are not time varying. The basic result of the CAPM is that the SDF is a linear function of the investors' total wealth. In practical applications, the proxy for total wealth is assumed to be the return on the market portfolio of equities, R_m. This then gives us the familiar expression for the CAPM:

$$E(r) = R_f + \beta(R_m - R_f) \tag{1.3}$$

Equation (1.3) is one version of equation (1.2), with $j = 1$ and $\lambda_j = E$ $(R_m - R_f)$. Roll (1977) suggests tests of the CAPM may be sensitive to the proxy used for investors' total wealth, because a broad equity portfolio does not represent a claim on all tradable wealth (see also Mayers 1973). Stambaugh (1982) uses a portfolio of equities, corporate and Treasury bonds, residential real estate, and other assets as a proxy for total wealth, and shows that empirical tests of the CAPM are insensitive to the composition of the market portfolio. Therefore, the use of a broad portfolio of equities only, as a proxy for total wealth in equation (1.3), has survived in common practice. The CAPM continues to be widely used and taught, despite much empirical evidence that its ability to explain the cross-section of stock returns is very poor (e.g., Fama and French 1992). Its continued use could be due to its theoretical intuition and ease of empirical implementation.

Equation (1.3) shows the static, or unconditional, CAPM in which the beta and risk premium do not vary over time. Conditional CAPM specifications allow variation in the beta and risk premium over the business cycle. This is because the price of risk, or required return per unit beta, is expected to increase in uncertain economic times. Risk, or beta, is also expected to increase in economic downturns because, for example, financial and operating leverage cannot be adjusted instantaneously. Empirical evidence on the performance of the conditional CAPM, relative to the unconditional CAPM, in explaining the cross-section of expected returns is mixed (e.g., Jagannathan and Wang 1996; Lettau and Ludvigson 2001; Lewellen and Nagel 2006; Roussanov 2010).

Intertemporal Capital Asset Pricing Model

The ICAPM of Merton (1973) models long-lived investors with stochastic variation in investment opportunities. The model suggests that investors care about not only current wealth, as in the CAPM, but also about future investment opportunities. Future investment opportunities are poor if expected returns decline, signaling that investors' capital will be less productive in the future. This suggests more will need to be saved to grow to a given target amount in the future, thereby reducing consumption today. However, a decline in expected returns is not unambiguously bad news: Because the discount rate declines, it raises the current value of the investor's portfolio. The net effect of a decline in expected returns could be bad news for a long-horizon investor, who cares about long-horizon returns, but good news for a short-horizon investor who intends to consume most of his capital in the near future.

In the ICAPM, future investment opportunities are riskier if future return volatilities are expected to increase. The ICAPM predicts that investors will try to hedge against adverse shocks to current wealth as in the CAPM, and also against adverse shocks to the mean and variance of future investment opportunities. In empirical implementation, the ICAPM can also be expressed as a linear function of state variables or risk factors. These risk factors predict changes in investment opportunities.

Fama and French (1993) developed a popular empirical model in which expected returns are a linear function of returns on the market portfolio and size and book-to-market risk factors. This model is now a workhorse in empirical academic research because of its power in explaining the cross-section of expected stock returns. Empirical evidence suggests the size and book-to-market factors predict changes in future investment opportunities (Liew and Vassalou 2000; Vassalou 2003; Li, Vassalou, and Xing 2006; Petkova 2006), indicating the Fama and French (1993) model is an ICAPM-type model. Campbell and Vuolteenaho (2004) and Khan (2008) also test ICAPM models using macroeconomic risk factors and valuation spreads—term structure and value spreads—that predict changes in future investment opportunities. These authors present evidence that their models explain a substantial portion of the cross-sectional variation in expected returns.

Arbitrage Pricing Theory

The arbitrage pricing theory (APT) of Ross (1976) observes that there is substantial common movement in stocks' returns. The sources of this co-movement are called factors. Stocks co-move because they are exposed to or correlated with these factors. The portion of stock returns uncorrelated with these factors is called the idiosyncratic return. If returns are a linear function of these factors, the idiosyncratic returns are on average zero and uncorrelated with the factors, and the law of one price holds, then the SDF in equation (1.1) can be written as a linear function of these factors (Cochrane 2011). In other words, the factors price all assets because any stock return can be synthesized by a portfolio of the factors. The idiosyncratic return is not expected to be priced (i.e., to be compensated by a risk premium) since it is diversifiable by investors holding portfolios of stocks.

The APT does not tell us the identity or number of factors. For this, we turn to statistical techniques, such as factor analysis, or to economic theory. The latter suggests macroeconomic variables related to the business cycle as risk factors. One empirical example of a linear factor specification based on the APT is Chen, Roll, and Ross (1986), who use the term *spread,* the default spread, unexpected inflation, and industrial production as risk factors.

Production-Based Models

The CAPM and ICAPM were developed by considering the optimizing behavior of consumers or investors. Production-based models, in contrast, solve for the first-order conditions of firms optimizing their production-investment decision. A firm can invest in physical assets to produce more goods next period, or it can invest in financial assets. At the margin, the two rates of return must be equal. Hence we can solve for the expected return on financial assets (e.g., stocks) by solving the firm's production-investment optimization. Production-based models are not distinct from consumption-based models. They are simply the other side of the same coin, but they lead to useful insights and testable restrictions on expected returns (Cochrane 1991). Another advantage is that investments are more variable and cyclical than consumption, and since stock returns are highly variable and cyclical, variation in investments rather than variation in consumption is likely to have higher explanatory power for stock return variation.

Production-based asset pricing was first developed, along with supporting evidence, by Cochrane (1991). Lamont (2000) provides additional evidence, as does Kogan (2004), who also extends the theory. A number of cross-sectional expected return models have been motivated by the production-based theory. Cochrane (1996), an early example, uses residential and nonresidential gross fixed investment returns as factors, and reports that this model performs about as well as the CAPM and the Chen, Roll, and Ross (1986) model in explaining cross-sectional variation in stock returns. Subsequent models perform better. Li, Vassalou, and Xing (2006) specify investment growth rates in four sectors as risk factors: households, nonfarm nonfinancial corporate business, nonfarm noncorporate business, and financial business. Their model performs as well as the Fama and

French (1993) and Lettau and Ludvigson (2001) models. Chen, Novy-Marx, and Zhang (2010) specify three risk factors—excess returns on the market portfolio, an investment factor-mimicking portfolio, and a profitability factor-mimicking portfolio—and they report that their model outperforms the Fama and French (1993) model in explaining the cross-section of stock returns. Their model also explains a number of empirical regularities previously considered anomalous. In summary, production-based asset pricing has resulted in some promising cross-sectional models of expected returns.

Firm-Specific Expected Return Estimates

The models described in the preceding section are typically used to estimate expected returns for portfolios of stocks rather than for individual stocks. This is because expected return estimates for individual stocks are very noisy or imprecise (Fama and French 1997), but estimation noise is lower for portfolios of stocks. There are two reasons for imprecise firm-specific estimates of expected returns: (1) reliable estimation requires a longer time series of data than is available for many firms, and (2) individual stock betas are likely more variable over time, which introduces further uncertainty in estimation.

In many investment applications, a firm-specific expected return estimate is not required. For example, a portfolio manager evaluating an investment signal, say the book-to-price ratio (B/P), is interested in the expected return on high and low B/P portfolios. Subtracting the model-implied expected return from the realized average return yields an estimate of the strategy's alpha. Similarly, for performance evaluation, the expected return (and subsequently alpha) on the portfolio of stocks under management is needed. Where a firm-specific expected return estimate for some stock S is required, one can estimate the expected return for a portfolio of stocks that are matched to S on various characteristics such as size, book-to-market, industry, and other variables, and then use the expected return on this portfolio as the expected return for S.

Implied Cost of Capital

The price of a stock is a function of its expected cash flows and its discount rate. If we take the observed market price of a stock as the true or accurate price, and we have estimates of expected cash flows, we can calculate the discount rate that forces the pricing equation to hold. This inferred discount rate is called the implied cost of capital (ICOC). Examples of this approach to calculating expected returns include Gebhardt, Lee, and Swaminathan (2001) and Ohlson and Juettner-Nauroth (2005). However, the validity of ICOC estimates as measures of expected return is unclear, because empirical evidence on the ability of ICOC estimates to predict future stock returns is mixed (Easton and Monahan 2005; Botosan, Plumlee, and Wen 2011).

In summary, given that there is a trade-off between risk and expected return, accurately measuring risk is important in order to accurately price stocks, calibrate portfolio risk, and measure investment performance. Therefore, a large part of the academic literature is devoted to increasing our understanding of risk and expected return, as surveyed in this appendix.

References

Barber, Brad, and John Lyon. 1997. Detecting long-run abnormal stock returns: The empirical power and specification of test statistics. *Journal of Financial Economics* 43: 341–372.

Barberis, Nicholas, Andrei Shleifer, and Robert Vishny. 1998. A model of investor sentiment. *Journal of Financial Economics* 49: 307–343.

Botosan, Christine, Marlene Plumlee, and He Wen. 2011. The relation between expected returns, realized returns and firm risk characteristics. Forthcoming, Contemporary Accounting Research.

Brav, Alon and J. B. Heaton. 2002. Competing theories of financial anomalies. *Review of Financial Studies* 15: 575–606.

Campbell, John, and Tuomo Vuolteenaho. 2004. Bad beta, good beta. *American Economic Review*, 94: 1249–275.

Chen, Long, Robert Novy-Marx, and Lu Zhang. 2010. An alternative three-factor model. Working paper, Washington University, University of Chicago, and Ohio State.

Chen, Nai-fu, Richard Roll, and Stephen Ross. 1986. Economic forces and the stock market. *Journal of Business* 59: 383–403.

Cochrane, John. 1991. Production-based asset pricing and the link between stock returns and economic fluctuations. *Journal of Finance* 46: 207–234.

Cochrane, John. 1996. A cross-sectional test of an investment-based asset pricing model. *Journal of Political Economy* 104: 572–621.

Cochrane, John. 2001. *Asset Pricing*. Princeton, NJ: Princeton University Press.

Coval, Joshua, and Erik Stafford. 2007. Asset firesales (and purchases) in equity markets. *Journal of Financial Economics* 86: 479–512.

Daniel, Kent, David Hirshleifer, and Avanidhar Subrahmanyam. 1998. Investor psychology and security market under- and overreactions. *Journal of Finance* 53: 1839–1885.

D'Avolio, Gene. 2002. The market for borrowing stocks. *Journal of Financial Economics* 66: 271–306.

DeBondt, Werner, and Richard Thaler. 1985. Does the stock market overreact? *Journal of Finance* 40: 793–805.

Easton, Peter, and Steven Monahan. 2005. An evaluation of the reliability of accounting-based measures of expected returns: A measurement error perspective. *The Accounting Review* 80: 501–538.

Fama, Eugene. 1965. The behavior of stock market prices. *Journal of Business* 38: 34–105.

Fama, Eugene. 1970. Efficient capital markets: A review of theory and empirical work. *Journal of Finance* 25: 383–417.

Fama, Eugene. 1998. Market efficiency, long-term returns, and behavioral finance. *Journal of Financial Economics* 49: 283–306.

Fama, Eugene, and Kenneth French. 1992. The cross-section of expected stock returns. *Journal of Finance* 47: 427–465.

Fama, Eugene, and Kenneth French. 1993. Common risk factors in the returns on stocks and bonds. *Journal of Financial Economics* 33: 3–56.

Fama, Eugene, and Kenneth French. 1997. Industry costs of equity. *Journal of Financial Economics* 43: 153–193.

Gebhardt, William, Charles Lee, and Bhaskaran Swaminathan. Toward an implied cost of capital. *Journal of Accounting Research* 39: 135–176.

Greenwood, Robin. 2005. Short- and long-term demand curves for stocks: Theory and evidence on the dynamics of arbitrage. *Journal of Financial Economics* 75: 607–649.

Grossman, Sanford, and Joseph Stiglitz. 1980. On the impossibility of informationally efficient markets. *American Economic Review* 70: 393–408.

Hansen, Lars Peter, and Scott Richards. 1987. The role of conditioning information in deducing testable restrictions implied by dynamic asset pricing models. *Econometrica* 55: 587–614.

Hong, Harrison, and Jeremy Stein. 1999. A unified theory of underreaction, momentum trading and overreaction in asset markets. *Journal of Finance* 54: 2143–2184.

Jagannathan, Ravi, and Zhenyu Wang. 1996. The conditional CAPM and the cross-section of expected returns. *Journal of Finance* 51: 3–53.

Kahneman, Daniel, and Amos Tversky. 1979. Prospect theory: An analysis of decision under risk. *Econometrica* 47: 263–291.

Khan, Mozaffar. 2008. Are accruals mispriced? Evidence from tests of an intertemporal capital asset pricing model. *Journal of Accounting and Economics*, 45: 55–77.

Khan, Mozaffar, Leonid Kogan, and George Serafeim. 2011. Mutual fund trading pressure: Firm-level stock price impact and the timing of SEOs. Forthcoming, Journal of Finance.

Kogan, Leonid. 2004. Asset prices and real investment. *Journal of Financial Economics* 73: 411–431.

Kothari, S. P., and Jerold Warner. 1997. Measuring long horizon security price performance. *Journal of Financial Economics* 43: 301–339.

Kuhn, Thomas. 1962. *The structure of scientific revolutions*. Chicago: University of Chicago Press.

Lakonishok, Josef, Andrei Shleifer, and Robert Vishny. 1994. Contrarian investment, extrapolation, and risk. *Journal of Finance* 49: 1541–1578.

Lamont, Owen. 2000. Investment plans and stock returns. *Journal of Finance* 55: 2719–2745.

Leamer, Edward. 1978. *Specification searches*. New York: Wiley.

Lee, Charles, Andrei Shleifer, and Richard Thaler. 1991. Investor sentiment and the closed-end fund puzzle. *Journal of Finance* 46: 75–110.

Lettau, Martin, and Sydney Ludvigson. 2001. Resurrecting the (C)CAPM: A cross-sectional test when risk premia are time-varying. *Journal of Political Economy* 109: 1238–1287.

Lewellen, Jonathan, and Stefan Nagel. 2006. The conditional CAPM does not explain asset pricing anomalies. *Journal of Financial Economics* 82: 289–314.

Li, Qing, Maria Vassalou, and Yuhang Xing. 2006. Sector investment growth rates and the cross-section of equity returns. *Journal of Business* 79: 1637–1665.

Liew, Jimmy, and Maria Vassalou. 2000. Can book-to-market, size, and momentum be risk factors that predict economic growth? *Journal of Financial Economics* 57: 221–245.

Lintner, John. 1965. The valuation of risky assets and the selection of risky investment in stock portfolios and capital budgets. *Review of Economics and Statistics* 47: 13–37.

Lo, Andrew. 2004. The adaptive markets hypothesis: market efficiency from an evolutionary perspective. *Journal of Portfolio Management* 30: 15–29.

Lo, Andrew. 2005. Reconciling efficient markets with behavioral finance: The adaptive markets hypothesis. Working paper, MIT.

Lo, Andrew, and A. Craig MacKinlay. 1990. Data-snooping biases in tests of financial asset pricing models. *Review of Financial Studies* 3: 431–467.

Loughran, Tim, and Jay Ritter. 2000. Uniformly least powerful tests of market efficiency. *Journal of Financial Economics* 55: 361–389.

Lowenstein, Roger. 2001. *When genius failed*. London: Fourth Estate.

Lyon, John, Brad Barber, and Chi-Ling Tsai. 1999. Improved methods for tests of long-run abnormal stock returns. *Journal of Finance* 59: 165–201.

Mandelbrot, Benoit. 1966. Forecasts of future prices, unbiased markets and martingale models. *Journal of Business* 39: 242–255.

Mayers, David. 1973. Non-marketable assets and the determination of capital asset prices in the absence of a riskless asset. *Journal of Business* 46: 258–267.

Merton, Robert C. 1973. An intertemporal capital asset pricing model. *Econometrica* 41: 867–887.

Merton, Robert C. 1987. A simple model of capital market equilibrium with incomplete information. *Journal of Finance* 42: 483–510.

Mitchell, Mark, and Erik Stafford. 2000. Managerial decisions and long-term stock price performance. *Journal of Business* 73: 287–329.

Nekrasov, Alexander, Pervin Shroff, and Rajdeep Singh. 2010. Tests of long-term abnormal performance: analysis of power. Working paper, University of Minnesota and UC-Irvine.

Odean, Terence. 1998. Are investors reluctant to realize their losses? *Journal of Finance* 53: 1775–1798.

Ohlson, James, and Beate Juettner-Nauroth. 2005. Expected EPS and EPS growth as determinants of value. *Review of Accounting Studies* 10: 349–365.

Petkova, Ralitsa. 2006. Do the Fama-French factors proxy for innovations in predictive variables? *Journal of Finance* 61: 581–612.

Roll, Richard. 1977. A critique of the asset pricing theory's tests: Part I. *Journal of Financial Economics* 4: 129–176.

Roll, Richard. 1988. R^2. *Journal of Finance* 43: 541–566.

Ross, Stephen. 1976. The arbitrage theory of capital asset pricing. *Journal of Economic Theory* 13: 341–360.

Ross, Stephen. 1978. A simple approach to the valuation of risky streams. *Journal of Business* 51: 453–475.

Ross, Stephen. 2005. *Neoclassical finance*. Princeton, NJ: Princeton University Press.

Roussanov, Nikolai. 2010. Composition of wealth, conditioning information and the cross-section of stock returns. Working paper, University of Pennsylvania.

Samuelson, Paul. 1965. Proof that properly anticipated prices fluctuate randomly. *Industrial Management Review* 6: 41–49.

Schwert, G. William. 2003. Anomalies and market efficiency. In *Handbook of the Economics of Finance*, ed. Constantinides, Harris, and Stulz. New York: Elsevier.

Sharpe, William. 1964. Capital asset prices: A theory of market equilibrium under conditions of risk. *Journal of Finance* 19: 425–442.

Shiller, Robert. 1981. Do stock prices move too much to be justified by subsequent changes in dividends? *American Economic Review* 71: 421–436.

Shleifer, Andrei. 1986. Do demand curves for stocks slope down? *Journal of Finance* 41: 579–590.

Shleifer, Andrei. 2000. _Inefficient markets: An introduction to behavioral finance._ New York: Oxford University Press.

Stambaugh, Robert. 1982. On the exclusion of assets from tests of the two-parameter model. _Journal of Financial Economics_ 10: 237–268.

Thaler, Richard (ed.). 1993. _Advances in behavioral finance._ New York: Russell Sage.

Vassalou, Maria. 2003. News related to future GDP growth as a risk factor in equity returns. _Journal of Financial Economics_ 68: 47–73.

Go to http://hema.zacks.com for abstracts and links to papers.

CHAPTER 2

The Accrual Anomaly

Patricia M. Dechow, Natalya V. Khimich, and Richard G. Sloan

The accrual anomaly is unique among asset pricing anomalies in several respects. First, at the time of its discovery, it was the most robust anomaly ever discovered. Second, the anomalous asset pricing behavior associated with accruals has gradually declined in the years since its original discovery. Third, the accrual anomaly is not really an anomaly at all. In fact, the original research documenting the accrual anomaly predicted that it would be there. The term *anomaly* is usually reserved for behavior that deviates from existing theories, but when Sloan (1996) first documented the accrual anomaly, he was testing a well-known theory and found that it was supported.

Sloan (1996) set out to test the theory that investors fixate too heavily on corporate earnings in establishing stock prices. This theory can be traced back at least as far as Graham and Dodd (1934, pp. 350–352) and has been widely espoused ever since. What changed in the meantime was that some prominent finance academics developed their own new theory, which they called the efficient market hypothesis, and they soon declared any evidence inconsistent with their theory to be anomalous. Meanwhile, their academic accounting brethren concluded that if stock prices were closely linked to accounting earnings, it must be because earnings did a great job of summarizing intrinsic value. For a while, everyone was happy with this state of affairs. Finance academics could take comfort in the great efficiency of capital markets, and accounting academics could take comfort in the usefulness of accounting earnings in enhancing capital market efficiency.

So what have accruals got to do with all of this? And what are accruals anyway? In a nutshell, accruals are the piece of earnings that is "made up" by accountants. The other piece of earnings consists of the actual cash flows that a company has generated from its operations. Of course, accountants have rules that guide the measurement of accruals, and auditors are meant to make sure that these rules are followed. However, at the end of the day, which piece of earnings do you trust more—the cash piece or the accrual piece? If you chose the cash piece, you are in good company, because that is what Graham and Dodd (1934) chose. In fact, the first part of Sloan (1996) demonstrates that you should trust the cash piece more. The study then investigates whether investors have figured this out. The answer is a resounding no. As previously postulated by Graham and Dodd, investors just seemed to fixate on earnings.

In this review, we walk you through Sloan's original 1996 research paper and related subsequent developments. We start off by providing a couple of examples to illustrate the nature of accruals and the intuition behind Sloan's tests. We then summarize Sloan's original research. This is followed by a summary of subsequent research that corroborates and extends Sloan's original research. We next summarize research that challenges Sloan's results and explanations. In reading this particular section, you should remember who we are (Sloan and colleagues). Finally, we discuss some practical aspects of the accrual anomaly, including implementation issues and potential refinements.

What Are Accruals?

In order to illustrate exactly what accruals are and how they affect earnings, we begin with a simple example. Let us assume that Peter and Paul are two budding entrepreneurs who each decide to set up lemonade stands.

Peter starts his first day of business by buying $100 of lemonade, $10 of cups, and renting a lemonade stand for $10/day. This costs him a total of $120, all of which he pays for in cash. By the end of the day, he has sold all of his lemonade and used all his cups. All his customers pay him in cash and his total cash proceeds are $200. Figure 2.1 summarizes the financial statements that Peter produces at the end of this first day. His first day's earnings are pretty simple to compute. He ends the day with net income of $200 − $120 = $80. Peter's balance sheet is also very simple. Peter started his business by contributing $120 in cash (the other side of the balance sheet records his equity ownership stake). He finished the first day with $200 in cash, and so his earnings were $80, his operating cash flows were $80 and his equity ownership stake increased by $80.

Peter				Paul			
Income statement	**Day 1**			**Income statement**	**Day 1**		
Revenue	200			Revenue	200		
Expenses				Expenses			
Lemonade	100			Lemonade	100		
Cups	10			Cups	10		
Rent of lemonade stand	10			Depreciation of lemonade stand	10		
Total expenses	*120*			*Total expenses*	*120*		
Net Income	**80**			**Net Income**	**80**		
Balance sheet				**Balance sheet**			
Assets	**Beg.**	**End**		**Assets**	**Beg.**	**End**	
Cash	120	200		Cash	2100	100	
	–	–		Accounts receivable	–	100	
	–	–		Inventory	–	990	
	–	–		Property, plant and equipment	–	990	
Total Assets	**120**	**200**		**Total Assets**	**2100**	**2180**	
Equity	**120**	**200**		**Equity**	**2100**	**2180**	
Statement of cash flows (direct)	**Day 1**			**Statement of cash flows (direct)**	**Day 1**		
Cash from operations				*Cash from operations*			
Cash revenue	200			Cash revenue	100		
Purchases of inventory	(110)			Purchase of inventory	(1,100)		
Rent of lemonade stand	(10)						
Total cash from operations	**80**			**Total cash from operations**	**(1,000)**		
Cash from investing				*Cash from investing*			
				Purchase of lemonade stand	(1,000)		
Total change in cash	**80**			**Total change in cash**	**(2,000)**		
Beginning cash balance	120			Beginning cash balance	2100		
Ending cash balance	200			Ending cash balance	100		
Statement of cash flows (indirect)	**Day 1**			**Statement of cash flows (indirect)**	**Day 1**		
Cash from operations				*Cash from operations*			
Earnings	80			Earnings	80		
Less increase in accruals	0			Add depreciation	10		
				Less increase in receivables	(100)		
				Less increase in inventory	(990)		
Total cash from operations	**80**			**Total cash from operations**	**(1,000)**		
Cash from investing				*Cash from investing*			
	0			Purchase of lemonade stand	(1,000)		
Total change in cash	**80**			**Total change in cash**	**(2,000)**		
Beginning cash balance	120			Beginning cash balance	2100		
Ending cash balance	200			Ending cash balance	100		
Cash component of net income		80		Cash component of net income		(2,000)	
Accrual component of net income		0		Accrual component of net income		2080	
Net income		80		Net income		80	

FIGURE 2.1 Financial Statements for Peter and Paul's Lemonade Stands

Paul, on the other hand, starts his first day by buying $1,000 of lemonade, $100 of cups, and a fancy new lemonade stand for $1,000. This costs him a total of $2,100, all of which he pays for in cash. By the end of the first day, he has sold about 10% of his lemonade and has used up about 10% of his cups. Paul also sold his lemonade for a total of $200, but half of his customers were short on cash and so he agreed that they could stop by and pay him the next day, collecting only $100 in cash on his first day. His lemonade stand is now a bit sticky, but it is holding up well and he hopes to get a further 99 days of usage out of it.

Unlike Peter, Paul needs an accountant to help him determine his earnings. One thing he knows for sure is that he is now out of pocket $2,000 in cash, because he had to invest $2,100 to start the business and only collected $100 of cash on the first day. However, he still has heaps of lemonade and cups and a nearly new lemonade stand. Paul's accountant tells him that, because he sold about 10% of his lemonade and used about 10% of his cups, the remaining lemonade is worth about $900 and the remaining cups are worth about $90, so Paul has $990 worth of inventory. Paul explains to his accountant that he is still owed $100 for the day's lemonade sales and that he expects to collect the cash tomorrow. The accountant says, "Are you sure these customers will come back and pay you?" Paul says, "Are you calling me a liar?" at which point the accountant promptly tells Paul that he also has $100 worth of accounts receivable. The accountant also notices the sticky lemonade stand and says, "Is this yours?" Paul says, "Yes, and I expect to get another 99 days use out of that beauty," upon which the accountant tells Paul that he has "property, plant, and equipment" worth $990.

After hitting a few buttons on his calculator, the accountant tells Paul he now has a balance sheet with $2,080 worth of noncash assets ($990 of inventory plus $100 of accounts receivable plus $990 of fixed assets). When Paul started the day, he had no noncash assets. The increase in noncash assets for the period is therefore $2,080. This increase in noncash assets represents the accruals for the period. The accountant tells Paul that a quick way to figure out his earnings for the period is to add the accruals to the net cash flows for the period. Cash is –$2,000 and accruals are $2,080, and so his first day's net income is also $80.

Figure 2.1 provides the financial statements for the two businesses. As you can see, Peter and Paul both generated earnings of $80. Moreover, they are both in the same line of business, but their first day's operations were far from the same. Peter's income of $80 is all made of a net cash inflow. Paul's income, in contrast, is made up of $2,080 worth of accruals less $2,000 worth of net cash outflows. Intuitively, while Paul had a net cash outflow of $2,000, the accrual accounting process tells us that his business also generated $2,080 of anticipated future benefits. These anticipated future benefits are recorded as assets on the balance sheet. Their existence and valuation is determined by applying generally accepted accounting principles (GAAP) to information about the business that Paul has provided to his accountant.

In the context of this example, both Graham and Dodd (1934) and Sloan (1996) argued that Paul's earnings are more uncertain, because they depend on accounting estimates of future benefits. For example, what if Paul's customers don't come back and pay him tomorrow? Or what if some of his lemonade inventory goes missing? In either case, $80 will have turned out to be too high an estimate of the earnings that was ultimately generated on the first day. Of course, it is also possible that Paul could end up making more than $80. A grateful customer could come back and pay Paul more than is owed, or Paul could discover he had more lemonade than he thought. This latter scenario would make for a nice dream, but it is, unfortunately, not a very good description of reality. In most cases of businesses with soaring inventory and receivables, these assets turn out to be worth less than their initial carrying value. We will examine one such case in the next subsection. For this reason, we often say that earnings like Paul's are of lower quality than earnings like Peter's. Peter's earnings have been realized in cash, while Paul's earnings consist primarily of accruals, which anticipate the realization of estimated future benefits. When we see a business in which most of the earnings come from accruals, it is more likely that some of the anticipated benefits will not be realized and so earnings will turn out to have been overstated.

Graham and Dodd (1934) supported their arguments with some illustrative cases. Sloan (1996) was able to take advantage of computerized databases to provide more systematic support using a large sample of thousands of stocks trading on a major U.S. exchange since the 1950s. We discuss exactly how he did this in the next section.

A Case Study

We are now in a position to describe how to measure accruals for any company using computerized financial data, such as that supplied by Compustat. Sloan's original measure of accruals focuses on changes in current asset and current liability accounts on the balance sheet. We illustrate the computation of accruals using KB Home as a case study. KB Home is one of the largest homebuilders in the United States, with a big presence in states such as Florida, California, and Arizona. KB Home expanded aggressively during the booming housing market of 2002–2006 and has since hit upon hard times. It is a classic example of how the examination of accruals can assist in the evaluation of the quality of a company's earnings. The pertinent data for KB Home are provided in Figure 2.2. Note that we have only extracted the current asset and current liability data that are required to compute Sloan's original measure of accruals.

The first step in the calculation of Sloan's measure of accruals is the computation of current net operating assets. Current net operating assets is defined as current operating assets less current operating liabilities. Figure 2.2 shows that Compustat reports current assets in 4 categories (cash, accounts receivable, inventories, and other current assets). Of these, we exclude cash, because cash is a financial as opposed to an operating asset.

Financial Statement Figures in Millions of U.S. Dollars

Year Ended	Line	2002	2003	2004	2005	2006	2007	2008	2009
Current assets									
Cash & ST Investments	1	$330.0	$138.1	$234.2	$154.0	$654.6	$1,343.7	$1,256.9	$1,292.3
Accounts Receivable	2	982.5	642.1	662.7	584.3	662.4	298.4	359.0	339.3
Inventories	3	2,173.5	2,883.5	4,143.3	6,128.3	6,454.8	3,312.4	2,106.7	1,501.4
Other Current Assets	4	0.0	0.0	0.0	0.0	0.0	0.0	0.0	0.0
Current Assets (Add line 1 through 4)	5	3,486.0	3,663.7	5,040.1	6,866.6	7,771.8	4,954.6	3,722.6	3,133.0
Current liabilities									
ST Debt & Curr. Portion LT Debt	6	516.9	329.6	86.0	130.3	503.6	221.0	296.4	18.5
Accounts Payable	7	521.3	554.4	749.1	892.7	1,071.3	699.9	541.3	341.0
Income Tax Payable	8	0.0	0.0	0.0	0.0	0.0	0.0	0.0	12.5
Other Current Liabilities	9	466.9	606.4	855.9	1,393.2	1,706.3	993.6	730.9	554.9
Current Liabilities (Add line 6 through 9)	10	1,505.1	1,490.4	1,691.0	2,416.2	3,281.1	1,914.5	1,568.5	926.9
Current net operating assets *(line 5 – line 1) – (line 10 – line 6 – line 8)*	*11*	*2,167.8*	*2,364.8*	*3,200.9*	*4,426.7*	*4,339.6*	*1,917.3*	*1,193.5*	*944.8*
Net income	12	314.4	370.8	480.9	842.4	482.4	–1,414.8	–976.1	–101.8
Accrual component of net income (change in 11)	*13*		*197.0*	*836.1*	*1,225.8*	*–87.1*	*–2,422.3*	*–723.8*	*–248.7*
Implied cash component of net income (line 12 - line 13)	*14*		*173.7*	*–355.2*	*–383.4*	*569.4*	*1,007.5*	*–252.3*	*146.9*
Stock price (in U.S. dollars)		22.35	34.44	43.95	69.77	51.69	20.89	11.63	13.55

FIGURE 2.2 KB Homes Accrual Worksheet

Current liabilities are also reported in 4 categories (short-term debt, accounts payable, income tax payable, and other current liabilities). Of these, we exclude short-term debt, because this is a form of financing rather than an obligation arising from the firm's operations.[1]

Sloan also excluded taxes payable for similar reasons. We could argue whether taxes payable is a form of financing or an operating obligation, but as a practical matter it is usually pretty small and makes little difference. Thus, we compute current net operating assets as follows:

Current Net Operating Assets = (Current Assets − Cash)

− (Current Liabilities − Short-Term Debt − Income Taxes Payable)

Figure 2.2 computes KB Home's current net operating assets from 2002 through 2009. You can see that they gradually rise from 2,167.8 in 2002 to a high of 4,426.7 in 2005 and subsequently plummet to 944.8 in 2009. You can also see that the biggest determinant of operating assets is inventories, which largely consists of partially finished houses and finished houses that have yet to be sold. By now, you can probably see a similarity between Paul's lemonade business and KB Home's homebuilding business. In both cases, they often sell only a small proportion of their total inventory in any given period. Consequently, their earnings depend critically on how they value their remaining inventory. Moreover, monetization of earnings hinges on their ability to sell the remaining inventory for more than it is valued on the balance sheet.

Returning to the computation of accruals, the computed amounts of net operating assets represent end of period balances of accountants' estimates of expected future benefits. To compute the accrual component of periodic earnings, we need to take the change in these balances over the period in question. Like Sloan, we focus on annual earnings, and so we compute accruals by taking the change in net operating assets over the year:

Accruals = Current Net Operating Assets (End of This Year)

− Current Net Operating Assets (End of Previous Year)

You can see the accrual computations for KB Homes in Figure 2.2. Accruals grow from 197.0 in 2003 to 1,225.8 in 2005 and then turn negative for 2006 to 2009. Let's try and understand why accruals are so big and positive in 2005. Scanning through the current asset accounts, you should

---

[1]Cash includes cash and other short-term investments, and short-term debt includes short-term debt and the current portion of long-term debt. Another term you will see used for current net operating assets is *noncash working capital* (this is the term Sloan used in his original paper). We use these two terms interchangeably, but you should be careful to always check how accruals are defined, because definitions vary considerably (as we will discuss later in the review).

quickly notice that 2005 was characterized by a dramatic increase in inventory, from 4,143.4 at the end of 2004 to 6,128.3 at the end of 2005. In other words, although KB Home probably sold a lot of homes in 2005, it also constructed $2 billion worth more homes than it sold. Moreover, it had also been building more homes than it sold in previous years, such that it had a total unsold home inventory in excess of $6 billion at the end of 2005.

Next, let's look at KB Home's reported net income. Net income gradually increased from 314.4 in 2002 to 842.4 in 2005, leveled off to 482.4 in 2006, plummeted to −1,414.8 in 2007 and has been negative ever since. Figure 2.3a plots the patterns in accruals and net income. You can see that they are similar. Both grew from 2002 to 2005 and then dramatically reversed course. Figure 2.3b plots the cash flow component of earnings, which tends to move in the opposite direction to accruals. KB Home's high accruals and low cash flows in 2005 alert us to the potentially low quality of its earnings.

Let's take a closer look at KB Home's 2005 net income. In that year, reported income was 842.4, but accruals were 1,225.8. This means that the implied cash component of earnings was −383.4. Therefore, although KB Home reported record net income, its cash component of earnings was negative. That is, the record net income was attributable to accounting accruals. However, how do we know the anticipated future benefits associated with these accruals are going to be realized? Shouldn't we be somewhat alarmed that KB Home now has to unload over $6 billion in unsold homes before this net income is fully realized in cash? This was Sloan's key argument. If net income is high only because accruals are high, then perhaps it is less likely that this net income will ultimately be realized in the form of cash. In particular, if some of the benefits that are anticipated by the accruals are not subsequently realized in the form of cash, the associated accruals will have to be reversed and charged off against future earnings. This is exactly what happened to KB Homes. In 2007, it wrote off around $1 billion worth of inventory, which is the main reason its accruals and net income were so negative in that year.

At this point, you may be thinking to yourself, "Isn't this an unusual case, because 2007 happened to be when the U.S. housing market went bust?" If so, you are both right and wrong. You are right in that high accruals are not always followed by accrual reversals and lower net income, but you are wrong in that Sloan found that this pattern was observed on average. So, although KB Home represents an extreme example, this is the basic pattern that Sloan documented for the typical high accrual firm. We cover Sloan's (1996) results in the next section.

Let's finish this section by taking a look to see whether the stock market seemed to figure things out in the case of KB Home. Figure 2.3c plots KB Home's stock price using a suitable scale on the right-hand side of the

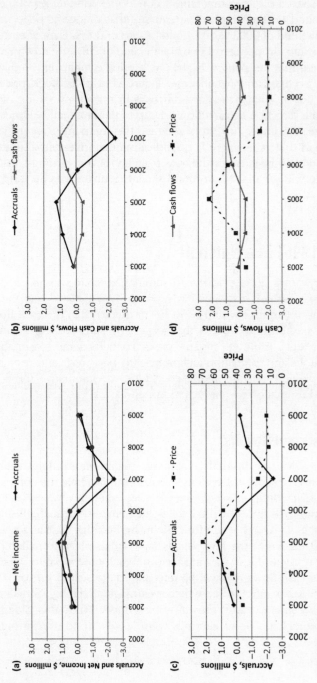

FIGURE 2.3 Time-Series Plots of KB Home's Net Income, Accruals, Cash Flows, and Stock Price from 2003 to 2009

31

graph to make it easily comparable to the corresponding accrual data that is also plotted on the graph. You can see that the stock price rose from $22.35 at the end of 2002 to $69.77 at the end of 2005. Thereafter it began a gradual decline, dropping to $11.63 by the end of 2008. By now, you should have noticed that the pattern in the stock price is amazingly similar to the pattern in accruals and net income. Figure 2.3d plots stock prices along with cash flows. What you can see here is that stock prices are moving in the opposite direction to cash flows. Despite the fact that 2005 net income was all due to accruals, investors assigned the company a record valuation at the end of that year. There is no indication that investors discounted the 2005 net income because of the lower quality of the earnings. In the next section, we will see that Sloan found similar results across his large sample of firms.

Sloan (1996) in a Nutshell

We are now in a good position to summarize Sloan's (1996) accrual paper. We have already explained why Sloan hypothesized that the accrual component of earnings would be of lower quality than the cash flow component of earnings. We begin this section by summarizing Sloan's basic tests and results. Although Sloan's paper contains some reasonably complex equations and estimation techniques, the basic tests and results can be readily explained. For the interested reader, we summarize the equations and related estimation techniques in Appendix 2.1.

Basic Tests and Results

In order to systematically analyze earnings quality across a large set of firms, Sloan first had to standardize all the measures to facilitate the comparison of firms with vastly different sizes. Sloan accomplished this by scaling earnings, accruals, and cash flows by total assets. Remember that accruals are essentially changes in assets. Therefore, Sloan figured that if changes in assets were large relative to the level of assets, accruals must be making a large contribution to earnings.[2] Moving forward, each time we refer to earnings, accruals, or cash flows, we will be referring to the scaled version.

Next, Sloan wanted to see whether earnings driven by accruals were of lower quality than earnings driven by cash flows. To do this, Sloan looked to see whether high (low) earnings were less likely to remain high (low)

---

[2]Hafzalla, Lundholm, and Van Winkle (2011) argue that directly scaling by earnings produces better results.

if the earnings were driven by accruals. We conduct an updated version of Sloan's analysis, which can be summarized as follows:

1. Compute earnings, accruals, and cash flows for a sample of firm-years from the COMPUSTAT database between 1970 and 2007.
2. Within each fiscal year, rank observations from lowest to highest based on earnings.
3. Assign firm-years into deciles based on the rank of earnings, with decile 1 consisting of the lowest-ranked 10% and decile 10 consisting of the highest-ranked 10%.
4. Compute the average level of earnings for firm-years in each decile.
5. Track the average level of earnings for the corresponding set of firm-years in the surrounding 10 years (5 years either side of the ranking year).
6. Construct a plot of average earnings over the 11 years for the highest and lowest deciles.

This is what academics refer to as an event-time plot. It enables us to understand the persistence of extreme earnings performance.

Panel a of Figure 2.4 reports the resulting plot. Two things are worth noting. First, the spread in earnings between the highest and lowest deciles is greatest in year 0. This is because we selected the firms based on earnings performance in this year. Second, earnings performance for the two extreme deciles tends to slowly drift back together over the surrounding years. However, note that the two lines are still quite far from converging even after 5 years. This plot tells us that earnings performance is highly persistent. If a firm has high earnings performance this year, it is expected to continue to have high earnings performance for several years into the future.

The next thing that Sloan did was to perform the same six steps discussed earlier for earnings, but with just one change. In step 2, he ranked the observations based on the magnitude of the *accrual* component of earnings. Figure 2.4b provides our replication of his results. There are two things of note. First, the spread in earnings is again greatest in year 0. This is because we have ranked on accruals in year 0, and accruals are a component of earnings. Second and more important, the rate at which the earnings converge in the surrounding years is much faster than in the previous plot. In fact, the convergence is pretty much complete after 5 years. In other words, earnings performance that is driven by high accruals is not very persistent.

To drive this point home, Sloan next performed the same set of steps, but ranked on the *cash flow* component of earnings in step 2. Figure 2.4c provides our replication of these results. It is very clear that earnings converge much more slowly in this plot. So earnings that are attributable

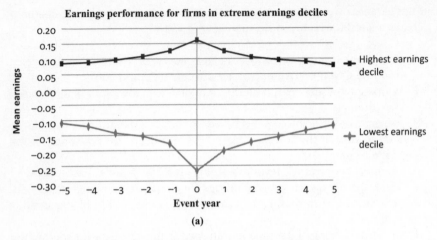

Earnings performance for firms in extreme earnings deciles

(a)

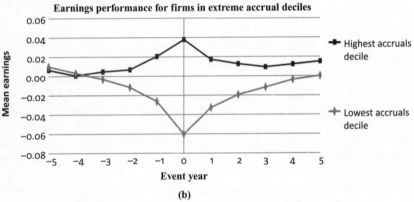

Earnings performance for firms in extreme accrual deciles

(b)

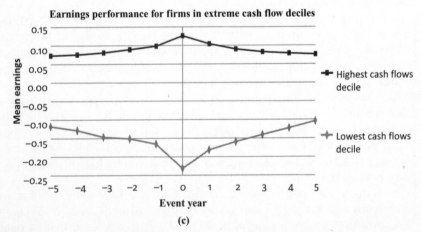

Earnings performance for firms in extreme cash flow deciles

(c)

FIGURE 2.4 Time-Series Plots of Earnings Performance for Extreme Deciles of Earnings, Accruals, and Cash Flows

to cash flows are very persistent, whereas earnings that are attributable to accruals are much less persistent.

To summarize, Figure 2.4 demonstrates that, if we see a company with high earnings today, we can expect that it will also have reasonably high earnings in the future. However, if we really want to assess the likelihood of it staying high, we should also check whether the current high earnings are driven by accruals or cash flows. If it is driven by accruals, it is much less likely to stay high, whereas if it is driven by cash flows, it is much more likely to stay high. The earnings of Paul's business and KB Home in 2005 are both examples of cases in which high earnings were driven by high accruals. This is a warning sign that the earnings are likely to fall in the future.

The other main question that Sloan's study addresses is whether investors use information in accruals and cash flows to forecast the persistence of earnings. In other words, do stock prices act as though investors already know that firms with high accruals are likely to experience relatively large drops in future earnings? The way that Sloan did this was to look at the subsequent stock returns earned by portfolios of firms with extreme earnings, accruals, and cash flows respectively. Previous research had already shown that stock prices were strongly positively related to earnings. If investors understood that firms with high accruals were likely to have lower future earnings, then we shouldn't expect to see abnormal future returns for a portfolio of high accrual firms. However, if investors failed to heed the warnings offered by the high accruals, we would expect to see unusually low future returns to a portfolio of high accrual firms. We conduct an updated version of Sloan's tests as follows:

1. Compute accruals for a sample of firm-years on the COMPUSTAT database between 1970 and 2007.
2. Within each fiscal year, rank observations from lowest to highest based on accruals.
3. Assign firm years into deciles based on the rank of accruals, with decile 1 consisting of the lowest-ranked 10% and decile 10 consisting of the highest-ranked 10%.
4. Compute the subsequent annual stock returns for firm-year observation beginning 4 months after the fiscal year end (the 4-month rule allows for financial statement information for the fiscal year to be made available to investors).
5. Compute the subsequent annual equally weighted portfolio returns for each accrual decile.

Panel A of Table 2.1 provides the results. The table reports the annual returns for each accrual portfolio over the 3 years subsequent to their being assigned to that accrual portfolio. Visual inspection of the returns indicates that the highest accrual portfolio has the lowest future return in year $t + 1$

TABLE 2.1 Mean Portfolio Raw Returns for a Sample of 60,009 Firm-Years from 1970 to 2007

Panel A: Accruals Decile Hedge Portfolio Returns				Panel B: Cash Flows Decile Hedge Portfolio Returns			
Raw Returns					Raw Returns		
Rank of Accruals	t + 1	t + 2	t + 3	Rank of Cash Flows	t + 1	t + 2	t + 3
Lowest 1	0.212	0.171	0.171	Lowest 1	0.143	0.159	0.162
2	0.184	0.158	0.182	2	0.151	0.163	0.165
3	0.166	0.148	0.175	3	0.186	0.168	0.169
4	0.168	0.153	0.157	4	0.160	0.148	0.172
5	0.154	0.152	0.158	5	0.146	0.140	0.185
6	0.170	0.131	0.157	6	0.146	0.137	0.175
7	0.149	0.153	0.197	7	0.154	0.138	0.173
8	0.151	0.144	0.154	8	0.161	0.133	0.161
9	0.126	0.126	0.178	9	0.162	0.143	0.171
Highest 10	0.102	0.128	0.161	Highest 10	0.171	0.134	0.158
Hedge (1–10)	**0.110**	**0.043**	**0.010**	**Hedge (10–1)**	**0.028**	**–0.025**	**–0.004**

Note: Portfolios are formed annually by assigning firms into deciles based on the magnitude of accruals (Panel A) or cash flows (Panel B).

Accrual is the change in noncash current assets less the change in current liabilities (exclusive of short-term debt and tax payable), divided by average assets. Cash flow is equal to earnings before extraordinary items less accruals, divided by average assets.

and t + 2. These returns are exactly what would be expected if investors did not anticipate the greater likelihood of future earnings declines for high accrual firms. We note in passing that the strength of these results is somewhat weaker than those originally reported by Sloan. As we discuss in more detail later, this is because investors appear to have learned about the quality of the accrual component since Sloan's study. At the very bottom of Panel A of Table 2.1, we report the hedge returns to an investment strategy of going long in the lowest accrual portfolio and short in the highest accrual portfolio (i.e., buying the stocks where earnings are expected to go up and short-selling the stocks where earnings are expected to go down). The hedge return is 11% over the subsequent year.

We have focused on accruals so far. However, we could apply the same logic to cash flows with the opposite prediction. If investors don't discriminate between the accrual and cash flow components of earnings, then they won't realize that a firm with low cash flows will have more persistently low cash flows in the future. As such, we would expect there to be lower subsequent returns to a portfolio of firms formed on low cash flows. Panel B of Table 2.1 provides the results of replicating the stock return analysis for portfolios formed on cash flows instead of accruals. Cash

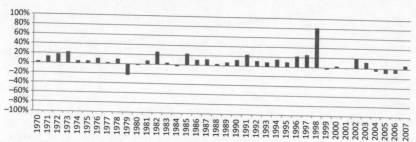

FIGURE 2.5   Accrual Strategy Hedge Portfolio Returns for a Sample of 60,009 Firm-Years from 1970 to 2006 (Positive in 30 out of 38 Years)

flows are calculated as the difference between earnings and accruals. The results indicate that investors do not fully anticipate the higher persistence of the cash component of earnings. For example, the lowest cash flow portfolio has the lowest subsequent returns in year t + 1. The hedge returns are smaller for the cash flow strategy (2.8%). Why the difference? Accruals and cash flows are not perfectly negatively correlated so the two hedge portfolios are selecting different firms. In fact, the overlap of firms selected in the hedge portfolios is only around 60%.

The returns reported in Table 2.1 are the average returns from 1970 to 2007. What if the results are all driven by one or two spectacular years? How risky is the strategy? Figure 2.5 addresses these questions by providing the hedge returns to the accrual strategy by year. The results indicate that the annual hedge returns are positive in all but one of the years prior to 1996 (the year Sloan's study was published). It has been a very low risk strategy. In fact, a recent paper by Hirshleifer, Hou, and Teoh (2011) finds that the risk/return trade-off offered by the accrual strategy dominates all other contenders, including the overall equity premium and the well-known Fama & French size and book-to-market strategies. After 1996 the pattern gradually becomes more mixed. What happened? A paper by Green, Hand, and Soliman (2010) argues that the accrual anomaly is likely to have been arbitraged away as sophisticated investors attempted to exploit Sloan's results. This is more than just a conjecture, as the accrual anomaly has been a favorite strategy of large quantitative investors.

Figure 2.6 provides the annual hedge returns to the cash flow strategy. The returns to this strategy appear to be somewhat more volatile than the accrual strategy, generating very negative returns in 1998 and 2002. However, the hedge returns are still positive in 29 of the 38 years.

We have now summarized Sloan's key ideas, tests, and results. The paper itself contains a couple of additional sets of analysis. First, Sloan develops and estimates a set of equations to formally test the ideas outlined earlier. For the technically minded, we summarize these equations in

FIGURE 2.6 Cash Flows Strategy Hedge Portfolio Returns for a Sample of 60,009 Firm-Years from 1970 to 2007 (Positive in 29 out of 38 Years)

Appendix 2.1. For the rest of us, there are really just two important insights from that analysis. First, Sloan verified that the key results outlined earlier were statistically significant. Second, Sloan was able to demonstrate that the magnitude of the predictable stock returns reported in Table 2.1 is consistent with investors fixating on earnings. In other words, he estimates by how much stocks would be mispriced if investors were to fixate on earnings, and then shows that this corresponds nicely with the actual mispricing amount.

He also examined whether the predictable returns documented in Table 2.1 were concentrated around subsequent earnings announcements. If the predictable stock returns arise because investors do not anticipate the more rapid mean reversion of the accrual component of earnings, then we would expect investors to learn about this when subsequent earnings are announced. These tests were another way that Sloan could corroborate the idea that investors were fixated on earnings. Sloan found that around half of the predictable returns were concentrated around subsequent earnings announcements. Interestingly, he found that the predictable returns were nearly all concentrated at earnings announcements for low accrual firms (for which earnings tend to increase) but not for high accrual firms (for which earnings tend to decrease). Sloan attributed the latter result to the fact that firms are more likely to preannounce bad earnings news (see Skinner 1994).

Extensions of Sloan (1996)

Sloan (1996) generated a lot of interest among both academics and practitioners and has become one of the most highly cited accounting research papers. The paper struck a raw nerve with academics who still clung to the efficient markets hypothesis. We will examine their reaction in more detail later. This led Sloan and others to seek ways to corroborate the original findings. Moreover, because of the obvious practical appeal of Sloan's findings, additional research was conducted to try and extend his findings to produce better measures of earnings quality and improved trading strategies. We review this research next.

Our review of this research is organized into five subsections. The first section summarizes research investigating whether sophisticated financial intermediaries, such as sell-side analysts, institutional investors, and auditors, appear to understand information in accruals. The second section examines research using broader definitions of accruals. You may recall that Sloan's original research only looks at working capital or current accruals. A natural extension is to look at noncurrent accruals, such as the capitalization of expenditures on property, plant, and equipment (PP&E) and business acquisitions. The third section summarizes research that examines situations in which Sloan's story indicates that the accrual anomaly should be particularly strong. For example, in subsets of firms where accruals are *relatively* less persistent than cash flows, we should see a *relatively* stronger accrual anomaly. The fourth section summarizes research using future information and events other than stock returns to corroborate the earnings quality story. For example, are high accrual firms more likely to get sued for manipulating earnings? Are they more likely to have subsequent asset write-downs? Finally, the chapter ends by examining the accrual anomaly around the world. Sloan's research uses U.S. data. Is the accrual component of earnings less persistent in other countries? If so, do investors in these other countries also fixate on earnings?

Do Sophisticated Financial Intermediaries Use Information in Accruals?

Bradshaw, Richardson, and Sloan (2001) seek to provide corroborating evidence for the earnings fixation hypothesis by looking at whether sell-side analysts and auditors use information in accruals. With respect to sell-side analysts, they looked at whether the earnings forecasts of these analysts anticipated the lower persistence of the accrual component of earnings. Their results indicate that sell-side analysts appear to be largely oblivious to the lower persistence of accruals. In other words, the analysts fixate on earnings. For example, Bradshaw et al. found that analysts' earnings forecasts for firms with high accruals were initially far too optimistic. Furthermore, even though they revised their forecasts down over time, they were still too optimistic immediately prior to the subsequent earnings announcement date.

Bradshaw et al. also looked to see whether auditors seem to use information in accruals. Auditors are meant to provide an opinion about whether firms' earnings fairly present the results of their operations. Recall from our earlier analysis that firms with high accruals tend to have overstated their earnings. Therefore, a smart auditor could presumably have figured this out and either warned investors by either issuing a qualified audit opinion or resigning. Yet Bradshaw et al. (2001) found no evidence of either a higher incidence of auditor qualifications or a higher incidence of auditor changes in firms with high accruals.

A related question is why didn't institutional investors identify the accrual anomaly and arbitrage it away? Lev and Nissim (2006) find that some active institutional investors do trade on the accrual anomaly but that the magnitude of their trading is relatively small. Lev and Nissim conclude that the majority of institutional investors avoid extreme-accruals firms because they have other attributes that are not desirable, including being illiquid and volatile stocks. Ali, Chen, Yao, and Yu (2008) provide evidence that some mutual funds have successfully implemented the accruals strategy in the U.S. market. In addition, consistent with institutional investors being more sophisticated than other investors, Collins, Gong, and Hribar (2003) document that stocks with high institutional ownership exhibit prices that more accurately reflect the persistence of accruals.

Finally, because institutional investors dominate corporate bond markets and the role of bond-rating agencies is to evaluate the quality of the underlying issuers, it is possible that the accrual anomaly could be weaker in bond markets. Bhojraj and Swaminathan (2008) investigate this issue and find that accrual anomaly is also robust in bond returns. The authors point out that this is somewhat surprising given that one would think that bondholders would look behind the earnings number and focus on cash flows. However, bondholders appear to misprice accruals in a similar manner to equity holders.

In summary, the available evidence indicates that sophisticated financial intermediaries do not fully utilize information in accruals about earnings quality. This evidence corroborates Sloan's original hypothesis that the anomaly persists because investors tend to fixate on earnings.

Using a Broader Definition of Accruals

Sloan's (1996) definition of accruals focused on the change in current net operating assets. Richardson, Sloan, Soliman, and Tuna (2005) expand the definition of accruals. They decompose the balance sheet into changes in current net operating assets, changes in noncurrent net operating assets, and changes in net financial assets. They argue that the aggregate change in both current and noncurrent net operating assets provides a more comprehensive measure of accruals. Appendix 2.2 illustrates their decomposition using Harley Davidson's balance sheets. Richardson et al. use data from 1962 to 2001 and form hedge portfolios (long lowest accrual decile, short highest accrual decile) for various accrual measures. For the change in noncash net operating assets, the hedge return is 18% per year. In contrast, when they use Sloan's original definition that includes only the change in current net operating assets, the hedge return is only 13.3%. Why does the broader definition produce stronger returns? The broader definition includes accountants' estimates of long-term future benefits. Recall that in Figure 2.1,

Paul spent $1,000 on a lemonade stand. Sloan's original definition of accruals would exclude this accrual because it only uses current accruals. Likewise, when WorldCom committed their multibillion-dollar fraud, they did so by incorrectly capitalizing cash expenses as PP&E. These long-term accruals are not incorporated in Sloan's original definition of accruals. Therefore, the broader definition should provide a more complete measure of accruals and a better measure of earnings quality.[3] Richardson et al.'s results support the efficacy of the broader measure of accruals.

A related paper by Hirshleifer, Hou, Teoh, and Zhang (2004) suggests that Sloan's accrual metric can also be improved by incorporating accruals from prior years. Recall that Sloan only considers accruals made over the past year. This choice is somewhat arbitrary. Why not look at the last quarter or the last 5 years? Fortunately, Sloan's persistence tests support the use of a year, because the lower persistence of accruals appears to largely manifest itself over the next 1 to 3 years. Hirshleifer et al. argue that aggregating accruals over the entire life of the firm should produce a better measure of earnings quality and claim to provide supporting evidence. Richardson, Sloan, and Tuna (2006) cast doubt on the interpretation of the evidence in Hirshleifer et al. (2004). They note that Hirshleifer et al. essentially divide aggregate accruals in the current year by aggregate accruals in the previous year and that this is equivalent to measuring accruals over one year (because accruals from earlier periods are in the numerator and denominator and so will cancel out). Nevertheless, Richardson et al. consider deflating by accruals from even earlier years and find that deflating by accruals from two years earlier provides a slightly better measure of earnings quality. Thus, their evidence suggests that earnings quality is best measured by aggregating accruals over the past two years.[4]

Where Is the Accrual Anomaly Strongest?

Thomas and Zhang (2002) examine the individual balance sheet components of Sloan's accrual measure and attempt to identify which component is primarily responsible for accrual anomaly. They find that inventory

---

[3]In a similar vein, Cooper et al. (2008) document a negative relation between total asset growth and subsequent abnormal returns. Growth in total assets is highly correlated with the change in net operating assets (remember that this latter measure is deflated by total assets). Moreover, Richardson et al. (2005) demonstrate that measures of accruals incorporating operating liabilities and excluding financial assets (which are the two main differences between total assets and net operating assets) results in a measure of accruals that better reflects earnings quality.

[4]Based on their evidence, it would seem that the optimal accruals measure would aggregate accruals over more than one year, but place increasingly less weight on accruals from earlier years. Intuitively speaking, we place less weight on earlier years' accruals, because there is a greater possibility that they have already reversed and impacted earnings.

accruals exhibit the most robust relation with future stock returns. Chan, Chan, Jegadeesh, and Lakonishok (2006) document a similar finding. There is no clear explanation for this result, though it is likely due to both the economic magnitude of inventory accruals and the reluctance of managers to write down inventory in the face of slowing demand.

Researchers in accounting have also developed models using regression analysis to decompose accruals into a normal component that is due to the growth in the economic activities of the firm and a "discretionary" component that is more likely to misstate future benefits. Xie (2001) shows that the discretionary component of accruals is less persistent than the normal component of accruals. He also shows that future predictable returns are stronger for the discretionary component. The key takeaway from his paper is that we can get a better measure of earnings quality by eliminating accruals that appear to be economically justified. Chan, Chan, Jegadeesh, and Lakonishok (2006) provide similar evidence. They also investigate whether the accrual strategy works better in industries that have larger working capital accrual requirements. They find the strategy is positive in 29 out of 32 industries and the spread tends to be larger in industries where working capital is a more important component of total assets. The industries where the hedge returns are largest during their sample period are construction, 16.2%; toys, 10.9%; computers, 9.4%; household, 9.1%; electrical equipment, 8.6%; and rubber, 8.6%. The strategy does not work in drugs, mines, or energy.

Finally, Shi and Zhang (2011) investigate some direct implications of Sloan's explanation for the magnitude of the accrual anomaly. They point out that if Sloan's explanation is correct, the accrual anomaly should be strongest for firms where the accrual component of earnings is relatively less persistent than the cash flow component; and stock prices have a greater response to earnings surprises.

Shi and Zhang (2011) first show that both of these characteristics appear to vary across firms. They then show that incorporating this variation significantly increases the returns to the accrual trading strategy. For example, the accrual hedge portfolio returns for firms with the lowest relative accrual persistence and highest earnings response coefficients exceed an annualized average return of 60%. Appendix 2.1 provides more details on Shi and Zhang's research design.

Investigation of Subsequent Events Following Extreme Accruals

Several papers investigate the years following extreme accruals to provide additional insights about why the accrual component of earnings is less persistent than the cash component of earnings. This research also helps to identify the types of future events that drive the returns to the accrual anomaly. As mentioned earlier, Thomas and Zhang (2002) find that the accrual anomaly is strongest for inventory accruals. The question is why? Allen et al. (2010) address this question by showing that extreme inventory accruals are particularly likely to experience extreme subsequent reversals. In particular, they find that firms with big inventory increases are much more likely to report inventory write-downs in subsequent years. This is exactly what we saw happen to KB Homes in Figure 2.2. Chan, Chan, Jegadeesh, and Lakonishok (2006) perform a similar analysis on high accrual firms and find that a greater proportion of these firms end up reporting negative special items over the next 3 years.

Richardson, Sloan, Soliman, and Tuna (2006) investigate whether high accrual firms are more likely to have manipulated their earnings. Specifically, they investigate whether high accrual firms are more likely to have subsequent SEC enforcement actions taken against them for overstating earnings. Their results are consistent with this prediction. Dechow, Ge, Larson, and Sloan (2011) provide similar evidence using a more comprehensive sample of SEC enforcement actions. Both of these studies show that firms accused of manipulating earnings have unusually high accruals. The accounts most often alleged to be subject to manipulation are accounts receivable and inventory. In addition, the high accruals for these manipulation firms reverse and become sharply negative in subsequent years.

In related research, Dechow and Ge (2006) focus specifically on low accrual firms and argue that, when low accruals are driven by special items (i.e., write-offs and other unusual negative items), the low accruals will be less persistent (earnings will improve more quickly). Their evidence is consistent with this prediction. They find that the positive future returns are much higher for low accrual firms with special items than for other low accrual firms. This is somewhat surprising, because managers have an incentive to highlight the temporary nature of the negative special items to investors. Dechow and Ge (2006) find that low accrual firms with negative special items tend to have performed particularly poorly and have lost popularity with analysts and investors. They conclude that investors overreacted to bad news related to negative special items and are subsequently positively surprised when performance improves.

The Accrual Anomaly around the World

The accrual anomaly has been examined in other countries besides the United States, providing supporting evidence of its robustness. It is not just a freak occurrence in U.S. markets. Table 2.2 is extracted from Leippold and Lohre (2010) and summarizes the key results of their study and a related study by Pincus et al. (2007). The accrual anomaly generates positive hedge returns in 22 out of 26 countries (85%) in the Leippold and Lohre study.

TABLE 2.2 Studies on the Global Accrual Anomaly

	Leippold and Lohre (2010)	Pincus et al. (2007)
Panel A: Data Characteristics		
Balance sheet data	DS	GV
Return data	DS	GV Issues
Period	1994–2008	1994–2002
Sample size	96,309 FY	62,027 FY
FY per year	6,879 FY	6,892 FY
Accruals method	BSM	BSM
Panel B: Common Law Countries' Alphas		
Australia	**8.28**	**17.88**
Canada	5.40	**8.28**
Hong Kong	**25.92**	5.04
India	*11.64*	4.70
Ireland	−0.36	−
Malaysia	0.60	**8.64**
New Zeland	6.24	−
Singapore	3.12	1.44
Thailand	**13.56**	**20.64**
UK	*3.00*	**9.96**
US	**7.92**	**8.40**
Panel C: Code Law Countries' Alphas		
Belgium	−7.80	−
Denmark	**17.28**	*8.52*
France	4.56	*8.16*
Germany	**5.76**	*6.60*
Greece	3.84	−
Indonesia	19.08	−12.60
Italy	**11.04**	*11.76*
Japan	**3.96**	**5.76**
Netherlands	3.36	2.16
Norway	4.56	−
South Korea	**10.20**	−
Spain	−0.12	−6.96
Sweden	5.76	9.24
Switzerland	**11.64**	4.92
Taiwan	−5.52	−0.48
Total number of countries	26	20
Number of countries with positive hedge returns	22	17
Percent of countries with positive hedge	85%	85%
Number of countries with statistically significant positive hedge return (p-value <0.1)	12	11

Alpha is the intercept of the regression of the accrual hedge portfolio return on the market portfolio, size, and book-to-market portfolios, and it essentially represents the abnormal hedge portfolio return adjusted for Fama and French risk factors. Alphas that are significant at a 10%-level are in italics, alphas significant at a 5%-level or better are in boldface. Alphas are given in percentage terms. GV denotes Global Vantage (Industrial/Commercial), Comp. denotes Compustat, DS denotes Datastream, and BSM stands for Balance Sheet Method. CGB-BMI denotes the Citigroup Bank Broad Market Indexes.

Of these, 12 are significant at the 10% level. For the Pincus et al. study, the accrual hedge return is positive in 17 out of 20 countries (85%) and significant in 11 of them. Chan, Chan, Jegadeesh, and Lakonishok (2006) also show that the accrual anomaly exists in the U.K., which is consistent with the studies reported in Table 2.2.

There are several things to consider when examining international evidence. First, the general takeaway from international research is that the accrual anomaly appears stronger in common law countries than in civil law countries. This suggests that it holds more strongly in countries with established capital markets that have similar accounting and legal systems to the United States. Second, the number of observations varies considerably across countries with the United States and the United Kingdom having far more observations than other countries. Therefore, low test power is a possible explanation for the lack of significance in countries with less established markets. Finally, related to our discussion of Shi and Zhang (2011) earlier, the accrual anomaly is expected to be stronger in countries that have both (1) stronger reactions to earnings news; and (2) where accruals are *relatively* less persistent than cash flows. Therefore, even if investors in all countries fixate on earnings, we would still expect variation across countries in the returns to the accrual anomaly.

Alternative Explanations for the Accrual Anomaly

We start this section by noting that the large body of evidence discussed in the previous section systematically supports Sloan's original explanation. With all this corroborating evidence, you might wonder whether there could conceivably be a different explanation that is consistent with the same set of results. However, because market efficiency is such an entrenched paradigm, many researchers have sought to provide alternative explanations to try and preserve it. We group these explanations into three categories. The first two categories are consistent with the efficient markets hypothesis. These include risk-based explanations and research design issues. The third category does not necessarily question the anomaly itself, but provides a different interpretation that relates to investor pricing of growth.

Risk-Based Explanations

Risk-based explanations are the natural default explanation of efficient market aficionados for any anomaly. The basic idea is that stocks with predictably higher (lower) returns must be more (less) risky. Investors are assumed to have already figured this out and have priced the stocks accordingly. In order to make a compelling case that the accrual anomaly is attributable to risk, one first has to come up with a story about why investors find low (high) accrual stock more (less) risky. Ideally, one would like to identify the underlying risk factor and show that it subsumes accruals in predicting future returns. The next step is to explain why the evidence from the previous two sections is also consistent with the risk-based explanation. Existing research in this area generally does a poor job on both counts.

Neither the standard CAPM nor three-factor Fama-French model explains the returns to the accrual anomaly. In fact, Sloan (1996) checked to see whether existing risk metrics subsumed the accrual anomaly, and they did not. So researchers have tried to find new risk factors that could potentially subsume the accrual anomaly. Khan (2008) proposes a four-factor risk model, which is essentially the standard Fama-French three-factor model with the excess return on the market portfolio decomposed into discount-rate news and cash-flow news. He also uses quintiles in place of deciles to construct accrual hedge portfolios. After doing so, he finds that the economic and statistical significance of the accrual anomaly is diminished. Khan then claims that the four-factor model captures rationally priced economic and financial distress characteristics that are correlated with accruals. Khan's research suffers from at least 3 shortcomings. First, he conducts low power tests. By incorporating additional factors and using quintiles in place of deciles, we would mechanically expect the economic and statistical significance of the accrual anomaly to decline even if Sloan's hypothesis is true. Second, Khan doesn't explicitly identify the characteristics that are supposedly captured by accruals. He doesn't measure them directly and show that they subsume the accrual anomaly. Finally he doesn't explain the other evidence from the previous section that is also consistent with Sloan's explanation.

Hirshleifer et al. (2011) cast further doubt on the risk explanation in general and Khan's explanation in particular. The authors follow Fama and French (1993) methodology and construct an accrual factor mimicking portfolio, that is, a portfolio that goes long in low accruals firms and short in high accruals firms. They label it the "conservative minus aggressive" (CMA) portfolio. The accrual factor is analogous to the "small minus big" (SMB) and "high minus low" (HML) factors of the three-factor Fama-French model. The basic idea is that, if risk explains the accrual anomaly, then firms whose returns co-move with the accrual factor should have higher returns. However, their statistical tests fail to confirm such a prediction. In contrast, the authors find that the level of accruals predicts returns irrespective of the covariation of the returns with the CMA factor. Hirshleifer et al. conclude that investors misvalue accruals and cast doubt on the rational risk-based explanation.

Research Design Issues

The accrual anomaly has been successfully replicated. In fact, documenting the accrual anomaly is an exercise that is often given to accounting PhD students to hone their computing skills. It is in the data. If you don't find it, you did something wrong. However, it is still possible that there is some sort of research design error, such as the use of information that wouldn't really have been available to investors in real time. In order to explore this possibility, Livnat and Santicchia (2006) use a unique point-in-time database containing originally reported, unrestated financial data and they also use actual SEC filing dates to begin investing on this information. Their results corroborate Sloan's original results using standard Compustat data and a 4-month lag to allow for SEC filings, so hindsight bias doesn't appear to be a problem.

A paper by Kraft, Leone, and Wasley (2006) shows that deleting extreme future stock returns causes the accrual anomaly to disappear. The authors claim that this evidence is inconsistent with Sloan's explanation for the accrual anomaly, but subsequent research by Teoh and Zhang (2009) points out that there is a natural explanation for the results in Kraft et al. (2006) and that Kraft et al. are wrong in claiming that their evidence is inconsistent with Sloan's explanation for the accrual anomaly. To see why, first note that Kraft et al. are not removing data errors but actual cases where firms had spectacularly high future returns. Because firms with extreme accruals tend to have more volatile returns, removing spectacular performers causes the average returns to be lower for extreme accrual firms. Of course, an investor would love to have known which firms were going to have spectacular stock returns, but Kraft et al. only identify these firms with the benefit of hindsight. It seems ironic that Kraft et al. could only make the accrual anomaly disappear by using a flawed research design that incorporates significant hindsight bias.

Growth-Based Explanations

Growth-based explanations for the accrual anomaly are the most difficult to refute, because the explanations themselves are poorly defined.[5] There is no doubt that accruals represent a type of growth. Specifically, they represent growth in management's estimates of the future benefits that will accrue

---

[5]Cooper et al. (2008) document a negative relation between firm total asset growth and future stock returns; Fairfield, Whisenant, and Yohn (2004) document a negative relation between changes in net operating assets and future returns; thus both studies use growth proxies that capture accruals. Zhang (2007) uses employee growth, but employee growth does not subsume the accrual anomaly (see Chu 2011).

to a firm. Sloan (1996) argues that when accruals are unusually high, the expected future benefits are less likely to materialize, causing future earnings to be lower. Fairfield, Whisenant, and Yohn (2003) provide an alternative explanation for this finding. They argue that diminishing returns to new investment cause the lower future earnings and stock returns. Under their story, accountants are correctly measuring the future benefits. However, increases in the number of units produced and sold lead to lower prices and hence lower future profitability. In the language of an economist, a shift to the right in the supply curve pushes the equilibrium market clearing price down the downward sloping demand curve.

If the Fairfield et al. (2003) explanation were true, one would expect more direct measures of quantity sold to be better at predicting future reductions in earnings and stock returns. For example, growth in sales should have stronger implications for earnings persistence and stock returns. However, evidence in Xie (2001), Chan, Chan, Jegadeesh, and Lakonishok (2006) and Richardson, Sloan, Soliman, and Tuna (2006) shows that accruals that are *unrelated* to contemporaneous sales are better at predicting future returns than those accruals that are related to sales. This evidence is inconsistent with the growth explanation and consistent with Sloan's original explanation. In addition, much of the evidence presented is difficult to reconcile with the growth explanation. For example, Allen et al. (2010) find that predictable returns are attributable to extreme accrual reversals, which is more consistent with the earnings quality explanation than the diminishing returns to scale explanation. Finally, a recent paper by Chu (2011) finds evidence that is consistent with Sloan's explanation but inconsistent with the growth explanation. Chu identifies a set of firms that operate with negative working capital (current assets are less than current liabilities). For such firms, growth in units sold and net operating accruals tend to move in opposite directions. This is because current liabilities grow more than current assets as the firm grows sales. Thus, Chu identifies a unique setting where the earnings quality and growth explanations have conflicting predictions. Chu's results support the earnings-quality explanation. She finds that firms with low operating accruals have high sales growth, but such firms have higher future earnings and positive future stock returns. The growth explanation would predict that high sales growth firms would have low future earnings and lower future returns.

A different growth-related explanation is offered in Desai et al. (2004). This study suggests that high accruals identify "glamour" stock, whereas low accruals identify "value" stock. They show that the ratio of cash flow to price is positively related to future stock returns and subsumes the accrual anomaly. They suggest that this evidence is consistent with investors over extrapolating growth prospects in high accrual firms rather than with earnings fixation. Yet their cash flow to price ratio should capture both investor fixation on earnings (because cash flows are the more persistent component of earnings) and the well-known value glamour anomaly (because they deflate by price). In other words, they seem to combine two existing anomalies rather than demonstrating that one subsumes the other.

Finally, Wu, Zhang, and Zhang (2010) provide what they call the q-theory hypothesis to explain the accrual anomaly. Intuitively, their idea is based on the idea that the discount rates used by firms' managers to evaluate investments vary considerably both across firms and over time. So if a manager wakes up one morning to discover that her firm's discount rate has dropped, the manager will increase investment (causing high accruals), and then diminishing returns to new investment will set in, leading to both lower future earnings and stock returns. Note that the q-theory allows for a *potentially* rational link between accruals and future returns. If these movements in discount rates occur for rational reasons, then rationally lower discount rates should lead to rationally higher accruals and rationally lower future returns. Of course, all these predictions would still hold if discount rates jumped about for irrational reasons. For example, money that poured into the Internet sector during the tech bubble of the late 1990s caused increased investment and lower future returns, but many observers attribute the tech bubble to irrationally low discount rates (e.g., Shiller 2000).

The evidence in support of q-theory presented by Wu et al. (2010) suffers from many of the shortcomings discussed earlier. First, the underlying reason for the variation in discount rates is not identified. Second, the evidence in Hirshleifer et al. (2011) suggests that it is the accrual characteristic rather than the accrual factor that predicts future stock returns. This makes it difficult to attribute any related variation in discount rates to rationally priced risk. Third, the finding that the accrual anomaly is not subsumed by other measures of growth is difficult to reconcile with diminishing returns to new investment driving the accrual anomaly.

A final problem for the q-theory is that its predictions apply to all investments made by firms, including investments in R&D and marketing. R&D and marketing investments are particularly interesting, because they must be immediately expensed for accounting purposes even though they result in expected future benefits. Thus, the q-theory predicts these investments will have a negative relation with future earnings and stock returns, whereas the earnings fixation theory predicts a positive relation (because they must be immediately expensed, causing current earnings to be lower). The evidence supports the earnings fixation theory and is inconsistent with the q-theory. Chan, Lakonishok, and Sougiannis (2001) find no evidence that high R&D firms have lower future returns and some evidence that they have higher future returns. Penman and Zhang (2002) show that firms with unusually high R&D and marketing expenditures have higher future earnings and stock returns.

Summing Up on Competing Explanations

So where does all this leave us? Here is our opinion. First, the accrual anomaly is unlikely to be attributable to rationally priced risk. The idea that investors are rationally pricing some sort of risk that has eluded academics for many years seems far-fetched. The possibility that research design flaws drive the accrual anomaly also seems far-fetched. However, the growth explanation is more difficult to rule out. There is little doubt in our minds that there are diminishing returns to new investment and that investors and managers sometimes overinvest in response to behavioral biases such as irrational exuberance. Can the accrual anomaly be completely explained by growth-related explanations? We think not. A large body of evidence ties the accrual anomaly to the earnings fixation explanation. Moreover, the fact that we do not observe similar anomalies for investments that have to be expensed immediately for accounting purposes contradicts the growth explanation and corroborates the earnings fixation explanation.

It seems likely to us that both the growth and earnings fixation explanations are at work and often reinforce each other. The recent financial crisis provides a good case in point. In the lead-up to the crisis, many banks were able to report strong profits by recklessly issuing loans that were unlikely to be repaid. The banks capitalized the promised future payments of these loans on their balance sheets, resulting in high accruals and earnings.[6] They were able to report high earnings because they did not adequately allow for the likelihood that the promised payments would not be made. Moreover, these very profits encouraged the banks to make even more reckless loans and encouraged investors to supply them with even more capital. In other words, fixation on earnings was a primary determinant of overinvestment in bad loans. If the banks had increased their allowance for loan losses so as to indicate that the loans were expected to be unprofitable, banks and investors would have been less likely to continue investing in bad loans. In other words, overinvestment is much more likely when the accounting overstates the future benefits associated with current investment. This highlights the critical importance of having good accounting principles

---

[6]Interestingly, many of the banks also went to great lengths to place the receivables in special purpose entities that allowed them to remove the associated accruals from the balance sheet and in many cases booked even higher earnings through the recording of associated "gains on sale" (see Dechow, Myers, and Shakespeare 2010).

that prevent managers from overstating the expected future benefits from current investment.

Practical Implications

So can you make money from the accrual anomaly? Well, we have both good and bad news. We'll start with the bad news. Mashruwala, Rajgopal, and Shevlin (2006) show that the accrual anomaly is concentrated in small thinly traded stocks with volatile stock returns and so involves considerable arbitrage risk. Also, recall that the hedge portfolio strategies constructed in accrual research involve short positions. In practice, these short positions could be difficult and costly to implement. Thus, although the accruals anomaly is one of the most robust anomalies ever discovered, the risks and costs involved in exploiting it are significant.

However, to make things worse, a recent paper by Green et al. (2010) indicates that the accrual anomaly started to disappear around the year 2000 (that's 4 years after the publication of Sloan's original paper). They conjecture that the decline of the accrual anomaly is at least partly due to hedge funds trying to exploit the anomaly. Anecdotal evidence supports their conjecture. For example, several of the academics who conducted early research on the accrual anomaly were subsequently hired by hedge funds.

So now that we have told you the accrual anomaly has been largely arbitraged away, what is the good news? The good news lies back in Sloan's original 1996 paper. Sloan's original research was motivated by the idea that good fundamental analysis should facilitate the evaluation of the quality of earnings. If other investors haven't done their homework, it should also facilitate the identification of mispriced securities.

Simply ranking firms on accruals hardly constitutes good fundamental analysis. What made Sloan's approach so novel at the time was that it could easily be applied using standardized financial statements in computerized databases. In other words, Sloan did some very sloppy fundamental analysis, but he did it on a very large number of firms in an expedient manner. What Sloan did is very easy to copy, so it stands to reason that investors caught on to it and arbitraged it away. His results, however, serve to highlight the potential gains from more thorough fundamental analysis that can distinguish between "bad" accruals that will reverse and "good" accruals that correctly anticipate future benefits.

Thorough fundamental analysis involves getting to know a firm and conducting a detailed evaluation of its financial statements. Such analysis, properly conducted, will never go out of style and is essential for keeping securities markets reasonably efficient. We expect that the lasting lesson from Sloan (1996) will be that leading edge fundamental analysis will always facilitate the evaluation of earnings quality and the identification of mispriced securities. As time goes by, the technology of fundamental analysis should improve. This, in turn, should improve the efficiency of capital markets, which are the lifeblood of capitalist economies. If we are right, this should be good news for all of us!

Appendix 2.1: Estimation and Testing Framework Used in Sloan (1996)

This appendix summarizes Sloan's formal equations and statistical tests. Sloan (1996) used an econometric approach developed by Mishkin (1983) to infer investors' expectations from security prices. This technique has been used extensively by follow-up research. The technique estimates both a rational forecasting equation and a pricing equation from which the forecasting equation that is being used by investors is inferred. By comparing the estimated parameters from the rational forecasting equation to those in the pricing equation, we can test Sloan's hypothesis that investors fixate on earnings.

Sloan begins with the following basic earnings forecasting regression:

$$\text{Earnings}_{t+1} = \alpha_0 + \alpha_1 \text{Earnings}_t + \upsilon_{t+1} \qquad (2.1)$$

This equation indicates that we can forecast next year's earnings using this year's earnings. The estimated coefficient α_1 measures the persistence of earnings. Recall from Figure 2.4a that earnings are slowly mean reverting, which means that we expect α_1 to be somewhat less than one. Sloan reports that α_1 equals 0.84, indicating that approximately 84% of current year earnings persists into next year. If investors fixate on earnings and ignore information in accruals and cash flows, they should use this forecasting equation.

Sloan next decomposed earnings into cash and accrual components and examined the following forecasting equation. Recall from Figure 2.4 that the accrual component of earnings is less persistent than the cash component, so Sloan estimated the following modified version of equation (2.1):

$$\text{Earnings}_{t+1} = \gamma_0 + \gamma_1 \text{Accruals}_t + \gamma_2 \text{Cash Flows}_t + \upsilon_{t+1} \qquad (2.2)$$

Sloan hypothesized that γ_1 would be less than γ_2. This is just another way of saying he expected the accrual component to be less persistent than the cash component. Consistent with his hypothesis, he found that γ_1 was 0.77 and γ_2 was 0.91. In other words, only 77% of earnings that is made up of accruals persist into the next year, whereas 91% of earnings that is made up of cash flows persist into the next year. This result formalizes Sloan's hypothesis that the accrual component of earnings is of lower quality than the cash component.

The next step is to determine whether investors use forecasting equation (2.1) or forecasting equation (2.2). If investors fixate on earnings, as Sloan hypothesized, they should use (2.1). However, if they are more sophisticated and recognize that accruals are of lower quality than cash flows, they should use (2.2). To do this, Sloan estimates the following equation:

$$\text{Returns}_{t+1} = \beta v_{t+1}^* + \varepsilon_{t+1} = \beta(\text{Earnings}_{t+1} - \gamma_0^* - \gamma_1^* \text{ Accruals}_t$$
$$- \gamma_2^* \text{ Cash Flows}_t) + \varepsilon_{t+1} \tag{2.3}$$

This equation says that the security returns in year $t + 1$ respond to the unexpected portion of earnings in year $t + 1$, with β representing the valuation multiplier or earnings response coefficient. The expression in parentheses represents unexpected earnings, which is equal to actual earnings for period $t + 1$, less the forecast of earnings for period $t + 1$ using information about accruals and cash flows in period t. Note that the persistence coefficients in this equation represent those that are embedded in stock prices and are not necessarily equal to the rational coefficients in equation (2.2). If investors fixate on earnings, as in equation (2.1), then $\gamma_1^* = \gamma_2^* = \alpha_1 = 0.84$. If, however, investors understand the lower quality of the accrual component of earnings, then $\gamma_1^* = \gamma_1 = 0.77$ and $\gamma_2^* = \gamma_2 = 0.91$.

The estimated values of these parameters turned out to be $\gamma_1^* = 0.91$ and $\gamma_2^* = 0.83$. These point estimates are very close to those predicted by the earnings fixation story and are inconsistent with investors understanding the lower quality of the accrual component of earnings. Note that although the rational forecasting equation yields $\gamma_1 < \gamma_2$, the pricing equation yields $\gamma_1^* > \gamma_2^*$. This indicates that, if anything, investors think the accrual component of earnings is *more* persistent than the cash component! It is important to note that the difference between γ_1^* and γ_2^* is not statistically significant, so the data are consistent with the hypothesis that investors fixate on earnings.

One final point we make in closing regards the Mishkin estimation framework. Subsequent research has leveled criticisms at the use of this framework (e.g., Kraft, Leone, and Wasley (2007) and Lewellen (2010)). Equations (2.1), (2.2), and (2.3) could have been estimated using ordinary least squares (OLS). The main issue that would be encountered using standard OLS would be the lack of direct estimates and associated standard errors for γ_1^* and γ_2^*. This is because OLS estimation would be of the following form:

$$\text{Returns}_{t+1} = \beta\text{Earnings}_{t+1} - \beta\gamma_0^* - \beta\gamma_1^* \text{Accruals}_t - \beta\gamma_2^* \text{Cash Flows}_t + \varepsilon_{t+1}$$

$$(2.4)$$

and so would return estimates of $\beta\gamma_1^*$ and $\beta\gamma_2^*$. The Mishkin framework extracts the underlying parameter estimates by using nonlinear least squares estimation, but is asymptotically equivalent to OLS. Thus, the Mishkin approach allows us to directly estimate and test hypotheses relating to fixation on earnings.

The criticism made by Kraft, Leone, and Wasley (2007) and Lewellen (2010) is that something else could be correlated with both accruals and future stock returns and this "something else" could be the real cause of all the results. This is what is commonly known in the academic circles as a correlated omitted variable. However, unless "something else" can be identified and a compelling reason offered about why it should be correlated with future returns, this sort of criticism is empty.

Finally, if you refer back to equation (2.3), you will see that the magnitude of the predictable returns associated with accruals is determined by three parameters. The first is β, the valuation multiplier. The bigger the stock returns to an earnings surprise, the greater the predictable returns to a predictable earnings surprise. The second is γ_1, the persistence of the accrual component of earnings. The lower the persistence of the accrual component of earnings, the stronger the negative relation between accruals and future stock returns. The third is γ_2, the persistence of the cash flow component of earnings. The higher the persistence of the cash flow component of earnings, the stronger the negative relation between accruals and future stock returns (because investors fixate on earnings and higher cash flow persistence leads to higher earnings persistence). Shi and Zhang (2011) check to see whether the accrual anomaly is in fact higher where Sloan's hypothesis predicts it will be. They find that the accrual anomaly is higher both when β is higher and when $(\gamma_2 - \gamma_1)$ is higher. An investment strategy going long (short) in low (high) accrual firms with high β and $(\gamma_2 - \gamma_1)$ yields hedge portfolio returns of an astounding 69% annualized return. It should, however, be noted that the breadth of this strategy is small and it tends to concentrate in smaller and more volatile securities.

Appendix 2.2: Details on the Broader Definition of Accruals

This appendix is provided to show you how to decompose a balance sheet into various categories of accruals. Figure 2.7 provides Harley Davison's balance sheet. We chose Harley Davidson because its balance sheet contains many different line items. As we mentioned in the simple example discussed at the beginning of the chapter, all line items on the balance sheet are subject to accounting rules. Even cash is subject to accounting rules and measurement issues (e.g., foreign currency translation, definition and measurement of cash equivalents). However, some accounts are measured with more reliability than others. Richardson, Sloan, Soliman, and Tuna (2005) argue that the lower the reliability of measurements in an account, the more likely it will reflect future benefits with error and the lower the associated earnings persistence.

The first column of Figure 2.7 classifies each line item according to whether the line item relates to an operating or financing activity. Cash and short-term marketable securities are classified as financial assets, since they are financial in nature and unrelated to primary business operations. The remaining assets are classified as operating assets because they are related to the underlying business operations. Liabilities are classified as operating, with the exception of those representing debt financing, which are classified as financing. The second column reports the classification of the reliability of each line item given by Richardson et al. Operating assets are all classified as having low reliability. This is because they tend to involve subjective assessments on the part of management. For example, accounts receivable involves the assessment of credit risk and the associated allowance for uncollectibles. If these assessments are incorrect, earnings will be misstated and the misstatement will have reverse in another period. Liabilities, such as accounts payable, involve less subjective assessment and so have higher reliability. The key exceptions are pensions and other postretirement liabilities. Note that Harley Davidson has finance receivables held for sale and investment. Should these finance receivables be classified as financial assets or operating assets? We classify them as operating assets, because they arise from credit provided to customers and distributors and, therefore, their measurement directly impacts Harley's operating income.

We now define total accruals (TACC) as the change in all balance sheet accounts aside from cash. Total accruals consists of three categories (see bottom of Figure 2.7):

Change in noncash working capital (ΔWC) = Change in current operating assets (ΔCOA) − Change in current operating liabilities (ΔCOL)

Change in noncurrent net operating assets (ΔNCO) = Change in noncurrent operating assets (ΔNCOA) − Change in noncurrent operating liabilities (ΔNCOL)

Harley-Davidson, Inc. Consolidated Balance Sheets December 31, 2009 and 2008 (in thousands)

	Measurement reliability		**31-Dec-09**	**31-Dec-08**	**Difference**
		Assets			
		Current assets:			
Cash	High	Cash and cash equivalents	$ 1,630,433	$ 568,894	1,061,539
FinA	High	Marketable securities	39,685	0	39,685
COA	Low	Accounts receivable, net	269,371	265,319	4,052
COA	Low	Finance receivables held for sale	0	2,443,965	−2,443,965
		Finance receivables held for			
COA	Low	investment, net	1,436,114	1,378,461	57,653
COA	Low	Inventories	323,029	379,141	−56,112
		Assets of discontinued			
COA	Low	operations	181,211	238,715	−57,504
COA	Low	Deferred income taxes	179,685	123,327	56,358
		Prepaid expenses and other			
COA	Low	current assets	282,421	128,730	153,691
		Total current assets	**4,341,949**	**5,526,552**	**−1,184,603**
		Finance receivables held for			
NCOA	Low	investment, net	3,621,048	817,102	2,803,946
		Property, plant, and equipment,			
NCOA	Low	net	906,906	1,056,928	−150,022
NCOA	Low	Goodwill	31,400	60,131	−28,731
NCOA	Low	Deferred income taxes	177,504	288,240	−110,736
NCOA	Low	Other long-term assets	76,711	79,672	−2,961
			$ 9,155,518	$ 7,828,625	1,326,893
		Liabilities and Shareholders' Equity			
		Current liabilities:			
COL	High	Accounts payable	$ 162,515	$ 303,277	−140,762
COL	High	Accrued liabilities	514,084	503,466	10,618
		Liabilities of discontinued			
COL	High	operations	69,535	77,941	−8,406
FinL	High	Short-term debt	189,999	1,738,649	−1,548,650
		Current portion of long-term			
FinL	High	debt	1,332,091	0	1,332,091
		Total current liabilities	**2,268,224**	**2,623,333**	**−355,109**
FinL	High	Long-term debt	4,114,039	2,176,238	1,937,801
NCOL	Medium	Pension liability	245,332	484,003	−238,671
		Postretirement health care			
NCOL	Medium	liability	264,472	274,408	−9,936
NCOL	Medium	Other long-term liabilities	155,333	155,040	293
		Total noncurrent liabilities	**4,779,176**	**3,089,689**	**1,689,487**
		Total shareholders' equity	**2,108,118**	**2,115,603**	**−7,485**
			$ 9,155,518	$ 7,828,625	1,326,893

Accruals redefined

				%Average Assets
ΔWC	Medium	ΔCOA − ΔCOL	−2,147,277	−25.29%
ΔNCO	Low	ΔNCOA − ΔNCOL	2,759,810	32.50%
ΔNOA	Medium	ΔWC + ΔNCO	612,533	7.21%
ΔFin	High	ΔFinA − ΔFinL	−1,681,557	−19.80%
TACC	Medium	ΔWC + ΔNCO + ΔFin	−1,069,024	−12.59%
ΔCash	High		1,061,539	12.50%
ΔEquity	Medium		−7,485	

FIGURE 2.7 Broadening the Definition of Accruals Using the Balance Sheet

Change in net financial assets (ΔFin) = Change in financial assets (ΔFinA) − Change in financial liabilities (ΔFinL):

$$\Delta TACC = \Delta WC + \Delta NCO + \Delta Fin$$

Note that:

$$Equity = Assets - Liabilities = Cash + WC + NCO + Fin$$

And so:

$$\Delta Equity = \Delta Cash + \Delta WC + \Delta NCO + \Delta Fin$$

Now recall from your accounting classes that the change in the book value of equity equals income less net distributions of income (i.e., dividends):

$$\Delta Equity = Income - Dividends$$

where Dividends are the net cash distributions made to investors (dividends plus repurchases less equity issuances). Substituting (Income − Dividends) for ΔEquity and rearranging gives:

$$Income = Dividends + \Delta Cash + \Delta WC + \Delta NCO + \Delta Fin$$

This expression indicates that income can be decomposed into a cash component, composed of dividends plus the increase in the cash balance[7] and an accrual component composed of working capital accruals, noncurrent operating assets, and the change in net financial assets.

We can further define the change in net operating assets (ΔNOA) as:

$$\Delta NOA = \Delta WC + \Delta NCO$$

You can see from Figure 2.7 that the change in working capital (ΔWC), for Harley is −2,147,277, (−25.9% of average assets). This level of ΔWC is in the *bottom* 10% of all firms listed on Compustat. In contrast, the change in noncurrent net operating assets (ΔNCO) is 2,759,810, (32.5% of average assets). This level of ΔNCO is in the *top* 10% of all firms listed on Compustat. In contrast, the change in net operating assets (ΔNOA) is 612,533, (7% of

---

[7]Dechow, Richardson, and Sloan (2008) show that the portion of the cash component attributable to dividends is more persistent than the portion of the cash component attributable to the change in the cash balance. This insight can be used to construct even more refined measures of earnings quality and improved trading strategies.

average assets) and puts Harley Davidson in the middle of the Compustat distribution of ΔNOA. Thus, we get different signals of earnings quality using different measures of accruals and so what should we do?

A careful examination of the balance sheet (and a reading of the footnotes) can explain the conflicting signals. In the second quarter of 2009, Harley ended its practice of meeting accounting requirements to use "gain on sale" accounting for its receivables. This change in accounting practice did not necessarily reflect a change in Harley's underlying business, but it did change their balance sheet. Harley reclassified several billion dollars of receivables from held for sale (current assets) to held for investment (noncurrent assets) and this is a major driver of the different signals we obtained using working capital accruals versus noncurrent operating accruals.

The takeaway from this exercise is that it is important to understand what is driving extreme accruals before jumping to conclusions about earnings quality. In Harley's case, the extreme accruals were the result of a change in an accounting procedure, whereas in the KB Home case the extreme accruals were the result of slowing demand and associated inventory buildups. These are quite different reasons for extreme accruals and have different implications for future earnings.

A final issue is whether to use the balance sheet or the statement of cash flows to calculate accruals. We have used the balance sheet. Another procedure for estimating the components of accruals is as follows (where* indicates that the variable is obtained from the statement of cash flows):

$$\Delta WC^* = \text{Income} + \text{Depreciation and Amortization}^*$$
$$- \text{Cash from Operating Activities}^*$$
$$\Delta NOA^* = \text{Income} - \text{Cash from Operating Activities}^*$$
$$- \text{Cash from Investing Activities}^*$$
$$TACC^* = \text{Income} - \Delta Cash^* - \text{Dividends}$$

Which approach is better is unclear. The statement of cash flows doesn't list accruals relating to noncash activities (e.g., reclassifications between two noncash accounts, capital lease transactions, stock-based acquisitions). The bottom line is that the accrual anomaly is strongest using the balance sheet approach. This is presumably because accruals related to noncash activities also result in lower earnings quality. However, we always recommend looking at the statement of cash flows and understanding any differences (see also Collins and Hribar 2002). For example, in Harley's case, this would have alerted you to the fact that the drop in working capital accruals was attributable to a reclassification.

References

Ali, A., X. Chen, T. Yao, and T. Yu. 2008. Do mutual funds profit from the accruals anomaly? *Journal of Accounting Research* 46 (1): 1–26.

Allen, E., J. Larson, R. Chad, and R. G. Sloan. 2010 Accrual reversals, earnings, and stock returns. Working paper.

Bhojraj, S., and B. Swaminathan. 2009. How does the corporate bond market value capital investments and accruals? *Review of Accounting Studies* 14 (1): 31–62.

Bradshaw, M. T., S. A. Richardson, and R. G. Sloan. 2001. Do analysts and auditors use information in accruals? *Journal of Accounting Research* 39 (1): 45–74.

Chan, K., L. K. C. Chan, N. Jegadeesh, and J. Lakonishok. 2006. Earnings quality and stock returns, *Journal of Business* 79 (3): 1041–1082.

Chu, J. 2011. Does growth subsume the implications of accruals for future performance? Working paper.

Collins, D. W., and P. Hribar. 2002. Errors in estimating accruals: Implications for empirical research. *Journal of Accounting Research* 40: 105–134.

Collins, D., G. Gong, and P. Hribar. 2003. Investor sophistication and the mispricing of accruals. *Review of Accounting Studies* 8 (2–3): 251–276.

Cooper, M. J., H. Gulen, and M. J. Schill. 2008. Asset growth and the cross-section of stock returns. *Journal of Finance* 63 (4): 1609–1651.

Dechow, P. M., and W. Ge. 2006. The persistence of earnings and cash flows and the role of special items: Implications for the accrual anomaly. *Review of Accounting Studies* 11: 253–296.

Dechow, P. M., S. A Richardson, and R. G. Sloan. 2008. The persistence and pricing of the cash component of earnings. *Journal of Accounting Research* 46 (1): 537–566.

Dechow, P. M., W. Ge, C. R. Larson, and R. G. Sloan. 2011. Predicting material accounting misstatements. In *Contemporary Accounting Research*, Forthcoming.

Desai, H. M., S. Rajgopal, and M. Venkatachalam. 2004. Value-glamour and accruals mispricing: One anomaly or two? *The Accounting Review* 79 (2): 355–385.

Fairfield, P. M., J. S. Whisenant, and T. L. Yohn. 2003. Accrued earnings and growth: Implications for future profitability and market mispricing. *Accounting Review* 78 (1): 353–371.

Graham, B., and D. Dodd. 1934. *Security analysis: Principles and technique.* 1st ed. New York and London: McGraw-Hill.

Green, J., J. R. M. Hand, and M. Soliman. 2010. Going, going, gone? The demise of the accruals anomaly, *Management Science* (forthcoming).

Hafzalla, N., R. Lundholm, and E. Van Winkle. 2011. Percent accruals. *Accounting Review* 86 (1): 209–236.

Hirshleifer, D. A., K. Hou, S. Teoh, and Y. Zhang. 2004. Do investors over-value firms with bloated balance sheets? *Journal of Accounting and Economics* 38: 297–331.

Hirshleifer, D. A., K. Hou, and S. H. Teoh. 2011. The accrual anomaly: Risk or mispricing? *Management Science* (forthcoming).

Khan, M. 2008. Are accruals mispriced: Evidence from tests of an intertemporal capital asset pricing model. *Journal of Accounting and Economics* 45 (1): 55–77.

Kraft, A., A. Leone, and C. Wasley. 2006. An analysis of the theories and explanations offered for the mispricing of accruals and accrual components. *Journal of Accounting Research* 44 (2): 297–339.

Kraft, A., A. Leone, and C. Wasley. 2007. Regression-based tests of the market pricing of accounting numbers: The Mishkin test and ordinary least squares. *Journal of Accounting Research* 45 (5): 1081–1114.

Leippold, M., and H. Lohre. 2010. Data snooping and the global accrual anomaly. Working paper. 2010, EFA 2007 Ljubljana Meetings Paper.

Lev, B., and D. Nissim. 2006. The persistence of the accruals anomaly. *Contemporary Accounting Research* 23 (1): 193–226.

Livnat, J., and M. Santicchia. 2006. Cash flows, accruals and future returns. *Financial Analysts Journal* 62 (4): 48–61.

Mashruwala, C., S. Rajgopal, and T. Shevlin, 2006. Why is the accrual anomaly not arbitraged away? The role of idiosyncratic risk and transaction costs. *Journal of Accounting and Economics* 42 (1–2): 3–33.

Mishkin, F. 1983. A rational expectations approach to macroeconomics: Testing policy ineffectiveness and efficient-markets models, The University of Chicago Press, Chicago, IL, 60637, for the National Bureau of Economic Research, Inc.

Pincus, M., S. Rajgopal, and M. Venkatachalam. 2007. The accrual anomaly: International evidence. *Accounting Review* 82 (1): 169–203.

Richardson, S. A., R. G. Sloan, M. T. Soliman, and I. Tuna. 2005. Accrual reliability, earnings persistence and stock prices. *Journal of Accounting & Economics* 39 (3): 437–485.

Richardson, S. A., R. G. Sloan, M. T. Soliman, and I. Tuna. 2006. The implications of accounting distortions and growth for accruals and profitability. *Accounting Review* 81 (3): 713–743.

Shi, L., and H. Zhang. 2011. Can the earnings fixation hypothesis explain the accrual anomaly? *The Review of Accounting Studies* (forthcoming).

Skinner, D. J. 1994. Why firms voluntarily disclose bad news? *Journal of Accounting Research*, 32 (1) (Spring): 38–60.

Sloan, R. G. 1996. Do stock prices fully reflect information in accruals and cash flows about future earnings? *The Accounting Review* 71 (3): 289–315.

Sloan, R. G., P. M. Dechow, A. P. Hutton, and J. H. Kim. 2010. Detecting earnings management: A new approach. Working paper. Available at SSRN: http://ssrn.com/abstract=1735168.

Teoh, S. H., and Y. Zhang. 2009. Data truncation bias, loss firms, and accounting anomalies. AAA 2006 Financial Accounting and Reporting Section (FARS) Meeting Paper. Available at SSRN: http://ssrn.com/abstract=817764.

Thomas, J. K., and H. Zhang. 2002. Inventory changes and future returns. *Review of Accounting Studies* 7 (1): 63–187.

Xie, H. 2001. The mispricing of abnormal accruals. *The Accounting Review* 76: 357–373.

Go to http://hema.zacks.com for abstracts and links to papers.

CHAPTER 3

The Analyst Recommendation and Earnings Forecast Anomaly

George Serafeim

S ome of the first anomalies discovered that contradicted the theory of an efficient market were related to the information provided by analysts. Analyst related anomalies violate the semi strong market efficiency hypothesis if analyst recommendations and earnings forecasts can be used to predict future prices. This is because analyst recommendations and forecasts are publicly available information and, as a result, anyone can trade on this information soon after its release. A review of the evidence of profitable investment strategies that exploit analysts' output is provided. The results show that investment opportunities exist for a subset of stocks and analysts. However, transaction costs are a formidable impediment that investors should take into account when they consider the profitability of these strategies.

Role of Research Analysts

Information is a critical element of a well-functioning market. Accumulating information allows an individual to make a better decision and potentially trade a certain asset at a more favorable price. Therefore, investors spend considerable amounts of money to buy analysis from information intermediaries such as security analysts. In 2006, U.S. and U.K. investment firms spent $7.1 billion on sell-side research (Tabb Group 2006).

Because of the magnitude of the economic resources that are spent on security analysis there is considerable debate about the value that analysts add to the market. Some view analysts as important agents through whom information is impounded in stock prices and the efficiency of stock markets is improved (Gleeson and Lee 2003; Kelly and Ljungqvist 2007). Others view analysts as zero value or even value destroying agents because their interests are not aligned with the interests of the investors (James and Karceski 2006; Lin and McNichols 1998; Chen and Matsumoto 2006). Although there is no clear consensus about the value added by analysts, we have evidence that analyst research affects stock prices and, therefore, the allocation of the resources in the economy. Previous research has shown that recommendations and earnings forecasts move stock prices (Stickel 1995; Womack 1996). However, this belief has been recently challenged by studies that show that recommendation revisions are in response to corporate events and on average associated with insignificant price reactions (Altinkilic and Hansen 2009; Loh and Stulz 2010).

Investment Recommendations

Analysts issue investment recommendations in the form of strong buy, buy, hold, underperform, or sell within company reports. These recommendations essentially summarize their opinion about the fundamental value of a firm relative to the stock market value. The higher the fundamental value, as measured by the residual-income model,[1] compared to the current market value of the firm, the more optimistic the recommendation of the analyst should be. However, there is evidence that this is not the case. Prior studies have found that ratios of fundamental value as a percentage of market value are not positively associated with the optimism of analyst recommendations (Bradshaw 2004; Barniv et al. 2009). Rather, analysts, potentially because of limited information processing ability, seem to rely on simple valuation heuristics in making recommendations.

Moreover, other studies document that the level of recommendations is a product of analyst bias because of conflict of interests. Investment banking (Dugar and Nathan 1995; Lin and McNichols 1998; Michaely and Womack 1999; Lin, McNichols and O'Brien 2005), brokerage business (Cowen, Groysberg, and Healy 2006), and access to management (Chen and Matsumoto 2006) have been suggested to bias analysts toward issuing more optimistic

---

[1]The residual-income model calculates the value of the firm as the sum of the book value of equity and a stream of residual incomes discounted by the equity cost of capital for each firm. Residual income is equal to net income minus the product of equity cost of capital and beginning of period book value of equity.

recommendations. Both limited information processing ability and conflicts of interest raise the possibility that analyst recommendations are not useful in predicting future stock returns.

However, for an investor to generate abnormal investment performance by taking into account recommendations, the analyst recommendations must have some predictive ability of future stock returns and either (1) the stock market fails to rapidly react and fully incorporate the information released by analyst recommendations or (2) the stock market fails to understand differences in analyst ability to identify mispriced stocks.

Evidence on Recommendation Profitability

Many studies have considered the investment potential of a trading strategy that buys stocks recommended as or upgraded to strong buy or buy, and sells stocks recommended as or downgraded to underperform or sell. The assumption underlying these studies is that the stock market might not fully account for the information released by analyst recommendations, and, as a result, an investment opportunity exists for an investor who follows these recommendations.

Figure 3.1 shows the performance of two portfolios of stocks. Each stock, in the beginning of the quarter, is sorted according to the average analyst recommendations. The top 10% of stocks with the most optimistic recommendations are assigned to portfolio top, and the bottom 10% of stocks with the most pessimistic recommendations are assigned to portfolio bottom. Portfolios are rebalanced quarterly.

The top portfolio outperforms the bottom portfolio in 14 years out of 21. The cumulative performance of a portfolio that buys stocks from the top

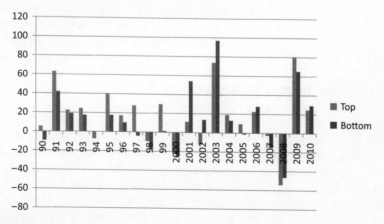

FIGURE 3.1 Performance of Analyst Recommendations

portfolio and sells stocks from the bottom portfolio is equal to 46% over the past 21 years. Interestingly the cumulative performance is much higher in the 1990s, with the portfolio generating a return of 344%.

Table 3.1 shows annualized returns for trading strategies that exploit the level of or the change in investment recommendations (see Tables 3.2 to 3.8 in the chapter appendix for more detailed analysis). All studies find that, before transaction costs, the investment strategy delivers positive abnormal performance. For example, Barber et al. (2001) find that the investment strategy that buys stocks with most (least) favorable consensus recommendations earns an annualized abnormal return of +9.4%. However, after accounting for transaction costs, the strategy delivers a performance that is equal to −3.1%. Moreover, trading soon after the publication of the recommendations is very important. The return from the investment strategy before trading costs decreases to +6.3% if weekly rebalancing is used instead of daily rebalancing. The investment returns of the strategies diminish quickly if an investor delays trading even for one day. The same trading strategy would deliver +6.1% before transaction costs if an investor trades with a one-week delay instead of trading the next day from the issuance of recommendations. Consistent with these findings, Green (2006) examines the returns to strategies that trade on recommendations that are available to subscribing investors before they become widely disseminated, and shows that these strategies produce an annualized abnormal return of 30%.

However, the profitability of investment strategies that follow recommendations is highly volatile. Groysberg, Healy, Serafeim et al. (2010) show that, for 85 large brokerage houses with continued operations from 1997 to 2004, the average abnormal return in any year ranged between −1% and 20%. Barber et al. (2003) document even more dramatic volatility in the profitability of the investment strategy. They compute market-adjusted returns for the period from 1986 to 2001, and they show that year-by-year returns range from −24.7% to 24%. This intertemporal return profile might be less desirable for investors who prefer a smooth performance over time.

THE INFLUENCE OF FIRM CHARACTERISTICS Studies have investigated firm characteristics that enhance the value of recommendations. Almost all studies find that most of the abnormal performance is concentrated on small firms. For example, Barber et al. (2001) find that their investment strategy delivers an annualized abnormal return of +19.6% before transaction costs. Moreover, the size of the recommended firms is able to explain differences in the profitability of recommendations across brokerage houses (Groysberg, Healy, Serafeim et al. 2010). This is consistent with the view that the stock market is less efficient for smaller firms because the information environment is worse (Lang and Lundholm 1993) and with the fact that many

TABLE 3.1 Returns to Recommendation Strategies

Study	Portfolio	Period	Strategy	Return	Benchmark
Barber, Lehavy, McNichols, Trueman 2001, *Journal of Finance*	Value-weighted	1985–1996	Buy (sell) stocks with most (least) favorable consensus recommendation (DAILY REBALANCING-NEXT DAY TRADE)	9.4%	4-factor model
Barber, Lehavy, McNichols, Trueman 2001, *Journal of Finance*	Value-weighted	1985–1996	Buy (sell) stocks with most (least) favorable consensus recommendation (DAILY REBALANCING-NEXT DAY TRADE-NET OF TRANSACTION COSTS)	–3.1%	4-factor model
Barber, Lehavy, McNichols, Trueman 2001, *Journal of Finance*	Value-weighted	1985–1996	Buy (sell) stocks with most (least) favorable consensus recommendation (WEEKLY REBALANCING-NEXT DAY TRADE)	6.3%	4-factor model
Barber, Lehavy, McNichols, Trueman 2001, *Journal of Finance*	Value-weighted	1985–1996	Buy (sell) stocks with most (least) favorable consensus recommendation (DAILY REBALANCING-ONE WEEK DELAY IN TRADE)	6.1%	4-factor model
Li 2005, *Journal of Accounting and Economics*	Equally weighted	1994–2000	Buy stocks with a strong buy rating	Mean: 3.1% Median: 1.9% One portfolio for all analysts: 5%	6-factor model
Li 2005, *Journal of Accounting and Economics*	Equally weighted	1994–2000	Sell stocks with an underperform or sell rating	Mean: 2.2% Median: 1.7% One portfolio for all analysts: 3.6%	6-factor model
Groysberg, Healy, Serafeim et al. 2010, Working paper	Equally weighted	1998–2004	Buy stocks with a buy or strong buy rating	1998: 11.1% 1999: 12.9% 2000: 20% 2001: 10.7% 2002: 6.5% 2003: 6.5% 2004: 5.3%	4-factor model

institutional investors who can act as arbitrageurs avoid trading on those stocks because of high transaction costs (Falkenstein 1996).

Other studies have explored whether the profitability of recommendations can be enhanced by exploiting fundamental firm characteristics that have been shown to predict future stock returns. Jegadeesh et al. (2004) show that an investment strategy on recommendation levels performs well only for stocks with favorable fundamental characteristics, such as high price momentum, high earnings-to-price ratio, high book-to-price ratio, low accruals, low growth, and low capital expenditures. Following investment recommendations for firms with favorable (unfavorable) fundamental information, such as the ones described earlier, delivers a market-adjusted return of +5.6% (−9.6%). Following changes in investment recommendations for firms with favorable (unfavorable) fundamental information delivers a market-adjusted return of +7.2% (+2.1%). Therefore, an investment strategy following analyst recommendations can be significantly enhanced by taking into account fundamental characteristics of the recommended firms.

THE INFLUENCE OF ANALYST AND BROKERAGE HOUSE CHARACTERISTICS Studies have also explored the role of personal characteristics of individual analysts in generating abnormal performance. Analysts differ on several dimensions such as experience in the task at hand, the complexity of the task they are performing, their ability to forecast firm fundamentals, and the environment they work in. If these factors affect their stock picking ability, then systematic differences might exist across analysts.

Conflicts of interest, created by brokerage or investment banking business, have often been suggested to reduce the investment value of recommendations. Barber et al. (2006) find that analysts who work for brokerage houses with stock recommendations that are less tilted toward buys issue recommendations that perform better. Upgrades to buy or strong buy from the least favorable brokerage houses (i.e., brokerage houses that, on average, issue more pessimistic recommendations) outperform by 6.5% upgrades issued by the most favorable brokerage houses. Similarly, initiations and resumptions of buy or strong buy ratings outperform by 4.6%. They argue that buy recommendations are more informative if they are issued by brokerage houses that are less optimistic overall. Embedded in their analysis is a view that the distribution of the ratings across brokerage houses is partially a result of differences in conflicts of interest with brokerage houses that issue more buys having more conflicts of interest. However, this result disappears after 2002 when the National Association of Securities Dealers required the publication of these ratings by brokerage houses, consistent with the stock market incorporating this information into the stock price reactions to the recommendations. Consistent with conflicts of interest from corporate finance business influencing the profitability of recommendations,

Barber, Lehavy, and Trueman (2007) find that investment banks' recommendations underperform recommendations of other brokerage houses by 8.2%.

Moreover, persistent abilities to predict future stock price performance might also be exploited to earn abnormal returns. If such abilities exist, then an investor might earn abnormal returns by following analysts who, in the previous time period, had the best performance. Li (2005) provides evidence that, even after taking into account transaction costs, an investor who follows the recommendations of analysts who were in the top performance decile in the previous quarter or year would earn a positive abnormal return of 9.1%. The best analysts tend to remain the best for at least two consecutive periods. Mikhail, Walther, and Willis (2004) also provide evidence of performance persistence but they fail to find evidence that a profitable investment opportunity exists by following analysts with the best performance. This might be attributed to the differences in methodology across the two papers. Mikhail, Walther, and Willis (2004) examine the performance of buy and strong buy recommendations collectively. In contrast, Li (2005) examines only the performance of strong buy recommendations and uses recommendations made by larger brokerage houses.

The forecast accuracy of individual analysts could also be another indicator of the profitability of analyst recommendations. If some analysts have superior ability of understanding and forecasting a firm's accounting performance, then this might translate into superior forecasting of stock performance. Loh and Mian (2006) confirm this intuition and find that a strategy that buys (sells) stocks that analysts in the top quintile of forecast accuracy recommend as buy or strong buy (sell or underperform) earns an abnormal return of +9.2%. Moreover, a strategy that sells (buys) stocks that analysts in the bottom quintile of forecast accuracy recommend as buy or strong buy (sell or underperform) earns an abnormal return of +6.5%. Ertimur, Sunder, and Sunder (2007) and Konchitchki and Simon (2010) also find that analysts issuing more accurate earnings forecasts also issue more profitable investment recommendations. Moreover, Ertimur, Sunder, and Sunder (2007) show that analysts who work for larger brokerage houses and cover fewer stocks issue more profitable recommendations.[2] Brown and Huang (2009) confirm the evidence that more accurate analysts issue more profitable recommendations but they show that consistency of forecast and recommendations is an even more important factor when evaluating the

---

[2]In contrast, Jung, Shane, and Yang (2009) examine recommendation profitability over the next 30 trading days from the issuance of the recommendation and find no relation between forecast accuracy and number of firms followed, and recommendation profitability. They argue that analysts who accompany their recommendations with long-term growth forecasts make more profitable recommendations. However, the economic effect of long-term growth issuance is small at 0.4%.

profitability of recommendations. They define analysts as consistent if the analyst's stock recommendation and earnings forecast are both above the prevailing consensus recommendation and forecast, and they show that consistent analysts outperform inconsistent analysts by +6.3% over 32 trading days starting one day before the issuance of the recommendation and the earnings forecast. However, their strategy is not implementable because they start calculating the portfolio performance before the recommendation and the earnings forecast are publicly announced.

Finally, a recent stream of literature explores the role of social networks on analysts' ability to collect superior information about firms. There is evidence that analysts can gain an information advantage through their position in social networks, allowing them to make more accurate, timely, and bold forecasts (Horton and Serafeim 2010) and enhance the value of their recommendations (Cohen, Frazzini, and Maloy 2010). Cohen, Frazzini, and Maloy (2010) show that a portfolio that buys (sells) stocks recommended as buys or strong buys by analysts that have attended the same university with a member of the board of directors (by analysts that have not attended the same university with a member of the board of directors) earns an annualized abnormal return in the U.S. market of 6.60% for the period between 1993 and 2006.[3] However, they show that Regulation Fair Disclosure limited the profitability of this strategy by prohibiting private information flows and thereby leveling the information playing field. It is interesting that, in the United Kingdom, where no such regulation exists, the profitability of this strategy is not affected. This raises the possibility that, in capital markets without regulations that limit selective disclosure, investors can benefit from identifying better-connected analysts.

Determinants of Recommendations

Although many studies have investigated the profitability of recommendations, we have little evidence about the determinants of recommendation levels or revisions. Most studies have focused on whether the level of recommendations is consistent with valuation models using fundamental analysis (Bradshaw 2004; Barniv 2009). In general, this line of research finds that, surprisingly, more favorable recommendations are associated with less favorable fundamental value-to-price ratios and vice versa. Also, these studies find that recommendations are associated with heuristic valuation metrics such as long-term growth or a simple price-to-one-year-ahead earnings ratio. Consistent with the evidence presented earlier, Jegadeesh et al. (2004) show

---

[3]This result does not extend to sell/underperform recommendations. A similar strategy does not yield abnormal returns that are reliably different from zero.

that recommendation optimism increases in price and earnings momentum and for growth firms.

In contrast to prior studies that focus on quantitative firm characteristics, Groysberg, Healy, Nohria et al. (2010) explore qualitative determinants of analyst recommendations. They use a proprietary dataset with 967 analysts ranking 837 companies to judge how analyst recommendations are related to firms' industry competitiveness, strategic choices, and internal capabilities. Groysberg, Healy, Nohria et al. (2010) find that recommendations are associated primarily with prior stock price performance, industry growth, and top management quality, followed by a commitment to a low price strategy, and internal capabilities such as strategy execution capability and innovation leadership.

Studies have also explored how recommendations are revised, focusing primarily on stock price movements before the revision. Conrad et al. (2006) find that, following large stock price increases, analysts are equally likely to upgrade or downgrade. However, following large stock price declines, analysts are more likely to downgrade, consistent with conflicts of interest affecting recommendations. Jegadeesh et al. (2004) show that recommendation revision optimism increases in price and earnings momentum and has an unclear relation with firm growth characteristics.

Who Trades on Recommendations?

Having established the significance of investment recommendations, we turn to the question of who trades on those recommendations. Answering this question is interesting because investors differ in their ability to process information and react quickly to new information. Institutional investors are seen as more efficient information processors, and they are able to execute trades more effectively.

Prior research has shown that both retail and institutional investors react to announcements of recommendations.[4] However, institutional investors trade more than retail investors on downgrades and sell recommendations. In contrast, retail investors trade more on upgrades and buy recommendations (Malmendier and Shanthikumar 2007; Mikhail, Walther, and Willis 2007). This asymmetry reflects the inability of retail investors to fully account for the tendency of analysts to convey positive news and withhold bad news. This tendency makes issuance of pessimistic recommendations more informative than issuance of optimistic recommendations. As a result, institutional (retail) investors earn positive (negative) returns from trading on recommendations. Institutional (retail) investors earn +5.1% (−0.9%) buying stocks with strong buy/buy recommendations and +5.2% (+0.4%)

---

[4]These studies use as a proxy the size of the trade for whether an investor is a retail or institutional.

selling stocks with hold/sell recommendations over the subsequent five days from the recommendation (Mikhail, Walther, and Willis 2007). Similarly, institutional (retail) investors earn $+5.4\%$ $(+0.4\%)$ buying stocks that are upgraded and $+4.9\%$ (-3.7%) selling stocks that are downgraded over the subsequent 5 days from the recommendation (Mikhail, Walther, and Willis 2007). The results of Christophe, Ferri, and Hsieh (2010) also suggest that sophisticated investors are able to take advantage of analyst recommendations. They show that an abnormal level of short selling activity is concentrated a few days before analysts downgrade a stock and that this happens more likely because analysts provide tips to institutional investors about the forthcoming downgrade. Irvine, Lipson, and Puckett (2006) also find evidence in support of the argument that analysts provide institutional investors with tips about forthcoming changes in recommendations. They document abnormally high institutional trading volume and buying activity 5 days before recommendations are publicly released. Moreover, the buying activity is profitable with investors who buy stocks with forthcoming buy and strong buy initiations earnings on average 5.4% over the next month.

International Evidence

The previous sections review the evidence on the profitability of analyst recommendations in the U.S. market. Evidence on the value of analyst recommendations internationally is scarcer. The limited evidence we have suggests that U.S. analysts are more skilled in identifying mispriced stocks compared to their foreign counterparts. Jegadeesh and Kim (2006) examine the profitability of recommendations in seven large markets and show that recommendations are most profitable in the United States and Japan. They find that trading strategies based on the level of recommendations do not yield significant positive returns in any of the countries. Trading strategies based on recommendation revisions produce significant positive returns for the United States, Canada, France, and Japan. The United Kingdom and Germany also report significant positive returns, but these returns are more sensitive to the trading-strategy horizon. Returns in Italy are insignificant. Again, the evidence shows that most of the recommendation profitability is concentrated in small firms. Equally weighted portfolios that place more weight on small firms perform better than value-weighted portfolios that place more weight on large firms.

Other studies have shown that analyst recommendations have value in markets such as in India, Brazil, and Australia, but the analysis relies on small samples limiting the generalizability of results (Chakrabarti 2010; Eid and Rochman 2010; He 2010). Harvey et al. (2010) examine a large sample of analyst recommendations in European countries and find that a trading strategy that follows recommendations outperforms the market index for the period 2005 to 2009. Moreover, they show that buy recommendations have more value than sell recommendations. In contrast, Barniv et al. (2010) confirm the findings of Bradshaw (2004) in an international setting showing that recommendations are negatively related to fundamental value over price ratios and to future stock returns.

Overview of the Investment Performance of Recommendations

The review of the evidence on the profitability of analyst recommendations highlights some general rules that investors can apply to enhance the investment value of the recommendations.

- Recommendation revisions are more valuable than recommendation levels.
- Transaction costs significantly reduce the investment value of recommendations.
- The investment value of recommendations is concentrated primarily on small stocks.
- Taking into account fundamental characteristics of the covered firms that are able to predict future stock returns can enhance the profitability of recommendations.
- There are cross-sectional differences in analyst ability to find mispriced stocks.

Earnings Forecast Revisions

The most frequent output of analyst activity is a forecast of a firm's earnings. Analysts forecast earnings because earnings are the most important input of a valuation model. This is also the reason why investors can potentially benefit by obtaining information about future firm earnings. In other words, observing upward (downward) revisions of earnings forecasts should lead to upward (downward) revisions of fundamental valuations and potentially to rises (declines) in stock prices. However, misaligned analyst incentives and/or cognitive biases affect forecast revisions and diminish their value. For example, many studies document that analyst forecasts are, on average, optimistic (Francis and Philbrick 1993; McNichols and O'Brien 1997), fail to reflect the mean reverting tendency of accruals (Bradshaw, Richardson, and Sloan 2002), and do not fully incorporate information in earnings announcements (Abarbanell and Bernard 1992). This evidence raises the possibility that analyst forecasts are of limited value to investors.

Similar to the potential value of recommendations, for an investor to generate abnormal investment performance by taking into account forecast revisions, forecast revisions must have some predictive ability of future stock returns and either (1) the stock market fails to rapidly react and fully incorporate the information released by forecast revisions or (2) the stock market fails to understand differences in analyst ability to forecast future earnings.

Evidence on the Value of Forecast Revisions

Many studies have considered the investment potential of a trading strategy that buys stocks with upgraded forecasts and sells stocks with downgraded forecasts. The assumption underlying these studies is that the stock market might not fully account[5] for the information released by forecast revisions, and, as a result, an investment opportunity exists for an investor who follows these revisions.

Zacks (1979) finds that the error in EPS forecasts is more closely related to subsequent returns, compared to EPS forecasts. He concludes that returns are more closely related to changes in the consensus of EPS, rather than to changes in earnings. Similarly, Elton, Gruber, and Gultekin (1981) show that risk-adjusted excess returns are associated with stocks whose earnings have been underestimated by security analysts, and that the payoff from correctly forecasting EPS forecasts is greater than the gain from correctly forecasting EPS. Both results suggest that investors should focus on forecasting earnings forecast revisions rather than actual earnings.

Early studies document that trading strategies that exploit forecast revisions are profitable. Givoly and Lakonishok (1979) document that buying stocks with more than 5% upward revisions delivers an abnormal return of 17.3%, on an annual basis. After transaction costs, the annualized abnormal return of this portfolio is 4.3%. Trading on larger revisions yields more profitable strategies. The annualized abnormal return of a strategy that buys stocks with more than 10% upward revisions is 8.7% after transaction costs. Creating a zero investment portfolio by buying (selling) stocks with more than 5% or 10% upward (downward) revisions delivers an abnormal return of 3.7% or 6.1%, respectively, on an annual basis, before transaction costs. These findings are consistent with a market in which investors respond slowly to forecasted earnings. Hawkins, Chamberlin, and Daniel (1984) provide corroborating evidence of slow investor reaction. They construct a strategy that purchases the 20 stocks with the largest monthly increase in consensus forecast and find abnormal returns of +14.2% in the year subsequent to revisions. Stickel (1991) uses a considerably larger sample than

---

[5]The assumption of strategies that buy (sell) stocks with upward (downward) revisions is that the market underreacts to the forecast revisions. A strategy that sells (buys) stocks with upward (downward) revisions is consistent with the belief that the market overreacts to the forecast revisions.

previous papers and documents that buying (selling) stocks in the top (bottom) 5% of the consensus revision distribution yields an abnormal return of +8.2% (+5.5%) every 6 months. Chan, Jegadeesh, and Lakonishok (1996) find that a moving average of the forecast revision for the last 6 months is a good predictor of firms' future returns. Buying (selling) stocks with the largest upward (downward) revisions yields a zero-investment portfolio that generates a return of +9.7% over the next 12 months.

THE INFLUENCE OF FIRM CHARACTERISTICS   Studies have investigated firm characteristics that enhance the value of forecast revisions. Consistent with the findings on the value of recommendations, Elgers, Lo, and Pfeiffer (2001) show that forecast revisions are more profitable for small firms, and especially for firms with low analyst following. Consistent with investors underreacting to forecast revisions for thinly followed firms, Gleason and Lee (2003) also find that the value of forecast revisions is higher for firms followed by fewer analysts. Buying stocks with upward revisions that move the forecast away from (toward) the consensus and selling stocks with downward revisions that move the forecast away from (toward) the consensus earns an annualized return of +16.2% (+7.3%) for firms with low analyst coverage. The same strategy yields +8.4% (+2.8%) for firms with high analyst coverage.

Barth and Hutton (2004) show that taking into account the level of accounting accruals can significantly enhance the profitability of forecast revisions. They find that buying (selling) stocks at the bottom portfolio of accruals and upward revisions (highest portfolio of accruals and downward revisions) yields an abnormal return of 28.5%.[6] Part of this enhanced return is coming from ignoring upward revisions for stocks at the highest portfolio of accruals. Stocks with these characteristics earn an abnormal return of −10.4%.

THE INFLUENCE OF ANALYST AND BROKERAGE HOUSE CHARACTERISTICS   Studies have also explored the role of personal characteristics of individual analysts in generating abnormal performance. Gleason and Lee (2003) find that investor underreaction to analysts' earnings forecast revision is related to the boldness of the forecast. Specifically, they find that the drift in stock prices following forecast revisions are of higher magnitude (in the same direction as the revision) for high-innovation revisions as opposed to low-innovation (or herding) forecasts. Buying stocks with upward revisions that move the forecast away from (toward) the consensus and selling stocks with downward revisions that move the forecast away from (toward) the consensus

---

[6]However, most of this return seems to come from exploiting the accruals anomaly (Sloan 1996) and less from exploiting the forecast revision anomaly.

earns an annualized return of +9.4% (+3.3%). A significant portion of the drift is concentrated around the next 6 forecast revisions and subsequent earnings announcements consistent with investors delaying their responses until further confirmation of the information already provided by analysts' forecast revisions.[7]

Determinants of Forecast Revisions

Studies have explored why forecasts are revised, focusing primarily on stock price movements before the revision. The overall conclusion from this line of research is that the sign and magnitude of forecast revisions are positively associated with the sign and magnitude of past stock returns (Givoly and Lakonishok 1979; Brown, Foster, and Noreen 1985; Klein 1990), but the revisions do not fully incorporate the information in past stock returns (Lys and Sohn 1990; Abarbanell 1991). Moreover, analysts seem to revise their forecasts subsequent to quarterly earnings announcements and other corporate events (Stickel 1989), and in the same direction with dividend changes (Denis, Denis, and Sharin 1994).

Interestingly, an analyst's forecast revision can be predicted by forecast revisions made by other analysts between the previous and the forthcoming forecast, and the deviation between an analyst's previous forecast and the consensus forecast (Stickel 1990). These results can be interpreted as evidence of herding across analysts.

Abarbanell and Bushee (1997) examine whether analysts revise their forecasts by taking into account fundamental signals that predict future actual earnings growth. They find that analysts' forecast revisions incorporate the predictable mean reversion of earnings, changes in gross margins, changes in effective tax rate, and changes in the productivity of labor force. However, analysts appear to fail to reflect in forecast revisions changes in inventory that are informative about future earnings growth.

Groysberg, Healy, Nohria et al. (2010) explore qualitative determinants of analyst forecasts and find that analysts forecast higher earnings growth for firms in industries that are expected to experience growth and with low competitiveness, high ability in strategy execution, high quality of top management, leadership in innovation, high performance culture, and firms that offer a strong price proposition to their customers. They find little evidence that forecasted earnings growth is associated with governance quality,

---

[7] Gleason and Lee (2003) argue that the market appears to underreact to forecast revisions made by accurate analysts that have little visibility relative to forecast revisions made by accurate analysts with high visibility. However, the difference in performance of the portfolios that follow forecast revisions of these two groups of analysts is rather small.

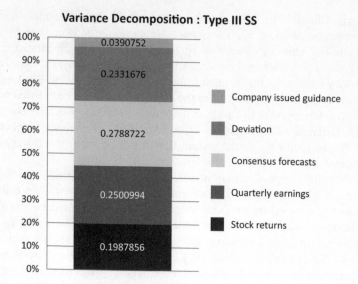

FIGURE 3.2   Relative Importance of Forecast Revision Determinants

existing financial resources, firms that compete based on differentiation, and the ability to understand competition, and communicate their strategy.

Figure 3.2 shows the results of a variance decomposition of forecast revisions of next year's earnings. To explain the sources of variance in forecast revisions of individual analysts, I use stock returns, announcements of quarterly earnings, changes in the consensus forecast, the deviation of the analyst's prior forecast from the contemporaneous consensus forecast, and issuance of management forecasts.[8] All these measures can trigger analyst

---

[8]An individual analyst's forecast revision for firm j in time t is measured as forecast for next year's earnings for firm j at time t minus forecast for next year's earnings for firm j at time $t - 1$. Change in consensus forecast. defined as the difference between the consensus forecast at time τ for firm j and the consensus forecast at time $\tau - 1$ for firm j, where time τ is the closest consensus date forecast prior to time t but after time $t - 1$ and time $\tau - 1$ is the closest consensus forecast to time τ that is after time $t - 1$. Deviation is defined as the consensus forecast at time $\tau - 2$ for firm j, where $\tau - 2$ is the closest consensus forecast date prior to $t - 1$ but after $t - 2$, less the earnings forecast by analyst i for firm j at time $t - 1$. Change in quarterly earnings equals actual quarterly earnings announcement at time τ for firm j, where time τ is prior to time t but after time $t - 1$ for quarter q, less the individual analyst's forecast of quarterly earnings for firm j for quarter q at time $t - 1$. Change in management forecasts equals the management forecast at time τ for firm j, where time τ is prior to time t but after time $t - 1$, less the individual analyst's forecast of earnings for firm j at time $t - 1$. Stock return equals the accumulated return for firm from time $t - 1$ to time t less the value weighted market return from time $t - 1$ to time t.

revisions. Changes in stock prices might inform analysts about change in future firm earnings, if analyst expectations change slower than investors' expectations. Announcements of quarterly earnings might change analyst expectations about future earnings. Changes in other analysts' expectations about future earnings might inform the focal analyst forecast. The deviation of the analyst's prior forecast from the contemporaneous consensus forecast might also determine revisions if analysts tend to herd toward the consensus. Finally, issuance of management forecasts updates analysts' expectations about future earnings, to the extent that those management forecasts are unanticipated.

The relative importance of the various sources of information is assessed in Figure 3.2 by tabulating the percent of the variation that is explained by each source divided by the total variation that is explained by the model. The model explains 54% of the total variation in forecast revisions. Most of the variation in an individual analyst's forecast revisions is explained by forecast revisions of other analysts (28%), consistent with analysts revising their forecasts because of common information. Announcements of quarterly earnings explain 25% of the total variation that is explained by the model, signaling that unexpected quarterly earnings cause analysts to revise their expectations about future earnings. Deviation explains 23%, consistent with analysts exhibiting a tendency to herd. Stock returns explain 20%. Changes in prices are informative about changes in analyst expectations of future earnings. Finally, unexpected management earnings forecasts explain only 4%, primarily because of the rare nature of management forecasts given the frequency of analyst forecast revisions.

International Evidence

The previous sections review the evidence on the profitability of analyst forecast revisions in the U.S. market. Several studies have explored the value of revisions in other capital markets. Bercel (1994) explores the value of revisions in France, the United Kingdom, Germany, Netherlands, Switzerland, and Japan. He finds that the trading strategy is most profitable in Netherlands, the United Kingdom, and Germany. Significant profits also exist in France but the profits are not significant in Japan and Switzerland. Hennessey (1995) reports that buying Canadian stocks with upgraded forecasts of more than 5% (10%) yields an abnormal return of +13.5% (+18.2%). However, selling Canadian stocks with downgraded forecasts does not generate any significant returns. Moreover, both upgrades and downgrades are preceded by, respectively, large positive and negative stock returns. Capstaff, Paudyal, and Rees (2009) examine the value of forecast revisions in the United Kingdom, Germany, and France and find opposite results to Hennessey. They find that stock prices drift downward after downgrades, but not upward after upgrades. They also show that the drift is most pronounced in the United Kingdom, followed by Germany, and then France.

Overview of the Investment Performance of Forecast Revisions

The review of the evidence on the profitability of analyst forecast revisions highlights some general rules that investors can apply to enhance the investment value of the revisions. They are:

- The value of forecast revisions increases in the magnitude of the revision.
- Transaction costs significantly reduce the investment value of forecast revisions.
- The investment value of forecast revisions is concentrated primarily on small stocks.
- Taking into account fundamental characteristics of the covered firms that are able to predict future stock returns can enhance the profitability of forecast revisions.
- There are cross-sectional differences in analyst ability to forecast earnings.

Appendix 3.1: Details of Returns to Recommendation Strategies

Tables 3.2–3.8 are continuations of Table 3.1. Each table details the returns to recommendations strategies discussed in this chapter based on different conditions or characteristics.

TABLE 3.2 Returns to Recommendation Strategies Conditional on Firm Characteristics

Study	Portfolio	Period	Strategy	Return	Benchmark
Barber, Lehavy, McNichols, Trueman 2001, *Journal of Finance*	Value-weighted	1985–1996	Buy (sell) stocks with most (least) favorable consensus recommendation (daily rebalancing-next day trade, small firms)	19.60%	4-factor model
Jegadeesh, Kim, Krische, Lee 2004, *Journal of Finance*	Equally weighted	1985–1998	Buy (sell) stocks with most (least) favorable consensus recommendation, conditional on favorable fundamental information	5.60%	Market adjusted
Jegadeesh, Kim, Krische, Lee 2004, *Journal of Finance*	Equally weighted	1985–1998	Buy (sell) stocks with most (least) favorable consensus recommendation, conditional on unfavorable fundamental information	−9.60%	Market adjusted
Jegadeesh, Kim, Krische, Lee 2004, *Journal of Finance*	Equally weighted	1985–1998	Buy (sell) stocks with most (least) favorable changes in consensus recommendation, conditional on favorable fundamental information	7.20%	Market adjusted
Jegadeesh, Kim, Krische, Lee 2004, *Journal of Finance*	Equally weighted	1985–1998	Buy (sell) stocks with most (least) favorable changes in consensus recommendation, conditional on unfavorable fundamental information	2.10%	Market adjusted

TABLE 3.3 Returns to Recommendation Strategies Conditional on Analyst/Brokerage House Characteristics

Study	Portfolio	Period	Strategy	Return	Benchmark
Barber, Lehavy, Trueman 2007, *Journal of Financial Economics*	Equally weighted	1996–mid-2003	Buy stocks that are upgraded to buy or strong buy or initiations/ resumptions/reiterations with a buy or strong buy rating	IB: 1.8% Non-IB: 10%	4-factor model
Barber, Lehavy, Trueman 2007, *Journal of Financial Economics*	Equally weighted	1996–mid-2003	Short stocks that are downgraded to hold, sell or strong sell or initiations/ resumptions/reiterations with a hold, sell or strong sell rating	IB: 4.9% Non-IB: 0.3%	4-factor model
Barber, Lehavy, McNichols, Trueman 2006, *Journal of Accounting and Economics*	Equally weighted	1996–mid-2003	Buy stocks that are upgraded to buy or strong buy	Least favorable houses: 10.6% Most favorable houses: 4.1%	4-factor model
Barber, Lehavy, McNichols, Trueman 2006, *Journal of Accounting and Economics*	Equally weighted	1996–mid-2003	Buy stocks for initiations/ resumptions/reiterations with a buy or strong buy rating	Least favorable houses: 3.6% Most favorable houses: −1%	4-factor model
Barber, Lehavy, McNichols, Trueman 2006, *Journal of Accounting and Economics*	Equally weighted	1996–mid-2003	Short stocks that are downgraded to hold, sell or strong sell	Least favorable houses: 5.4% Most favorable houses: 10.5%	4-factor model

(continued)

TABLE 3.3 (Continued)

Study	Portfolio	Period	Strategy	Return	Benchmark
Barber, Lehavy, McNichols, Trueman 2006, *Journal of Accounting and Economics*	Equally weighted	1996–mid-2003	Short stocks for initiations/resumptions with a hold, sell, or strong sell rating	Least favorable houses: 0% Most favorable houses: 8.4%	4-factor model
Li 2005, *Journal of Accounting and Economics*	Equally weighted	1994–2000	Buy stocks with a strong buy rating (Best performance analysts previous one year—5-day trading delay—net of transaction costs)	9.10%	6-factor model
Li 2005, *Journal of Accounting and Economics*	Equally weighted	1994–2000	Sell stocks with an underperform or sell rating (Best performance analysts previous one year—5-day trading delay, net of transaction costs)	5.80%	6-factor model
Loh and Mian 2006, *Journal of Financial Economics*	Value-weighted	1994–2001	Buy (sell) stocks with most (least) favorable consensus recommendation for analysts at the top quintile of forecast accuracy	9.20%	4-factor model
Loh and Mian 2006, *Journal of Financial Economics*	Value-weighted	1994–2001	Sell (buy) stocks with most (least) favorable consensus recommendation for analysts at the bottom quintile of forecast accuracy	6.50%	4-factor model

TABLE 3.4 Returns to Recommendation Strategies Internationally

Study	Portfolio	Period	Strategy	Return	Benchmark
Jegadeesh, Kim 2006, *Journal of Financial Markets*	Equally weighted	1994–mid-2002	Buy (sell) stocks that have been upgraded (downgraded) the previous month	U.S.: 32.9% U.K.: 15% Canada: 17.9% France: 12.1% Germany: 13.1% Italy: 6% Japan: 26.7%	CAPM
Jegadeesh, Kim 2006, *Journal of Financial Markets*	Value-weighted	1994–mid-2002	Buy (sell) stocks that have been upgraded (downgraded) the previous month	U.S.: 8.3% U.K.: 6.5% Canada: 5.7% France: −0.1% Germany: 3.4% Italy: 1.6% Japan: 4.5%	CAPM

TABLE 3.5 Returns to Forecast Revision Strategies

Study	Portfolio	Period	Strategy	Return	Benchmark
Givoly, Lakonishok 1979, *Journal of Accounting and Economics*	Equally weighted	1967–1974	Buy stocks with more than 5% upward revisions	17.3%	Market adjusted
Givoly, Lakonishok 1979, *Journal of Accounting and Economics*	Equally weighted	1967–1974	Buy stocks with more than 5% upward revisions, after transaction costs	4.3%	Market adjusted
Givoly, Lakonishok 1979, *Journal of Accounting and Economics*	Equally weighted	1967–1974	Buy stocks with more than 10% upward revisions—after transaction costs	8.7%	Market adjusted
Hawkins, Chamberlin, Daniel 1984, *Financial Analysts Journal*	Equally weighted	1975–1980	Buy the 20 stocks with the largest upward revisions	14.2%	Market adjusted
Stickel 1991, *The Accounting Review*	Equally weighted	1981–1985	Buy stocks in the top 5% of revisions	16.6%	Market adjusted
Stickel 1991, *The Accounting Review*	Equally weighted	1981–1985	Sell stocks in the bottom 5% of revisions	11.1%	Market adjusted
Chan, Jegadeesh, Lakonishok 1996, *Journal of Finance*	Equally weighted	1973–1993	Buying (selling) stocks in the top (bottom) decile of revisions	9.7%	Market adjusted

TABLE 3.6 Returns to Forecast Revision Strategies Conditional on Firm Characteristics

Study	Portfolio	Period	Strategy	Return	Benchmark
Gleason and Lee 2003, *The Acccounting Review*	Equally weighted	1994–1998	Buy stocks with upward revisions that move the forecast toward the consensus; high analyst coverage	2.8%	Size adjusted
Gleason and Lee 2003, *The Acccounting Review*	Equally weighted	1994–1998	Buy stocks with upward revisions that move the forecast toward the consensus; low analyst coverage	7.3%	Size adjusted
Gleason and Lee 2003, *The Acccounting Review*	Equally weighted	1994–1998	Buy stocks with upward revisions that move the forecast away from the consensus; high analyst coverage	8.4%	Size adjusted
Gleason and Lee 2003, *The Acccounting Review*	Equally weighted	1994–1998	Buy stocks with upward revisions that move the forecast away from the consensus; low analyst coverage	16.2%	Size adjusted
Barth, Hutton 2004, *Review of Accounting Studies*	Equally weighted	1981–1996	Buy (sell) stocks at the bottom decile of accruals and with upward revisions (top decile of accruals with downward revisions)	28.5%	Size adjusted

TABLE 3.7 Returns to Forecast Revision Strategies Conditional on Analyst/Brokerage House Characteristics

Study	Portfolio	Period	Strategy	Return	Benchmark
Gleason and Lee 2003, *The Acccounting Review*	Equally weighted	1994–1998	Buy stocks with upward revisions that move the forecast toward the consensus	3.3%	Size adjusted
Gleason and Lee 2003, *The Acccounting Review*	Equally weighted	1994–1998	Buy stocks with upward revisions that move the forecast away from the consensus	9.4%	Size adjusted

TABLE 3.8 Returns to Forecast Revision Strategies Internationally

Study	Portfolio	Period	Strategy	Return	Benchmark
Hennessey 1995, *Accounting and Business Research*	Equally weighted	1979–1988	Buy stocks with more than 5% upward revisions	Canada: 13.5%	Market adjusted
Capstaff, Paudyal, Rees 2010, Working paper	Equally weighted	1988–1998	Buy (sell) stocks with more than 10% upward (downward) revisions	U.K.: 31.5% France: 12.5% Germany: 21.8%	Market adjusted

References

Altinkilic, O., and R. Hansen. 2009. On the information role of stock recommendation revisions. *Journal of Financial Economics* 48: 17–36.

Bagnoli, M., M. Clement, M. Crawley, and S. Watts. 2009. The relative profitability of analysts' stock recommendations: What role does investor sentiment play? Working paper, University of Texas at Austin.

Barber, B., R. Lehavy, M. McNichols, and B. Trueman. 2001. Can investors profit from the prophets? Security analyst recommendations and stock returns. *Journal of Finance* 56: 531–563.

Barber, B., R. Lehavy, M. McNichols, and B. Trueman. 2003. Prophets and losses: Reassessing the returns to analysts' recommendations. *Financial Analyst Journal* 59: 2, 88–96.

Barber, B., R. Lehavy, M. McNichols, and B. Trueman. 2006. Buys, holds, and sells: The distribution of investment banks' stock ratings and the implications for the profitability of analysts' recommendations. *Journal of Accounting and Economics* 41: 87–117.

Barber, B., R. Lehavy, and B. Trueman. 2007. Comparing the stock recommendation performance of investment banks and independent research firms. *Journal of Financial Economics* 85: 490–517.

Bercel, A. 1994. Consensus expectations and international equity returns, *Financial Analysts Journal*, July–August, 76–80.

Bradshaw, M. 2004. How do analysts use their earnings forecasts in generating stock recommendations? *The Accounting Review* 79: 25–50.

Brown, L., and K. Huang. 2009. The impact of stock recommendation–earnings forecast consistency on forecast accuracy and recommendation profitability, Working paper, Georgetown University.

Carhart, M. 1997. On persistence in mutual fund performance. *Journal of Finance* 52: 57–82.

Chan, L., N. Jegadeesh, and J. Lakonishok. 1996. Momentum strategies, *Journal of Finance* 51: 1681–1713.

Chen, S., and D. Matsumoto. 2006. Favorable versus unfavorable recommendations: The impact on analyst access to management–provided information, *Journal of Accounting Research* 44: 657–689.

Cheng, Y., M. H. Liu, and J. Qian. 2006. Buy-side analysts, sell-side analysts, and investment decisions of money managers. *Journal of Financial and Quantitative Analysis* 41: 51–83.

Christophe, S., M. Ferri, and J. Hsieh. 2010. Informed trading before analyst downgrades: Evidence from short sellers. *Journal of Financial Economics* 95: 85–106.

Clement, M. 1999. Analyst forecast accuracy: Do ability, resources, and portfolio complexity matter? *Journal of Accounting and Economics* 27: 285–304.

Cohen, L., A. Frazzini, and C. Malloy. 2010. Sell-side school ties. *Journal of Finance* 65: 1409–1437.

Cowen, A., B. Groysberg, and P. Healy. 2006. Which types of analyst firms make more optimistic forecasts? *Journal of Accounting and Economics* 41: 119–146.

Dechow, P., A. Hutton, and R. Sloan. 2000. The relation between analysts' forecasts of long-term earnings growth and stock price performance following equity offerings. *Contemporary Accounting Research* 17: 1–32.

Denis, D., D. Denis, and A. Sarin. 1994. The information content of dividend changes: cash flow signaling, overinvestment and dividend clienteles. *Journal of Financial and Quantitative Analysis* 29: 567–587.

Dugar, A., and S. Nathan. 1995. The effect of investment banking relationships on financial analysts' earnings forecasts and investment recommendations. *Contemporary Accounting Research* 12: (1), 131–160.

Elton, J., M. Gruber, and M. Gultekin. 1981. Expectations and share prices. *Management Science* 27: 975–987.

Ertimur, Y., J. Sunder, and S. V. Sunder. 2007. Measure for measure: The relation between forecast accuracy and recommendation profitability of analysts. *Journal of Accounting Research* 45: 567–606.

Falkenstein, E. G. 1996. Preferences for stock characteristics as revealed by mutual fund portfolio holdings. *Journal of Finance* 51: 111–135.

Givoly, D., and J. Lakonishok. 1979. The information content of financial analysts' forecasts of earnings. *Journal of Accounting and Economics* 1: 165–185.

Green, C. 2006. The value of client access to analyst recommendations. *Journal of Financial and Quantitative Analysis* 41: 1–24.

Groysberg, B., P. Healy, G. Serafeim, D. Shanthikumar, and G. Yang. 2010. The performance of buy-side analyst recommendations. Working paper, Harvard Business School.

Groysberg, B., P. Healy, N. Nohria, and G. Serafeim. 2010. What determines analyst forecasts? *Financial Analysts Journal*, forthcoming.

Irvine, P., M. Lipson, and A. Puckett. 2007, Tipping. *Review of Financial Studies* 20: 741–768.

Jegadeesh, N., J. Kim, S. D. Krische, and C. M. C. Lee. 2004. Analyzing the analysts: When do recommendations add value? *Journal of Finance* 59: 1083–1124.

Jung, B., P. Shane, and Y. Yang. 2009. Do financial analysts' long-term growth forecasts reflect effective effort towards informative stock recommendations? Working paper, University of Colorado.

Klein, A. 1990. A direct test of the cognitive bias theory of share price reversals. *Journal of Accounting and Economics* 13: 155–166.

Lin, H., and M. McNichols. 1998. Underwriting relationships, analysts' earnings forecasts and investment recommendations. *Journal of Accounting and Economics* 25: 101–127.

Lin, H., M. McNichols, and P. O'Brien. 2005. Analyst impartiality and investment banking relationships. *Journal of Accounting Research* 43 (4): 623–650.

Loh, R. K., and G. M. Mian. 2006. Do accurate earnings forecasts facilitate superior investment recommendations? *Journal of Financial Economics* 80: 455–483.

Loh, R. K., and R. Stulz. 2010. When are stock recommendation changes influential? NBER working paper No. 14791.

Malmendier, U., and D. Shanthikumar. 2005. Do security analysts speak in two tongues? Working paper, Harvard Business School.

Michaely, R., and K. Womack. 1999. Conflicts of interest and the credibility of underwriter analyst recommendations. *The Review of Financial Studies* 12: 653–686.

Stickel, S. 1990. Predicting individual analyst earnings forecasts. *Journal of Accounting Research* 28: 409–417.

Stickel, S. 1991. Common stock returns surrounding earnings forecast revisions: more puzzling evidence. *The Accounting Review* 66: 402–416.

Stickel, S. 1995. The anatomy of the performance of buy and sell recommendations. *Financial Analysts Journal* 51: 25–39.

Tabb Group. 2006. The future of equity research: A 360 degree perspective.

Womack, K. 1996. Do brokerage analysts' recommendations have investment value? *Journal of Finance* 51: 137–167.

Zacks, L. 1979. EPS forecasts: Accuracy is not enough. *Financial Analysts Journal* March–April, 53–55.

Go to http://hema.zacks.com for abstracts and links to papers.

CHAPTER 4

Post-Earnings Announcement Drift and Related Anomalies

Daniel Taylor

S ince the 1970s, academics have been fascinated with the ability of earnings to predict future returns. It is well documented that stock prices drift in the direction of the earnings surprise several months after the firm announces earnings, a phenomenon referred to as post-earnings announcement drift. Post-earnings announcement drift is the topic of considerable academic research because it is at odds with an efficient market—the belief that the market quickly impounds all publicly available information into prices. Investment professionals and sophisticated investors have also become fascinated with the drift for obvious reason. At a basic level, post-earnings announcement drift implies that one can take minimal risk and beat the market by ranking stocks on the magnitude of their earnings surprises; buying those stocks at the top of the ranking and shorting those stocks at the bottom of the ranking. Although several firm characteristics are commonly thought to predict future returns (e.g., firm size, firm growth, dividend yield), earnings surprises are widely accepted as the strongest predictor, and their predictive power has survived 4 decades of academic scrutiny.[1] Indeed, estimates of the returns to a long-short

[1]In a defense of efficient markets, Fama (1998) questions the collective evidence that returns can be predicted on the basis of public information. However, unlike other evidence, Fama (1998) concludes that the evidence on post-earnings announcement drift is "above suspicion."

strategy based on taking long (short) positions in firms with extreme positive (negative) earnings surprises range from 2.84% to 6.88% per quarter (see Table 4.1).

The purpose of this chapter is to synthesize existing academic research on post-earnings announcement drift and related earnings-based trading strategies, with a view toward how investors might apply such research. Rather than an in depth analysis of the collective academic evidence, this chapter will focus on the economic significance and magnitude of the returns implied by trading strategies based on post-earnings announcement drift and how one might refine such strategies. As such, the chapter is written for readers with a basic grasp of statistics and a modest amount of institutional knowledge about investing. For those readers interested in detailed statistical evidence or additional commentary on a topic, wherever possible, references to the respective academic papers are provided.

The chapter is organized as follows. The first part of the chapter reviews the academic evidence on post-earnings announcement drift. First, it discusses the institutional history of post-earnings announcement drift, introduces terminology used throughout the chapter, and reviews the basic evidence on post-earnings announcement drift. Next it discusses how to measure an earnings surprise, how the measurement of an earnings surprise affects post-earnings announcement drift, and how managers might manipulate an earnings surprise. Finally, it discusses various theories as to why post-earnings announcement drift exists. The second part of the chapter discusses how investors can refine and apply strategies based on post-earnings announcement drift, in particular, how investors can refine post-earnings announcement drift using other publicly available information.

The Basics of the Anomaly

In 1968 the *Journal of Accounting Research* published a now seminal article by Professors Ray Ball and Philip Brown that ranked 261 firms each year from 1957 to 1965 on the change in earnings per share. Ball and Brown (1968) found, as expected, that those companies with the largest increase (decrease) in earnings during the year also had the largest increase (decrease) in stock price during the year. However, to their surprise, they also found that the stock prices of those companies with the largest increase (decrease) in earnings continued to rise (fall) over the 3 months after the earnings announcement.

Following this seminal article, a number of academic papers attempted to measure the unexpected component of earnings, or earnings surprise, and used this to explain the drift in prices. Because analysts' consensus

TABLE 4.1 Selected Academic Papers on Post-Earnings Announcement Drift

Paper	Period Studied	Measure of Surprise	Return Spread	Return Measure	Holding Period
Foster et al. (1984)	1974–1981	Seasonal random walk with drift	6.32%	Beta adjusted	Quarterly
Bernard and Thomas (1989)	1974–1986	Seasonal random walk with drift	4.20%	Size adjusted	Quarterly
Abarbanell and Bernard (1992)	1976–1986	Value Line forecast error	4.29%	Size adjusted	Quarterly
Chan et al. (1996)	1977–1993	Seasonal random walk	6.80%	Raw returns	6 months
Collins and Hribar (2000)	1988–1997	Seasonal random walk with drift	6.88%	Size adjusted	6 months
Chordia and Shivakumar (2005)	1972–2001	Seasonal random walk	5.52%	Raw returns	6 months
Chordia and Shivakumar (2006)	1972–1999	Seasonal random walk	5.40%	Raw returns	6 months
Doyle et al. (2006)	1988–2000	Analyst forecast error	13.95%	Raw returns	Annual
Jegadeesh and Livnat (2006)	1987–2003	Seasonal random walk with drift	5.55%	Size adjusted	6 months

(continued)

TABLE 4.1 (Continued)

Paper	Period Studied	Measure of Surprise	Return Spread	Return Measure	Holding Period
Sadka (2006)	1983–2001	Seasonal random walk with drift	2.84%	Beta adjusted	4 months
Battalio and Mendenhall (2007)	1993–2002	Seasonal random walk	9.37%	Size adjusted	Quarterly
Francis et al. (2007)	1982–2001	Analyst forecast error	5.00%	Beta adjusted	6 months
Lerman et al. (2007)	1987–2005	Analyst forecast error	4.27%	Size and book-to-market adjusted	Quarterly
Livnat and Mendenhall (2006)	1987–2003	Analyst forecast error	4.40%	Size and book-to-market adjusted	Quarterly
Ng et al. (2008)	1988–2005	Analyst forecast error	6.33%	Size adjusted	Quarterly
Brandt et al. (2008)	1987–2004	Announcement day return	3.27%	Size and book-to-market adjusted	Quarterly
Lerman et al. (2008)	1987–2006	Analyst forecast error	4.31%	Size and book-to-market adjusted	Quarterly

Estimates of the magnitude of post-earnings announcement drift for selected studies cited in the text. *Return Spread* refers to the difference in returns between firms with extreme positive and extreme negative surprises.

Raw returns refers to returns not adjusted for a benchmark.

Size adjusted refers to returns in excess of benchmark based on firm size.

Size and book-to-market adjusted refers to returns in excess of a benchmark based on both size and book-to-market.

Beta adjusted refers to returns that are independent of (or uncorrelated with) the market return.

forecasts of earnings did not exist during the 1970s, the early literature on post-earnings announcement drift calculated earnings surprise as the change in earnings relative to four quarters prior (i.e., relative to the same quarter in the prior year). This is commonly referred to as the forecast errors from a seasonal random walk model of earnings.[2]

During the 1980s, first Zacks and a few years later I/B/E/S (now part of Thomson Reuters) began providing professional investors with analysts' consensus forecasts of quarterly earnings. Shortly thereafter, earnings surprises calculated relative to analyst forecasts became one of the most widely used tools in quantitative portfolio management. By 1986, the quantitative research departments at both Sanford Bernstein and Prudential Securities were both calculating and publishing earnings surprises relative to analyst forecasts and, by the early 1990s, using data provided by Zacks and I/B/E/S, the practice became common in the academic literature.

Measuring Post-Earnings Announcement Drift

Historically, researchers have documented post-earnings announcement drift by ranking stocks on the difference between actual and expected earnings (i.e., the earnings surprise) and then tracking the returns to those stocks that have extreme positive and extreme negative values. The literature consistently indicates that firms with an earnings surprise in the top 10% (i.e., top decile) or top 20% (i.e., top quintile) outperform the market and that firms with an earnings surprise in the bottom 10% (i.e., bottom decile) or bottom 20% (i.e., bottom quintile) consistently underperform the market.

To study post-earnings announcement drift, researchers examine returns to what is known as a hedge portfolio—a portfolio that is long firms announcing an extreme positive earnings surprise and short firms announcing an extreme negative earnings surprise. The returns to the hedge portfolio capture what is known as the return spread, or the difference in returns between firms in the top and bottom decile (or quintile) of earnings surprise. To profit from firms with an extreme positive earnings surprise is straightforward; buy a diversified portfolio of all such firms. When a firm announces an earnings surprise in the top 10% or 20% of all earnings surprises, add it to the portfolio and hold it for 3 to 12 months. This results in a very large, well-diversified portfolio, because it entails taking a long position in one-tenth of the universe of stocks. For example, if one is restricted to the S&P 500, the portfolio would entail taking long positions in the 50 stocks

---

[2]Latane and Jones (1977) provide an excellent summary of the post-earnings announcement drift literature during the 1970s.

with the highest earnings surprise each quarter. To profit from firms with an extreme negative earnings surprise is relatively more difficult, because prices are expected to decline. In this case, one can take a short position in the desired stocks and close the short position 3 to 12 months later.[3]

Some subtleties regarding the various portfolios and their construction are worth noting. First, not all firms announce earnings simultaneously. So the distribution of earnings surprise for the current quarter is not known until after all firms have announced results. Because Firm A announces earnings before Firm B, at the time of Firm A's announcement it is impossible to tell where the earnings surprise falls in the ranking for the current quarter. To overcome this issue, one can use the distribution of earnings surprises in the same quarter in the prior year to group firms into portfolios. For example, if Firm A's Q1–2009 earnings surprise is in the top (bottom) 10% of all surprises in Q1–2008, then it is placed in the top (bottom) decile portfolio.

Second, the individual portfolios are subject to significant market risk. For example, both the extreme positive surprise portfolio and the extreme negative surprise portfolio will have exposure to market risk. Just like any other portfolio, the portfolio returns will fluctuate with the overall market, so the fact that these portfolios earn significant returns should not be surprising. The question is whether such portfolios perform better than the market or some other benchmark. Accordingly, in considering returns to such portfolios, researchers calculated market-adjusted or size-adjusted returns (see Table 4.1).

Third, the hedge portfolio has considerably less market risk than the individual long or short portfolios. This is because the market risk of the hedge portfolio is equal to the market risk of the top decile less the market risk of the bottom decile. As a result, the hedge portfolio itself has little to no market risk. Consistent with this, prior studies document that the return spread between firms announcing extreme positive and extreme negative earnings surprises is positive in almost every calendar year.

Evidence on Post-Earnings Announcement Drift

Ball and Brown (1968) were the first to document that returns drifted in the direction of the earnings surprise after the earnings announcements. Investigating this phenomenon further, Foster et al. (1984) report that stocks with extreme positive (negative) earnings surprises earn 3.23% (–3.09%)

---

[3]Some investors might find a short position of this nature difficult to sustain or even infeasible. In this case, investors can buy put options on the stock. Because a put option is the right to sell the stock at a specified price, as the price declines the put option will become more valuable. Later in this chapter we discuss methods to reduce the number of short positions.

over 60 trading days following the firm's quarterly earnings announcement, a spread of 6.32% each quarter or about 25% annualized. Foster et al. (1984) find that the spread varies with firm size and estimates the spread is 3.6% over the subsequent 60 days for large firms and 8.34% over the subsequent 60 days for small firms. In a now seminal paper investigating post-earnings announcement drift, Bernard and Thomas (1989) report a similar spread of 4.2% over the subsequent 60 days, or 18% on an annual basis. Bernard and Thomas (1989) find the spread is negative in only 6 quarters from 1974 to 1985 and that the spread was positive in 11 of the 16 quarters in which the NYSE index had negative returns. Like Foster et al. (1984), Bernard and Thomas (1989) also find the spread varies with firm size, and estimates the spread is 2.74% over the subsequent 60 days for large firms and 5.32% over the subsequent 60 days for small firms.

TEMPORAL CONSISTENCY OF DRIFT   Since Foster et al. (1984) and Bernard and Thomas (1989), several studies find that post-earnings announcement drift consistently occurs across multiple time periods. Collins and Hribar (2000) use data from 1988 to 1997 and report that the earnings surprise hedge portfolio earns 6.88% per quarter, and has negative returns in only 7 of 36 quarters. Chordia and Shivakumar (2006) use data from 1972 to 1999 and find that the earnings surprise hedge portfolio earns monthly returns of 0.96% from 1972 to 1979, 1.05% from 1980 to 1989, and 0.69% from 1990 to 1999. Ng et al. (2008) use data from 1988 to 2005 and find that firms with extreme positive (negative) earnings surprises earn 12.12% (–1.58%) over the 12 months following the earnings announcement. Moreover, Ng et al. (2008) report the spread between firms with extreme positive and extreme negative surprises is consistently positive in every year from 1988 to 2005 (see Figure 4.1).

As Table 4.1 illustrates, studies examining post-earnings announcement drift usually use samples of 10 years or more and, regardless of period studied, all find evidence of drift. Importantly, while the magnitude of the drift varies by study, the existence of the drift does not. Indeed, Table 4.1 suggests early studies using data from the late 1970s and early 1980s estimate the drift between 4.20% and 6.32% per quarter (e.g., Foster et al. 1984; Bernard and Thomas 1989; Abarbanell and Bernard 1992). Strikingly, later studies using data through 2005 and 2006 estimate a very similar range for the drift, between 4.27% and 6.33% per quarter (e.g., Lerman et al. 2007, 2008; Ng et al. 2008).

PERSISTENCE OF DRIFT   Several studies find that earnings surprises predict returns multiple years into the future.

For example, Bernard and Thomas (1989) measure earnings surprise using the change in earnings relative to 4 quarters prior, and show that

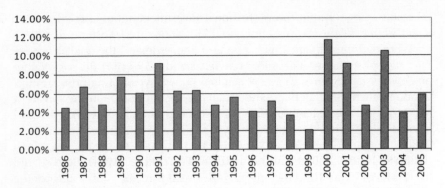

FIGURE 4.1   Return Spread by Calendar Year

Earnings surprise is calculated as the seasonal difference in net income before extraordinary items and scaled by market capitalization 4 quarters prior. Firms are ranked into quintiles at the time of the earnings announcement using the quintile breakpoints for the same calendar quarter in the prior year. Returns are calculated assuming positions are taken one day after the earnings announcement and held for 3 months.

the ability of earnings surprise to predict returns persists beyond the initial 60 days following the announcement, to the subsequent 6 months, 12 months, and 24 months after the earnings announcement. Bernard and Thomas (1989) find the return spread for firms with extreme positive and extreme negative earnings surprises is 5.32% (2.74%) over the first quarter for small (large) firms, 7.96% (4.02%) over 6 months, 9.90% (4.47%) over 12 months, and 9.99% (3.61%) over 24 months. However, over the 24 months following the announcement, Bernard and Thomas (1989) show that 53% (76%) of the drift for small (large) firms occurs in the first quarter following the announcement and that, of this, 13% (20%) occurs in the first 5 days. Doyle et al. (2006) measure earnings surprise using analyst forecast errors, and find that earnings surprises predict returns as far out as 36 months into the future. Doyle et al. (2006) estimate that the difference in return between extreme positive and negative surprises is 13.95% over 12 months, 19.89% over 24 months, and 23.69% over 36 months after the earnings announcement.

Several studies interpret the persistence of drift as stemming from the persistence (or autocorrelation) in earnings surprises. That is, the earnings surprise in the current quarter predicts the earnings surprise in future quarters. If investors are not aware that future surprises are predictable based on historical surprises, then the earning surprise in the current quarter will predict returns more than one quarter into the future (e.g., Bernard and

Thomas, 1989). Within the professional investment community, this effect is referred to as the "cockroach effect." This is an important feature of post-earnings announcement drift because it implies that investors attempting to exploit drift need not turn over their portfolio every quarter. Rather, the evidence suggests investors can buy and hold stocks over long horizons perhaps as long as 3 years. Such long-term positions greatly reduce the transaction costs associated with frequent portfolio turnover and active management.

CONCENTRATION OF DRIFT AROUND FUTURE EARNINGS ANNOUNCEMENTS Research also shows that a significant portion of the drift occurs around next quarter's earnings announcement. That is, the earnings surprise this quarter predicts the returns around next quarter's earnings announcements. Specifically, Bernard and Thomas (1989) estimate that, for small (large) firms, the earnings surprise hedge portfolio earns 5.32% (2.74%) over the 60 days following the earnings announcement and 2.14% (0.68%) over the 5 days ending on next quarter's earnings announcement date. In this case, the portfolio return in the 5 days around the next earnings announcement accounts for 40% (25%) of the quarterly drift. Brandt et al. (2008) report a similar but diminished result. Brandt et al. (2008) find that the earnings surprise hedge portfolio earns 3.23% over the 60 days following the earnings announcement and 0.46% over the 3-day period centered on the next earnings announcement. This suggests that investors wishing to maximize returns to a post-earnings announcement drift strategy need to be vigilant and execute the strategy within a few days of the earnings announcement. Doing so will earn higher returns than delaying. However, because the drift persists over as much as 36 months, research suggests diminished but still relatively large returns can be earned by trading over the course of the quarter (e.g., Doyle et al. 2006).

Measuring Earnings Surprises

Measuring the magnitude of an earnings surprise is not as straightforward as it seems. Earnings surprise is defined as the difference between reported earnings and expected earnings. How does one define reported earnings, and how does one measure expected earnings? It turns out that the answers to these questions affect not only the magnitude of the earnings surprise, but also the returns to post-earnings announcement drift.

Generally Accepted Accounting Principles (GAAP) define the earnings reported on financial statements, commonly referred to as GAAP earnings. However, in press releases and conference calls, managers and analysts often report earnings excluding items that appear in GAAP earnings (e.g., special items, stock-based compensation expense, etc.). Unlike GAAP earnings, the use and definition of these non-GAAP earnings numbers, popularly referred to as pro forma earnings, varies from firm to firm.[4]

Conceptually, post-earnings announcement drift can be based on any definition of earnings and earnings expectations. However, whatever the definition of earnings, expected earnings should be computed on the same basis as reported earnings. For example, using GAAP earnings to measure reported earnings, but using pro forma earnings forecasts to measure expected earnings will result in an earnings surprise that captures both the surprise as well as the difference in the earnings definitions. For example, suppose GAAP earnings are $1 and the analysts' pro forma forecast is $1.05 excluding $0.10 stock-based compensation expense. Then the earnings surprise would seem to be −$0.05, but after adjusting earnings to be on the same basis, the surprise is really $0.05 (true surprise = unadjusted surprise + amount of excluded expense). The distinction between GAAP and pro forma earnings is very important because analysts often forecast pro forma earnings numbers.[5]

Academic research uses various definitions of earnings and various measures of earnings expectations to compute earnings surprise and calculate post-earnings announcement drift. The earliest work used a seasonal random walk model of GAAP earnings. The seasonal random walk model is appealing in its simplicity; expected earnings for the quarter are the earnings for the same quarter in the prior year.[6] Over the years, there have also been many studies that measure earnings expectations using consensus forecasts provided by I/B/E/S, by Zacks, and by individual analysts. For example, Abarbanell and Bernard (1992) use Value Line forecasts of earnings to

---

[4]The fact that the definition of pro forma earnings varies by firm can cause significant comparability issues. These issues are accentuated when data aggregators do not force a standard definition of pro forma earnings across firms. For example, the consensus forecast from I/B/E/S (now Thomson Reuters) will include stock-based compensation expense for one firm, but it will exclude stock-based compensation expense for another (Lambert 2004; Barth et al. 2010). To address this issue, beginning in 1978 Zacks Investment Research adjusted both analyst estimates and reported earnings to conform with a definition of "earnings from continuing operations before extraordinary items," and in 2000, Standard & Poor's promulgated a standardized earnings definition called "core earnings."

[5]For example, Abarbanell and Bernard (1992) report results that differ between measuring reported earnings using GAAP and expected earnings using Value Line, and measuring reported and expected earnings using Value Line. This suggests that Value Line earnings differ from GAAP earnings.

[6]Several studies also use a straightforward extension of the seasonal random walk model, and model the seasonal random walk forecast error as a function of the prior period's forecast error, but Foster (1977) and Foster et al. (1984) found little difference between these models. Later studies use the former almost exclusively.

measure expectations. Abarbanell and Bernard (1992) estimate firms with Value Line forecast errors in the top (bottom) quintile earn 1.91% (−2.38%) over the following quarter and 3.47% (−4.65%) over the following year. Similarly, Doyle et al. (2006) and Livnat and Mendenhall (2006) use analyst forecast errors to measure earnings surprise. Doyle et al. (2006) estimate that firms with analyst forecast errors in the top (bottom) decile earn 9.37% (−4.58%) over the 12 months following the earnings announcement, and 14.93% (−4.96%) over the 24 months following the earnings announcement. Moreover, Doyle et al. (2006) report that the spread in returns between these two groups of firms, on average 19.89%, is positive in every quarter from 1988 to 2002. Comparing the predictive ability of seasonal random walk forecast errors to analyst forecast errors, Livnat and Mendenhall (2006) estimate firms with seasonal random walk forecast errors in the top (bottom) quintile earn 0.8% (−2.38%) over the following quarter, and firms with analyst forecast errors in the top (bottom) quintile earn 1.70% (−2.70%) over the following quarter.

Still another measure of earnings surprise is the return on or around the day of the earnings announcement (i.e., the announcement period return). One important feature of this measure is that the announcement period return will capture the reaction to all value-relevant news, not just earnings news. For example, if the earnings announcement coincided with other corporate disclosures, then the announcement period return would pick up both the reaction to earnings and the reaction to the other disclosures. Ultimately, it is not clear *ex ante* whether including the reaction to this other information would lead to increased or decreased drift. Using returns over the 3-day period centered on the earnings announcement, Brandt et al. (2008) find that firms in the top and bottom quintile of announcement period returns earn 4.61% (−2.94%) over the following year, whereas firms in the top (bottom) quintile of seasonal random walk forecast errors earn 2.70% (−3.48%) over the following year.

Of course, one can use multiple measures of earnings surprise. It is possible to refine post-earnings announcement drift by focusing on those firms announcing extreme surprises under multiple definitions of earnings surprise. For example, Livnat and Mendenhall (2006) find that firms with both seasonal random walk forecast errors in the top (bottom) quintile *and* analyst forecast errors in the top (bottom) quintile earn 3.40% (−3.50%) over the following quarter. Lerman et al. (2007) estimate the hedge portfolio based on firms with seasonal random walk forecast errors in the top (bottom) quintile *and* analyst forecast errors in the top (bottom) quintile earns 5.80% over the following quarter. Similarly, Brandt et al. (2008) estimate firms with both seasonal random walk forecast errors in the top (bottom) quintile *and* announcement period returns in the top (bottom) quintile earn 7.24% (−5.24%) over the following year.

Manipulation of Surprise

Managers can manipulate the earnings surprise in three ways. First, managers can directly manage realized earnings. Such earnings management is not necessarily illegal. Offering end-of-quarter coupons or promotions is common among retailers, and it is one way in which firms manage earnings upward, so-called real earnings management. Alternatively, firms can manage earnings using leeway in GAAP to choose more favorable accounting assumptions (e.g., depreciation, allowance for doubtful accounts). Using a measure of the quality of the non-cash component of earnings, the component affected by changes in accounting assumptions, Francis et al. (2007) show that post-earnings announcement drift is concentrated in firms with low-quality earnings. Francis et al. (2007) find that the earnings surprise hedge portfolio earns 0.95% per month in firms with low-quality earnings and 0.05% per month in firms with high-quality earnings.

Second, managers can manipulate the earnings surprise by manipulating analyst expectations. It is widely alleged that managers have incentives to "walk down" analyst forecasts to achieve a forecast that is easier to beat. Consistent with this, Richardson et al. (2004) find that analyst forecasts are downward bias for companies whose managers subsequently sell shares after the earnings announcement. This suggests managers walk down analysts' forecasts so that the forecasts are easier to beat, and managers, in turn, can sell their shares at an inflated price. On average, however, academic research suggests that analysts are optimistic—not pessimistic—and that analyst upward (downward) revisions portend positive (negative) future returns.

Third, managers can manipulate the earnings surprise by manipulating the definition of pro forma earnings. In contrast to GAAP earnings, because there is no generally accepted definition of pro forma earnings, managers can manipulate the definition of pro forma earnings as they see fit. Research shows that managers often define pro forma earnings in such a way so as to give the appearance of improved performance and smoother earnings. For example, Barth et al. (2010) find that managers exclude items (e.g., stock-based compensation expense) when doing so will allow them to beat earnings expectations and lead to smoother earnings. Despite the possibility of such manipulation, studies in the literature largely agree that earnings surprises calculated using pro forma earnings are associated with greater drift than earnings surprises calculated using GAAP earnings (e.g., Doyle et al. 2006; Livnat and Mendenhall 2006; Lerman et al. 2007).

Sources of Post-Earnings Announcement Drift

Post-earnings announcement drift is an incredibly robust phenomenon that has been documented across more than 4 decades of academic research.

However, the underlying causes of post-earnings announcement drift have only recently begun to be understood. Recent studies attempt to explain what causes the drift and why the drift persists. Studies that offer causal explanations for the drift can be grouped into two categories: those that offer rational explanations based on latent risks and those that offer behavioral explanations based on investor trading behavior. Studies that offer explanations for why the drift persists focus on transaction costs and other limits to arbitrage.

Rational Explanations

Several studies in the academic literature conjecture that post-earnings announcement drift is simply a manifestation of some latent risk. This is an important hypothesis, because it suggests the returns to post-earnings announcement drift strategies are actually compensation for risk. In order for risk to explain why firms with extreme positive (negative) earnings surprises earn extreme positive (negative) returns over the next several months, at least two conditions must hold. First, firms reporting extreme positive surprises must be *riskier* than firms reporting extreme negative surprises. Second, risk must be correlated with the timing of the earnings announcement. That is, since returns accrue *after* the earnings announcement, changes in risk must also occur *after* the announcement.

The first condition comes directly from traditional asset pricing theory: stocks that earn higher (lower) expected returns than the market must be higher (lower) risk. Several recent studies examine the relation between post-earnings announcement drift and risks related to macroeconomic conditions, divergence in opinions, and adverse selection.

Chordia and Shivakumar (2005, 2006) posit that drift may be capturing the difference in firms' exposure to macroeconomic conditions.[7] Consistent with a link between macroeconomic conditions and drift, Chordia and Shivakumar (2005) find drift is greatest following periods of high inflation. Specifically, Chordia and Shivakumar (2005) estimate the earnings surprise hedge portfolio earns on average 1.31% per month after periods of high inflation, and 0.71% after periods of low inflation. Similarly, Chordia and Shivakumar (2006) show that the returns to the earnings surprise hedge portfolio negatively predicts growth in industrial production, growth in real consumption, and growth in labor income over the future 12 months.

---

[7]Ball et al. (1993) make a similar argument. Chordia and Shivakumar (2005) interpret the association between inflation and future returns as consistent with investors underreacting to inflation. However, a large related literature suggests that inflation predicts returns because inflation captures information about business conditions and hence systematic risk.

Garfinkel and Sokobin (2007) build on rational asset pricing models that suggest that divergence in investors' opinions is an additional risk factor (e.g., Varian 1985) and posit that this omitted risk might explain the drift. Consistent with this, Garfinkel and Sokobin (2007) find that the drift is increasing in a measure of divergence in opinions: the difference between the average trading volume around the announcement and the average trading volume prior to the announcement. That is, the higher the unexpected volume around the earnings announcement, the higher the drift.

Sadka (2006) posits that the drift may be capturing the difference in firms' exposure to unexpected changes in market-wide liquidity. That is, Sadka (2006) conjectures that firms announcing extreme positive earnings surprises are more sensitive to fluctuations in market-wide liquidity than firms announcing extreme negative earnings surprises. Using the marginal cost of trading one additional share as the measure of exposure to market-wide liquidity, Sadka (2006) finds that the earnings surprise hedge portfolio earns 1.07% per month in firms with low liquidity and 0.80% per month in firms with high liquidity.

The second condition—that changes in risk are correlated with the timing of the announcement—is based on the fact that the drift occurs post-announcement. Despite several attempts, studies have been unable to find evidence of a significant shift in firm risk around earnings announcements. For example, Bernard and Thomas (1989) group firms into earning surprise deciles and examine the risk of each portfolio over several periods prior to and post-announcement. Although Bernard and Thomas (1989) find some evidence that firms reporting extreme positive surprises are riskier than firms reporting extreme negative surprises, Bernard and Thomas (1989) find no evidence that the risk changes before and after the earnings announcement. Similarly, Ball et al. (1993) find evidence of a positive relation between changes in risk and the earnings surprise *prior* to the earnings announcement, but they find no evidence of a relation between changes in risk and the earnings surprise *after* the announcement.

Behavioral Explanations

Rather than test risk-based explanations for post-earnings announcement drift, an alternative stream of literature tests whether drift is associated with the trading behavior of naive investors. Studies in this literature have had a great deal of success in explaining observed patterns in returns. Studies in this literature typically proxy for investor sophistication using trade size or quarterly institutional ownership, and test whether post-earnings announcement drift is decreasing in measures of sophistication. Bartov et al. (2000) use quarterly institutional ownership as a proxy for investor sophistication and find that institutional ownership is negatively associated with drift.

Similarly, Vega (2006) shows that the drift is concentrated in firms in which the probability of informed trade is low and media coverage is high.

Hirshleifer et al. (2009) and DellaVigna and Pollet (2009) conjecture that post-earnings announcement drift is the result of limited attention. That is, they conjecture that the drift occurs because investors have limited information processing abilities and are simply unable to process the information in the earnings announcement in a timely manner. DellaVigna and Pollet (2009) conjecture that investors are most distracted on Fridays and, therefore, that investors pay less attention to earnings announcements on Fridays. Consistent with this, DellaVigna and Pollet (2009) find that the earnings surprise hedge portfolio formed based on non-Friday announcements earns 5.14% over the next 75 trading days whereas the hedge portfolio formed on Friday announcements earns 9.76% over the next 75 trading days. Similarly, Hirshleifer et al. (2009) conjecture that investors are most distracted on days when many firms report earnings simultaneously. Consistent with this, Hirshleifer et al. (2009) find that, on days with few concurrent announcements, the earnings surprise hedge portfolio earns returns of 2.81% over the next quarter, but on days with many concurrent announcements, the hedge portfolio earns returns of 5.37%.

Using a dataset of the actual trades of individual retail investors, Taylor (2010a) investigates the relation between drift and both the amount and direction of retail investor trading. Taylor (2010a) finds that the drift is concentrated in those stocks where retail investors trade contrarian to the earnings surprise. That is, the upward drift following positive earnings surprises is largest when retail investors are net sellers, and the downward drift following negative earnings surprises is largest when retail investors are net buyers. Taylor (2010a) finds evidence of drift only in those stocks for which retail investors are contrarians, and that the drift is most pronounced in stocks for which individuals are contrarian *and* transaction costs are high. Collectively, these papers suggest that investors may be able to enhance the returns to a post-earnings announcement drift strategy by using intraday order flow or other measures to identify the trading of unsophisticated investors.

Transaction Costs

The role of transaction costs is important. If naive investors cause prices to deviate from fundamental values, then the deviation—and therefore the drift—should be the largest when arbitrage by sophisticated investors is constrained. Consistent with this, several studies suggest that post-earnings announcement drift is concentrated in stocks for which arbitrage is risky and transaction costs are high. Mendenhall (2004) examines whether post-earnings announcement drift is concentrated in firms that are risky for sophisticated investors to arbitrage. Using the variance of returns to measure arbitrage risk, Mendenhall (2004) finds that when arbitrage is very risky, stocks with extreme positive (negative) earnings surprises earn 5.21% (–5.46%) per quarter, and when arbitrage is least risky, stocks with extreme positive (negative) earnings surprises earn returns of 1.32% (–1.65%) per quarter. Ng et al. (2008) rank firms on the basis of several measures for transaction costs and find that post-earnings announcement drift is most pronounced when transaction costs are high. Ng et al. (2008) find that when transaction costs are highest (i.e., liquidity is lowest), stocks with extreme positive (negative) earnings surprises earn annualized returns of 9.92% (–4.93%), and when transaction costs are lowest (i.e., liquidity is highest), stocks with extreme positive (negative) earnings surprises earn annualized returns of 3.89% (–0.29%). Taking a broader definition of transaction costs that includes not only trading commission and the price impact of trades, but also margin maintenance requirements and short-sale constraints, Bushee and Raedy (2005) examine the cost to implementing a $350 million investment in various post-earnings announcement drift strategies. Bushee and Raedy (2005) find that such strategies are successful even after including implementation costs and disallowing short sales. Interestingly, because of margin calls required on short positions, Bushee and Raedy (2005) find that the profits to implementing a post-earnings announcement drift strategy where short sales are not allowed are higher than if short sales are allowed.

In contrast, Chordia et al. (2009) estimate that transaction costs on a $5 million investment accounts for between 66% and 100% of returns to a post-earnings announcement drift strategy. Battalio and Mendenhall (2007) report that assuming investors trade at the closing price of the date listed as the earnings announcement on the COMPUSTAT database will lead to an overstatement of drift by 2.66% per quarter and that trading at the close of the day following the date listed on the database will lead to an understatement of drift by 1.16% per quarter. Battalio and Mendenhall (2007) use the actual timing of earnings announcements on the Dow Jones News Wire to correct for this issue, and they estimate that an investor in the earnings surprise hedge portfolio could have earned at least 14% per year *after* transaction costs. In summarizing the foregoing evidence on transaction costs, Richardson et al. (2010) point out that the academic literature has grossly overestimated transaction costs, and they suggest that the actual transaction cost (including price impact) paid by institutional investors is about 0.25%.

Extensions

In addition to post-earnings announcement drift, academic research shows that several other firm characteristics predict returns. Several studies show that one can earn even higher returns by combining post-earnings announcement drift strategies with other earnings-based or nonearnings-based strategies.

Other Earnings-Based Strategies

Post-earnings announcement drift is fundamentally about the predictive ability of the earnings surprise. However, studies show that considering other properties of earnings can refine post-earnings announcement drift. Balakrishnan et al. (2010) conjecture that investors underreact not only to the earnings surprise, but also the level of earnings (post-loss/profit drift). Balakrishnan et al. (2010) sort stocks based on both the earnings surprise and the level of reported earnings, and find that the hedge portfolio formed on reported earnings earns 10.1% over the 6 months following the earnings announcement. Examining returns to combining the two strategies, Balakrishnan et al. (2010) estimate that firms with both extreme positive (negative) earnings surprises and extreme positive (negative) earnings earn 8.17% (−4.29%) over the 6 months following the announcement, a difference of 12.47%.

Several papers suggest additional extensions of post-earnings announcement drift based on the accrual components of earnings. It is well known that the accrual (i.e., non-cash) component of earnings negatively predicts future returns (e.g., Sloan 1996). Collins and Hribar (2000) sort stocks based on both the magnitude of earnings surprise and the magnitude of the accrual component of earnings. Collins and Hribar (2000) find that the earnings surprise hedge portfolio earns 6.88% over 6 months and that the accrual hedge portfolio earns 5.56% over 6 months.[8] Examining returns to combining the two strategies, Collins and Hribar (2000) estimate that firms with both extreme positive (negative) earnings surprises and extreme negative (positive) accruals earn 5.89% (−6.11%) over 6 months, a difference of 11.94%.

Related, Jegadeesh and Livnat (2006) decompose earnings into revenue and expense components. Jegadeesh and Livnat (2006) sort stocks based on both the earnings surprise and the revenue surprise, and they find that the earnings surprise hedge portfolio earns 5.55% over the 6 months following the earnings announcement, and the revenue surprise hedge portfolio earns 4.42% over the 6 months following the earnings announcement. Examining returns to combining the two strategies, Jegadeesh and Livnat (2006) estimate that firms with both extreme positive (negative) earnings surprises and extreme positive (negative) revenue surprises earn 5.29% (−2.81%) over the 6 months following the announcement, a difference of 8.10%.

---

[8]The accrual strategy takes a long position in low-accrual firms and a short position in high-accrual firms.

Other Nonearnings-Based Strategies

Several studies show that post-earnings announcement drift can be refined by considering nonearnings information in addition to the earnings surprise. The most well studied refinement entails combining post-earnings announcement drift and return momentum. Among others, Chan et al. (1996) show that the returns over the past 6 months predict future returns. Chan et al. (1996) sort stocks based on both the earnings surprise and return momentum over the past 6 months, and they find that the earnings surprise hedge portfolio earns an annual return of 7.5% and the momentum hedge portfolio earns an annual return of 15.4%. Examining returns to combining the two strategies, Chan et al. (1996) estimate that firms with both extreme positive (negative) earnings surprises and extreme positive (negative) return momentum earn 25.7% (14.2%) over the next year, a spread of 11.5%. However, Chordia and Shivakumar (2006) question whether the momentum strategy is distinct from post-earnings announcement drift. Chordia and Shivakumar (2006) show that returns to the momentum strategy are explained by post-earnings announcement drift but not vice versa. Chordia and Shivakumar (2006) estimate that the earnings surprise hedge portfolio earns 0.90% per month whereas the momentum hedge portfolio earns 0.76% per month, and that the earnings surprise hedge portfolio outperforms the momentum hedge portfolio in every 10-year period since 1972, except for the period 1980 to 1989.

Lerman et al. (2008) conjecture that post-earnings announcement drift is concentrated in firms in which a greater fraction of volume occurs on the announcement day. Lerman et al. (2008) sort stocks based on both the earnings surprise and the fraction of volume over the prior quarter that occurs on the earnings announcement. Lerman et al. (2008) report that the earnings surprise hedge portfolio earns 4.31% per quarter and the volume hedge portfolio earns 2.71% per quarter. Examining returns to combining the two strategies, Lerman et al. (2008) estimate that firms with both extreme positive (negative) earnings surprises and high (low) announcement period volume earn 4.97% (−2.67%) over the quarter, a spread of 7.64%.

Institutional Investors

Several studies document that institutional investors trade on, and profit from, post-earnings announcement drift. Ke and Ramalingegowda (2005) hypothesize and find that institutions making predominantly short-term investments trade based on post-earnings announcement drift. Ke and Ramalingegowda (2005) suggest the trading activities of such institutions generate annual returns of 22% after transaction costs. However, Ke and

Ramalingegowda (2005) report that despite these large returns, post-earnings announcement drift is not the predominant strategy, and that trading based on return momentum is four times more prevalent than post-earnings announcement drift. Additionally, Ke and Ramalingegowda (2005) find that institutions making predominantly short-term investments trade less aggressively in firms with high transaction costs, and that their trades help impound earnings information into prices, reducing the drift. Similarly, Campbell et al. (2009) also report that institutions appear to trade on post-earnings announcement drift. Campbell et al. (2009) report that institutions buy stocks in advance of positive earnings surprises and sell stocks in advance of negative earnings surprises. Consistent with stock-picking ability, Campbell et al. (2009) find that the price of stocks bought (sold) in anticipation of the earnings announcement drift upward (downward) following the announcement.

Although Ke and Ramalingegowda (2005) and Campbell et al. (2009) focus on institutional investors broadly defined, several studies focus exclusively on mutual funds. For example, Ali et al. (2009) estimate that the average actively managed mutual fund has a portfolio tilted in such a way so as to capture some of the returns to the drift. Ali et al. (2009) rank funds according to the tilt of their portfolio toward firms with extreme earnings surprises, and find that highly tilted funds outperform funds with no tilt by 1.97% per year. Relatedly, Baker et al. (2010) examine the extent to which trading on post-earnings announcement drift can explain mutual fund performance. Baker et al. (2010) find that stocks bought (sold) by the average mutual fund outperform (underperform) the market around subsequent earnings announcements. Baker et al. (2010) find that this spread amounts to about 0.38% annually, and that this accounts for 27.88% of performance of the average mutual fund trade. Strikingly, Baker et al. (2010) report that the subsequent earnings surprise of stocks bought by managers exceeds the subsequent earning surprise of stock sold by mangers in all 22 years in their sample.

Griffin et al. (2009) examine whether institutional investor trades predict earnings surprises because institutions have nonpublic information about future earnings or because institutions use public information to predict the earnings surprise. Griffin et al. (2009) find no evidence that institutional trading in the 5 and 10 days prior to the earnings announcement earn significant profits, but that trades on and immediately after the announcement day are highly profitable. This suggests that intuitional investors profit from post-earnings announcement drift not because they have foreknowledge about which companies will announce extreme earnings but because they trade in a timely manner following the announcement.

Collectively, the evidence supports the conclusion that at least a subset of institutions trade on and profit from post-earnings announcement drift.

However, this raises an important question that has far-reaching implications for securities regulators charged with investor protection: If institutions are profiting from trading on earnings information, who is losing? The answer: individual investors.

Individual Investors

Academic research on how individual investors use earnings information in their trading decisions is quite limited. However, a few studies consistently show that individual investors make systematic investing mistakes in general, and when processing earnings information. With regard to general investment decisions, Odean (1999) examines the profitability of individual investor trades at a discount broker and finds that stocks sold by individuals earn *higher* subsequent returns than stocks bought by individuals. Similarly, Barber and Odean (2000) find that investors at a large discount broker tilt their portfolios toward small value stocks, pay 3% in commissions and 1% in bid-ask spread, and that the average portfolio earns significant returns of −3.7% net of transaction costs. When aggregated across all individual investors in the economy, the magnitude of these losses is staggering. For example, using a comprehensive dataset of all individual investors in Taiwan, Barber et al. (2009) find that the annual net losses of individual investors is equivalent to 2.2% of Taiwan's GDP.

With regard to earnings, individuals are known to trade on earnings information but in a naive manner. Dey and Radhakrishna (2007) use data on actual orders from all individual investors on the NYSE for 144 firms over a 3-month period and find a surge in volume across all market participants at the time of the announcement. Strikingly, Dey and Radhakrishna (2007) find that individual investors account for 30.1% (11.2%) of all trades (trading volume) around earnings announcements. Despite increased individual investor trading activity around earnings announcements, studies in the experimental literature often show that individuals not only fail to understand the persistence of earnings (e.g., Maines and Hand 1996), but also overestimate their ability to interpret the information (e.g., Bloomfield et al. 1999). Confirming that individuals make systematic mistakes when trading on earnings information, Taylor (2010b) shows that around earnings announcements, individual investors' trades earn economically significant losses and that these losses are greater than losses to nonannouncement trades. Moreover, after partitioning investors by socioeconomic demographics, Taylor (2010b) finds that increased losses around the earnings announcements accrue primarily to nonaffluent, nonactively trading individual investors.

There are two ways individual investors might be able to use earnings information to improve the performance of their earnings-based trades and that of their overall investment portfolio. First, individual investors might consider refraining from trading around earnings announcements or other preplanned company news events. Around such events, there is likely to be a preponderance of more sophisticated traders who can more efficiently process the earnings information. This also entails canceling or monitoring any limit orders in effect at the time of the earnings announcement.

Second, individual investors might consider investing in an ETF or mutual fund that employs a trading strategy that exploits post-earnings announcement drift. Although an institutional investor can spend considerable resources on fundamental analysis and can bring considerable wealth to bear, individual investors have both limited time and limited wealth. For example, although large institutional investors can easily afford to manage a large, well-diversified portfolio of stocks (i.e., 30+), most individual investors who trade stocks on their own account simply cannot afford to purchase or manage such a large portfolio. Additionally, most individual investors cannot sustain the large, long-term short positions necessary to profit from firms with extreme negative earnings surprises, or are uncomfortable using put options as a substitute. For these reasons, it makes sense for individuals interested in pursuing a post-earnings announcement drift strategy to invest in a professionally managed mutual fund or ETF that exploits the drift, rather than trying to manage the strategy themselves.

There are considerable risks for individual investors attempting to manage the strategy on their own. Because most individuals do not have the wealth or expertise needed to sustain long-term short positions and trade 30+ stocks, their portfolios will be both unhedged (i.e., the long positions on firms announcing extreme positive surprises will not be offset by short positions on firms announcing extreme negative surprises) and underdiversified.

One way individuals may be able to reduce some of the risk from holding underdiversified portfolios and improve returns is by screening stocks based on multiple characteristics. As discussed earlier, a vast body of research investigates the characteristics of stocks for which post-earnings announcement drift is the most pronounced. This line of research suggests several refinements that earn even larger returns than traditional post-earnings announcement drift strategies. These refinements typically entail using additional public information to refine the set of investable stocks. Thus, one way that individuals can potentially reduce the risk from holding underdiversified portfolios is to screen stocks based on both the earnings surprise and characteristics known to be associated with pronounced drift. For example, post-earnings announcement drift is known to be concentrated among small firms and those with extreme past returns. Because screening firms based on market capitalization and past returns is relatively straightforward, individual investors could conceivably enhance the returns to a strategy that buys firms that are in the top 10% based on earnings surprise by focusing on stocks that are also in the top 10% based on prior 6-month return and that have low market capitalization. The advantage of using these two additional screens is that it shrinks the number of stocks that an investor needs to hold while simultaneously increasing the expected portfolio return. An additional advantage to restricting the strategy to smaller stocks is that large trades tend to move prices more in small stocks. As a result, large sophisticated investors will tend to avoid small stocks. The absence of large sophisticated investors means the drift will be more pronounced, presenting an opportunity for small sophisticated investors who do not move prices when they trade.

References

Abarbanell, J., and V. L. Bernard. 1992. Tests of analysts' overreaction/underreaction to earnings information as an explanation for anomalous stock price behavior. *Journal of Finance* 47 (3): 1181–1207.

Ali, A., S. Klasa, and O. Li. 2009. Institutional stakeholdings and better-informed traders at earnings announcements. *Journal of Accounting and Economics*, forthcoming.

Baker, M., L. Litov, J. A. Wachter, and J. Wurgler. 2010. Can mutual fund managers pick stocks? Evidence from their trades prior to earnings announcements. *Journal of Financial and Quantitative Analysis* 45: 1111–1131.

Balakrishnan, K., E. Bartov, and L. Faurel. 2010. Post loss/profit announcement drift. *Journal of Accounting and Economics* 50: 20–41.

Ball, R., and P. Brown. 1968. An empirical evaluation of accounting income numbers. *Journal of Accounting Research* 6 (2): 159–178.

Ball, R., S. P. Kothari, and R. L. Watts. 1993. Economic determinants of the relation between earnings changes and stock returns. *The Accounting Review* 68 (3): 622–638.

Barber, B., and T. Odean. 2000. Trading is hazardous to your wealth: The common stock investment performance of individual investors. *Journal of Finance* 55 (2): 773–806.

Barber, B., T. Odean, and N. Zhu. 2009. Do retail traders move markets? *Review of Financial Studies* 22: 151–186.

Barth, M., I. D. Gow, and D. J. Taylor. 2010. Non-GAAP and Street Earnings: Evidence from SFAS123R. Working paper.

Bartov, E., S. Radhakrishnan, and I. Krinsky. 2000. Investor sophistication and patterns in stock returns after earnings announcements. *The Accounting Review* 75: 43–63.

Battalio, R., and R. Mendenhall. 2007. Post-earnings announcement drift: Intra-day timing and liquidity costs. Working paper.

Bernard, V., and J. K. Thomas. 1989. Post-earnings-announcement drift: Delayed price response or risk premium? *Journal of Accounting Research* 27: 1–36.

Bloomfield, R., R. Libby, and M. Nelson. 1999. Confidence and the welfare of less-informed investors. *Accounting, Organizations, and Society* 24: 623–647.

Bradshaw, M. T., and R. G. Sloan. 2002. GAAP versus the street: An empirical assessment of two alternative definitions of earnings. *Journal of Accounting Research* 40 (1): 41–66.

Brandt, M., R. Kishore, P. Santa-Clara, and M. Venkatachalam. 2008. Earnings announcements are full of surprises. Working paper.

Bushee, B., and J. S. Raedy. 2005. Factors affecting the implementability of stock market trading strategies. Working paper.

Campbell, J. Y., T. Ramadorai, and A. Schwartz. 2009. Caught on tape: Institutional trading, stock returns, and earnings announcements. *Journal of Financial Economics* 92: 66–91.

Chan, L. K. C., N. Jegadeesh, and J. Lakonishok. 1996. Momentum strategies. *Journal of Finance* 51: 1681–1713.

Chordia, T., A. Goyal, G. Sadka, R. Sadka, and L. Shivakumar. 2009. Liquidity and the post-earnings announcement drift. *Financial Analysts Journal* 65 (4): 18–32.

Chordia, T., and L. Shivakumar. 2005. Inflation illusion and post-earnings-announcement drift. *Journal of Accounting Research* 43: 521–556.

Chordia, T., and L. Shivakumar. 2006. Earnings and price momentum. *Journal of Financial Economics* 80: 627–656.

Collins, D., and P. Hribar. 2000. Earnings-based and accrual-based market anomalies: One effect or two? *Journal of Accounting and Economics* 29: 101–123.

Dellavigna, S., and J. Pollet. 2009. Investor inattention and Friday earnings announcements. *Journal of Finance* 64 (2): 709–749.

Dey, M., and B. Radhakrishna. 2007. Who trades around earnings announcements? Evidence from TORQ Data. *Journal of Business Finance and Accounting* 34: 269–291.

Doyle, J. T., R. J. Lundholm, and M. T. Soliman. 2003. The predictive value of expenses excluded from pro forma earnings. *Review of Accounting Studies* 8 (2–3): 145–174.

Doyle, J., R. Lundholm, and M. Soliman. 2006. The extreme future stock returns following I/B/E/S earnings surprises. *Journal of Accounting Research* 44 (5): 849–887.

Fama, E. F. 1998. Market efficiency, long-term returns, and behavioral finance. *Journal of Financial Economics* 49: 283–306.

Foster, G. 1977. Quarterly accounting data: Time-series properties and predictive-ability results. *The Accounting Review* 52 (1): 1–21.

Foster, G., C. Olsen, and T. Shevlin. 1984. Earnings releases, anomalies, and the behavior of security returns. *The Accounting Review* 59 (4): 574–603.

Francis, J., R. Lafond, P. Olsson, and K. Schipper. 2007. Information uncertainty and post-earnings-announcement-drift. *Journal of Business Finance & Accounting* 34 (3–4): 403–433.

Garfinkel, J., and J. Sokobin. 2006. Volume, opinion divergence, and returns: A study of post-earnings announcement drift. *Journal of Accounting Research* 44 (1): 85–112.

Griffin, J. M., T. Shu, and S. Topaloglu. 2008. How informed are the smart guys? Working paper.

Hirshleifer, D., S. Lim, and S. Teoh. 2009. Driven to distraction: Extraneous events and underreaction to earnings news. *Journal of Finance*, forthcoming.

Jegadeesh, R., and J. Livnat. 2006. Revenue surprises and stock returns. *Journal of Accounting and Economics* 41: 147–171.

Ke, B., and S. Ramalingegowda. 2005. Do institutional investors exploit the post-earnings announcement drift? *Journal of Accounting and Economics* 39: 25–53.

Lambert, R. A. 2004. Discussion of analysts' treatment of non-recurring items in street earnings and loss function assumptions in rational expectations tests on financial analysts' earnings forecasts. *Journal of Accounting and Economics* 38 (1–3): 205–222.

Latane, H., and C. Jones. 1977. Standardized unexpected earnings—A progress report. *Journal of Finance* 32 (5): 1457–1465.

Lerman, A., J. Livnat, and R. R. Mendenhall. 2007. Double surprise into higher future returns. *Financial Analysts Journal* 63 (4): 63–71.

Lerman, A., J. Livnat, and R. R. Mendenhall. 2008. The high-volume return premium and post-earnings announcement drift. Working paper.

Livnat, J., and R. R. Mendenhall. 2006. Comparing the post-earnings announcement drift for surprises calculated from analyst and time series forecasts. *Journal of Accounting Research* 44 (1): 177–205.

Maines, L. A., and J. R. M. Hand. 1996. Individuals' perceptions and misperceptions of the time series properties of quarterly earnings. *The Accounting Review* 71 (3): 317–336.

Mendenhall, R. 2004. Arbitrage risk and post-earnings-announcement drift. *Journal of Business* 77 (4): 875–894.

Ng, J., T. Rusticus, and R. Verdi. 2008. Implications of transaction costs for the post-earnings-announcement drift. *Journal of Accounting Research* 46 (3): 661–696.

Odean, T. 1999. Do investors trade too much? *American Economic Review* 89: 1279–1289.

Richardson, S., S. H. Teoh, and P. D. Wysocki. 2004. The walk-down to beatable analyst forecasts: The role of equity issuance and insider trading incentives. *Contemporary Accounting Research* 21 (4): 885–924.

Richardson, S., I. Tuna, and P. Wysocki. 2010. Accounting anomalies and fundamental analysis: A review of recent research advances. *Journal of Accounting and Economics* 50: 410–454.

Sadka, R. 2006. Momentum and postearnings-announcement drift anomalies: The role of liquidity risk. *Journal of Financial Economics* 80: 309–349.

Sloan, R. 1996. Do stock prices fully reflect information in accruals and cash flows about future earnings? *The Accounting Review* 71: 289–315.

Taylor, D. 2010a. Retail investors and the adjustment of stock prices to earnings information. Working paper.

Taylor, D. 2010b. Individual investors and corporate earnings. Working paper.

Varian, H. 1985. Divergence of opinion in complete markets: A note. *Journal of Finance* 40: 309–317.

Vega, C. 2006. Stock price reaction to public and private information. *Journal of Financial Economics* 82: 103–133.

Go to http://hema.zacks.com for abstracts and links to papers.

CHAPTER 5

Fundamental Data Anomalies

Ian Gow

As discussed in Chapter 1, a key tenet of the efficient markets hypothesis (EMH) is that the value implications of financial statement information should be fully impounded into stock prices. As such, analysis of such "fundamental" information should not provide the analyst with the opportunity to earn excess returns or "beat the market." The EMH was a maintained hypothesis in accounting and finance research for several decades; evidence of the historical firmness of the belief in EMH among many researchers is given by the use of the term *anomaly* to describe any apparent departure from market efficiency. However, by the turn of the millennium, a growing body of evidence of a variety of anomalies had developed, making it difficult to maintain an unequivocal belief in its validity.

Much of the evidence that has shaken faith in the EMH relates to fundamental data. Foster, Olsen, and Shevlin (1984) and Bernard and Thomas (1989) provide evidence of *post-earnings announcement drift*, which refers to the apparent tendency of stock prices to continue to move in the direction of the earnings surprise for months after an earnings announcement. Sloan (1996) documents the *accrual anomaly*. Fama and French (1992) document several anomalies related to measures of fundamental value, such as earnings-to-price and book-to-market ratios. Each of these anomalies (or groups of anomalies) is sufficiently important to warrant a separate chapter in this volume. In Chapter 2, Patricia Dechow, Natalya V. Khimich and Richard Sloan discuss the accrual anomaly. In Chapter 4, Daniel Taylor covers post-earnings announcement drift. In Chapter 10, Oleg Rytchkov discusses the so-called value anomalies.

The goal of this chapter is to examine a number of strategies that use detailed fundamental information to predict future returns. Each strategy is drawn from academic research on the usefulness of fundamental analysis. What distinguishes most of the strategies examined in this chapter from fundamental-based strategies examined in other chapters is the use of multiple elements of fundamental analysis in constructing trading portfolios. For example, Piotroski (2000) constructs F_SCORE by summing statistics derived from 9 fundamental metrics, and Mohanram (2005) constructs GSCORE from 8 fundamental metrics.

It is interesting to note that the approaches considered in these papers more closely resemble approaches commonly used by practitioners to identify stocks for investment. For example, while purchasing high book-to-market (BM) firms has been shown to yield higher returns, Piotroski (2000, p. 4) notes "[sell-side] analysts do not recommend high BM firms when forming their buy/sell recommendations." In contrast, analysts will recommend firms who report above-average or increasing profits, measures which figure in both F_SCORE and GSCORE.

Fundamental Metrics

A number of measures of fundamental value have been proposed by practitioners. Given the long-recognized principle that the fundamental value of a share of common stock equals the present value of future dividends, a number of strategies focus on dividend yield, the level of annual dividends per share divided by the stock price. In their book, O'Higgins and Downs (1991) propose a strategy of buying those stocks from the Dow Jones Industrial Average with the highest dividend yield. Variants of this strategy go by names such as "Dow 10" or "Dogs of the Dow." The basic notion here is that current dividend levels provide a useful estimate of future dividend power and, critically, that the stock market fails fully to appreciate this (if it did, such stocks would be fairly priced and thus not necessarily the source of abnormal returns). A dividend yield-based strategy is included, along with other value-based strategies, in Fama and French (1993). Fama and French (1993) argue that apparent excess returns to a dividend-yield strategy are attributable to 3 risk factors, now called the Fama-French factors, and do not represent true abnormal returns. Hirschey (2000, p. 15) argues that the profitability of the "dogs of the Dow" strategy is a myth, and that it is "incredible . . . that modern financial markets could be that inefficient" that such a simple strategy could produce superior returns. However, it remains an open question whether more refined strategies based on dividends can produce true excess returns.

A number of papers have taken more sophisticated approaches to the construction of fundamental-based strategies. One style that is popular in academic research involves construction of a summary measure of the fundamental attractiveness of a stock. An early paper in this vein is Ou and Penman (1989), who devise a model to predict the probability of a firm having earnings increase in the next year, denoted as *Pr*. They then evaluate a trading strategy that goes long in stocks with *Pr* greater than 0.6 and shorts stocks with *Pr* less than or equal to 0.4. Forming portfolios at the end of the third month after fiscal year-end—to ensure that fundamental data are available—and holding for 24 months, this trading strategy yields a hedge return of 12.5% (after adjusting for size, the return is about 7.0%).

One concern with the approach taken in Ou and Penman (1989) is that it involves "data mining," which is defined by Tortoriello (2009) as "using computers to look for correlations between items in a database, without necessarily seeking to understand the underlying factors that cause and can alter those correlations." One reason to be concerned about this is that a user of this approach risks overfitting the data, that is, identifying a relationship that holds in the dataset examined but doesn't hold in other settings, in particular, when the candidate investment strategy is actually deployed. Consistent with this concern, Holthausen and Larcker (1992) show that the strategy used by Ou and Penman (1989) for the return sample period 1973–1983, does not work in the 1978–1999 period.

To address concerns about overfitting, subsequent studies have generally sought to motivate the financial ratios considered using either valuation theory, industry practice, or models drawn from behavioral finance. For example, Lev and Thiagarajan (1993) construct an "aggregate fundamental score" based on 12 fundamental signals identified from written pronouncements of financial analysts. The authors identify 12 fundamental signals from a search of professional publications, such as the *Wall Street Journal* and *Barron's*, and show that, from 1974 to 1988, these fundamental signals are consistently negatively associated with contemporaneous stock returns after controlling for changes in earnings.

Subsequent studies have not only refined this approach, but also examined whether detailed, contextual fundamental analysis can produce superior returns. Abarbanell and Bushee (1998) find that a portfolio constructed using 9 fundamental signals taken from Lev and Thiagarajan (1993) and Abarbanell and Bushee (1997) earns a cumulative abnormal return of 13.2%. Among the 9 signals, 3 have a statistically significant role: INV, measured as the difference between changes in sales and changes in inventory; GM, measured as the change in gross profit less the change in sales; and, S&A, measured as the change in sales less the change in selling and administrative expenses.[1]

---

[1]They also find a significant relation with capital expenditures, but with slightly lower level of statistical significance and with a sign contrary to that predicted from the analysis of Lev and Thiagarajan (1993) and Abarbanell and Bushee (1997). Specifically, they found that firms with higher-than-expected capital expenditures have lower future returns.

Two significant papers have used detailed analysis of fundamentals to refine the value anomaly discussed in Chapter 8. Piotroski (2000) examines the value of fundamental analysis within value stocks (i.e., those with low market-to-book ratios). On the other hand, Mohanram (2005) focuses on glamour stocks (i.e., those with high market-to-book ratios).

Piotroski (2000) notes that the typical value stock is financially distressed and that this distress is associated with low or declining levels of several fundamental variables, such as margins, profits, cash flows, liquidity, and financial leverage. This observation provides the basis for identifying nine financial statement signals used to distinguish among value firms. The 9 fundamental signals examined by Piotroski (2000) measure 3 areas of a firm's financial condition: profitability, financial leverage, and operating efficiency. Under profitability, Piotroski (2000) identifies ROA (return on assets), defined as net income before extraordinary items scaled by beginning total assets, CFO, defined as cash flow from operations scaled by beginning total assets, ΔROA, the current year's ROA less the prior year's ROA, and ACCRUAL, which equals ROA minus CFO.

Three variables relate to financial leverage: ΔLEVER is the change in the ratio of total long-term debt to average total assets, and ΔLIQUID equals the difference between the firm's ratio of current assets to current liabilities at end and at the beginning of the fiscal year. The indicator variable EQOFFER is equal to one if the firm did not issue common equity in the year preceding portfolio formation, zero otherwise.

The remaining two variables relate to operating efficiency: ΔMARGIN is the firm's current gross margin ratio (gross margin scaled by total sales) less the prior year's gross margin ratio, and ΔTURN is the change in a firm's current year asset turnover ratio (total sales scaled by beginning-of-the-year total assets).

To form portfolios, Piotroski (2000) first constructs a measure F_SCORE which gives one point for each positive value for ROA, ΔROA, CFO, ΔMARGIN, ΔTURN, ΔLEVER, and ΔLIQUID, one point for a negative value of ACCRUAL, and one point if EQOFFER equals one. The analysis in Piotroski (2000) focuses on returns earned on a hedge portfolio constructed by going long in stocks with high F_SCORE (i.e., F_SCORE of 8 or 9) and going short in stocks with low F_SCORE (i.e., 1 or 2). One-year market adjusted returns to such a portfolio constructed using all high BM firms average 23.0%, whereas 2-year returns reach 43.2%. Piotroski (2000) shows that this strategy is not explained by variables shown to be associated with returns, such as size, momentum, and trading volume. Additionally, returns based on F_SCORE are not explained by other investment anomalies, such as momentum or accruals.

Since the year 2000, Piotroski's scoring system has been the subject of articles in *Forbes* and *Bloomberg Businessweek*. In addition, a number of popular investment web sites—including Zacks.com, Graham Investor.com and OldSchoolValue.com, and magicdilligance.com—provide F_SCORE values for stocks and allow users to screen stocks using this metric.[2]

The approach of Mohanram (2005) is complementary to that of Piotroski, as Mohanram (2005, p. 133) "combines traditional fundamentals, such as earnings and cash flows, with measures tailored for growth firms, such as earnings stability, growth stability and intensity of R&D, capital expenditure and advertising, to create an index – GSCORE." Mohanram (2005) uses financial statement data to create signals related to two apparent inefficiencies related to the processing of information related to growth stocks: naive extrapolation of firm fundamentals (e.g., La Porta 1996, Dechow and Sloan 1997) and failure to incorporate the implications of accounting conservatism for future earnings (e.g., Penman and Zhang 2002). Like F_SCORE in Piotroski (2000), GSCORE is the sum of fundamental signals. The 8 signals, labeled G1 through G8, equal one if the following criteria are met: G1: ROA $\geq$ industry median; G2: CFROA $\geq$ industry median; G3: CFROA $\geq$ ROA; G4: VARROA $\leq$ industry median; G5: VARSSGR $\leq$ industry median; G6: RDINT $\geq$ industry median; G7: CAPINT $\geq$ industry median; G8: ADINT $\geq$ industry median, where ROA is net income scaled by average assets, CFROA is cash from operations scaled by average assets, VARROA and VARSGR are the variance of ROA and SGR, respectively, measured over the past 4 years using quarterly data. RDINT is R&D expenditure scaled by total assets. CAPINT is capital expenditure scaled by total assets. ADINT is advertising expenses divided by total assets. Industry medians are calculated at the 2-digit SIC level within low BM firms.

A long-short strategy based on GSCORE earns significant excess returns, though most of the returns come from the short side. Results are robust in partitions of size, analyst following, and liquidity, and they persist after controlling for momentum, book-to-market ratio, accruals, and size. High GSCORE firms have greater market reaction and analyst forecast surprises with respect to future earnings announcements, consistent with a mispricing explanation. Further, the results are inconsistent with a risk-based explanation as returns are positive in most years, and firms with lower risk earn higher returns.

Piotroski (2000) and Mohanram (2005) illustrate the importance of adapting fundamental analysis according to the context. Mohanran (2005) examines the performance of GSCORE when applied to high BM firms, as well as the performance of F_SCORE when applied to low BM firms, rather than to high BM firms as in Piotroski (2000). He finds that a trading strategy focused on low BM firms, but based on F_SCORE, provides a hedge return

---

[2]See www.investinganomalies.com under "Trading Strategies" for a more complete list of web sites that provide the F_SCORE.

of 9.8%. But Mohanram (2005, p. 165) argues that "this pales in comparison to both the success of GSCORE in low BM stocks and the success of F_SCORE in high BM stocks."

The preceding discussion focuses on academic studies, which often look at a limited number of measures or use combinations of simplified metrics such as the zero-or-one variables used to construct F_SCORE and GSCORE. More practitioner-oriented writers have considered refinements to some of these measures. For example, Tortoriello (2009) notes that "dividend yields that are too high often indicate a problem," and, thus, he focuses on the second quintile in his analysis of a dividend-based strategy. Additionally, with more and more firms using share buybacks as an alternative to paying dividends, Tortoriello refines the measure to be "dividend plus repurchase yield" and finds superior returns from a strategy based on this measure.

Like Piotroski (2000) and Mohanram (2005), Tortoriello (2009) also considers combination-based strategies. Consistent with the value of the kinds of fundamental-based strategies examined by Piotroski (2000) and Mohanram (2005), Tortoriello (2009) finds that 12 out of the top 15 2-factor strategies contain a valuation factor, and 5 of the top 15 include a profitability factor. Tortoriello (2009) also discusses methods for combining factors into strategies based on 3 or more factors, including statistical methods similar to those discussed in the early academic literature (e.g., Ou and Penman 1989), to yield even stronger performance. Of course, as with those early academic studies, a concern for investors is that the historical performance of a strategy be reproduced in future returns, which seems more likely if the strategy is based on solid principles.

Distress Risk

Another setting in which fundamental analysis has played a leading role is in prediction of bankruptcy and default. Seminal papers, such as Altman (1968) and Ohlson (1980), use financial ratio analysis to develop bankruptcy prediction models yielding risk indices that have come to be called Altman's Z-score and Ohlson's O-score, respectively. More recently, Campbell et al. (2008) find that bankrupt firms exhibit intuitive differences compared to healthy firms, such as recent losses, high debt levels, high volatility, limited cash, low market-to-book ratios, low stock prices, and relatively small market capitalization. These differences are similar to those used by Piotroski (2000) to guide his identification of variables for inclusion in his F_SCORE, as discussed earlier, with the basic motivation being that investors might enhance the returns on their portfolios if they could avoid or short stocks that are more likely to encounter financial distress.

Along these lines, Dichev (1998) examines the relations between Altman's Z-score and Ohlson's O-score and subsequent stock returns. The main focus of Dichev (1998) is the examination of whether the book-to-market ratio and size factors examined by Fama and French (1992) and covered in Chapter 8 of this volume can be explained as picking up financial distress. However, using Altman's Z-score and Ohlson's O-score as proxies for financial distress, Dichev (1998) finds that distress risk is actually *negatively* associated with subsequent returns. Put simply, firms with higher estimated probability of bankruptcy earn lower returns, rather than the higher returns that their increased risk would seem to require. Furthermore, Dichev (1998) finds evidence more consistent with a mispricing explanation for his results, rather than a risk-based explanation. In particular, the returns on a portfolio that goes long in the 70% of firms with low bankruptcy risk, and shorts the remaining 30% yields positive returns in 12 of the 15 years between 1981 and 1995, and in the remaining 3 years, the returns average 0.81%, which does not suggest that the pricing reflects avoidance of catastrophic losses.

More recent studies (e.g., Shumway 2001; Chava and Jarrow 2004; Campbell, Hilscher, and Szilagyi 2008) provide evidence consistent with Dichev (1998). For example, Campbell et al. (2008) sort stocks by failure probabilities into value-weighted portfolios, but find that average excess returns are strongly, and almost monotonically, negatively related with the probability of failure. The safest 5% of stocks have an average excess yearly return of 3.4% and a probability of failure of 0.34%; in contrast, the riskiest 1% of stocks have an average return of −17.0% and a probability of failure of 0.80%.

Portfolios are constructed that go long on stocks with relatively low failure risk and short on stocks with relatively high failure risk. A portfolio focused on the safest and riskiest 10% of stocks produces an average raw return of 10.0% per year. Furthermore, the poor performance of distressed stocks is more pronounced instead of less when risk adjustments are made, with alphas between 12.0% and 22.7% for CAPM, Fama-French 3-factor, and 4-factor models for the long-short strategy.

Campbell et al. (2008) identify a number of firm characteristics that vary with distress risk and argue that these, rather than variation in distress risk itself, may account for the variation in realized returns. However, the distress risk anomaly remains one of the more puzzling results in the literature.

Capital Investment and Growth Anomalies

Abarbanell and Bushee (1998) found evidence of a negative relation between capital expenditure and future stock returns, which they viewed as anomalous given the usual view that higher capital expenditures is to be interpreted as good news. Titman, Wei, and Xie (2004) point out that prior research shows that stock prices generally react favorably to announcements of major capital investment and attempt to provide an explanation for the apparent inconsistency. In summary, Titman, Wei, and Xie (2004, p. 678) provide evidence that they argue is "consistent with the idea that investors tend to underreact to the empire building implications of increased investment expenditures. Specifically, we find that firms that increase their investment expenditures the most tend to underperform their benchmarks over the following five years." In their empirical analysis, Titman, Wei, and Xie (2004) examine firms listed on NYSE, AMEX, and NASDAQ during July 1973 to June 1996, with annual net sales bigger than $10 million, positive book value of equity, and more than 2 years' history on Compustat. They then calculate abnormal capital investment (CI) as capital expenditure to sales in year $t - 1$ divided by average capital expenditure to sales for years $t - 4$ to $t - 2$, and partition sample firms into quintiles based on CI. The trading strategy examined in Titman, Wei, and Xie (2004) forms portfolios in July of year t by taking a long position in firms in the lowest quintile of CI and a short position in firms in the highest quintile of CI. According to the results in Table 1 of the paper, the hedge return is about 16.8% per year. The authors further show that the hedge returns are higher for firms with high cash flow and low debt-to-assets ratio, which is consistent with the empire-building explanation, because these firms likely have more flexibility in terms of capital expenditures.

A number of studies have examined very similar strategies to Titman, Wei, and Xie (2004). Anderson and Garcia-Feijóo (2006) also examine growth in capital expenditures and, for the period 1976 to 1999, find hedge returns of 0.32% to 0.57% per month from going long in stocks in the lowest quintile of prior investment growth and going short in stocks in the highest quintile (see Table III, p. 183). They also find that this result is not subsumed by size and book-to-market ratio. Cooper, Gulen, and Schill (2008) examine a broader measure of capital investment, namely, the growth in total assets in fiscal year prior to portfolio formation. From 1968 to 2003, the hedge return from going long in stocks in the lowest decile of asset growth and short in the stocks in the highest decile yields 1.05–1.73% per month over the first year following portfolio formation (see Table II, pp. 1618–1619). Cooper, Gulen, and Schill (2008) also provide evidence that this return is not subsumed by book-to-market ratio, size, prior returns, sales growth, or accruals.

Another measure related to capital investment is capital efficiency. A popular approach to understanding a firm's return on assets is the DuPont decomposition, which views return on assets as the product of profit margin (profit divided by sales) and asset turnover (sales divided by assets), which can be viewed as a measure of capital efficiency. Soliman (2008) examines whether market participants use information from a DuPont decomposition and the extent to which this information is quickly impounded into stock prices. The evidence in Soliman (2008) suggests that the market does react to components of the DuPont decomposition, but that the reaction to the capital efficiency (asset turnover) component is incomplete. In measuring asset turnover, Soliman (2008) focuses on ATO, which equals sales divided by average operating assets, defined as total assets minus the sum of cash, short-term investments, and nondebt liabilities. Soliman (2008) shows that an investment strategy based on changes in ATO yields abnormal hedge returns of between 5.2% and 7.8% per annum.

One appealing feature of anomalies related to capital expenditures and asset growth is that implementation by individual investors is feasible for a number of reasons. First, the calculation of measures such as CI and ATO is straightforward using data available on popular data services. Second, these trading strategies do not decay quickly; the results of Titman, Wei, and Xie (2004) suggest that the strategy based on capital investment yields positive hedge returns from year $t + 1$ to year $t + 5$ after portfolio formation. Finally, this kind of strategy appears to be incremental to other anomalies. One caveat is that Titman, Wei, and Xie (2004) find that the trading strategy they study yields *negative* hedge returns from 1984 to 1989, when hostile takeovers were common. Although the authors argue that this is consistent with the empire-building explanation, it does raise the question of whether future periods better resemble this period, or the periods that constitute the balance of their sample period; this question matters, because the profitability of the strategy hinges on the answer.

International Evidence

A careful reader will have noticed that the preceding discussed studies all relate to U.S. capital markets. This is probably a function of the scale of data—and concomitant statistical power—available to researchers due to the number of securities traded and maturity of U.S. capital markets. However, the reasoning used to identify anomalies in these studies seems equally applicable to other capital markets, and investors are likely less interested in statistical power and more concerned with identifying opportunities for excess returns. In fact, some anomalies may be more pronounced in international settings. Galdi and Lopes (2010) examine the profitability of using a variant of Piotroski's F_SCORE in Brazilian markets. They suggest that the hedge returns are likely to be greater, as the barriers to arbitrage are greater, especially for stocks outside the main index, due to limited liquidity and restrictions on short-selling in Brazilian markets. Consistent with this prediction, Galdi and Lopes (2010) estimate a 1-year (2-year) market-adjusted return of 26.7% (120.2%), considerably higher than the comparable returns reported by Piotroski (2010). Noma (2010) finds that a strategy based on F_SCORE also produces abnormal returns in Japan, with a 17.6% annual return to a hedge portfolio based on F_SCORE.

Fama and French (1998) examine the performance of a number of value-based strategies in international markets. Relevant to the strategies covered in this chapter, they find that the profitability of a dividend yield-based strategy is limited to a handful (including Japan and France) of the 13 countries they examine.

Conclusion

This chapter has discussed a number of significant studies that have shown that, contrary to the efficient markets hypothesis (EMH), investors can profit from trading on fundamental analysis. However, the studies collectively suggest that care should be taken in applying this analysis, as illustrated by the greater success of Piotroski's F_SCORE in the context of value firms, and the greater success of Mohanram's GSCORE for growth firms, with the strategies in each case being applied in the setting for which they were originally designed.

References

Abarbanell, J., and B. Bushee. 1997. Fundamental analysis, future earnings, and stock prices. *Journal of Accounting Research* 35 (1): 1–24.

Abarbanell, J., and B. Bushee. 1998. Abnormal returns to a fundamental analysis strategy. *Accounting Review* 73 (1): 19–45.

Altman, E. 1968. Financial ratios, discriminant analysis and the prediction of corporate bankruptcy. *Journal of Finance* 23 (4): 589–609.

Anderson, C., and L. Garcia-Feijóo. 2006. Empirical evidence on capital investment, growth options, and security returns. *Journal of Finance* 61: 171–194.

Bernard, V., and J. Thomas. 1989. Post-earnings announcement drift: De-layed price response or risk premium? *Journal of Accounting Research* 27 (Supplement): 1–36.

Brown, D., and B. Rowe. 2007. The productivity premium in equity returns. SSRN eLibrary.

Campbell, J., J. Hilscher, and J. Szilagyi. 2008. In search of distress risk. *Journal of Finance* 63 (6): 2899–2939.

Chava, S., and R. A. Jarrow. 2004. Bankruptcy prediction with industry effects. *Review of Finance* 8: 537–569.

Cooper, M., H. Gulen, and M. Schill. 2008. Asset growth and the cross-section of stock returns. *Journal of Finance* 63 (4): 1609–1651.

Dechow, P., and R. Sloan. 1997. Returns to contrarian investment strategies: Tests of naive expectations hypotheses. *Journal of Financial Economic*, 43: 3–27.

Dichev, I. 1998. Is the risk of bankruptcy a systematic risk? *Journal of Finance* 53 (3): 1131–1147.

Easton, P. 2007. Effect of analysts' optimism on estimates of the expected rate of return implied by earnings forecasts. *Journal of Accounting Research* 45 (5): 983–1015.

Fama, E., and K. French. 1988. Dividend yields and expected stock returns. *Journal of Financial Economics* 22: 3–25.

Fama, E., and K. French. 1992. The cross-section of expected stock returns. *Journal of Finance* 47 (2): 427–465.

Fama, E., and K. French. 1998. Value versus growth: The international evidence. *Journal of Finance* 53 (6): 1975–1999.

Foster, G., C. Olsen, and T. Shevlin. 1984. Earnings releases, anomalies, and the behavior of security returns. *Accounting Review* 59 (4): 574–603.

Galdi, F. C., and B. Lopes. 2010. Limits to arbitrage and value investing: Evidence from Brazil. Working paper, available at: http://ssrn.com/abstract=1099524.

Hirschey, M. 2000. The "dogs of the Dow" myth. *Financial Review* 35: 1–16.

Hirshleifer, D., K. Hou, S. Teoh, and Y. Zhang. 2004. Do investors overvalue firms with bloated balance sheets? *Journal of Accounting and Economics* 38: 297–331.

Holthausen, R., and D. Larcker. 1992. The prediction of stock returns using financial statement information. *Journal of Accounting and Economics* 15 (2–3): 373–411.

La Porta, R. 1996. Expectations and the cross-section of stock returns. *Journal of Finance* 51 (5): 1715–1742.

Lev, B., and S. Thiagarajan. 1993. Fundamental information analysis. *Journal of Accounting Research* 31 (2): 190–215.

Lewellen, J. 2004. Predicting returns with financial ratios. *Journal of Financial Economics* 74 (2): 209–235.

Mohanram, P. 2005. Separating winners from losers among low book-to-market stocks using financial statement analysis. *Review of Accounting Studies* 10: 133–170.

Noma, M. 2010. Value investing and financial statement analysis. *Hitosubashi Journal of Commerce and Management* 44: 29–46.

O'Higgins, M., and J. Downs. 1991. *Beating the Dow*. New York: Harper-Collins.

Ou, J., and S. Penman. 1989. Financial statement analysis and the prediction of stock returns. *Journal of Accounting and Economics* 11 (4): 295–329.

Penman, S., and X.-J. Zhang. 2002. Accounting conservatism, the quality of earnings, and stock returns. *Accounting Review* 77 (2): 237–264.

Piotroski, J. 2000. Value investing: The use of historical financial statement information to separate winners from losers. *Journal of Accounting Research* 38: 1–41.

Shumway, T. 2001. Forecasting bankruptcy more accurately: A simple hazard model. *Journal of Business.*

Sloan, R. 1996. Do stock prices fully reflect information in accruals and cash flows about future earnings? *Accounting Review* 71 (3): 289–315.

Soliman, M. 2008. The use of DuPont analysis by market participants. *Accounting Review* 83: 823–853.

Titman, S., K. Wei, and F. Xie. 2004. Capital investments and stock returns. *Journal of Financial and Quantitative Analysis* 39 (4): 677–700.

Tortoriello, R. 2009. *Quantitative strategies for achieving alpha.* New York: McGraw-Hill.

Go to http://hema.zacks.com for abstracts and links to papers.

CHAPTER 6

Net Stock Anomalies

Daniel Cohen, Thomas Lys, and Tzachi Zach

A large body of academic research has studied the stock price behavior before, in response to, and after significant corporate events. Such events include initial public offerings (IPOs), seasoned equity offerings (SEOs), stock repurchases, issuance of debt, dividend initiation and omission, mergers and acquisitions, spin-offs, and so on. This review focuses on several of these events and on the stock price behavior following them. It is by no means an exhaustive summary of all the research done to date but instead focuses on several studies that sparked and generated a voluminous subsequent body of research. The interested reader may refer to more comprehensive reviews of the related literature such as Fama (1998), Ritter (2003), and Schwert (2003).

The general pattern that emerges from the academic literature is that the stock prices of firms following corporate events tend to drift in predictable manners, for a period of up to five years. Such predictable and observed patterns seem to be inconsistent with market efficiency. As such, academic research, practitioners, investors, and others refer to these patterns as "anomalies." More formally, Schwert (2003) defines anomalies as, "empirical results that seem to be inconsistent with maintained theories of asset-pricing behavior. They indicate either market inefficiency (profit opportunities) or inadequacies in the underlying asset pricing model."

The specific anomalies reviewed in this chapter, which are called net stock anomalies, pertain to financing policy decisions made by U.S. firms. It is important to note that the literature has identified numerous settings in which other anomalies seem to exist. These specific anomalies are discussed separately in other chapters of this book. In general, the empirical evidence suggests that trading strategies initiated following the corporate financing events generate economically and statistically significant returns.

There are a few important issues to note when one evaluates the collective evidence on these anomalies. First, the empirical results originally documented in the specific studies we discuss are somewhat sensitive to the sample periods examined and as such their generalizability to future periods is not guaranteed. Second, statistical inferences based on long-term stock returns are generally regarded as less reliable because standard errors of such models increase and hence their reliability decreases as the length of the period increases. Third, when analyzing anomalies one needs to acknowledge that their documented existence relies on crucial assumptions regarding expected returns—the asset pricing model used to compute abnormal stock returns. This particular issue is often referred in the academic literature as a joint test of both the market efficiency hypothesis and the adequacy of the underlying asset pricing model. In practice, one needs to note the specifics of the research design, such as the benchmarks used by the researcher to assess the reliability and implications of the documented empirical findings. Finally, it is important to note that the documented anomalies may not be independent of each other—they may be documentation of a common phenomenon, or may be related to anomalies outside the corporate financing decision setting. In other words, a priori it is difficult to evaluate the degree of overlap between the different anomalies and whether there is an unidentified common factor driving some or all the anomalies recognized in the literature.

The next section summarizes the main findings in the literature pertaining to net stock anomalies for each one of the main corporate financing activities identified in the literature.

Initial Public Offerings

Initial Public Offerings (IPOs) are one of the most significant financing activities carried out by firms to raise capital. Ritter (1991) analyzed the 3-year benchmark-adjusted returns of firms issuing IPOs. His sample consisted of 1,526 IPOs issued between 1975 and 1984 listed on AMEX-NYSE or NASDAQ. Ritter (1991) used two different techniques to calculate abnormal returns. The first calculates the cumulative average adjusted returns, which assumes monthly portfolio rebalancing. The average adjusted returns are calculated each month using either one of the following benchmarks: CRSP value-weighted NASDAQ index, CRSP value-weighted AMEX-NYSE index, industry- and size-matched firms, and the index of smallest size decile of NYSE firms. The cumulative average adjusted returns are then computed by adding the average adjusted returns over all months. Using this method, the cumulative average adjusted returns were −29.13% for the 36 months following the IPO.

Second, Ritter computes 3-year abnormal buy-and-hold returns as the difference between IPO firms (34.5%) and a set of firms matched by industry and size (61.9%). Thus, IPO firms underperform the industry- and size-matched firms by 27.4%. Ritter (1991) concludes that the IPO issuing firms underperform their peer firms in both the buy-and-hold and the monthly rebalancing strategies. Ritter conjectures that this mispricing may be due to firms going public when investors are too optimistic about their prospects.

Several studies seek to extend Ritter's initial work and, more importantly, offer some evidence for Ritter's original conjecture regarding investors' overoptimism. For example, Teoh, Welch, and Wong (1998) analyze the effect of earnings management on the long-run market performance of IPOs, thus focusing on the possible sources of investors' overoptimism. They argue that investors may not be aware of earnings management activities prior to IPOs and as a consequence would base their expectations of future performance on financial information that does not reflect accurately the underlying economic performance of the firm. Their results indicate that, for IPOs issued between 1980 and 1992, IPOs in the most aggressive quartile of earnings management (using discretionary accruals) have a 3-year abnormal stock return approximately 20% less than IPO issuers in the most conservative earnings-management quartile. These findings are consistent with the assertion that investors were too optimistic at the time of the IPO because they were misled by financial information. The post-IPO negative stock performance is suggestive of investors' gradual understanding that they overvalued the firm at the time of the IPO.

In a related study, Purnanandam and Swaminathan (2004) also analyze the IPOs issued between 1980 and 1997 and find them to be overvalued. Their findings suggest that the level of overvaluation ranges from 14% to 50% depending on peer-matching criteria. The authors conclude that IPO investors were deceived by optimistic growth forecasts and pay insufficient attention to profitability in valuing IPOs.

Brav and Gompers (1997) investigate the sources of IPOs' underperformance documented in prior literature by focusing on venture-capital-backed IPOs (issued between 1972 and 1992) versus non-venture-backed IPOs (issued between 1975 and 1992). Their results show that over a 5-year period, venture-capital-backed IPOs exhibit returns of 44.6%, but still underperformed the NYSE/AMEX equal weighted benchmark by 16.2%. In contrast, non-venture-backed IPOs earned returns of 22.5% and underperformed the same index by 33.2% over 5 years. These results lead the authors to conclude that most of the documented IPOs' underperformance (and mispricing) stems from the non-venture-backed IPOs, especially from the smaller firms.

Baker and Wurgler (2000) seek to explain the anomalous returns. They focus on the market-timing hypothesis. They show that the equity share in the total volume of debt and equity issuances is a good predictor of future market returns. Periods of high equity share are followed by low market returns, in a long sample extending from 1928 to 1997. According to the market–timing hypothesis, this pattern in market returns is caused by managers' ability to time their equity issuances to coincide with what they see in real time as market peaks. They argue that such explanation defies market efficiency. In contrast, Schultz (2003) shows that the documented underperformance of IPOs is expected to occur even in an efficient market. His argument centers around the fact that IPOs seem to cluster and occur in periods in which firms seem to be able to raise funds at good prices. As a result, IPOs concentrate in periods that *ex-post* represent market peaks, without managers being able to identify these peaks *ex-ante*. This representation is important because it stands in contrast to the market-timing explanation, which attributed to managers the ability to *ex-ante* identify market peaks and thus, time the market in deciding when to issue equity.

In summary, although the results pertaining to IPOs suggest that a trading strategy might generate significant stock returns, it is important to understand that the results are not uniform across studies and/or subsamples of firms. As such, one needs to be cautious in generalizing that the documented anomalous returns could be translated into profitable trading strategies in every IPO setting.

Seasoned Equity Offerings

Seasoned Equity Offerings (SEOs) present another interesting anomaly that challenges the efficient market hypothesis. Similar to the IPO setting, research has shown that firms that issued equity through an SEO, experience negative stock returns in the years following the equity issues. For example, Loughran and Ritter (1995) and Spiess and Affleck-Graves (1995) show that, on average, SEO firms underperform for a period of 3 to 5 years following the equity issuance. Loughran and Ritter (1995) find that for the period 1970–1990, SEO firms significantly underperformed nonissuing firms matched on size by 59.4% over a 5-year period, and Spiess and Affleck-Graves (1995) show that the SEO firms underperform their peers by an average of 31% to 39%, depending on the type of matching criteria. In addition, Loughran and Ritter (1995) show that the stock returns in the year preceding the SEO are on average +72%. One interpretation that is consistent with the return pattern documented in these studies is the market-timing explanation. Under this view, managers exploit their information advantage relative to outsiders to time their SEOs at opportune times when their stock is most likely to be overvalued. A variation of this explanation suggests that investors' overoptimism about the firm's prospects is due to managers' manipulation of reported earnings. Under this argument, investors overextrapolate the inflated reported earnings into the future, giving rise to overpricing of equity that managers exploit (see Teoh, Welch, and Wong 1998; Rangan 1998; and Shivakumar 2000).

Similar to the IPO setting, the literature has been debating whether the documented SEO underperformance is a clear indication against the efficient market hypothesis. The bad-model problem is at the center of much of this debate (e.g., Fama 1998; Mitchell and Stafford 2000). According to Fama (1998), the reliability of long-run abnormal stock returns depends heavily on the underlying model used to compute normal stock returns. Even if the errors in the model used are relatively small in short window tests, they get compounded and magnified as one extends the window analyzed. However, a related argument advanced in the literature offers an explanation of why one should expect measurement problems in the asset pricing model to be correlated with the existence of an equity offering. In other words, the risk of the firm engaging in an SEO changes in response to the corporate event. For example, Eckbo, Masulis, and Norli (2000) argue that the decreased leverage after an equity issue lowers the systematic risk of the equity issuers. In summary, given the caveats identified earlier, as with the IPO setting, one needs to be cautious in inferring that anomalous stock returns can be systematically exploited around SEOs.

Debt Issuances

In addition to issuing equity, firms often utilize the economically significant public debt markets in raising capital. Spiess and Affleck-Graves (1999) analyze stock return performance of firms issuing both straight debt as well as convertible debt. The authors conclude that straight debt issuances are associated with an average abnormal negative stock return of 14.3% for a period of 5 years, although these are not statistically significant (the median is significant). However, the documented results become statistically significant for smaller and younger firms.

As for convertible debt, it was found that issuers underperform a matched sample by a statistically significant 36.9% for a period of 5 years. In both types of debt issuances, the authors find stronger evidence for issuances that occurred during "hot periods," that is, periods with large volume of debt issuances. The authors base their evidence on a sample spanning 1975 to 1989 as reported in the Investment Dealers' Digest Directory of Corporate Financing. For straight debt issuances, using other benchmarks, such as a 3-factor model, the authors report a Jensen alpha of about 0.3% per month, but only relative to an equally weighted market portfolio and not relative to a value-weighted market portfolio. The Jensen alpha reported is slightly higher for convertible debt issuers. The authors argue that just like equity offerings, debt equity offerings are also signals of firms' overvaluations.

In a related study, Affleck-Graves and Miller (2003) analyze stock returns following calls of both straight and convertible debt in the period extending from 1945 to 1995 and find that these firms outperform their peers. The evidence suggests that abnormal stock returns for the straight debt call sample is between 0.18% and 0.34% per month, depending on the benchmark used for a period of 5 years following the debt call event. As for convertible debt, the authors find mixed evidence following the calls of convertible debt.

In addition to obtaining debt financing from the public debt market, firms can raise capital through private debt. Focusing on bank loans (private debt issuances), Billett, Flannery, and Garfinkel (2006) document similar evidence as the one reported in Spiess and Affleck-Graves (1999). In particular, they report that firms announcing bank loans earn negative abnormal stock returns ranging between 26% and 33% over the subsequent 3 years, depending on the benchmark asset pricing model used. The authors find some cross-sectional variations in stock returns, along the size of the bank loans. Larger loans are associated with worse stock performance.

Share Repurchases and Tender Offers

The literature documented significant abnormal stock returns following open market share repurchases as well as self-tender offer announcements. Empirical research has shown that significant abnormal stock returns can be earned by following a simple trading strategy around these specific corporate events. One of the earliest studies to examine the anomalous stock price behavior around repurchase tender offers is Lakonishok and Vermaelen (1990). The evidence in their study suggests that, by following a simple trading strategy around repurchase tender offers, one can generate abnormal stock returns of more than 9% in a period of less than one week. The authors argue that since the strategy carries very little risk and it does not involve any sophisticated analysis, its performance runs contrary to the efficient market hypothesis and thus meets the criteria of being characterized as an anomaly. The authors conjecture that a plausible reason for the persistence of this specific anomaly is that repurchase tender offers are relatively rare corporate events. In addition, Lakonishok and Vermaelen (1990) document that a portfolio of repurchasing firms earns significant positive abnormal stock returns after the repurchase. The authors show that this effect is mainly driven by the behavior of small firms that generate an abnormal return of approximately 24% in the 22 months after the expiration of the offer. It is important to note that this is mainly concentrated in small firms. The behavior observed for large firms is significantly different as larger firms experience positive abnormal stock returns before the repurchase announcement and zero abnormal returns afterward. The authors infer that their findings are consistent with the observation that tender offer stock repurchases by large firms are part of a wide corporate restructuring strategy rather than a signal of firm undervaluation.

In a subsequent study focusing on open share repurchases, Ikenberry, Lakonishok, and Vermaelen (1995) document that, for a sample of over 1,200 open share repurchases between 1980 and 1990, the average abnormal return after the initial announcements was 12.1% per year in the 4-year period following such an announcement. For stocks whose open market repurchase is more likely to be the result of undervaluation, the average abnormal return is 45.3%. Thus, similar to equity issuances, abnormal stock returns seem to drift in the same direction as the initial stock price reaction. Because open market share repurchases are the opposite of equity issuances, the sign of the documented abnormal stock returns is positive, rather than negative. The authors compute abnormal stock returns using four different benchmarks: equally weighted market index, value-weighted market index, size-based adjustment, and a size and book-to-market adjustment. They also use 3-factor alphas as an additional benchmark.

The results of both Lakonishok and Vermaelen (1990) and Ikenberry, Lakonishok, and Vermaelen (1995) are consistent with the hypothesis that, on average, the capital market has underestimated the value of the information that is signaled through repurchase announcements and that the repurchasing firms have repurchased their shares at suppressed prices. As with prior studies documenting anomalous stock returns around certain corporate events, some caveats are in order. Specifically, as Fama (1998) and Schwert (2003) argue, it is possible that the findings of the studies focusing on shares repurchases are an artifact of chance and/or they are sample specific. In other words, it is not clear whether one can replicate the anomalous stock price behavior in future periods either because the original findings were a result of data mining or because investors learned and arbitraged the anomalous returns away.

To address the concerns raised by Fama (1998) and Schwert (2003), Peyer and Vermaelen (2009) first test whether the share repurchase and tender offers anomalies persist using a larger sample and more recent data than in previous studies. The first conclusion that the authors reach is that the buy-back anomalies have not disappeared and, therefore, were not time or sample specific. The authors claim that arbitrageurs have not been able to exploit this strategy and following the strategies highlighted in earlier studies can still generate the returns. The authors reexamined the buyback anomalies using 3,481 open market repurchase programs announced during 1991–2001 and 261 fixed price tender offers announced between 1987 and 2001. As noted by the authors, long-run abnormal stock returns after open market share repurchase programs are still as large and economically significant as the earlier studies documented, especially for value firms. The authors emphasize that their conclusion still holds after they incorporate the criticism of Fama (1998) and Mitchell and Stafford (2000) who claim that the buy-and-hold stock return methodology used in Ikenberry, Lakonishok, and Vermaelen (1995) is biased. In addition, the recent evidence in Peyer and Vermaelen (2009) is also consistent with the findings of Lakonishok and Vermaelen (1990) with regard to tender offers. The new evidence suggests that the average abnormal stock return from trading around the expiration date of tender offers is 8.6%, and 84% of the trades produce positive abnormal returns.

The authors emphasize, as in the original studies, that the repurchase trading strategy is obviously not risky. As a result, Peyer and Vermaelen (2009) investigate the sources of the buyback anomalies and examine why these anomalies persist for an extended period of time. The authors entertain numerous hypotheses and conclude that the evidence is most consistent with investors overreacting to bad news announcements prior to the buyback programs. They further examine why it takes a long period of time for the "mispricing" to be eliminated. One novel and insightful explanation the authors offer is labeled as the "analyst mistake" hypothesis. This hypothesis suggests that the firm's repurchase program is a response to a mistake made by financial analysts who follow the firm. Because it appears that analysts will not admit that they made a mistake, investors who follow these professionals are not going to revise their expectations regarding the prospects of the company. Overall, the evidence in Peyer and Vermaelen (2009) seems to resolve the long debate regarding the reasons managers choose to repurchase their firms' stock. Some have argued that managers repurchase stock to substitute for dividends or to manage reported earnings per share. In contrast, survey evidence (e.g., Brav et al. 2005) suggests that the most important reason for share repurchases is exploiting undervaluation. Peyer and Vermaelen (2009) seem to support the managers' view.

Dividend Initiation and Omissions

Dividend initiations and omissions are corporate financing activities with possibly strong signaling effects. Numerous researchers have compared the signaling effect of dividend initiations and omissions to the signaling effect of positive and negative earnings surprises. These researchers claim that the stock return performance of firms initiating or omitting dividends is consistent with the stock return performance associated with positive and negative earnings surprises.

Michaely, Thaler, and Womack (1995) analyze stock returns of firms initiating or omitting cash dividend payments to shareholders. Their sample spans 1964 to 1988 and consists of NYSE/AMEX companies that initiated dividends during this period. The authors define initiation of cash dividends as the first cash dividend payment reported on the CRSP master file. First, the authors find a positive and significant stock price reaction to the announcements of initiating dividends and negative and significant stock price reaction to dividends omissions. The stock price reaction magnitude seems to be asymmetric as it is greater for dividend omissions than for dividend initiations. In the 3 years following these corporate events, stock prices drift in the same direction as the original reaction. The market-adjusted stock returns of firms initiating dividends are 7.5% after 1 year and 24.8% after 3 years of the dividend announcement, measured starting on the second day of the announcement. For firms omitting dividends, the authors find market adjusted stock returns of -11% after 1 year and -15.3% after 3 years of announcement, measured starting on the second day of the announcement. The authors define abnormal stock returns as buy-and-hold returns of the stock less the buy-and-hold return of either the equally weighted CRSP index including dividends, the appropriate CRSP market-capitalization decile, the equally weighted market index adjusted for the beta of each stock, or a matching firm in the same industry that is closest in market capitalization. Thus, based on these findings, investors can generate significant abnormal returns by going long in a portfolio of firms initiating dividends and going short in firms omitting dividends.

In the year prior to the dividend announcements, Michaely, Thaler, and Womack (1995) find that firms initiating dividends have an average abnormal stock return of 15.1% whereas firms omitting dividends have an average abnormal stock return of -31.8%. Thus, building on these results, it seems that well-performing firms have a tendency of initiating dividends whereas poorly performing firms have a tendency of omitting dividends. The authors also calculated the abnormal stock returns during the 3-day announcement period. They document that the dividend initiators generate an abnormal stock return of 3.4% whereas the firms omitting dividends generate a negative abnormal return of -7.0% during the 3-day announcement period. In summary, the announcement of either initiations or omissions of dividends has a significant effect on the stock return performance both in the long and the short term, which can be capitalized by capital market participants.

Michaely, Thaler, and Womack (1995) try to address concerns that their documented findings are subsumed by an other well-known accounting anomaly, the postearnings announcement drift (PEAD). They conclude that the documented postdividend drift is indeed distinct and more pronounced than the drift following earnings surprises. The trading rule the authors offer seems to generate significant returns in 22 out of the 25 years they analyze.

The documented long-term drift following dividend announcements, again, challenges the efficient market hypothesis. Although these results are surprising, they are consistent with the studies documenting drifts following other corporate events (e.g., Ikenberry, Lakonishok, and Vermaelen 1995; and Loughran and Ritter 1995).

Private Equity Placement

Building on the evidence and explanations offered in the studies discussed so far, Hertzel, Lemmon, Linck, and Rees (2002) seek to provide further evidence on investor behavior and expectations around equity issuances by examining the stock price performance for a sample of publicly traded firms that engage in a private placement of equity. Using a sample of 619 publicly traded firms that announce private placements of equity during a period between 1980 and 1996, the authors find that the positive announcement period stock returns are followed by abnormally low stock returns. The authors document that relative to a size and book-to-market matched sample of control firms, the average 3-year buy-and-hold abnormal return is −23.8%, a level of underperformance that is similar to studies focusing on IPOs (e.g., Ritter 1991; Loughran and Ritter 1995) and SEOs (e.g., Loughran and Ritter 1995; Spiess and Affleck-Graves 1995). This evidence suggests that investors are overoptimistic about the future prospects of the firms that issue equity, regardless of the issuance method used. In addition, the authors' overall findings seem inconsistent with the underreaction hypothesis. Finally, the authors document that private issues seem to follow periods of relatively poor operating performance, which is the opposite for public offerings. Overall, the evidence in Hertzel, Lemmon, Linck, and Rees (2002) is not consistent with a behavioral explanation that poor long-run performance is due to the tendency of investors to overweight recent performance when forming expectations about future performance. Given that firms that issue equity privately tend to invest more than a control group, both before and after the private issue, one can infer that both managers and investors may be too optimistic about the investment opportunities facing these firms.

Overall Net External Financing

The studies reviewed so far specifically identified and focused on a single corporate financing event. Identifying the corporate financing event was typically done using corporate directories, searching through news articles that match the event, or using databases that specialize in tracking particular corporate events (e.g., IPOs and SEOs). Unlike these approaches, an alternative way to collectively identify corporate financing events is through their effects on firms' financial statements. Bradshaw, Richardson, and Sloan (2006) adopt such an approach and develop a comprehensive and parsimonious measure of net corporate financing, based on financial statement data retrieved from Compustat. Specifically, Bradshaw, Richardson, and Sloan's (2006) major innovation is their focus on net external financing activities rather than individual components of corporate financing activities (e.g., debt versus equity) chosen by firms. They define their measure of net external financing activities as net cash received from the sale or purchase of common and preferred stock less cash dividends paid plus the net cash received from the issuance or retirement of debt. The authors find that their measure is a strong predictor of future stock returns. Using a trading strategy that is based on the top decile of net cash inflows from financing (i.e., issuers) and the bottom decile of net cash outflows from financing (i.e., repurchasers), the authors document that such a hedge portfolio generates an average annual return of 15.5%. This magnitude exceeds the hedge portfolio return based on the individual components of net external financing. The overall evidence in Bradshaw, Richardson, and Sloan (2006) implies that investors do not correctly infer the negative relation between financing activities and future performance.

The authors seek to distinguish between risk and misvaluations as potential explanations for the association between future stock returns and firms' corporate financing activities. They find a systematic positive relation between net external financing and optimism in analysts' earnings forecasts. Furthermore, the results suggest that analysts' optimism is related to the type of security issued: Overoptimism for debt issuance is restricted to short-term earnings forecasts, whereas overoptimism for equity issuance is also related to long-term earnings forecasts, growth, stock recommendations, and target prices. The preceding findings lead the authors to conclude that analysts play a central role in the overpricing of security issuances. Overall, the documented findings are consistent with the misvaluation hypothesis under which firms time their corporate financing activities to exploit temporary misvaluations of firms' securities in capital markets. In addition, the authors consider an alternative hypothesis, the wealth-transfer hypothesis, which refers to wealth transfers between shareholders and bondholders. Their results suggest that changes in debt are negatively related to future stock returns. Given that they find negative stock returns following new security issuances, their overall evidence is consistent with the firm misvaluation hypothesis but not with the wealth transfer hypothesis.

Cohen and Lys (2006) question whether one can refer to the evidence in Bradshaw, Richardson, and Sloan as an external financing anomaly that is distinct from and independent of other anomalies identified in the literature. Cohen and Lys (2006) note that, by design, the authors' analysis is closely related to the accrual-anomaly literature: The cash flow identity implies that financing and operating cash flows are negatively related. Moreover, operating cash flows equal net income minus accruals. In other words, accounting accruals are increases in the amount of net operating assets on a company's balance sheet. As a result, it is important to establish whether the evidence in Bradshaw, Richardson, and Sloan is incremental to or is subsumed by the results of the accrual anomaly (Sloan, 1996). Indeed, the results in Cohen and Lys (2006) suggest that an alternative interpretation to the findings reported in Bradshaw, Richardson, and Sloan might be that the "external financing activities anomaly" documented by the authors is just a reflection of the well-known and widely cited accrual anomaly. This interpretation is not new. Zach (2003), exploring characteristics that cause or are correlated with extreme accruals, finds that extreme accrual firms are more likely to have experienced specific corporate financing events, such as IPOs, seasoned-equity offerings, mergers and acquisitions, restructurings, and divestitures. Given that these corporate events are known to be related to abnormal future stock returns, Zach (2003) examines to what extent the accrual anomaly overlaps with the external financing anomaly. He provides evidence suggesting that the accrual's hedge returns strategy decreases by 25% once mergers and divestitures are excluded. Cohen and Lys (2006) show that, once one controls for the accrual anomaly, the external financing anomaly no longer persists. This result is not surprising as accounting accruals are increases in the amount of net operating assets on a company's balance sheet. Since accounting accruals represent the other side of the balance sheet from financing liabilities, a firm that has high accounting accruals (i.e., a large amount of net operating assets) is likely to have higher amounts of external financing. Overall, the evidence suggests that the negative relation documented between net external financing activities and future stock returns is consistent with the overinvestment hypothesis rather than with the market-timing hypothesis.

In a recent paper Billett, Flannery, and Garfinkel (2011) try to offer an alternative explanation to the observed underperformance of firms raising external funds. Recall that the literature has argued that overvaluation and market inefficiency may explain this phenomenon. On the other hand, Fama (1998) argues that the underlying asset pricing models used to calculate the long-run abnormal stock returns are flawed. Billett, Flannery, and Garfinkel (2011) emphasize that the separate studies in the literature to date focus on a single type of external claim issuance without controlling for the sample firms' other financing activities. For example, if a firm engages in an SEO and at the same time obtains financing from a bank, a study focusing on a single type of financing activity will fail to control for the other activity. This being the case, if one were to study the long-run stock performance of the SEO he or she will fail to observe and control for the bank loan, or any other financing activity that the firm engaged in during the SEO analysis window. In addition, subsequent financing activities undertaken by a single firm may proxy for specific underlying characteristics of the issuing firm and not the issuance of claims. This suggests that prior studies that chose to focus on a claim-specific corporate event will suffer from a classic omitted variable problem since firms that repeatedly access capital markets might be significantly different from those firms that do not access capital markets that frequently.

Therefore, the authors investigate whether the prior documented underperformance is associated with claim type or, instead, with the tendency to issue multiple claim types, that is, access capital markets frequently. The evidence provided suggests that external financing per se does not relate to future underperformance but that underperformance is more a function of the variety and frequency of firms' issuance activities. The results in Billett, Flannery, and Garfinkel (2011) are, therefore, important as they provide new insights about the performance observed following external financing activities and allow us to interpret evidence from earlier studies in a more comprehensive context.

Mergers and Acquisitions

Mergers and acquisitions have been one of the most researched areas in the finance literature. A significant number of studies have addressed issues related to mergers and acquisitions. Among them are studies evaluating the performance of the acquiring or the target firms after the acquisition.

Agrawal, Jaffe, and Mandelkar (1992) examine an exhaustive sample of mergers and acquisitions over the period between 1955 and 1997. They report that the acquiring firms in mergers generate an average negative abnormal stock return of 10.26% over a 5-year period following the merger. This general result poses a challenge to the efficient market hypothesis. This finding also casts doubt on studies that evaluate the benefits of mergers merely through examining stock price reactions to initial announcements of mergers. Interestingly, the authors do not find evidence that their findings are a result of the capital markets slowly adjusting to the merger event.

Schwert (1996) examines mergers during a sample period between 1975 and 1991. He finds a significant negative abnormal return of 7% in the year following the announcement of the bid. He concludes that this drift is explained by an unusually high stock price performance of the bidders in the years prior to the acquisitions. Schwert (1996) emphasizes that these findings have important implications for measuring normal stock returns in the period prior to the bid announcements. When researchers estimate an asset-pricing model in the period prior to a corporate event, the maintained assumption is that the stock performance in that period and the event itself are independent and thus uncorrelated. If this maintained assumption does not hold, a researcher faces a selection bias that casts doubt on the results documented and inferences that can be drawn. As Schwert (2003) notes, "The unusually positive performance of bidders' stocks before the bid is an example of sample selection bias: the decisions of bidder firms to pursue acquisitions is correlated with their past stock price performance."

Loughran and Vijh (1997) analyze 947 acquisitions between 1970 and 1989 and find that postacquisition stock returns strongly depend on the form of payment used in the merger. Cash tender offers are followed by a significant positive excess stock return of 61.7% in the 5-year period following the merger. On the other hand, stock mergers earn a significant negative excess stock return of 25% over the same period of time following the merger. Importantly, Loughran and Vijh (1997) examine the preacquisition stock price performance to gauge at the overall wealth effect of the target's shareholders. They find that, on average, the target's shareholders do not earn significantly positive excess returns.

Rau and Vermaelen (1998) use more refined methods of calculating abnormal stock returns and examine a sample of over 3,000 mergers and over 300 tender offers over the period 1980–1991. They find that acquirers in mergers earn a statistically significant negative excess return of -4% in the 3 years following the merger. In contrast, acquirers in tender offers earn a significant positive excess return of 9% in the same period following the merger. The authors also find that the documented abnormal returns are consistent with a performance extrapolation hypothesis. In particular, the capital market overextrapolates the past performance of the bidder in evaluating the acquisition. This gives rise to the observed pattern that abnormal returns are more pronounced in firms that are referred to as glamour firms. These specific firms are characterized as having low book-to-market ratios, high past stock returns, and high past growth in earnings. Glamour acquirers earn statistically significant negative abnormal returns of -17% in mergers and insignificant abnormal returns of 4% in tender offers.

International Evidence

The research around share issuances or repurchases and subsequent stock returns has focused mostly on the U.S. capital markets. One of the main criticisms of the general findings of anomalous stock returns following certain corporate events is that they are a result of data mining, especially relying on U.S. data. To alleviate this concern, researchers have decided to shift their focus to alternative settings other than the U.S. capital markets with the objective of trying to replicate some of the anomalies outside the United States.

For example, McLean, Pontiff, and Watanabe (2009) analyze whether the effect of share issuance and repurchases is present among non-U.S. firms and compare that to the results documented in studies that focused on the United States. In addition, the authors seek to investigate what might explain cross-country differences in the issuance effect by focusing on proxies for equity market development, level of investor protection, short-sale constraints, buy-back restrictions, and earnings management. McLean, Pontiff, and Watanabe (2009) use a sample of firms from 41 countries (other than the United States) and examine the existence of an international issuance effect over a 25-year period between 1981 and 2006. Using a net issuance measure that reflects both share issuances and share repurchases, the authors find a significant issuance effect in non-U.S. capital markets. Similar to the U.S. evidence, issuance predictability has greater statistical significance than either size or momentum, and it seems to be of the same magnitude as the book-to-market effect. As the U.S. evidence suggests, the issuance effect in international markets seems to hold both across small and large firms. However, unlike the U.S. evidence, the issuance effect seems to be driven more by low stock returns after share issuances rather than positive stock returns following share repurchases.

The authors also find that the issuance effect is stronger in countries with greater issuance activity, greater stock market development, stronger investor protection laws, and less earnings management. The authors infer that the issuance effect is stronger in countries in which it is less costly for firms to issue and repurchase shares. These specific cross-country results seem to be consistent with the market timing explanation in which issuance costs seem to affect firms' abilities to time markets.

Other Explanations for the Abnormal Returns

The discussion thus far has mentioned several general explanations that were offered in the literature to the observed stock price patterns following corporate financing events. These included challenges to the market efficiency hypothesis, in that some explanations suggested that investors are not able to incorporate relevant pieces of news into stock prices in a timely manner or that managers are able to time their equity issuances to coincide with periods of high prices. Managers were also hypothesized to intentionally mislead investors by managing earnings prior to some of these events. Other explanations that are still consistent with market efficiency focused on methodology issues related to possible misspecifications of the asset pricing models used. On that front, researchers expended considerable efforts to improve on these models. These efforts contributed to the asset pricing literature as well, because the anomalous results challenged researchers to produce richer and more sophisticated models, and develop more comprehensive theories. For example, Li, Livdan, and Zhang (2009) observe that corporate events result in changes in firms' real investments. They then evaluate what changes these real investments can lead to, and whether these changes relate in any way to the pricing of their securities. They show that investment and discount rates are negatively correlated and argue that optimal investment carried out following these events is an important determinant of the anomalous stock price patterns we observe. The reason for the observed anomalous returns is that the asset-pricing models used do not account for the shifts in expected returns that occur concurrently with changes in real investments.

Another possible explanation offered in the literature to the anomalous returns is related to methodology but not necessarily to the asset pricing model. For example, Kothari, Sabino, and Zach (2005) discuss the issue of survival and extreme performance. They argue that an empirical challenge in measuring long-term returns is that some firms that begin the period do not survive the entire long-term window. Because this nonsurvival is not random in some settings and is related to performance, they show in simulations that such nonsurvival may result in abnormal returns that are not necessarily an indication that pricing at the time of the event was inefficient or erroneous. The issue of survival raises important research design issues in how to measure the returns of firms that do not survive the entire period.

References

Affleck-Graves, J., and R. Miller. 2003. The information content of calls of debt: Evidence from long-run stock returns. *Journal of Financial Research* 26 (4): 421–447.

Agrawal, A., J. Jaffe, and G. Mandelkar. 1992. The post-merger performance of acquiring firms: A re-examination of an anomaly. *Journal of Finance* 47 (4): 1605–1621.

Baker, M., and J. Wurgler. 2000. The equity share in new issues and aggregate stock returns. *Journal of Finance* 55 (5): 2219–2257.

Billett, M., M. Flannery, and J. Garfinkel. 2006. Are bank loans special? Evidence on the post-announcement performance of bank borrowers. *Journal of Financial and Quantitative Analysis* 41 (4): 733–751.

Billett, M., M. Flannery, and J. Garfinkel. 2011. Frequent issuers' influence on long-run post-issuance returns. *Journal of Financial Economics* 99 (3): 349–364.

Bradshaw, M., S. Richardson, and R. Sloan. 2006. The relation between corporate financing activities, analysts' forecasts and stock returns. *Journal of Accounting & Economics* 42 (1): 53–85.

Brav, A., and P. Gompers. 1997. Myth or reality? The long-run underperformance of initial public offerings: Evidence from venture and non-venture capital-backed companies. *Journal of Finance* 52 (5): 1791–1821.

Brav, A., J. Graham, and C. Harvey. 2005. Payout in the 21st century. *Journal of Financial Economics* 77 (3): 483–527.

Cohen, D., and T. Lys. 2006. Weighing the evidence on the relation between external corporate financing activities, accruals, and stock returns. *Journal of Accounting & Economics* 42 (1): 87–105.

Eckbo, E., R. Masulis, and O. Norli. 2000. Seasoned public offerings: Resolution of the "new issues puzzle." *Journal of Financial Economics* 56 (2): 251–291.

Fama, E. 1998. Market efficiency, long-term returns, and behavioral finance. *Journal of Financial Economics* 49 (3): 283–306.

Hertzel, M., M. Lemmon, J. Linck, and L. Rees. 2002. Long-run performance following private placement of equity. *Journal of Finance* 57 (6): 2595–2617.

Ikenberry, D., J. Lakonishok, and T. Vermaelen. 1995. Market underreaction to open market share repurchases. *Journal of Financial Economics* 39 (1): 181–208.

Kothari, S. P., J. Sabino, and T. Zach. 2005. Implications of survival and data trimming for tests of market efficiency. *Journal of Accounting & Economics* 39 (1): 129–161.

Lakonishok, J., and T. Vermaelen. 1990. Anomalous price behavior around repurchase tender offers. *Journal of Finance* 45 (2): 455–477.

Li, E., D. Livdan, and L. Zhang. 2009. Anomailes. *Review of Financial Studies* 22 (11): 4301–4334.

Loughran, T., and J. Ritter. 1995. The new issues puzzle. *Journal of Finance* 50 (1): 23–51.

Loughran, T., and A. Vijh. 1997. Do long-term shareholders benefit from corporate acquisitions? *Journal of Finance* 52 (5): 1765–1790.

McLean, R. D., J. Pontiff, and A. Watanabe. 2009. Share issuance and cross-sectional returns: International evidence. *Journal of Financial Economics* 94 (1): 1–17.2

Michaely, R., R. Thaler, and K. Womack. 1995. Price reactions to dividend initiations and omissions: Overreaction or drift? *Journal of Finance* 50 (2): 573–608.

Mitchell, M., and E. Stafford. 2000. Managerial decisions and long-term stock price performance. *Journal of Business* 73 (3): 287–329.

Peyer, U, and T. Vermaelen. 2009. The nature and persistence of buyback anomalies. *Review of Financial Studies* 22 (4): 1693–1745.

Purnanandam, A., and B. Swaminathan. 2004. Are IPOS really underpriced? *Review of Financial Studies* 17 (3): 811–848.

Rangan, S. 1998. Earnings management and the performance of seasoned equity offerings. *Journal of Financial Economics* 50 (1): 101–122.

Rau, P. R., and T. Vermaelen. 1998. Glamour, value and the post-acquisition performance of acquiring firms. *Journal of Financial Economics* 49 (2): 223–253.

Ritter, J. 1991. The long-run performance of initial public offerings. *Journal of Finance* 46 (1): 3–27.

Ritter, J. 2003. Investment banking and securitites issuance. In *Handbook of Economics and Finance*, Chapter 5, edited by G. M. Constantinides, M. Harris, and R. Stulz. Amsterdam: Elsevier.

Schultz, P. 2003. Pseudo market timing and the long-run underperformance of IPOs. *Journal of Finance* 58 (2): 483–517.

Schwert, G. W. 1996. Markup pricing in mergers and acquisitions. *Journal of Financial Economics* 41 (1): 153–192.

Schwert, G. W. 2003. Anomalies and market efficiency. In *Handbook of Economics and Finance*, Chapter 15, edited by G. M. Constantinides, M. Harris, and R. Stulz. Amsterdam: Elsevier.

Shivakumar, L. 2000. Do firms mislead investors by overstating earnings before seasoned equity offerings? *Journal of Accounting & Economics* 29 (3): 339–371.

Sloan, R. 1996. Do stock prices fully reflect information in accruals and cash flows about future earnings? *The Accounting Review* 71 (3): 289–315.

Spiess, K., and J. Affleck-Graves. 1995. Underperformance in long-run stock returns following seasoned equity offerings. *Journal of Financial Economics* 38: 243–267.

Spiess, K., and J. Affleck-Graves. 1999. The long-run performance of stock returns following debt offerings. *Journal of Financial Economics* 54 (1): 45–73.

Teoh, S. H., I. Welch, and T. J. Wong. 1998. Earnings management and the long-run market performance of initial public offerings. *Journal of Finance* 53 (6): 1935–1974.

Zach, T. 2003. Inside the accrual anomaly. PhD Dissertation. University of Rochester.

Go to http://hema.zacks.com for abstracts and links to papers.

CHAPTER 7

The Insider Trading Anomaly

Ian Dogan

Insider trading is among the most profitable stock market anomalies, delivering superior returns for more than 40 years. It can be implemented successfully not only in the United States but in several other countries. Insiders have access to nonpublic detailed information about recent and imminent developments in their companies, so they have the expertise to judge the effects of material nonpublic information on their business results and stock returns. In fact, it wouldn't be an exaggeration to claim there's no one out there who's more informed than an insider is. Moreover, insiders have the essential background to utilize this advantage. As a result, it's not a big surprise insiders profit from their transactions. The abnormal returns are not limited to small and risky stocks; several hundred millions of dollars can be invested profitably in large cap stocks as well. Naturally, there's significant demand for insider trading data by individuals and institutional investors.

This chapter provides a brief definition of insider trading, explains laws and regulations governing insider transactions, addresses why insider transactions are profitable, and explores the challenges of imitating insiders. Summaries of notable studies on this topic are shown, as well as a detailed documentation of insider trading returns covering a 27-year period, the longest among existing studies. Results summarized by year, firm size, different holding periods, and different industries will be analyzed. A brief summary of international results and recent developments in this field is also provided.

The chapter also presents a long/short investment strategy based on insider transactions that can be implemented by institutional investors. This strategy invests in liquid medium and large capitalization stocks, and takes into account transaction costs, implementation costs, and historically delivered double-digit excess returns.

Overview of Insider Filings

The large shareholders who hold more than 10% of a stock's outstanding shares, all members of the board of directors, the CEO, CFO, and other highest-level officers are considered insiders. Attorneys, underwriters, and consultants to these highest-level officers and directors are also considered insiders. Because these people may have access to material, nonpublic information, they have to report their transactions to the SEC for public scrutiny. It is illegal for them to trade based on material nonpublic information, but they are allowed to trade otherwise.

However, regulators cannot always know whether insiders illegally use nonpublic information in their transactions, so they don't prosecute insiders unless insiders trade right before major corporate announcements, such as mergers, acquisitions, or quarterly earnings. Insiders know that they will get caught if they trade days before major announcements and also know that they have a free pass if they trade months before major announcements.

A recent study by Agrawal and Nasser (2010) examined 3,700 targets of takeovers during the 1988–2006 period and found that both insider purchases and sales fell 6 months prior to the takeover announcement. However, insider sales fell much more than insider purchases, and insiders profited from the knowledge of the upcoming takeovers by abstaining from selling.

Another study by Li and Zhang (2006) documented similar very early insider activity before financial restatement announcements. They observed little net insider selling around the announcement (one quarter prior to the announcement); however, they provide evidence of net insider selling 2 to 8 quarters before the announcement.

Therefore, it seems that insiders do trade based on their nonpublic knowledge, and, as we show in this chapter, outsiders can profit legally by imitating insiders' purchases.

Documentation of the Anomaly

The analysis of insider trading returns is not new. In 1968, Lorie and Niederhoffer published one of the earliest papers on the profitability of insider trading with a relatively proper methodological approach. Since, at that time, insider data was not in machine readable form, they used statistical sampling from manual filings and manually calculated their results. Until 1968, academic studies had not found any evidence of significant abnormal returns to insider transactions. However, the SEC and investors believed just the opposite. Lorie and Niederhoffer's study came at a time when the "efficient market hypothesis" was conceived. They wanted to investigate the validity of the SEC's and investment community's conviction that insiders were illegally profiting from insider trading. They found that, under the intensive trading criteria (for which the number of buyers is at least two more than the number of sellers or vice versa), insiders will outperform the market over the following 6 months.

The next test of insider profitability was done by Jaffe (1974) who did not find abnormal returns for the zero investment portfolio[1] that's long in companies with more insider purchases and short in companies with more insider sales in a given month. Reducing the sample to only large transactions (at least $20,000) also didn't change his conclusion. However, when he employed intensive trading criteria, for which there had to be at least 3 buyers from each company to be included in the long portfolio and 3 sellers from each company to be included in the short portfolio, he found abnormal returns of 5.07% in the first 8 months following the transactions. When he included each company in the portfolio 2 months after the transaction,[2] he still found abnormal returns of 4.84% over the following 8 months and concluded that outsiders can also enjoy abnormal profits by imitating insiders.

Seyhun (1986) published perhaps the most complete analysis of insider trading. He covered the period from 1975 to 1981 and used a better methodology by incorporating the "size effect" to measure the abnormal returns more accurately. Seyhun found abnormal returns of 4.3% over the first 300 days following the transaction for firms with more insider purchases than sales, and −2.2% for the same period for firms with more insider sales than purchases. He noted that employing intensive trading criteria yielded similar results. He also investigated the determinants of these returns. He found that all insider types have statistically abnormal returns where officer-directors have the highest and officers have the lowest abnormal returns. Large shareholders have higher abnormal returns than officers, even though the difference is not statistically significant. He found that insider type (officers, directors, large shareholders or a combination of such), firm size, and transaction size are separate determinants of insiders' abnormal returns.

---

[1]Zero investment portfolio approach combines the returns to insider purchases and sales. If abnormal returns to insider purchases is 4% and abnormal returns to insider sales is 2%, zero investment portfolio approach will yield an abnormal return of 6%.

[2]Prior to 2002, Sarbanes-Oxley Act insiders had anywhere between 10 and 40 days to report their transactions. Late reporting was also tolerated.

However, he cautioned the readers that these variables explained only 1% of the variation of abnormal returns, and even when companies are selected based on these variables, outsiders can't profit from publicly available information.

Lakonishok and Lee (2001) corrected for size and book-to-market effects. They used net-purchase ratios, which are similar to Jaffe's intensive trading criterion. The difference between strong buy and strong sell portfolios, which excluded transactions of large shareholders, was 4.8% for the first year following the transactions. They didn't find any abnormal returns for large shareholders.

Jeng, Metrick, and Zeckhauser's 2003 study focused on abnormal returns earned by insiders themselves. They started to calculate abnormal returns as soon as the insiders made the transactions, not when the transactions became public. Insiders earned an annual raw return over the 6 months following the trade of 11.2 percentage points above the market, and more than 6 percentage points above the market when size and book-to-market effects were taken into account (one third of this abnormal return was observed during the first month). Note that they didn't use any intensive trading criteria; they just imitated insider transactions and gave each firm a weight in proportion to the amount insiders spent on purchases. Their results showed that purchases in small firms don't earn significantly higher returns than do purchases in large firms, and that purchases of top executives don't earn significantly higher abnormal returns than do purchases of other insiders. Finally, they did not find any abnormal returns to insider sales.

Results for the 1978–2005 Period

The results reported in this section use a large insider-trading database,[3] which covers 27 years of insider transactions. Firstly we replicate Jeng's methodology for the 1978–2005 period, and we find that the average monthly raw return is only 35 basis points greater than the S&P 500. This is (annually) nearly 7 percentage points less than the 11.2% figure suggested by Jeng et al. Table 7.1 and Figure 7.1 show the return details of this methodology.

It's obvious that imitating Jeng et al.'s methodology doesn't present attractive returns, even though it's still better than index funds. Other previous insider trading studies found higher returns when they employed some form of an intensive trading criterion. One insider may be wrong in his conviction to buy, whereas several insiders buying around the same time signal a greater conviction. Limiting the dataset to only those transactions with

---

[3]This database is a compilation of Ownership Reporting System (ORS) data and author's own data.

TABLE 7.1   Strategy Statistics—Insider Purchases—1978 to 2005

	Insider Purchases	S&P 500 Total Return
Average return	1.48%	1.13%
Median monthly return	1.73%	1.35%
Standard deviation	6.21%	4.38%
Worst month	−38.58%	−21.61%
Best month	22.67%	13.53%
Sharpe ratio	0.55	0.50
Correlation with S&P 500	0.75	1.00
No. of positive months	215	212
No. of negative months	121	124

at least 3 insiders buying in a 3-month period nearly doubles the monthly excess returns, and the annual raw return for these stocks is 7.7 percentage points higher than the S&P 500. Table 7.2 and Figure 7.2 summarize these results over the full period, and Figure 7.2 shows the returns over sequential 4-year intervals.

These results clearly show that insider purchases are profitable. One central question in market anomaly research is whether these results are real or merely an outcome of data mining. Efficient markets theorists usually raise two arguments against stock market anomalies: The observed anomaly is a result of either risky trades or data mining (i.e., coincidence). Insider trading profits are more likely to be a result of private information than excessive risk. The insider trading anomaly has been around since the 1970s, and several studies covering different nonoverlapping time periods

Insider trading returns
4-year intervals 1978–2005

FIGURE 7.1   Insider Purchase Returns from 1978 to 2005

TABLE 7.2   Strategy Statistics—Intense Insider Purchases

	Insider Purchases (Consensus)	S&P 500 Total Return
Average return	1.78%	1.16%
Median monthly return	1.73%	1.36%
Standard deviation	6.95%	4.37%
Worst month	−25.68%	−21.61%
Best month	25.29%	13.53%
Sharpe ratio	0.63	0.52
Correlation with S&P 500	0.64	1.00
No. of positive months	211	212
No. of negative months	123	122

document abnormal returns to insider trading. If the anomaly was a result of data mining, there wouldn't be abnormal returns observed nearly 40 years after they were first documented. International studies also confirm this phenomenon in several other countries.

How Consistent Is the Anomaly Year by Year?

Even though insider trading strategies handily beat the market index over the full time period, there are many years in which the insider strategies underperformed. In particular, during the 3 consecutive years between 1996 and 1998, both strategies displayed so far underperformed the S&P 500 by more than 10%. There are very few investors who can stomach this kind of

FIGURE 7.2   Intense Insider Purchase Returns from 1978–2005

abysmal performance 3 years in a row, which is a weakness of this strategy. On the other hand, this is a blessing for the investor with a long-term focus. Wild swings in return performance of insider transactions keep professional fund managers away from the strategy. In 12 out of 28 years, the S&P 500 Total Return index performed better than the stocks intensively bought by insiders. Table 7.3 shows the annual returns for the strategy using all insider purchases, the S&P 500 Total Return index, and the strategy limited by intensive trading criterion.

TABLE 7.3 Year-by-Year Returns of Two Insider Purchase Strategies

Year	Insider Purchases (%)	S&P500TR(%)	Insider Purchases (Consensus) (%)
1978	43.2	6.3	25.3
1979	40.8	18.6	39.5
1980	17.7	32.6	6.0
1981	−2.1	−5.1	16.6
1982	7.3	22.0	11.1
1983	49.6	22.3	85.7
1984	−2.0	6.7	14.1
1985	24.3	32.0	23.3
1986	17.9	18.3	14.1
1987	−15.6	5.1	8.8
1988	18.3	17.0	26.8
1989	14.1	31.4	19.2
1990	−11.2	−3.2	20.6
1991	40.3	30.7	52.0
1992	31.2	7.7	30.9
1993	43.6	9.8	37.5
1994	−0.7	1.4	−2.8
1995	37.0	37.6	47.1
1996	16.8	23.2	10.9
1997	21.9	33.5	21.8
1998	9.1	29.0	4.2
1999	26.4	20.9	22.4
2000	−18.3	−8.8	−29.1
2001	27.1	−11.8	33.2
2002	−18.8	−22.1	−11.7
2003	58.0	28.7	85.5
2004	23.7	11.0	8.8
2005	15.4	5.1	0.0

Cumulative excess returns
Days 0 through 252

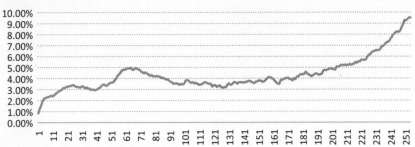

FIGURE 7.3   Cumulative Excess Returns

When Are Returns Generated during the 1-Year Holding Periods?

A look at the daily stock return minus S&P 500 Total Return in Figure 7.3 shows that most of the excess returns are realized within the first month. Cumulative daily excess return increases until the end of the third month, and then declines for the next 3 months.[4] This suggests that the market reacts positively to insider purchases and stock prices initially increase. Six months after the initial insider purchase, stock prices once again start to increase and register a 1% per month excess return for the following 6 months. This indicates that insiders anticipate forthcoming favorable events 6 to 9 months in advance.

Figure 7.4 shows that nearly 2.5% of the 5% month-end abnormal return is realized within the first 10 days. Therefore, nimble traders and small funds can greatly benefit from utilizing insider trading transactions, whereas large funds are disadvantaged.

---

[4]The returns presented in the previous sections had 6-month holding periods, and, at each point in time, we had several different companies in our portfolio whose stock had been intensively bought by insiders in the past 6 months. This methodology is called the rolling portfolio method and reflects the experience of a fund manager or an investor imitating insider transactions. To understand how stocks behave each day after insider purchases, we grouped all insider stocks into one sample and started calculating returns for each day separately. The day-1 return is calculated by averaging all stocks' excess returns for the first day after the trade. Consequently this methodology gives more weight to those years in which there are more insider purchases, whereas our rolling portfolio approach gives each time period equal weight, so the returns presented here do not exactly match the returns presented in the previous sections.

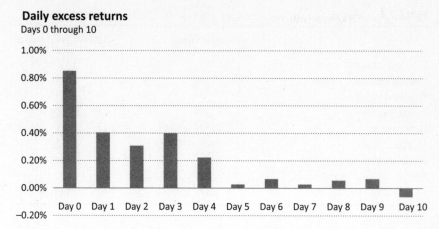

FIGURE 7.4   Daily Excess Returns

Most of the transactions for this analysis come from transactions that were consumed before the 2002 Sarbanes Oxley Act. Nevertheless, return patterns and magnitudes are not very different in the latter period.

Returns in Small Cap versus Large Cap

Abnormal returns to insider trading can be observed mainly because there is an information asymmetry between market participants and insiders.[5] Theoretically, insider trading returns should be higher when information asymmetry is larger. This is usually the case in smaller firms where there are only a few analysts (if any at all) following the companies. Analysis shows that small companies have nearly 50 basis points per month higher raw returns than large companies. Table 7.4 summarizes the performance of large companies that are intensively bought by insiders. These companies still outperform the market index. Figure 7.5 displays the performance of these stocks in four year increments.

Small companies, on the other hand, have outstanding returns and beat the market index by 91 basis points per month. Naturally, some of these companies are microcap stocks and/or low liquidity stocks and can't be bought in large quantities. That's why each company is given a weight that is in proportion to insiders' open market transactions. Because insiders

---

[5]Another reason is the motivation effect; unlike other investors, insiders can work harder and improve their companies' performance and stock returns. However, without getting into the details, it can be said that information effect is more dominant than motivation effect and points to much higher returns.

TABLE 7.4   Strategy Statistics—Large Cap, Intense Purchases

	Consensus (Large)	S&P 500 Total Return
Average return	1.57%	1.16%
Median monthly return	1.73%	1.36%
Standard deviation	7.33%	4.37%
Worst month	−28.14%	−21.61%
Best month	24.81%	13.53%
Sharpe ratio	0.50	0.52
Correlation with S&P 500	0.60	1.00
No. of Positive Months	200	212
No. of Negative Months	134	122

can't buy large quantities in illiquid stocks in the open market as well, results for the most part bypass this problem. The summary of results is shown in Table 7.5. Figure 7.6 displays the performance of these stocks in four year increments.

It's not very difficult to set up a small fund (up to $100 million in assets) to mimic insider transactions in small firms. The following graph shows this strategy would beat the S&P 500 Total Return index in almost all 4-year time periods.

Does It Work on the Short Side?

Insider sales are less likely to be driven by private information. As the stock- and options-based compensation methods became widespread,

Insider trading consensus (large) returns
4-year intervals 1978–2005

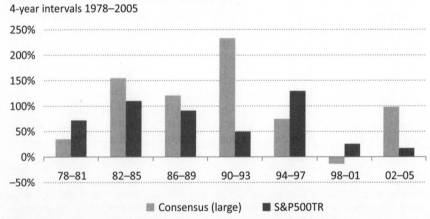

FIGURE 7.5   Intense Insider Purchases, Large Cap, from 1978 to 2005

TABLE 7.5   Strategy Statistics—Small Cap—Intense Insider Purchases

	Consensus (Small)	S&P 500 Total Return
Average return	2.04%	1.13%
Median monthly return	1.73%	1.36%
Standard deviation	7.78%	4.37%
Worst month	−30.22%	−21.61%
Best month	36.75%	13.53%
Sharpe ratio	0.68	0.50
Correlation with S&P 500	0.59	1.00
No. of positive months	207	209
No. of negative months	124	122

insiders needed to sell more for diversification and liquidity purposes. As a result, insider sales overall are usually uninformative. However, it is possible to find subsets of insider sales transactions that will underperform the market in the following 6–12 months.

In 2000, the SEC provided insiders the opportunity to trade practically without fear of prosecution by enacting Rule 10b5–1. If insiders enter into an explicit contract and transfer the trade execution authority to an uninformed third party by providing an explicit written algorithm for trade execution, then they can trade during restricted trade windows, trade as much as they want, and trade at the prices they determine. This rule enables insiders to trade based on their material private information about distant corporate events because they can claim that they weren't in possession of material information when they preplanned the trades. A recent study by Jagolinzer

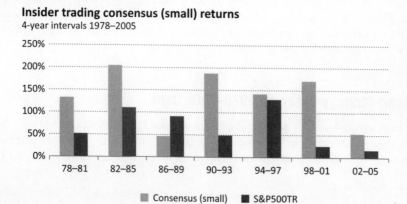

Insider trading consensus (small) returns
4-year intervals 1978–2005

FIGURE 7.6   Intense Insider Purchases, Small Cap, 4-Year Intervals, 1978–2005

(2009) analyzed returns to insider sales executed under Rule 10b5–1 and found that during a 6-month holding period, insiders have a statistically significant 30-basis-points negative return.[6]

Another potential area in which examining insider sales transactions may lead to abnormal returns is earnings restatements. A 2008 study by Agrawal and Cooper investigating insider sales transactions before accounting scandals concludes that top managers of restating firms sell substantially more stock during the misstated period. This phenomenon is more pronounced at firms with more serious restatements and large declines in stock prices after the announcement. Such results suggest that a signaling mechanism may be developed to determine these firms in advance.

Insider sales may be based on private information in growth firms with a long history of consecutive increases in quarterly earnings. Another study by Ke, Huddart, and Petroni (2002) examined insider trading in these growth firms that break the streak and disappoint investors. The decline in stock price is usually larger when expectations and the decline in earnings are higher. In these firms, insiders don't trade immediately before the announcement, but there's an increase in frequency of insider sales three to nine quarters before the announcement.

One of the interesting studies on performance of insider sales focuses on insider sales before insiders' home purchases (Liu and Yermack, 2007). Insider sales 2 months prior to home purchases have an abnormal return of −5.4% during the following 20 trading days. This is also not a short-lived signal; insiders' large home purchases have around −1% per month abnormal returns for a period of 36 months.

The bottom line is that some insiders illegally sell their stock holdings when they know that they have been artificially inflating earnings or earnings will be declining in the future, or when bankruptcy is inevitable. So far, limited research done in this field shows insider selling is more intense when insiders are in possession of future bad news. In general, most insider sales are not informative, but it's still possible to develop an investment strategy for the short side of the portfolio.

Short Strategy Based on 1978–2005 Data

Again, overall insider sales transactions do not have any abnormal returns. However, it's possible to screen through to eliminate uninformative transactions and get a good list of companies to short. The strategy shown in

---

[6]We do not use this strategy in our own trading because there are only a few years of data to test this strategy.

TABLE 7.6 Strategy Statistics—Short Insider Sales

	Sales Portfolio	S&P 500 Total Return
Average return	0.61%	1.13%
Median monthly return	0.77%	1.36%
Standard deviation	6.18%	4.37%
Worst month	−19.93%	−21.61%
Best month	20.09%	13.53%
Sharpe ratio	0.06	0.50
Correlation with S&P 500	0.82	1.00
No. of positive months	186	209
No. of negative months	143	122

Table 7.6 uses an intensive selling criterion (at least three insiders selling during the prior 3-month period), eliminates small transactions (total number of shares sold during the prior 3-month period is at least 25,000), limits the companies to sectors where insider selling was more successful (basic materials, utilities, transportation), and only includes large companies, because it may not be easy to short sell small- or medium-size companies. Additionally, only stocks with no insiders buying during the prior 3-month period are included. Shorting the stocks that satisfy these screens and holding the positions for a year produces the results shown in Table 7.6.

This subset of insider sales underperforms the S&P 500 Total Return index by around 6 percentage points per year. The results are not sensitive

Insider trading sales portfolio returns
4-year intervals 1978–2005

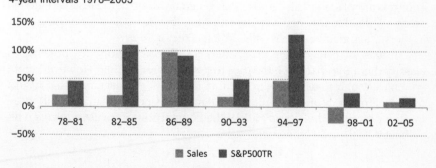

FIGURE 7.7 Returns for Shorting Insider Sales

to initiating these positions immediately after insider sales. If the sales portfolio was formed with a 90-day lag, the average monthly raw return of the sales portfolio would have been 67 basis points instead of 61.

In almost all 4-year time periods, this strategy underperforms the S&P 500 and has negative returns in 143 months and positive returns in 186 months. However, it shouldn't be forgotten that the 1978–2005 period is a long bull market and it is very normal that this strategy has positive returns. Zooming in on the 1998–2005 time period, during which stock returns were relatively lower, this strategy had negative raw returns as well (see Figure 7.7).

Do Returns Vary by Industry?

The source of the abnormal returns to insider trading mainly is the information asymmetry between market participants and insiders. In certain industries (i.e., technology) information asymmetry is larger. Insiders are more knowledgeable than analysts or investors about the future prospects of their industries and/or companies. In other industries (i.e., consumer cyclicals and capital goods) information asymmetry is smaller. This may be a result of regulation where returns are steady but upside potential is limited, or in mature companies and markets where profits depend on predicting the course of business cycles. As a result of these differences, some variation in returns to insiders across industries can be observed. Each company in the database is assigned to one of 10 sectors based on their SIC number.[7]

The results show that the 5 sectors with the highest average monthly returns are transportation, consumer staples, technology, financial, and services. Capital goods, basic materials, energy, consumer cyclical, and utilities have lower returns to insiders. These results are more or less as expected. Consumer staples may not be expected to be in the top group, but pharmaceuticals are placed in this group. This is certainly one of the least researched areas of insider trading. Yet, results hint that it's still a promising one. Table 7.7 summarizes the results for each sector.

Instead of categorizing companies into broad sectors, it's possible to classify them into narrow industries to get a clearer picture. However, there weren't enough transactions in the first half of the dataset, and that results in a small number of companies (and sometimes no companies at all) to be in the portfolios. This doesn't allow the comparison of industry results with sufficient statistical confidence.

---

[7]http://mba.tuck.dartmouth.edu/pages/faculty/ken.french/Data_Library/det_49_ind_port.html.

TABLE 7.7 Performance of Insider Purchases by Sector

	Transportation	Consumer Staples	Technology	Finance	Services	Utilities	Energy	Basic Materials	Consumer Cyclical	Capital Goods
Average return	2.28%	2.25%	2.03%	1.93%	1.93%	1.73%	1.54%	1.52%	1.46%	1.32%
Median monthly return	1.92%	2.61%	1.38%	1.83%	1.78%	1.43%	1.86%	1.29%	1.89%	1.06%
Standard deviation	9.82%	8.02%	10.24%	5.62%	9.51%	8.81%	8.59%	8.99%	6.40%	8.47%
Worst month	−32%	−39%	−26%	−24%	−31%	−43%	−43%	−46%	−32%	−32%
Best month	77%	36%	45%	19%	43%	49%	33%	46%	27%	25%
Sharpe ratio	0.63	0.75	0.52	0.88	0.52	0.48	0.42	0.39	0.52	0.33
Correlation with S&P 500	0.47	0.54	0.65	0.65	0.54	0.57	0.42	0.51	0.65	0.57
No. of positive months	219	218	201	231	202	191	198	196	210	189
No. of negative months	116	118	135	105	134	142	135	140	126	145

Institutional Investors

When insiders are buying, either individual investors or institutional investors must be selling to insiders. A 2008 study by Sias and Whidbee analyzed the dynamics of insider transactions and found that in aggregate, institutional investors trade in the opposite direction of insiders. On the other hand, individual investors trade in the same direction as insiders. This is mainly a result of institutions' preference for momentum trading and insiders being contrarians.

There isn't any research that looks at institutional investors' use of insider transactions data in their decision processes. However, because there are several data services[8] providing insider trading data to the asset management industry, it is safe to assume that institutional investors are using this data. (During the past several years the author of this chapter advised banks and hedge funds how to use insider trading data in their investment strategies. One of the clients was a multibillion-dollar hedge fund that managed a $200 million portfolio based on insider transactions.)

Usually, hedge fund managers don't tell how they pick their investments, but successful hedge fund manager Joel Greenblatt (1997), founder of Gotham Capital lets us peek into his stock-picking process and reveals that he takes into account insider trading data when he says:

> *Insider participation is one of the key areas to look for when picking and choosing between spinoffs—for me, the most important area. Are the managers of new spinoff incentivized along the same lines as shareholders? Will they receive a large part of their potential compensation in stock, restricted stock, or options? Is there a plan for them to acquire more? When all the required public documents about the spinoff have been filed, I usually look at this area first.*

This clearly lends support to the idea that institutional investors take insider transactions into account.

Individual Investors

Insider trading transactions have been the focus of investors for a very long time. Academic insider trading research goes back more than 40 years. Likewise there were several newsletters targeting individual investors. *Insiders' Chronicle*, one of these newsletters, was started in October 1976 and stayed

---

[8]Thomson Reuters, Zacks, Bloomberg, Vickers, and the Washington Service are the primary providers of insider data.

in the business until 1999. Then it was acquired by First Call/Thomson Financial and became Thomson Financial's insider trading data service. *Vickers Weekly Insider Report, Consensus of Insiders, Insiders,* and *Market Logic* were also among the list of newsletters that recommend stocks based on insider transactions. For instance, *Insiders*[9] newsletter rated several hundred stocks and a number of sectors, listed stocks that are heavily bought or sold, displayed an index of insider trading activity, and published a portfolio of recommended stocks.

Hulbert Financial Digest, which tracks the performance of prominent newsletters, reported that the portfolio of stocks recommended by *Insiders Chronicle* increased by 118.9% between January 1985 and June 1992, while the S&P 500 Total Return index increased by 216.7% during the same time period. Moreover, *Insiders Chronicle* recommended portfolio had a beta of 1.9, suggesting that most of the stocks in the recommended list were small or microcap stocks. Hulbert reported that *Market Logic,* another newsletter recommending stocks based on insider trading, increased by 339.2% between June 1980 and June 1992. Again, the S&P 500 Total Return index increased by 483% during the same time period. Considering our results show that insider trading was profitable, the lag between insider transactions and publication of the buy recommendations and subjective recommendations of newsletter editors must have contributed to the dismal performance of these newsletters.

Today, there are dozens of paid subscription services providing insider transactions data almost instantaneously. There are also free online services, such as InsiderMonkey.com, providing real-time data on insider transactions. Publications such as *Wall Street Journal* or *Barron's* have sections covering the notable insider transactions that happened over the most recent few days or week.

Relation to Other Anomalies

Insider trading is more prevalent in small and somewhat distressed companies. This chapter has so far shown the source of abnormal returns to insider trading is information asymmetry and insiders have information advantage especially in small and distressed firms. As a result of this, some of the abnormal returns to insider trading have been attributed to size effect and book-to-market effect in the past 25 years. Academicians consider small firms and firms with high book-to-market ratios very risky, and explain the higher returns to these firms as an outcome of this higher risk. This may seem like a plausible explanation if one is an outsider with

---

[9]October 1987 issue of *Kiplinger's Personal Finance.*

limited information about these companies. However, when insiders of these small and distressed companies trade and subsequently earn abnormal returns, one shouldn't claim insiders earned abnormal returns because they assumed excessive risks. Insiders profit because they utilize their private information. Knowing the outcome or the actual probabilities of potential outcomes beforehand really limits the use of excessive risk. That's why it's not appropriate to attribute some of the abnormal returns from insider trading to size effect or book-to-market effect. On the other hand, it might be more appropriate to attribute some of the abnormal returns to small and distressed firms to insider trading.

Another well-documented anomaly in the stock market is momentum effect. Insiders are contrarian investors; they generally buy when prices are declining, not increasing. That's why abnormal returns to insider trading cannot be explained by using momentum effect. Most recent academic papers on insider trading erroneously adjust returns to accommodate size, book-to-market, and momentum effects. This isn't necessary when it comes to insider trading.

Although there are not any published articles analyzing insider transactions in firms with high sales-to-market value ratios or high profit margins, there is a study by Hsieh, Lilian, and Wang (2005) jointly evaluating insider transactions and analyst recommendations. The results indicate that analyst upgrades lead to 25 basis points per month abnormal return over the next 12 months when insiders are net buyers. When insiders are net sellers, analyst downgrades do not lead to any abnormal returns. These results indicate that when analysts join insiders in their assessment of the company, they are usually late to the party. Analyst downgrades lead to abnormal negative returns only when there are no insider transactions. Another useful result of this study is that analyst downgrades cancel the effect of insider purchases. In companies in which insiders are net buyers, stock downgrades lead to 12-basis-points abnormal return per month. However, this number is not statistically different from zero.

International Evidence

Insider trading is profitable not only in the United States, but in several other countries. In Germany, Dymke and Walter (2007) show that insider purchases have a 1-month abnormal return of 4.4% and insider sales underperform by 1.5% during the first month. Outsiders mimicking insider purchases would earn abnormal returns of about 2.8%, whereas corresponding number for insider sales is 1.4%. In Netherlands, Biesta et al. (2003) show that insider transactions are among the world's most profitable. Insider purchase portfolios have abnormal returns of 9% over 6 months, whereas insider sale portfolios underperform by more than 7% over 6 months. In Italy, Bajo and Petracci (2006) also find similar magnitude of abnormal returns and report that the insider purchase portfolio has an abnormal return of 9% over the next 3 months, and the insider sales portfolio has a −6% abnormal return over 3 months and −9% abnormal return over 6 months. Cheuk, Fan, and So (2006) report abnormal returns associated with legal insider transactions in Hong Kong and Wisniewski and Bohl (2005) find abnormal returns to insider trading on the Warsaw Stock Exchange in Poland.

In the United Kingdom Gregory, Matatko, Tonks, and Purkis (1994) find abnormal returns are concentrated in smaller companies; however, mimicking those returns does not yield exceptionally high returns to outsiders. In Spain, where there is a 39-day delay between insider transactions and announcement of those transactions, Del Brio, De Miguel, and Perote (2001) find that insiders earn excess profits whereas outsiders mimicking insiders do not. In Switzerland, Zingg, Lang, and Wyttenbach (2007) show that the insider purchase portfolio has an abnormal return of 1.6% over the next 30 trading days and that outsiders mimicking insiders can earn 1% abnormal returns assuming zero transaction costs but insider sales are not profitable. New Zealand is also one of these countries where insiders earn significantly large abnormal returns whereas outsiders do not because of significant delays in reporting as shown by Etebari, Tourani-Rad, and Gilbert (2004).

On the other hand, Eckbo and Smith (1999) find zero or negative abnormal performance for insider trades on the Oslo Stock Exchange. Nevertheless, there is overwhelming evidence that insider trading is exceptionally profitable for insiders. In several countries outsiders mimicking insider transactions can also profit handsomely. These results support our thesis that abnormal returns to insider trading are not a result of data mining or a statistical fluke.

Can Insider Data Predict S&P 500 Returns?

The previous sections suggest that insider trading can be used as a stock-picking strategy and it delivers superior returns over long investment horizons. However, this does not imply that aggregate insider trading can be used to predict the market returns. Although intensively bought and sold stocks outperform the market, if the total magnitude of these transactions pales in comparison to the uninformed insider transactions, then aggregate insider transactions may fail to deliver meaningful signals to predict the market.

Fortunately, previous research by Seyhun (1988) and Lakonishok (2001) show that aggregate insider trading predicts future stock market returns. Seyhun used a limited dataset, while Lakonishok's results are more comprehensive. Each month, Lakonishok aggregated total number of purchases and sales during the prior 6-month period and calculated net purchase ratio (NPR) which is the ratio of purchases minus sales to purchases plus sales. Then each month's NPR is ranked together with 59 NPRs of the previous 59 months. The 12 months that have the highest NPR are hypothesized to signal higher returns for the stock market, and the 12 months at the bottom of the list are hypothesized to signal lower returns for the stock market. The transactions of large shareholders are excluded, but including them does not change the nature of final results.

First of all, the results clearly show that insiders are contrarian traders. The bottom 20% of NPRs have the highest net insider sales; they also have the highest preceding 12-month stock market return. The stock market increased an average of 29.5% during the previous 12 months for this group. The top 20% of NPRs have the highest net insider purchases; they also have the lowest preceding 12-month stock market return. The stock market increased an average of 5.6% during the previous 12 months. Clearly insiders sell after large increases in stock market and they buy after poor performance.

The stock market in general has an average 12-month increase of only 7.2% after the months with the lowest 20% of NPRs. The stock market increases an average of 21% after months with the highest 20% of NPRs. The NPRs in the middle (60% of the total) are followed by an average 12-month stock market return of about 17%. So, aggregate insider trading is more successful in predicting forthcoming poor stock market performance, but it can also be used with moderate success to predict large stock market increases. Aggregate insider transactions have a promising potential to be used as a market-timing tool.

Latest Developments

One of the changes brought by Sarbanes-Oxley Act of 2002 was the new requirement about the timely reporting of insider trading transactions. Previously insiders had anywhere between 10 to 40 days to report their transactions. Several insiders used to report their transactions even later than the official deadlines, yet the SEC wasn't assessing penalties toward these people. Even though insiders themselves made abnormal profits, outsiders may not copycat these transactions because of run-ups in prices during the time between the transactions and reporting.

Today insiders have only 2 business days to report their transactions. Moreover, since June 30, 2003, insider transactions are filed electronically and can be accessed through SEC's web site. This significant change now provides more opportunities for outsiders to mimic insiders' transactions.

However, more timely reporting may potentially alter the way insiders ex-ploit their private information. Some might refrain from trading, others might accelerate their transaction to utilize their information before their trades became public. Hence, the return patterns to insider trading might have significantly changed after the enactment of Sarbanes-Oxley Act.

A 2010 study by Brochet focuses on insider transactions that occurred between 1997 and 2006. Before Sarbanes Oxley Act, average 3-day cu-mulative abnormal return to insider purchases was 0.59 percent; after the Sarbanes Oxley Act, it has been 1.89 percent. Post SOX, cumulative abnor-mal return is 0.71 percent on day 0, 0.81 percent on day 1, 0.37 percent on day 2, 0.21 percent on day 3, and 0.17 percent on day 4. Average 3-day cumulative abnormal return to insider sales was −0.28 percent pre SOX and −0.11 percent after SOX. The 3-day window in these analyses starts on the day of the filing, not the trade day. The average cumulative abnormal return between transaction date and filing date is also as much as another 1 percentage point.

Long/Short Strategy for Institutional Investors

As we have seen previously, individual investors have the opportunity to profit from insider data by day trading or by investing in micro to small cap stocks. However, institutional investors with portfolios of $100 million or more are limited to buying and shorting mid and large cap companies. This section outlines a long/short investment strategy solely based on insider purchase and sales transactions shown in Table 7.8.

The long side of the portfolio has to be constructed quickly because stock prices react to insider purchases, but the short side of the portfolio

TABLE 7.8 Strategy Statistics for Long/Short Mid–Large Cap Insider Portfolio

	Long/Short Portfolio	S&P 500 Total Return
Average return	1.60%	1.13%
Median monthly return	0.66%	1.35%
Standard deviation	7.24%	4.38%
Worst month	−21.21%	−21.61%
Best month	51.08%	13.53%
Sharpe ratio	0.52	0.50
Correlation with S&P 500	0.00	1.00
No. of positive months	182	212
No. of negative months	148	124

Note: These results do not include transaction costs.

Daily excess returns
Days 0 through 10

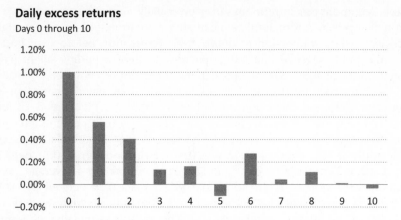

FIGURE 7.8   Daily Excess Returns of Long/Short Insider Portfolio

can be constructed gradually, thereby limiting the market impact of the transactions. The assumptions used in this strategy are (1) that the net cost of developing and maintaining the short side of the portfolio is about 2% per year, and (2) 2 round-trip transactions are made per year and the total cost of these transactions is 6% per year.

If the transaction cost of the purchase transactions happens to be greater than 3% each, then the holding period can be extended from six months to twelve months which will cut the transaction costs by half. The average return for each of the first 10 days after the stock is purchased is shown in Figure 7.8. Because the long positions in this portfolio increase faster than the rest of the insider purchases, the assumption of 3% transaction cost for each of these positions is reasonable.

Figure 7.9 presents cumulative average daily returns for each day after the stock is included in the purchase portfolio. The graph shows that excess returns keep increasing beyond the initial 6-month period (the first 126 trading days). A 6-month holding period is used because, over the 27 years, redeploying capital in new companies that satisfied our criteria achieves higher returns. These results imply that patience is a virtue and that price impact can be minimized when selling these stocks.

Overall, the long side of the portfolio has an average monthly return of 2.16% between 1978 and 2005. The short side of the portfolio has an average monthly return of 0.61% during the same time period. The long/short portfolio is constructed such that it has zero correlation with the S&P 500 Total Return index. As a result, the portfolio is 100% long and 90% short. The strength of this portfolio is that it has high average returns and it is not correlated with the market. The weaknesses are its high volatility and inconsistency. Even though it has zero market exposure, its standard deviation is more than 50% above the market's standard deviation. There

Cumulative excess returns
Days 0 through 252

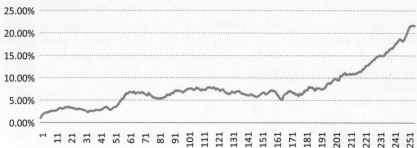

FIGURE 7.9 Cumulative Excess Return for Long/Short Insider Portfolio

Note: The graph could give you the impression that it may be better to hold stocks for 12 months rather than 6 months. However, these results are dominated by certain time periods where returns in the second half of the year were relatively higher. When we equally weigh each time period, rather than each transaction, shorter holding periods lead to higher returns.

have been long time periods in the past when the portfolio underperformed the market even though, on the average, it beats the market. There are also long periods of time where this portfolio performed spectacularly. This also contributed to its high standard deviation. Keep in mind that this is a market-neutral strategy and should not be regarded as an alternative to index funds (see Figure 7.10).

The short portfolio used in the long/short strategy is discussed earlier in the chapter. The long portfolio is comprised of companies that have a larger market cap than the median NYSE firm and operate in one of the following

Long/short portfolio returns
4-year intervals 1978–2005

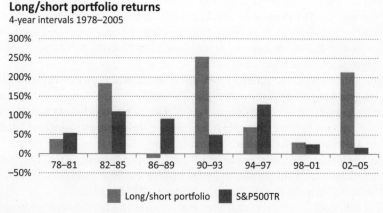

FIGURE 7.10 Four-Year Returns of Long/Short Portfolio

sectors: transportation, technology, consumer staples, services, financial. The portfolio also requires 3 insider purchases in the 3 months preceding the insider purchases. After taking into account an annual 8% transaction cost, the long/short insider trading portfolio achieves a more than 10% annual return. The results for longer holding periods have not been tabulated here for the sake of brevity, but the long/short insider trading portfolio with 12-month holding period achieves an 8% average annual return and has lower volatility.

References

Agrawal, Anup, and Tommy Cooper. Insider Trading Before Accounting Scandals (March 1, 2008). EFA 2008 Athens Meetings Paper. Available at SSRN: http://ssrn.com/abstract=929413.

Agrawal, Anup, and Tareque Nasser. Insider Trading in Takeover Targets. July 15, 2010. Available at SSRN: http://ssrn.com/abstract=1517373.

Bettis, J. C., J. L. Coles, and M. L. Lemmon. 2000. Corporate policies restricting trading by insiders. *Journal of Financial Economics* 57, 191–220.

Biesta, Mathijs A., Ronald Q. Doeswijk, and Han A. Donker. September 2003. The Profitability of Insider Trades in the Dutch Stock Market. Available at SSRN: http://ssrn.com/abstract=498042.

Brochet, F. 2010. Information content of insider trades before and after the Sarbanes-Oxley act. *Accounting Review* 85 (2): 419.

Cheuk, M.-Y., D. K. Fan, and R. W. So. 2006. Insider trading in Hong Kong: Some stylized facts. *Pacific-Basin Finance Journal* 14 (1): 73–90.

Del Brío, Esther, Alberto De Miguel, and Javier Perote (n.d.). Insider Trading in the Spanish Stock Market. EFMA 2001 Lugano Meetings. Available at SSRN: http://ssrn.com/abstract=267011.

Dymke, Bjoern M., and Andreas Walter. (2008). Insider trading in Germany—Do corporate insiders exploit inside information? July 13, 2007. 2nd Annual Conference on Empirical Legal Studies Paper; *BuR Business Research Journal*, 1 (2) December 2008. Available at SSRN: http://ssrn.com/abstract=956066.

Eckbo, B. E., and D. C. Smith. 1998. The conditional performance of insider trades. *Journal of Finance* 53 (2): 467–498.

Emanuele Bajo, Barbara Petracci. 2006. Do what insiders do: Abnormal performances after the release of insiders' relevant transactions. *Studies in Economics and Financ*, 23 (2): 94–118.

Etebari, Ahmad, Alireza Tourani-Rad, and Aaron Gilbert. 2004. Disclosure regulation and the profitability of insider trading: Evidence from New Zealand. *Pacific-Basin Finance Journal* 12 (5): 479–502.

Greenblatt, Joel. 1997. *You can be a stock market genius: Uncover the secret hiding places of stock market profits.* New York: Simon & Schuster.

Gregory, A., J. Matatko, I. Tonks, and R. Purkis. 1994. U.K. directors' trading: The impact of dealings in smaller firms. *Economic Journal* 104: 37–53.

Hsieh, Jim, Lilian K. Ng, and Qinghai Wang. April 12, 2005. How Informative are Analyst Recommendations and Insider Trades? AFA 2006 Boston Meetings Paper. Available at SSRN: http://ssrn.com/abstract=687584.

Jaffe, Jeffrey F. 1974. Special information and insider trading. *The Journal of Business* 47: 410–428.

Jagolinzer, Alan D. Sec Rule 10b5–1 and insiders' strategic trade. February 1, 2009. Management Science, February 2009. Available at SSRN: http://ssrn.com/abstract=541502 or doi:10.2139/ssrn.541502.

Jeng, Leslie A., Andrew Metrick, and Richard Zeckhauser. May 2003. Estimating the returns to insider trading: A performance-evaluation perspective. *The Review of Economics and Statistics* 85 (2): 453.

Ke, Bin, Steven J. Huddart, and Kathy R. Petroni. March 2002. What insiders know about future earnings and how they use it: Evidence from insider trades. Available at SSRN: http://ssrn.com/abstract=278055.

Lakonishok, J., and I. Lee. Spring 2001. Are insider trades informative, *The review of financial studies* 14 (1): 79.

Li, Oliver Zhen, and Yuan Zhang. October 2006. Financial restatement announcements and insider trading. Available at SSRN: http://ssrn.com/abstract=929539.

Liu, Crocker H., and David Yermack. October 17, 2007. Where are the shareholders' mansions? CEOs' home purchases, stock sales, and subsequent company performance. Available at SSRN: http://ssrn.com/abstract=970413.

Lorie, James H., and Victor Niederhoffer. April 1968. Predictive and statistical properties of insider trading. *Journal of Law and Economics* 11: 35–51.

Seyhun, H. Nejat. 1986. Insiders' profits, cost of trading, and market efficiency, *Journal of Financial Economics* 16: 189–212.

Seyhun, N. 1988. The information content of aggregate insider trading. *Journal of Business* 61: 1–24.

Sias, Richard W., and David A. Whidbee. October 20, 2008. Insider trades and demand by institutional and individual investors Available at SSRN: http://ssrn.com/abstract=917140.

Wisniewski, T. P., and M. T. Bohl. 2005. The information content of registered insider trading under lax law enforcement. *International Review of Law and Economics* 25 (2): 169–185.

Zingg, Andreas, Sebastian Lang, and Daniela Wyttenbach. January 2007. Insider trading in the Swiss stock market Available at SSRN: http://ssrn.com/abstract=1091348.

Go to http://hema.zacks.com for abstracts and links to papers.

CHAPTER 8

Momentum: The Technical Analysis Anomaly

Lee M. Dunham

Technical analysis, or charting, has a long history in finance. In this chapter, we take an in-depth look at some of the numerous academic studies completed over the past century that have investigated the profitability of various trading strategies based on past price patterns. As we will find out, the general consensus among these past studies is that two interesting patterns in stock returns tend to surface from the data over time: short-term to medium-term momentum, and long-term reversals. Momentum in stock returns is generally described as the continuation of those stocks that have performed well recently to do well over the subsequent 1–12 months. On the contrary, long-term reversals refer to the pattern of winning (loser) stocks tending to become losers (winners) in the long run, usually 3–5 years.

Readers of the chapter who are traders will be happy to learn that hedge portfolios based on short-term and medium-term momentum generate average returns of about 1% per month, or 12% annually. To arrive at this return estimate, researchers use past return data to simply sort stocks into deciles based on their recent return performance (typically measured over the prior 6 months) and then assess the relative performance of these decile portfolios over a subsequent holding period, ranging anywhere from one to twelve months. In summary, most past studies reveal that the top decile portfolio (the set of stocks that were the best performers over the recent past) tend to continue to outperform, and the bottom decile (the set of stocks that were the worst performers over the recent past) continue to be losers. Therefore, researchers suggest the optimal strategy is to create a hedge portfolio by taking a long position in the top decile (recent winners) and a short position in the bottom decile (recent losers); this long-short hedge portfolio generates an average return of about 1% per month over holding periods ranging from 1 to 12 months. As we will see, these returns typically continue to be statistically positive even after controlling for risk.

For those readers of the chapter who have a longer-term time horizon, we document that long-short hedge portfolios based on long-term reversals also tend to generate statistically positive returns. To assess the profitability of trading strategies based on long-term reversals, researchers again sort stocks into deciles based on their past return performance (typically measured over a longer period, such as the past 3 years), and then assess the relative performance of these decile portfolios over a longer-term holding period, ranging anywhere from 3 to 5 years. Contrary to the short-term momentum findings, these past studies document that the bottom decile portfolio (the set of stocks that were the worst past performers) tend to reverse this past poor performance and become winners, and the top decile (the set of stocks that were the best past performers) tend to reverse and become losers. These empirical findings suggest the optimal strategy is to create a hedge portfolio by taking a long position in the bottom decile (recent losers) and shorting the top decile (recent winners). Past studies document an average return from such a strategy of about 7% per year over a holding period of 3 years. Interestingly though, recent research has suggested these returns become statistically insignificant after controlling for risk.

To offer a preview of the empirical evidence relating to momentum found in this chapter, Figure 8.1 illustrates the cumulative dollar returns for 2 momentum strategies during the 1970–2008 time period. For the short-term momentum series, at the end of each *month* during the 1970–2008 time period, stocks are sorted into deciles based on their return performance over the past 10 months. Then, the performance of a long-short, equally weighted hedge portfolio, defined as the return difference between the top (best performing) and bottom (worst performing) deciles, is evaluated over the following *month*. The cumulative dollar return illustrated in Figure 8.1 depicts the growth of $1 invested in such a strategy starting in January 1970. Of course, this simple illustration assumes monthly portfolio rebalancing, which, of course, may be cost prohibitive; however, the point here is to illustrate that such a strategy delivers positive returns over time.

Results for the medium-term momentum strategy illustrated in Figure 8.1 are formulated in a similar manner. At the end of each *year* during the 1970–2008 time period, stocks are sorted into deciles based on their return performance over the past 10 months. Then, the performance of a long-short, equally weighted hedge portfolio, defined as the return difference between the top (best performing) and bottom (worst performing) deciles, is evaluated over the following *year*. Even though both strategies are highly

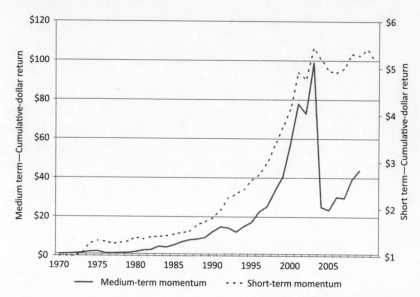

FIGURE 8.1 Short-Term and Medium-Term Momentum-Based Strategy 1970–2008
Data Source: Kenneth French's Data Library.

correlated, the cumulative returns are quite different in scale. Also, there is a period of time during the 2003–2005 period when both the short-term and long-term momentum strategies did not perform well. However, when taken in aggregate, Figure 8.1 clearly illustrates the positive return performance over time generated by the 2 momentum strategies.

Figure 8.2 shows a similar graph for a long-term reversal strategy. For the short-term momentum series, at the end of each *year* during the 1970–2008 time period, stocks are sorted into deciles based on their return performance over the past *four years*. Then, the performance of a long-short, equally weighted hedge portfolio, defined as the return difference between the bottom (worst performing) and top (best performing) deciles, is evaluated over the following *year*. The cumulative dollar return illustrated in Figure 8.2 depicts the growth of $1 invested in such a strategy starting in January 1970. The results in Figure 8.2 illustrate the positive return performance over time generated by the long-term reversal strategy. It should be noted that whereas the returns for the reversal strategy in Figure 8.2 are based on a 1-year holding period, as previously noted, past studies tend to examine returns of long-term reversal strategies over longer holding periods, such as 3 to 5 years. As we will find out, the results from such studies tend to reveal a positive return pattern similar to that in Figure 8.2. We now take a look back into the history of technical analysis.

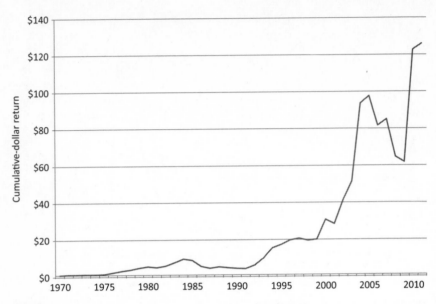

FIGURE 8.2   Long-Term Reversal-Based Strategy 1970–2008

Data Source: Kenneth French's Data Library.

History of Technical Analysis and Momentum

Technical analysis has deep roots in finance. If stock prices either overreact or underreact to information, then successful trading strategies that select stocks based on past returns will exist, and pursuing such strategies may be profitable. Traditionally defined as the process of detecting patterns in stock prices in order to predict future prices, many have used technical analysis extensively in an attempt to develop trading rules and strategies to beat the market for over 50 years. More specifically, Lo et al. (2000) succinctly state: "The general goal of technical analysis is to identify regularities in the time series of prices by extracting nonlinear patterns from noisy data." This chapter provides a synthesis of the technical analysis literature, starting with a brief history of technical analysis. The chapter then offers a detailed discussion of momentum and reversal anomalies found in financial markets.

Technical analysis dates back to the end of the twentieth century with the work of Charles Dow, who many consider to be the founding father of modern technical analysis. As the founder and editor of the *Wall Street Journal* (*WSJ*) before his death in 1902, Dow described his views on using the rails and industrials averages to assist in identifying trends and speculation through a series of *WSJ* editorials. Interestingly, Dow actually never explicitly presented his ideas as a trading tool. After his death, William P.

Hamilton, who was an understudy of Dow at the *WSJ* and assumed the role of editorship of the *WSJ* after Dow's death, began the development of Dow theory. In short, Dow theory describes various market movements, trends, and definitive signals given by the observed relationship between the industrials average and the rails average. Hamilton authored his own series of *WSJ* and *Barron's* editorials on Dow theory and eventually he published his Dow theory ideas in a book called *The Stock Market Barometer*. After Hamilton's death in 1930, Robert Rhea and E. George Schaefer went on to expound on the Dow theory over the following 20 years. Today, the theory is still used by market participants where the transports average is now used in lieu of the original rails average.

About this same time, a young trader, W. D. Gann, was honing his own charting strategy. In November 1928, Gann famously predicted the market crash of September 1929 in his supply and demand letter entitled "1929 Annual Stock Forecast" by charting cycles using his strategy of overlaying angles to charts to detect price patterns. Years later, in 1935, he would publish the details of his charting strategy in "The Basis of My Forecasting Method," in which he insisted on inspecting angles when price and time were in a 1:1 ratio. A few years later, in 1938, Ralph Nelson Elliott published "The Wave Principle," in which he proposed that historic stock prices follow specific patterns, or waves, thus allowing for the prediction of future prices. This early technical analysis served as a springboard for additional charting theories. In the 1950s, trading based on technical analysis grew in popularity with the help of pioneers like Gerald Tsai and Walter Deemer whose funds were profiting handsomely via chart-based strategies. In 1964, Edmund Tabell and Anthony Tabell published their article "The Case for Technical Analysis" further supporting the usage of charting strategies and advocating their utility to predict future returns.

Just as these strategies were becoming more developed, technical analysis hit a brick wall. In 1970, Eugene Fama stated very clearly, in "Efficient Capital Markets: A Review of Theory and Empirical Work," that academics agreed that the market was "weakly efficient" and that there were no patterns in past prices that could be used to predict future prices. Many articles, including Jensen (1978), Kemp and Reid (1971), and Grossman (1976), supported Fama's position in the 1970s. In 1973, Burton Malkiel further eschewed charting by writing "under scientific scrutiny, chart reading must share a pedestal with alchemy" in his now-famous *A Random Walk Down Wall Street*. There were the occasional voices of support throughout the 1980s including an article by Pruitt and White (1988); however, charting remained more of an outlying strategy. In the 1980s, John Bollinger created the concept of Bollinger Bands, which consists of a band plus or minus a certain standard deviation away from a moving average. However, by the 1990s, most professional investors ignored technical analysis although individual investors continued to utilize it. Some brokerage firms employed a lone analyst to produce technical-based stock research as a dwindling pool of investors continued to employ charting strategies such as head-and-shoulders.

A major change in the academic attitude toward technical analysis occurred in August 2000 with the publication of "Foundations of Technical Analysis: Computational Algorithms, Statistical Inference, and Empirical Implementation" by Professor Andrew Lo, Harry Mamaysky, and Jiang Wang (2000) at MIT. This seminal paper utilized highly sophisticated statistical techniques to analyze the more subjective geometric shapes and patterns characteristic of technical analysis. By finding that several technical indicators do, in fact, have practical value, the language of technical analysis changed from support and resistance to positive and negative autocorrelation and effectively shifted the paradigm from the old world of technical analysis into the new, academically respectable regime of momentum and reversal anomalies. Effectively, the work of Lo et al. (2000) acted as a translation of the charting language into an academic language.

Assessing Momentum and Reversal in Stock Prices

The assessment of momentum and reversals in stock prices in early studies of stock price behavior was mostly based on serial autocorrelation tests and other empirical tests of time-series data. More recently, the assessment of momentum and reversals in stock prices has actually become a somewhat standardized process starting with the influential work of DeBondt and Thaler (1985) and Jegadeesh and Titman (1993, 2001). In general, momentum and reversals in stock prices is evaluated by sorting stocks into portfolios based on their past return performance and then evaluating the future performance of these portfolios. Although the process of forming winner and loser portfolios to assess momentum and reversals in stock prices is fairly standardized in the literature, the decisions of how to construct the winner and loser portfolios (equally weighted vs. value-weighted) and how to measure risk-adjusted return performance (CAPM, Fama-French 3-factor risk models) remain topics of debate. However, in most of the subsequent work to be discussed in this chapter, the portfolio formation process can be summarized as follows: Sort stocks into winner and loser portfolios on the basis of past returns over the past J months and then hold the portfolios for K months.

More precisely, the J-month/K-month strategy is constructed as follows: At the beginning of each month, stocks are ranked in ascending order on the basis of their past returns over the past J months. Based on these rankings, equally weighted decile portfolios are constructed; the decile portfolio with the highest return is called the winner portfolio, and the portfolio with the lowest return is called the loser portfolio. A momentum (reversal) portfolio is then created by buying (shorting) the winner portfolio and shorting (buying) the loser portfolio and then evaluating the performance of this zero-cost, long-short portfolio over the next K months. So, for example, a 6/6 momentum strategy is a momentum strategy that sorts stocks based on their past 6-month returns and creates a long-short portfolio by buying the winner portfolio and shorting the loser portfolio (as defined earlier) and holding the position for 6 months. Similarly, a 1/12 momentum strategy is one that sorts stocks based on past 1-month returns, buys the winner portfolio and shorts the loser portfolio, and holds the long-short portfolio for 1 year. Lastly, a 36/36 reversal strategy is one that sorts stocks based on past 3-year returns, buys the loser portfolio, and shorts the winner portfolio, and holds the long-short portfolio for 3 years. In more recent studies, research has focused on trying to improve on this J-month/K-month strategy, such as skipping a week between the J-month ranking period and the K-month evaluation period, using sorts other than deciles (e.g., the top 30% and the bottom 30%), and even conditioning the strategy on a firm characteristic, such as trading volume or idiosyncratic volatility.

Early Influential Work on Momentum and Reversals

Perhaps the seminal study of patterns in stock prices was the work of DeBondt and Thaler (1985) who examine patterns in individual stock prices. The authors find strong evidence that recent good performing stocks become poor performers over 3-year and 5-year holdings and vice versa. Using data from January 1933 to December 1980, DeBondt and Thaler (1985) sort stocks based on their prior 36-month abnormal returns and form winner and loser portfolios that consist of the best performing decile and worst performing decile, respectively. The authors then examine the subsequent long-term performance of these 2 portfolios over the next 36 months (essentially a 36/36 reversal strategy). DeBondt and Thaler (1985) find that the loser portfolio cumulatively outperforms the winner portfolio by an average of 24.6% for the 36 months after portfolio formation. Interestingly, most of this abnormal performance (19.6%) comes from the reversal of the prior poor performance of the loser's portfolio stocks while the winner's portfolio underperforms (−5.0%). In fact, the difference in return performance between the loser portfolio and winner portfolio generally increases with the length of the holding period. Also, the results are not driven by the choice of sorting on 36-month prior returns or the 36-month holding period; similar results also hold for 5-year ranking and holding periods. The authors interpret these results as evidence that stock prices exhibit persistent long-run reversals and find the results consistent with experimental psychology studies, which suggest that most people overreact to unexpected and dramatic news events.

One implication of the work of DeBondt and Thaler (1985) is that a zero-cost strategy of shorting the winner portfolio and using the short proceeds to buy the loser portfolio earns a very large abnormal return with minimal investment. Interestingly, DeBondt and Thaler (1985) show that their contrarian strategy results of buying losers and selling winners is insensitive to the choice of the then-accepted models of abnormal returns (CAPM and Sharpe-Lintner) and to the choice of using the month of December to sort stocks into portfolios.

In summary, DeBondt and Thaler conclude that the difference in returns for these two portfolios was due to overreaction in security prices as the extreme losers become too cheap and bounce back, whereas the extreme winners become too expensive and earn lower subsequent returns. In a more exhaustive follow-up study, DeBondt and Thaler (1987) continue to find evidence of long-term reversals in individual stock returns. Again, the empirical evidence here strongly suggests that stock prices exhibit long-run reversals.

Poterba and Summers (1988) examine stock price behavior and find evidence of momentum over short horizons and reversals over longer horizons. Using annual data from 1871 to 1985 and monthly return data from 1926 to 1985, the authors utilize variance ratio tests and reject the hypothesis that stock prices follow a random walk, which, of course, implies stock price predictability. Specifically, the authors find evidence that stock prices tend to exhibit positive autocorrelation (or momentum) over shorter periods (less than one year) and negative autocorrelation (or reversals) over longer horizons. Of course, the evidence of negative autocorrelation in stock prices documented by the authors is consistent with the earlier findings of DeBondt and Thaler (1985, 1987). Interestingly, Poterba and Summers (1988) also examine mostly post–World War II monthly return data from 17 other equity markets and find that the stock returns of most of these markets exhibit similar time-series properties.

At the start of the 1990s, there was fairly compelling empirical evidence that stock prices exhibited long-run reversals and some evidence of short-term negative autocorrelation. At this time, studies of stock price behavior began to focus on short-term predictability. This line of research, focused on short-term price behavior, began with the work of Jegadeesh (1990) and Lehmann (1990) who examine stock return predictability over very short time horizons of one week to one month. Using monthly return data from January 1929 to December 1982, Jegadeesh (1990) performs serial autocorrelation tests and finds that the first-order autocorrelation in monthly stock returns is negative and statistically significant, whereas autocorrelation is positive at longer lags. These results suggest that returns exhibit reversals within 1 month but exhibit momentum over time horizons of 2 months to 1 year. Furthermore, these results hold even after controlling for firm size. Lehmann (1990), using data from January 1962 to December 1986, examines weekly returns and finds that portfolios of securities that earned positive returns in one week typically earned negative returns the following week and vice versa. The author shows that a zero-cost strategy of buying the loser portfolio and shorting the winner portfolio generates a positive return about 90% of the time.

Jegadeesh and Titman (1993) perform an analysis similar to DeBondt and Thaler (1985) but with a focus on a shorter-term investment horizon. Using data from January 1965 to December 1989, Jegadeesh and Titman sort stocks into winner and loser decile portfolios based on their returns over the past 1, 2, 3, or 4 quarters; then they examine the subsequent performance of these 2 portfolios over holding periods varying from 1 to 4 quarters (a total of 16 momentum strategies ranging from a 1/1 strategy to a 12/12 strategy). The authors also examine the same 16 momentum strategies but with a slight variation; sort the stocks into winners and losers portfolios but defer the start of the holding period by one week.

Interestingly, unlike the long-term reversal trends found by DeBondt and Thaler (1985, 1987), the authors find evidence of short-term momentum; that is, the winner portfolio continues to outperform the loser portfolio over time horizons of 3 months to a year. For the 12/3 strategy, the winner portfolio outperforms the loser portfolio by an average of 1.31% per month over the 3-month holding period. The same strategy but with the one-week lag increases the winner's outperformance to 1.49% per month over the 3 months.

When forming the winners and losers portfolios based on the return performance over the past 6 months ($J = 6$ months), the winner portfolio outperforms the loser portfolio by about 1% per month irrespective of the length of the holding period ($K = 1, 2, 3$ or 4 months). So, this evidence of short-term momentum in stock returns appears to be robust to the choice of the ranking period length or the length of the holding period. In general, Jegadeesh and Titman (1993) show that, over holding periods of 3–12 months, stocks that performed well over the previous 3–12 months continued to outperform over the next 3–12 months. More importantly, irrespective of the ranking period length and holding period length, a zero-cost strategy of shorting the loser portfolio and going long the winner portfolio earns, statistically, positive returns. Also, the authors show that the outperformance of the winner's portfolio over the loser's portfolio continues to hold after controlling for firm size (both large and small stocks exhibit momentum return patterns) and also when using risk-adjusted returns (using the CAPM model).

The authors conclude that, even after considering a one-way transaction cost of 0.5%, the 6/6 momentum strategy results in a risk-adjusted, annualized return of 9.29%. Interestingly, most of this abnormal performance comes from the continued strong performance of the winner portfolio and less from the performance of the loser portfolio. This finding of the winner portfolio driving the performance of the zero-cost long-short portfolio is in stark contrast to the findings of DeBondt and Thaler (1985) where the reversal of the loser portfolio mostly drove the outperformance of the long-short portfolio.

In a follow-up study, Jegadeesh and Titman (2001) show that the momentum strategies of buying the winner portfolio and shorting the loser portfolio continue to be profitable using data from January 1990 to December 1998. Similar to their 1993 study, Jegadeesh and Titman sort stocks into winner and loser decile portfolios that consists of the best performing and worst performing deciles, respectively, based on their shorter past return performance. This time, the authors sort stocks into winner and loser portfolios based only on their returns over the past 6 months, then examine the subsequent performance of these two portfolios over a 6-month holding period (6/6 strategy). The results show that the winner portfolio outperforms the loser portfolio by 1.39% per month over the 6-month holding period; again, most of the outperformance is due to the continued performance of the winner portfolio. Using the whole sample period of January 1965 to December 1998, the winner portfolio outperforms the loser portfolio by a significant 1.23% per month over the 6-month holding period. These results continue to hold after controlling for size (both large and small stocks exhibit momentum return patterns) and risk (using CAPM or the Fama-French 3-factor model). In fact, the Fama-French 3-factor risk-adjusted return of 1.36% per month is actually higher than the raw return difference of 1.23%. Interestingly, for some subsamples of the data and depending on the choice of raw returns or risk-adjusted returns, Jegadeesh and Titman (2001) find that the momentum profits do tend to dissipate over time when the holding period is extended beyond a year. However, the momentum profits documented for holding periods less than a year are insensitive to the choice of subsample period and whether one uses raw returns or risk-adjusted returns.

Hong, Lim, and Stein (2000) construct momentum portfolios in a very similar way to those of Jegadeesh and Titman (1993). However, rather than focusing on the extreme top and bottom deciles when ranking stocks and categorizing winner and loser portfolios, Hong et al. (2000) evaluate a 6/6 momentum strategy where the winner and loser portfolios are characterized as the best and worst performing thirtieth percentiles, respectively. Using data from January 1980 to December 1996, the authors document that this long-short, zero-cost momentum portfolio generates a monthly return of 0.53% per month over the 6-month holding period. The authors then sort the stocks into deciles by firm size as measured by market capitalization and find an inverted U-shaped pattern to momentum returns across the deciles; momentum returns for long-short momentum portfolios appear to be nonexistent for the smallest and largest stocks but significantly positive for medium-sized stocks. Interestingly, most of the momentum profits across the size deciles comes from the loser portfolio. This is in stark contrast to the results of Jegadeesh and Titman (1993, 2001) who document that the winner portfolio was mostly responsible for momentum returns. Hong et al. (2000) also sort the stocks into 3 categories based on analyst coverage: top 30%, middle 40%, and bottom 30%. Comparing the top and bottom 30%, the authors find that momentum returns are statistically larger for stocks with lower analyst coverage. Hong et al. (2000) also investigate momentum returns after double-sorting stocks into firm size classes and the same 3 analyst coverage categories. As one moves progressively from small to large size classes, the overall momentum effect shrinks, and the difference in momentum returns between the low and high analyst categories tend to shrink as well. The authors suggest these results to be consistent with the notion that momentum stems from gradual information flow.

Returning to the famous study of Lo, Mamaysky, and Wang (2000), which we mentioned earlier, we note that the authors develop a pattern-recognition algorithm by utilizing a smoothing technique known as non-parametric kernel regression to identify nonlinear patterns in the time series of prices. In attempting to develop a systematic approach to pattern detection, Lo et al. (2000) are trying to address the fact that most technical patterns "observed" by practitioners are fairly subjective; that is, even the most commonly accepted patterns such as head-and-shoulders are not uniformly defined. What one trader sees as a clear head-and-shoulders pattern is merely noise to another trader. By making the pattern detection process more systematic, the authors attempt to standardize the more common price patterns used by traders by removing some of the subjective elements inherent in pattern detection.

The authors use this systematic approach to detect technical patterns in individual stock prices using data from January 1962 to December 1996. Specifically, the authors focus their efforts on 10 commonly used technical patterns: head-and-shoulders, inverse head-and-shoulders, broadening tops and bottoms, triangle tops and bottoms, rectangle tops and bottoms, and double tops and bottoms. The authors break the 1962–1996 sample period into seven 5-year subsample periods (1962–1966, 1967–1971, etc.) and, in each subsample period, randomly select 10 stocks from each of 5 market-capitalization quintiles. This sampling process results in a total of 50 stocks in each subsample across the 7 subsample periods. To determine whether the pattern detection methodology actually provides useful information to traders, the authors compare the return distribution conditional on the occurrence of a particular pattern with the corresponding unconditional return distribution. In summary, Lo et al. (2000) document that certain technical patterns, when applied over multiple time periods, do appear to offer incremental information that can be used to add to the investment process. It is important to note that the authors' assessment of the informativeness of technical trading is not a measure of profitability; that is, although their results suggest that technical trading can aid the investment process, they did not assess the profitability of such trading rules. Interestingly, in a discussion article of Lo et al. (2000), Jegadeesh (2000) shows that the trading rules developed by Lo et al. (2000) are actually not statistically profitable. Regardless, it is generally accepted that the work of Lo, Mamaysky, and Wang (2000) transformed the consensus opinion of academics on technical trading from one of general disbelief to a respectable regime of momentum and reversal anomalies.

Could the momentum and reversal trends found in these past studies be explained by the risk of such trading strategies? In an important paper, Fama and French (1996) document that their now famed 3-factor risk model fully explains the long-term reversals documented in past studies; however, their model cannot fully explain medium-term momentum. That is, Fama and French (1996) conclude that, after controlling for risk, returns from long-term reversal strategies become insignificant but momentum strategies remain profitable on a risk-adjusted basis.

Improving Upon Momentum Strategies

As with any investment strategy, practitioners and academics continue to search over the various momentum strategies put forth in the literature to see if they can be improved. Arena, Haggard, and Yan (2008) suggest that momentum-based returns are highest when trading high idiosyncratic volatility (iVol) stocks. IVol is specifically defined as the standard deviation of the residual when regressing the returns of an individual stock on the returns of the broader market and is used as a proxy to measure underreaction to firm-specific information.

Using data from January 1965 to December 2002, Arena et al. (2008) construct momentum portfolios utilizing the aforementioned strategy of Jegadeesh and Titman (2001). The authors sort stocks into winner and loser portfolios based on their returns over the past 6 months, and then examine the subsequent performance of these two portfolios over a 6-month holding period (6/6 strategy). To test whether momentum profits are related to iVol, the authors first sort the sample of stocks based on iVol into 3 portfolios: low iVol, medium iVol, and high iVol. Within each iVol portfolio, the stocks are then sorted into deciles based on their past 6-month returns following Jegadeesh and Titman (2001). The top return decile is considered the winner's portfolio and the lowest return decile is deemed the loser's portfolio. A momentum portfolio is then constructed within each iVol portfolio by buying the winner's portfolio and shorting the loser's portfolio, and the performance of this zero-cost, long-short portfolio is then evaluated over a 6-month holding. Arena et al. (2008) find that the momentum returns from these 3 long-short portfolios conditional on iVol and past returns are all statistically significant, and increase monotonically across the iVol portfolios, moving from a 0.55% monthly return for the low iVol portfolio to a 1.43% monthly return for the high iVol portfolio. The incremental monthly return of 0.88% (10.56% annually) provided by the high iVol portfolio is both statistically and economically significant. On a risk-adjusted basis using the Fama-French 3-factor model, the authors show that the difference in abnormal return between the high iVol portfolio (1.62% monthly abnormal return) and the low iVol portfolio (0.65% monthly abnormal return) is 0.97% per month over the 6-month holding period, which is actually larger than the raw return difference of 0.88%.

To be sure that iVol is the key variable driving the momentum results and not some other firm characteristics, Arena et al. (2008) examine results that control for size, share price, turnover, beta, price delay, and distress risk. Ultimately, each test shows that the results are not influenced by any of the aforementioned factors. In addition, the authors test 15 alternative momentum strategies with various ranking period and holding period lengths. For each strategy, the momentum returns of the high minus low iVol portfolios were all positive, and 12 were statistically significant. As a final robustness check, the authors also examine slightly different measures of iVol, and their main results are essentially unchanged. Arena et al. (2008) ultimately conclude that a momentum-based trading strategy with stocks conditioned on iVol can yield incrementally higher momentum returns.

Vassalou and Apedjinou (2004) document a strong relationship between price momentum and a variable they define as corporate innovation. Corporate innovation (CI) is defined as the proportion of a firm's change in gross profit margin that is not explained by the change in growth in labor and capital it utilizes. In short, the authors find that portfolios sorted on the basis of corporate innovation have very similar properties to those sorted on the basis of past returns.

Using data from January 1967 to December 2002, the authors construct momentum portfolios following the methodology and Jegadeesh and Titman (2001) by sorting stocks based on the corporate innovation variable as measured over the past 2 quarters. The authors construct portfolios of buying the winner high-CI decile and shorting the loser low-CI decile, and holding the portfolio for a 6-month period. The average monthly return of the zero-cost, long-short portfolio is 0.76% per month over the 6-month holding period. To facilitate comparison, the authors also compute the momentum returns for the Jegadeesh and Titman (2001) 6/6 strategy and find it earns a monthly return of 0.57%. Also, the authors find that momentum returns are positive and significant for a host of other momentum strategies. However, the authors document that the momentum returns decline as the holding period increases. This result is similar to previous studies indicating that momentum profits tend to dissipate over longer-term horizons as mean reversion in prices begins to take shape. Regardless, Vassalou and Apedjinou (2004) find that the winner's (loser's) portfolio based on the highest (lowest) past returns are also firms with the highest (lowest) levels of corporate innovation.

Moving Averages

In a very early paper, Levy (1967) suggested that a simple trading rule that buys stocks with prices that are substantially higher than their average price over the past 27 months is very profitable on a risk-adjusted basis. Although Jensen and Bennington (1970) later argued that the trading rule suggested by Levy was a result of data mining and did not outperform a buy-and-hold strategy out of sample, the use of moving averages has become a focal point of practitioners over time as a means of predicting future return performance. In essence, the momentum strategy of Jegadeesh and Titman (1993, 2001) is a moving-average-based strategy where stocks are ranked based on performance.

Reilly and Norton (2003) suggest a trading rule that assesses the relationship between a stock's short-term moving average and its long-term moving average. Specifically, they develop a trading rule by which stocks are bought when the short-term moving average line crosses the long-term moving average line from below and sell stocks when the short-term moving average line crosses the long-term moving average line from above. In a more recent paper, Park (2010) follows this logic and documents that the ratio of short-term to long-term moving averages has a meaningful amount of predictive power for future returns. Park (2010) shows that the 50-day/200-day moving average ratio is an actual improvement over the momentum strategies of Jegadeesh and Titman (1993) and George and Hwang (2004).

Using data from January 1964 to December 2004, Park (2010) sorts stocks based on the 50-day/200-day moving average ratio, and those stocks with ratios in the top decile (or top thirtieth percentile) are deemed winners whereas stocks with ratios in the bottom decile (or bottom thirtieth percentile) are labeled losers. The performance of this zero-cost, long-short portfolio is then evaluated over a 6-month holding period similar to Jegadeesh and Titman (2001). Park finds that when using decile portfolios, on a raw return basis, the long-short, moving-average ratio momentum strategy generates 1.45% per month over the 6-month holding period: 1.81% per month for the winners and 0.36% per month for the losers. To facilitate comparison, Park (2010) reports that the Jegadeesh and Titman (2001) and the George and Hwang (2004) momentum strategies earn 1.23% per month (1.72% for the winners and 0.49% for the losers) and 1.15% per month (1.43% for the winners and 0.28% for the losers), respectively, over the 6-month holding period. Thus, Park's (2010) moving average momentum strategy outperforms both the Jegadeesh and Titman (1993) and the George and Hwang (2004) momentum strategies on both the winner and loser sides of the trade, although only the differences on the winner side of the trade are statistically significant. However, when using the thirtieth percentile portfolios, none of the differences in performance for the 3 momentum strategies are statistically significant.

On a risk-adjusted basis, using the Fama-French 3-factor model, Park's (2010) long-short, moving average momentum strategy generates a 1.64% per month return over the 6-month holding period, which is actually higher than the raw return of 1.45% per month. This risk-adjusted return is higher than the risk-adjusted monthly returns of 1.40% and 1.64%, for the Jegadeesh and Titman (1993) and the George and Hwang (2004) momentum strategies, respectively. Also, the moving average ratio momentum strategy used by Park (2010) also appears to be robust to using other measures of the moving average ratio; that is, momentum profits remain if the 1-day, 5-day, 20-day, or 50-day moving average is used as the short-term moving average and if the 250-day moving average is used as the long-term moving average. To determine which strategy has higher predictive power for future returns, Park (2010) double-sorts each of the momentum strategies by comparing two strategies at a time and extracting one portfolio's variable within the other portfolio's quintiles. Results lead Park (2010) to conclude that the moving-average ratio variable is the strongest predictor of future returns.

52-Week High/Low

Another of the techniques used by technical traders is to compare a stock's current price to its 52-week high and low. This was tested by George and Hwang (2004) who developed a strategy that selects stocks based on the ratio of the current price relative to its past 52-week high. Using data from January 1963 to December 2001, the authors sort stocks monthly based on this ratio, and those stocks with ratios in the top thirtieth percentile are deemed winners whereas stocks with ratios in the bottom thirtieth percentile are labeled losers. The authors construct a zero-cost momentum portfolio by buying the winner portfolio and shorting the losers portfolio, and evaluate the performance of the portfolio over a 6-month holding period similar to Jegadeesh and Titman (2001). Results show that the long-short portfolio generates 0.45% per month, with the winner's portfolio average return of 1.51% being about 50% more than the loser's portfolio average return of 1.06%. To facilitate comparison, George and Hwang (2004) show that this monthly return is in line with the 0.48% average monthly return generated by the long-short momentum strategy of Jegadeesh and Titman (2001). George and Hwang (2004) also demonstrate that the nearness to the past 52-week high price is a better predictor for future returns than the past 6-month return used by Jegadeesh and Titman (2001). Lastly, the return from this 52-week high momentum strategy does not reverse in the long run, as was the case in the results of Jegadeesh and Titman (1993, 2001).

Momentum at Industry Levels

There have been some studies put forth in the literature to suggest that the momentum found in individual stock returns may actually be industry driven. Moskowitz and Grinblatt (1999) suggest that the momentum effect over intermediate holding periods (6–12 months) is stronger when viewed by industry rather than by individual stocks and conclude that momentum in individual stock returns is actually driven by momentum in industry returns. Using monthly data from July 1963 to July 1995, the authors form 20 value-weighted industry portfolios based on 2-digit standard industrial classification (SIC) codes. Similar to Jegadeesh and Titman (1993), the authors rank industry portfolios based on their past 6-month returns and then create zero-cost, long-short portfolios by buying the top 3 winner industries and shorting the bottom 3 loser industries. The authors find that industry portfolios exhibit significant momentum, and industry-based momentum strategies are more profitable than strategies that are based on individual stocks. Interestingly, Moskowitz and Grinblatt (1999) find that momentum in individual stock returns is weak and insignificant after adjusting for industry momentum. Another interesting finding here is that the profitability of industry momentum appears to be driven by the winner's portfolio whereas the bulk of momentum profits from individual stocks in their sample is driven by the losers portfolio. Similar to the findings of Jegadeesh and Titman (1993), when looking out over longer time horizons, the authors find that most of this short-term momentum is reversed for both industry returns and individual stock returns.

O'Neal (2000) also suggests that intermediate-term momentum in individual stocks is driven by the performance of its industry. To investigate further, the author explores trading strategies utilizing industry-sector mutual funds using data from May 1989 to April 1999 provided by 31 Fidelity Select Portfolios sector funds. The author follows the methodology of Jegadeesh and Titman (1993) and examines a host of momentum strategies that consider ranking and holding period lengths of 3, 6, and 12 months.

First, the author considers a single-fund investment strategy where the 31 sector funds are sorted based on past return and momentum profits of investing only in the best performing fund are examined. So, for example, for the 6/6 strategy, the fund with the best return over the past 6 months is bought and held for 6 months. At the end of the 6-month holding period, the position is sold and the best performing fund over the past 6 months is purchased, and this process is replicated through the sample period to create a series of returns. Results from this analysis confirm the existence of momentum in these sector funds.

O'Neal (2000) also constructs momentum portfolio strategies similar to Moskowitz and Grinblatt (1999) by buying the best performing 3 (or 6) sector funds (high portfolio) and shorting the worst performing 3 (or 6) sector funds (low portfolio). For all ranking and holding periods examined, results show strong evidence of industry momentum with the average difference between high and low portfolios at 8.6% on an annualized basis with the results being a bit stronger when the holding period is 12 months instead of 6 months. One further advantage of the study is that O'Neal (2000) factors transaction costs for these sector funds into the analysis. Ultimately, O'Neal (2000) is able to neatly show via trading in sector mutual funds that industry momentum is prevalent over the intermediate term.

Lewellen (2002) studies momentum in stock returns at the aggregate level with an emphasis on the role of industry, firm size, and the book-to-market factor. The author finds that portfolios created based on size and book-to-market value (BTM) exhibit momentum equally as strong as individual stocks and industry portfolios. Following the methodology of Jegadeesh and Titman (1993), the author examines the profitability of portfolio-based momentum strategies by constructing various portfolios based on individual stock performance, industry performance, size, book-to-market, and also double-sorted size/book-to-market. Using monthly return data from January 1941 (results relating to book-to-market portfolios start in May 1963) to December 1999, the author documents average monthly momentum returns over a 5-month holding period that range from 0.38%–0.41% for industry portfolios, 0.46%–0.53% for size portfolios, and 0.38%–0.50% for size/book-to-market double-sorted portfolios. All these momentum returns are statistically significant. Lewellen (2002) concludes from this analysis that momentum returns cannot be attributed simply to firm-specific returns but rather to macroeconomic factors because portfolio-based analysis essentially eliminates firm-specific risk.

Momentum and Mutual Funds

In a more recent study, Sapp (2010) follows the 52-week high methodology of George and Hwang (2004) to assess the performance of momentum strategies in mutual funds. Using monthly data on a large sample of domestic equity mutual funds from January 1970 to December 2004, the author finds evidence of persistent raw and risk-adjusted momentum returns. Specifically, Sapp (2010) finds that the return performance of a momentum strategy that selects funds based on the ratio of the fund's current NAV relative to its past 52-week high rivals that of the Jegadeesh and Titman (1993, 2001) momentum strategy of selecting funds based on fund return performance over the past 6 months. When sorting funds into winner and loser deciles based on the ratio of current fund NAV relative to its past 52-week high and holding for 6 months, Sapp (2010) finds that the long-short portfolio generates a risk-adjusted return of 0.33% per month, with the winner's portfolio average return of 0.20% earning significantly more than the loser's portfolio average return of −0.13%. To facilitate comparison, the Jegadeesh and Titman (1993, 2001) 6/6 momentum strategy generates a risk-adjusted return of 0.40% per month with the winner decile earning 0.24% per month and the loser decile earning −0.16% per month. Similar results are reported when funds with ratios in the top thirtieth percentile are deemed winners while funds with ratios in the bottom thirtieth percentile are labeled losers.

Sapp (2010) points out that mutual fund shares cannot be shorted and, therefore, constructing the long-short momentum portfolio for mutual funds is merely hypothetical. However, given that most of the risk-adjusted momentum return is generated by the winner decile, the author suggests one can utilize the ratio of the fund's current NAV relative to its past 52-week high to form long-only winner portfolios and generate average annual raw returns of 15.60%, 15.96%, and 15.36%, respectively, for holding periods of 3 months, 6 months, and 12 months, respectively. After adjusting for risk using the Fama-French 3-factor model, these raw returns reduce to 3.72%, 3.60%, and 2.64%, respectively. Lastly, consistent with most previous studies, Sapp (2010) shows that the momentum profits in mutual funds tend to erode as the holding period lengthens and mostly disappear for holding periods longer than a year.

Is Technical Analysis Profitable?

Although trading commissions are generally lower today and are typically based on a fixed-cost structure, these costs were not a trivial amount before the 1990s and were generally on a per-share basis. It was the deregulation of brokerage commissions by the SEC on May 1, 1975, that terminated fixed commissions and allowed commissions to be set by market competition. The deregulation, coupled with the surge in online trading via the Internet during the late 1990s and early 2000s, ultimately led to the cheaper costs of trading we benefit from today.

Large stocks tend to incur less transaction costs than small stocks, mostly due to higher liquidity, and, as a result, lower bid-ask spreads and price-impact costs. Furthermore, commissions on thinly traded stocks may be considerably more than those of their highly liquid counterparts. Accordingly, this would suggest that the profits from momentum-based trading strategies would dissipate more quickly for large stocks in comparison to small stocks. Furthermore, the institutional costs of short-selling stocks would suggest that the profits from a momentum-based strategy of buying recent winners would dissipate more quickly than shorting recent losers. Perhaps the most important question in this literature is whether there are momentum or reversal strategies that can actually be implemented and still be profitable after consideration of transaction costs. That question remains hotly contested as researchers debate how to measure transaction costs.

Recall that, using data from January 1965 to December 1998, Jegadeesh and Titman (2001) document a fairly compelling short-term momentum-based trading strategy that provides an approximate 1.36% per month risk-adjusted return over a 6-month holding period. Even after consideration of one-way 0.5% transaction costs that the authors used in their 1993 paper, this strategy appears profitable. However, Lesmond, Schill, and Zhou (2004) suggest that the measure of transaction costs used by Jegadeesh and Titman (1993) was inadequate. Specifically, the strategy of Jegadeesh and Titman require four trades per 6-month holding period (opening and closing positions for both the winners and losers), and these extreme decile winner's and loser's portfolios consist mostly of relatively illiquid stocks. Thus, Lesmond et al. (2004) argue that the one-way transaction costs of 0.5% are considerably too low. In their work, Lesmond et al. (2004) consider a battery of transaction costs estimates, and their results leave us questioning how much, if any, of that momentum return remains after incorporating adequate transaction costs for implementing such a strategy.

Lesmond et al. (2004) revisit the work of Jegadeesh and Titman (1993, 2001) and Hong, Lim, and Stein (2000) and more vigorously examine the impact of transaction costs on their documented abnormal momentum returns. One interesting finding in the work of Jegadeesh and Titman (2001) was that, when examining large stocks and small stocks separately, the momentum abnormal returns that accrued to small stocks were larger than those of large stocks. That finding is important because small stocks tend to incur more transaction costs than large stocks, mostly due to larger bid-ask spreads for smaller stocks. To assess the impact of trading costs on the momentum returns of Jegadeesh and Titman (1993, 2001), Lesmond et al. (2004) utilize four different methods for estimating transaction costs. The authors document that, for large capitalization stocks, round-trip (entering and unwinding a position) trading-cost estimates are generally between 1% and 2%. For small capitalization stocks, trading costs are substantially higher, generally between 5% and 9% per roundtrip trade. Lesmond et al. (2004) suggest that transaction costs for most strategies examined are generally north of 1.5% per trade, substantially higher than the 0.5% suggested by Jegadeesh and Titman (1993). These results lead the authors to conclude that these higher trading costs wipe out most if not all of the abnormal returns realized from the momentum strategy.

Lesmond et al. (2004) also assess the impact of these higher transaction costs on the results of Jegadeesh and Titman (2001) by forming size-based quintile portfolios and share turnover-based quintile portfolios. Perhaps, since it is generally the case that large stocks have lower transaction costs, momentum-based strategies may be profitable after transaction costs only for large stocks. Similarly, for small stocks whose transaction costs are higher, momentum-based trading may not be profitable. However, all size-based portfolio strategies examined by Lesmond et al. (2004) show that the trading costs outweigh the returns for each of the portfolios constructed. The authors also sort on share turnover based on the idea that shares with higher (lower) turnover are more (less) liquid and, therefore, have lower (higher) transaction costs. However, similar to the size-based results, turnover-based portfolios appear to also wipe out the majority of momentum profits. The authors also cleverly attempt to construct momentum portfolios that would yield minimal trading costs by sorting the sample into portfolios based on trading costs. Again, the profits for these strategies after transaction costs are not very compelling. In summary, Lesmond et al. (2004) strongly conclude that the profit from common momentum-based strategies is all but wiped out once more accurate transaction costs are incorporated into the analysis. Results of Hanna and Ready (2005) and Grundy and Martin (2001) also lend further support to Lesmond et al. (2004) by doubting the profitability of momentum investing after consideration of transaction costs.

Korajczyk and Sadka (2004) also research the impact of transaction costs on abnormal returns for a set of common momentum-based strategies. Using data from February 1967 to December 1999, the authors investigate a variety of portfolio creation strategies based on the momentum strategies of Jegadeesh and Titman (1993) and utilize four estimates of transaction costs based on the bid-ask spread. Two of the estimates of transaction costs are proportional to portfolio size and two are not. Unlike most studies that typically form equal-weighted portfolios to assess momentum returns, the authors consider four primary portfolio creation strategies: equal-weighted (EW), value-weighted (VW), liquidity-weighted (LW), and a 50/50 VW/LW hybrid. Also, the authors choose to only take long positions in the winner portfolio unlike most previous research that constructs long-short portfolios by taking long positions in the past winners and short positions in the past losers. The justification for this decision is that the trading costs for short selling transactions are typically more expensive in comparison to long-only positions.

The authors focus their analysis to two specific, profitable strategies: the 11/1/3 (stocks ranked by past 11-month returns and one week later a 3-month holding period begins) and the 5/1/6 (stocks ranked by past 5-month returns and 1 week later a 6-month holding period begins). For the 11/1/3 strategy, abnormal returns from the Fama-French 3-factor model, not including transaction costs, are 0.80% per month for the EW portfolio and 0.57% per month for the VW portfolio. Incorporating transaction costs that are proportional to the size of the portfolio, these values decrease to 0.40%–0.45% per month for the VW portfolios and 0.54%–0.61% for the EW portfolios; these net abnormal returns are statistically significant. For the 5/1/6 strategy, abnormal returns, not including transaction costs, are 0.59% per month for the EW portfolio and 0.33% per month for the VW portfolio. After proportional transaction costs are considered, these values decrease to 0.35%–0.41% per month for the EW portfolios and 0.17%–0.22% for the EW portfolios.

Korajczyk and Sadka (2004) also examine the impact of nonproportional trading costs. However, in this analysis, rather than focus on monthly abnormal momentum returns, the authors focus on the level of breakeven initial investment from executing momentum strategies. The EW portfolio has a very low and unattractive breakeven point because it includes an equal weighting of liquid and illiquid stocks, where illiquid stocks are generally more expensive to trade. In third place, the VW portfolio breaks even at an initial investment of around $2 billion. The LW and 50/50 LW/VW portfolios tie for best performance with a breakeven level of initial investment of approximately $5 billion and an optimal investment of $2.5 billion. Though the authors' analysis does not consider the cost of commissions paid, the authors suggest this omission would not materially alter the results. Though the relative portfolio sizes for optimal cost/return utilizing a momentum-based strategy are not large, it is shown that the strategy can still be incorporated to produce an abnormal return even when considering transaction costs.

Institutional Investors

The behavioral finance literature suggests that there may be differences in investor behavior between institutional investors and individual investors. Institutional investors are suggested to engage in herd behavior and follow positive feedback trading strategies, such as momentum strategies, and even go as far as "window dress" a portfolio by buying recent winners and selling losers before a portfolio holdings reporting date. Furthermore, institutional investors are likely to prefer stocks with low transaction costs and high liquidity (Falkenstein 1996; Gompers and Metrick 2001). Individual investors have been found to hold losers too long and sell winners too soon—called the disposition effect (Shefrin and Statman 1985; Barber and Odean 2000; Grinblatt and Keloharju 2001), and only sell stocks that have experienced recent positive returns (Griffin, Harris, and Topaloglu 2003). The implication of such behavior is that individual investors are likely to be considered more as contrarian investors and less as momentum-based investors.

Grinblatt, Titman, and Wermers (1995) document that mutual fund managers tend to pursue momentum-based strategies. The authors examine quarterly holdings of 155 mutual funds over the 1975–1984 period and examine the impact of herding and momentum investing on fund performance. Grinblatt et al. (1995) characterize the portfolio choices of these funds by the degree to which they follow a momentum strategy and purchase stocks based on past returns, and also by the degree to which they herd, defined as a certain group of funds buying or selling the same securities at approximately the same time. The authors find that most funds tend to purchase stocks based on their past returns and do engage in some level of herding behavior, albeit not a level to be considered economically significant. In summary, the average level of herding and number of funds following momentum-based strategies were both statistically significant but not considerably large.

Badrinath and Wahal (2002) also investigate the use of momentum-based trading strategies by institutional investors and conclude that there does not appear to be systematic evidence of implementing these strategies at the institution or firm level. The authors examined the quarterly holdings of all institutions that filed a form 13-F with the SEC between the third quarter of 1987 and 1995. This included 3,800 firms and their respective institutions. First, momentum-based trading was inspected at the institution level for only holdings with a consistent presence. The weight of each security was compared each quarter and ultimately the authors found no real evidence of momentum-based strategies being used to tilt the ratio of holdings from quarter to quarter. Next, those securities that were entered into or exited altogether were investigated. It appears there is strong evidence of entry/exit momentum-based trading at the institutional level. Combining these two results, Badrinath and Wahal (2002) conclude that there is some evidence of momentum-based trading occurring at the institutional level on a quarterly basis, albeit not a significant amount. When aggregating this institutional data to conduct firm-level analysis there is no evidence to suggest momentum-based trading. Given there appears to be some momentum-based trading at the institutional level, this suggests that some institutions are entering into contrarian trades that are canceling out the effect of the minor momentum-based traders.

Explanations for Momentum and Reversals

A number of explanations have been put forth in the literature to explain the momentum anomaly. In general, these explanations typically fall into one of two categories: risk-based and investor behavior-based arguments. The risk-based argument is based on the idea that high-risk investments should earn higher returns. Thus, it could be the case that momentum returns are merely compensation to investors for the inherent high risk of momentum portfolios or compensation for some unique risk associated with momentum investing. However, as some of the aforementioned research has shown, it appears that momentum returns remain significant even after controlling for risk. In an important paper, Fama and French (1996) document that their 3-factor risk model fully explains the long-term reversals documented in past studies; however, their model cannot fully explain medium-term momentum. That is, Fama and French (1996) conclude that, after controlling for risk, returns from long-term reversal strategies become insignificant but momentum strategies remain profitable on a risk-adjusted basis. Furthermore, to date, there has not been any unique risk factor identified that explains the momentum return phenomenon. In short, most academics agree that the risk-based story is weak at best.

A number of papers have also focused on investor behavior as an explanation for the momentum anomaly. In a very influential paper that laid the groundwork for the behavioral finance literature, Kahneman and Tversky (1979) developed prospect theory. Based largely on their theory, it is now well established that investors typically do not treat gains and losses symmetrically; that is, the pain of regret exceeds the joy of pride for most humans. Therefore, a 30% decline in stocks causes much more pain than a 30% increase causes joy. This sort of asymmetric treatment of gains and losses may play a role in the timing decisions of investors and may lead to investors selling winners too soon and holding losers too long. The implications of the disposition effect are far-reaching in the sense that it may cause investors to react slowly to new information. That is, when good news is announced, the price of a stock may not immediately rise to its true value because of premature selling or lack of buying. Similarly, when bad news is announced, the price falls less than it should because of a lack of sellers due to some investors being reluctant to close losing positions. As a result, investors may underreact to new information and be slow to overreact to new information.

Hong and Stein (1999) present a model of investor behavior based on the existence of two types of rational agents: "newswatchers" and "momentum traders." In their model, newswatchers trade on fundamental information whereas momentum traders make trades based on past price movements. New, fundamental information diffuses gradually across the newswatchers and this causes prices to underreact and display positive autocorrelation (momentum). The momentum in prices incentivizes the momentum traders to enter the market; their simple trading strategies based on past prices eventually drive prices above fundamental value, leading prices to overreact and display negative autocorrelations over longer horizons (reversals) as prices move back to fundamental value. In such a model, Hong and Stein (1999) conclude that certain trading strategies based on past prices may in fact be profitable.

Other studies have tried to explain momentum and reversals using models in which investors possess certain psychological biases, namely, investor overconfidence, biased self-attribution, and confirmatory bias. Daniel, Hirshleifer, and Subrahmanyan (1998) suggest that overreaction and underreaction in the market are due to investor overconfidence and biased self-attribution. When investors are overconfident, they overvalue the accuracy of their private information. This overconfidence leads these investors to overreact to new information, causing prices to overreact and ultimately driving the price away from the fundamental value. In the long run, the market realizes the overvalued stocks and makes necessary corrections. Furthermore, when public information confirms the investor's private information, investor confidence increases by more than the decline in confidence when the public and private information are not in line. The combination of initial overreaction by investors and eventual price corrections leads to momentum over short to intermediate time horizons followed by reversals over longer investment horizons.

In a more recent paper, Friesen, Weller, and Dunham (2009) present a theoretical model that offers an explanation to the observed momentum and reversal patterns in stock returns and for the documented success of trend-following and pattern-based technical trading rules. Their model introduces a single cognitive bias into the model, that of confirmation bias. Confirmatory bias is a phenomenon that refers to the search for, or the interpretation of evidence in ways that favor existing beliefs or expectations. In their model, information arrival is modeled with signals of various magnitudes, arriving at differing frequencies. Large, observed signals that arrive infrequently are interpreted rationally by investors. However, investors' interpretations of subsequent signals that arrive more frequently but are less informative are biased by the recently observed large signals. To better understand, suppose there is a quarterly earnings announcement (infrequent signal) and that, after objectively assessing the information, an investor chooses to buy the firm's stock. Soon after the purchase, the investor is exposed to numerous information stories on a daily basis (infrequent signals) that provide both good and bad news about the firm. The authors' model suggests that an investor will overweight the good news and underweight the bad news as the subsequent good news "confirms" the original objective decision to purchase the stock. As a result, similar to Hong and Stein (1999), their model predicts that strategies based on past prices may indeed be profitable.

The authors' model generates price patterns that have the predictive power for future stock returns claimed by technical analysts, and thus provides a theoretical foundation for several price patterns commonly used by technical analysts. The model also produces the well-documented pattern of price momentum, which can be exploited by trend-following technical rules such as those based on the comparison of short-run and long-run moving averages. Most importantly, their model predicts that returns exhibit price reversals over very short horizons, price momentum over intermediate horizons, and again reversals over long horizons. Based on the aforementioned work on momentum and reversals, the authors' model conforms to the empirical properties of U.S. equity prices.

Hvidkjaer (2006) suggests that price momentum could be driven by the behavior of small investors. Specifically, the author suggests that momentum could be driven by initial buying pressure or delayed selling pressure among loser stocks, and initial selling pressure or delayed buying pressure among winner stocks. Using actual investor transaction data from January 1983 to December 2002, Hvidkjaer (2006) separately examines trading behavior of large and small investors with an emphasis on trade imbalance and finds that the two groups of traders exhibit quite different trading behavior. Specifically, by examining buying and selling pressures for both momentum winners and losers, the author documents evidence to be consistent with both initial underreaction and delayed reaction among small traders but not large traders and that trade imbalances are especially high for high-volume stocks suggesting that volume may be a predictor of momentum.

Interestingly, evidence from Lee and Swaminathan (2000) does suggest that a stock's past trading volume is a good predictor of both the magnitude and persistence of future momentum returns. Following the methodology of Jegadeesh and Titman (1993), the authors begin by creating portfolios double-sorted by past returns and trading volume. Analysis of these portfolios shows that, conditional on past returns, firms with low trading volume tend to outperform their high volume counterparts over the next year. Low volume losers outperform high volume losers by 1.02% per month for a 9/6 strategy, and low volume winners outperform high volume winners by 0.26% per month for the same 9/6 strategy. This result holds for numerous momentum strategies of various ranking and holding period lengths. Furthermore, the authors find evidence of long-term reversals, and document that high (low) volume winners (losers) experience faster momentum reversals. In conclusion, the authors suggest that the trading behavior of small investors at least offers a partial explanation of the momentum phenomenon.

Lastly, Chordia and Shivakumar (2002) suggest macroeconomic variables as the source of momentum in stock returns. In short, the authors find that the profitability of common momentum-based trading strategies is explained by common macroeconomic factors (dividend yield, default spread, yield on 3-month Treasury bill, and term structure spread) that are related to the business cycle. Using data from July 1926 to December 1994, the authors investigate performance of momentum-based strategies over expansionary and recessionary business cycles and document that such strategies generate significant positive returns only during the expansionary periods over the 1926–1994 period. Furthermore, during recession periods, momentum profits are actually negative and statistically insignificant. This result leads the authors to conclude that momentum returns can mostly be explained by changes in the business cycle.

International Evidence

The first to examine the momentum effect in international markets was Rouwenhorst (1998). The author uses individual stock return data from 12 European markets for the 1978–1995 period and finds evidence that momentum returns are not just a U.S. phenomenon. Rouwenhorst (1998) documents that a zero-cost, long-short strategy of buying winners (best performing decile) and shorting losers (worst performing decile) based on past return generates a return of about 1% per month over a 6-month holding period. This evidence of momentum over the intermediate term (12 months) is present in all 12 European markets, and the results hold across size deciles although momentum appears stronger for small firms. Furthermore, the momentum returns are not fully explained by standard risk models. In a follow up study, Rouwenhorst (1999) examines momentum in 20 emerging markets and again finds evidence of momentum strategies being profitable. Griffin, Ji, and Martin (2003) examine momentum strategies in 39 different non-U.S. equity markets and find significant evidence of large momentum profits in most markets; interestingly, the authors find that momentum profits only weakly co-move across these markets. The authors interpret this as evidence that macroeconomic factors are not likely driving momentum.

Chan, Hameed, and Tong (2000) investigate the profitability of utilizing momentum strategies on international stock indices while including the effect of exchange rate movements. Portfolios are weighted based on previous performance and exchange rate as all profits are converted back into U.S. dollars. Their assessment of various momentum strategies ultimately leads to the conclusion that the momentum profits are statistically significant, especially when holding periods are one month or less. For a 2-week holding period, the difference between the weekly returns of the winners and losers is 0.48% whereas that decreases to 0.25% for a 4-week holding period. More recently, Huang (2006) uses index returns on broad indexes for a sample of 17 countries over the 1969–1999 period and also finds evidence of momentum in international markets but only in up markets.

In addition to the work of Rouwenhorst (1998, 1999), positive momentum returns have been reported for several European markets (Liu, Strong, and Xu 1999; Schiereck, DeBondt, and Weber 1999; Bird and Whitaker 2003; Doukas and McKnight 2005; Agyei-Ampomah 2007), for the Australian market (Marshall and Cahan 2005), and for emerging markets (Hart, Zwart, and van Dijk 2005). Following the methodology of Jegadeesh and Titman (1993), Liu et al. (1999) document evidence of momentum in the United Kingdom and Schiereck et al. (1999) find evidence of momentum in Germany. Doukas and McKnight (2005) task themselves with determining whether short-term momentum strategies are profitable and significant in thirteen European markets and whether the momentum is the result of gradual information diffusion. The authors conclude that momentum is present and significant in 8 of the 13 markets. Additionally, they are able to confidently state that gradual information diffusion is driving European momentum.

In the Asian markets, Chiu, Titman, and Wei (2000) examine momentum profits in 8 Asian markets with a focus on ownership and legal systems. The authors find that momentum strategies are profitable in all markets except Japan. Hameed and Kusnadi (2002) explore the prevalence of momentum among 6 Asian stock markets, specifically Hong Kong, Malaysia, Singapore, Thailand, Taiwan, and South Korea. They construct country-neutral portfolios in a similar fashion to Jegadeesh and Titman (1993) over the sample period from 1979 to 1994 and find significant, yet small returns of 0.37% per month. However, after controlling for size and turnover, the results become insignificant. Liu and Lee (2001) report medium-term reversals in Japan and no evidence of momentum.

Other studies in the international momentum literature focus on explanations for momentum in non-U.S. markets. Fong, Wong, and Lean (2005) look at whether risk-based explanations for momentum exist by utilizing a stochastic dominance test on portfolios constructed from 24 Morgan Stanley Capital International indices. The results of these tests help conclude that momentum is a global phenomenon, winners dominate losers for substantial periods, and for most periods it is the loser portfolio that is reversing while the winner is ongoing. Van Dijk and Huibers (2002) study the root cause of momentum within the European market and determine it is due to analyst underreaction to new earnings information. News regarding earnings surprises, revisions, and expected growth appeared to be systematically related to price movements. Thus, utilizing momentum strategies within the European markets can be a profitable endeavor as momentum persists.

References

Agyei-Ampomah, S. 2007. The post-cost profitability of momentum trading strategies: Further evidence from the UK. *European Financial Management* 13: 776–802.

Arena, Matteo, K. S. Haggard, and Xuemin Yan. 2008. Price momentum and idiosyncratic risk. *The Financial Review* 43: 159–190.

Badrinath, S., and S. Wahal. 2002. Momentum trading by institutions. *Journal of Finance* 57: 2449–2478.

Barber, Brad M., and Terrance Odean. 2000. Trading is hazardous to your wealth: The common stock investment performance of individual investors. *Journal of Finance* 55: 773–806.

Bird, Ron, and Jonathan Whitaker. 2003. The performance of value and momentum investment portfolios: Recent experience in the major European markets. *Journal of Asset Management* 4: 221–246.

Brock, William, Josef Lakonishok, and Blake LeBaron. 1992. Simple technical trading rules and the stochastic properties of stock returns. *Journal of Finance* 47: 1731–1764.

Chan, Kalok, A. Hameed, and W. Tong. 2000. Profitability of momentum strategies in the international equity markets. *Journal of Financial and Quantitative Analysis* 35: 153–172.

Chopra, Navin, Josef Lakonishok, and Jay Ritter. 1992. Measuring abnormal performance: Do stocks overreact? *Journal of Financial Economics* 31: 235–268.

Chordia, Tarun, and Lakshmanan Shivakumar. 2002. Momentum, business cycle, and time-varying expected returns. *Journal of Finance* 57: 955–1019.

Chui, A., S. Titman, and K. Wei. 2000. Momentum, ownership structure, and financial crises: An analysis of Asian stock markets. University of Texas–Austin working paper.

Conrad, J., G. Kaul, and M. Nimalendran. 1991. Components of short-horizon individual security returns. *Journal of Financial Economics* 29: 365–384.

Cooper, M. 1999. Filter rules based on price and volume in individual security overreaction. *Review of Financial Studies* 12: 901–935.

Daniel, Kent, David Hirshleifer, and Avanidhar Subrahmanyam. 1998. Investor psychology and security market under- and over-reactions. *Journal of Finance* 53: 1839–1885.

DeBondt, Werner, and Richard Thaler. 1985. Does the stock market overreact? *Journal of Finance* 40: 793–805.

DeBondt, Werner, and Richard Thaler. 1987. Further evidence on investor overreaction and stock market seasonality. *Journal of Finance* 42: 557–581.

Dijk, Ronald van, and Fred Huibers. 2002. European price momentum and analyst behavior. *Financial Analyst Journal* 58: 96–105.

Dooley, M., and J. Schafer. 1983. Analysis of short-run exchange rate behavior: March 1973 to November 1981. In: *Exchange Rate and Trade Instability: Causes Consequences and Remedies*, edited by D. Bigman, and T. Taya. Cambridge, UK: Ballinger.

Doukas, J. A., and P. J. McKnight. 2005. European momentum strategies, information diffusion, and investor conservatism. *European Financial Management* 11: 313–338.

Dueker, M., and C. J. Neely. 2007. Can Markov switching rules predict foreign exchange returns? *Journal of Banking and Finance* 31: 279–296.

Elliott, Ralph N. 1938. The wave principle. In *R.N. Elliott's masterworks: The definitive collection*, edited by Robert R. Prechter. Gainesville, GA: New Classic Libraries.

Falkenstein, Eric G. 1996. Preferences for stock characteristics as revealed by mutual fund portfolio holdings. *Journal of Finance* 51: 111–135.

Fama, Eugene. 1970. Efficient capital markets: A review of theory and empirical work. *Journal of Finance*, 25: 383–417.

Fama, Eugene, and Kenneth French. 1996. Multifactor explanations of asset pricing anomalies. *Journal of Finance* 51: 55–84.

Fong, W. M., W. K. Wong, and H. H. Lean. 2005. International momentum strategies: a stochastic dominance approach. *Journal of Financial Markets* 8: 89–109.

Friesen, Geoff C., Paul Weller, and Lee M. Dunham. 2009. Price trends and patterns in technical analysis: A theoretical and empirical examination. *Journal of Banking and Finance* 33: 1089–1100.

Gann, William D. 1929. 1929 annual stock forecast. In *Supply and demand letter*. New York: W.D. Gann Scientific Service.

Gann, William D., 1935. *The basis of my forecasting method*. New York: W.D. Gann.

George, T., and C. Y. Hwang. 2004. The 52-week high and momentum investing. *Journal of Finance* 59: 2145–2176.

Gompers, Paul A., and Andrew Metrick, 2001. Institutional investors and equity prices. *Quarterly Journal of Economics* 116: 229–259.

Griffin, John, Jeff Harris, and Selim Topaloglu. 2003. The dynamics of institutional and individual trading. *Journal of Finance* 58: 2285–2320.

Griffin, John M., Xiuqing Ji, and Spencer Martin. 2003. Momentum investing and business cycle risk: Evidence from pole to pole. *Journal of Finance* 20: 2515–2547.

Grinblatt, Mark, and Matti Keloharju. 2001. What makes investors trade? *Journal of Finance* 56: 589–615.

Grinblatt, M., S. Titman, and R. Wermers. 1995. Momentum investment strategies, portfolio performance, and herding: a study of mutual fund behavior. *American Economic Review* 85: 1088–1105.

Grossman, Sanford J. 1976. On the efficiency of competitive stock markets where traders have diverse information. *Journal of Finance* 31: 573–584.

Grundy, B. D., and J. S. Martin, 2001. Understanding the nature of the risks and the source of the rewards to momentum investing. *The Review of Financial Studies* 14: 29–78.

Gutierrez R., Jr., and E. Kelley. 2008. The long-lasting momentum in weekly returns. *Journal of Finance* 63: 415–447.

Hameed A., and Y. Kusnadi. 2002. Momentum strategies: evidence from pacific basin stock markets. *Journal of Financial Research* 25: 383–397.

Hamilton, William P. 1922. *The stock market barometer.* New York: Harper and Row.

Hanna, J. D., and M. Ready. 2005. Profitable predictability in the cross-section of stock returns. *Journal of Financial Economics* 78: 463–505.

Hart, J. V. D., G. D. Zwart, and D. V. Dijk. 2005. The success of stock selection strategies in emerging markets: Is it risk or behavioral bias? *Emerging Markets Review* 6: 238–262.

Hong, Harrison, T. Lim, and Jeremy Stein. 2000. Bad new travels slowly: size, analyst coverage, and the profitability of momentum strategies. *Journal of Finance* 55: 265–296.

Hong, Harrison, and Jeremy Stein. 1999. A unified theory of underreaction, momentum trading and overreaction in asset markets. *Journal of Finance* 54: 2143–2184.

Huang, D. 2006. Market states and international momentum strategies. *Quarterly Review of Economics and Finance* 46: 437–446.

Hvidkjaer, Soeren. 2006. A trade-based analysis of momentum. *Review of Financial Studies* 19: 457–491.

Jegadeesh, Narasimhan. 1990. Evidence of predictable behavior of security returns. *Journal of Finance* 45: 881–898.

Jegadeesh, Narasimhan. 2000. Discussion of foundations of technical analysis. *Journal of Finance* 55: 1765–1770.

Jegadeesh, Narasimhan, and Sheridan Titman. 1993. Returns to buying winners and selling losers: Implications for stock market efficiency. *Journal of Finance* 48: 65–91.

Jegadeesh, Narasimhan, and Sheridan Titman. 1995. Overreaction, delayed reaction and contrarian profits. *Review of Financial Studies* 8: 973–993.

Jegadeesh, N., and S. Titman. 2001. Profitability of momentum strategies: An evaluation of alternative explanations. *The Journal of Finance* 56: 699–720.

Jensen, Michael C. 1978. Some anomalous evidence regarding market efficiency. *Journal of Financial Economics* 6: 95–101.

Jensen, Michael C., and George Bennington. 1970. Random walks and technical theories: Some additional evidence. *Journal of Finance* 25: 469–482.

Kahneman, D., and A. Tversky. 1979. Prospect theory: An analysis of decisions under risk. *Econometrica* 47: 313–327.

Kemp, Alexander G., and Gavin C. Reid. 1971. The random walk hypothesis and the recent bahaviour of equity prices in Britain. *Economica* 38: 28–51.

Korajczyk, Robert A., and Ronnie Sadka. 2004. Are momentum profits robust to trading costs? *Journal of Finance* 59: 1039–1082.

Lee, C. M., and B. Swaminathan. 2000. Price momentum and trading volume. *Journal of Finance* 55: 2017–2069.

Lehmann, Bruce. 1990. Fads, martingales and market efficiency. *Quarterly Journal of Economics* 105: 1–28.

Lesmond, David, Michael, Schill, and Chunsheng Zhou. 2004. The illusory nature of momentum profits. *Journal of Financial Economics* 71: 349–380.

Levich, R., and L. Thomas. 1993. The significance of technical trading rule profits in the foreign exchange market: A bootstrap approach. *Journal of International Money and Finance* 12: 451–474.

Levy, Robery. 1967. Relative strength as a criterion for investment selection. *Journal of Finance* 22: 595–610.

Lewellen, Jonathan. 2002. Momentum and autocorrelation in stock returns. *Review of Financial Studies* 15: 533–564.

Liu, C., and Y. Lee. 2001. Does the momentum strategy work universally? Evidence from the Japanese stock market. *Asia-Pacific Financial Markets* 8: 321–339.

Liu, W., N. Strong, and Xu Xinzhong. 1999. The profitability of momentum investing. *Journal of Business Finance and Accounting* 26: 1043–1091.

Lo, A., H. Mamaysky, and J. Wang. 2000. Foundations of technical analysis: Computations algorithms, statistical inference and empirical implementation. *Journal of Finance* 55: 1705–1765.

Malkiel, Burton G. 1973. *A random walk down Wall Street: The time-tested strategy for successful investing*. New York: W.W. Norton.

Marshall, B. R., and R. M. Cahan. 2005. Is the 52-week high momentum strategy profitable outside the US? *Applied Financial Economics* 15: 1259–1267.

Moskowitz, Tobias, and M. Grinblatt. 1999. Do industries explain momentum? *Journal of Finance* 54: 1249–1290.

Neely, C. J., Paul A. Weller, and R. Dittmar. 1997. Is technical analysis in the foreign exchange market profitable? A genetic programming approach. *Journal of Financial and Quantitative Analysis* 32: 405–426.

O'Neal, Edward S. 2000. Industry momentum and sector mutual funds. *Financial Analyst Journal* 56: 37–49.

Park, Seung-Chan. 2010. The moving average ratio and momentum. *The Financial Review* 45: 415–447.

Poterba, James M., and Lawrence H. Summers. 1988. Mean reversion in stock prices: evidence and implications. *Journal of Financial Economics* 22: 27–59.

Pruitt, Stephen, and Robert White. 1988. The CRISMA trading system: Who says technical analysis can't beat the market? *Journal of Portfolio Management* 14: 55–58.

Reilly, Frank K., and Edgar A. Norton. 2003. *Investments*, 6th ed. Florence, KY: South-Western, Thomson.

Rouwenhort, K. 1998. International Momentum Strategies. *Journal of Finance* 53: 267–284.

Rouwenhort, K. 1999. Local Return Factors and Turnover in Emerging Stock Markets. *Journal of Finance* 54: 1439–1464.

Sapp, Travis, 2010. The 52-week high, momentum, and predicting mutual fund returns. *Review of Quantitative Finance and Accounting*, forthcoming.

Schiereck, D., W. DeBondt, and M. Weber. 1999. Contrarian and momentum strategies in Germany. *Financial Analysts Journal* 55: 104–116.

Shefrin, H., and M. Statman. 1985. The disposition to sell winners too early and ride winners too long: Theory and evidence. *Journal of Finance* 40: 777–790.

Shen, Qian, Andrew C. Szakmary, and Subhash C. Sharma. 2007. An examination of momentum strategies in commodity futures markets. *Journal of Futures Markets* 27: 227–256.

Shen, Qian, Andrew C. Szakmary, and Subhash C. Sharma. 2010. Trend following trading strategies in commodities futures: A re-examination. *Journal of Banking and Finance* 34: 409–426.

Subrahmanyam, A. 2005. Distinguishing between rationales for short-horizon predictability in stock returns. *Financial Review* 40: 11–35.

Sweeney, R. 1986. Beating the foreign exchange market. *Journal of Finance* 41: 163–182.

Tabell, Anthony, and Edward Tabell. 1964. The case for technical analysis. *Financial Analysts Journal* 20: 67–76.

Van Dijk, R., and F. Huibers. 2002. European price momentum and analyst behavior. *Financial Analysts Journal* 58: 96–105.

Vassalou, Maria, and Kodjo Apedjinou, 2004. Corporate innovation, price momentum, and equity returns. Columbia University working paper.

Go to http://hema.zacks.com for abstracts and links to papers.

CHAPTER 9

Seasonal Anomalies

Constantine Dzhabarov and William T. Ziemba*

S easonality of stock markets has a long history despite the academic research being dominated by efficient market theory as surveyed by Fama (1970, 1991). Small firm effects were popularized by University of Chicago students Banz (1981), Reinganum (1981), Blume and Stambaugh (1983), Roll (1983), and Ritter (1988) among others.

Early surveys are in Lakonishok and Smidt (1988), Thaler (1992), and Ziemba (1994). The latter references considerable regularity of various seasonal anomalies in Japan as well as in the U.S. Jacobs and Levy (1988a, b, and c) have used seasonal and fundamental factor model derived anomalies to create a multibillion-dollar investment firm. Dimson (1988) and Keim and Ziemba (2000) present whole books with studies across the world. *The*

---

*Dedicated to the memory of Merton H. Miller, Ziemba's co-host in 1996 at the Graduate School of Business, University of Chicago, and to the memory of Chris Hensel, Ziemba's coauthor of many anomaly papers at the Frank Russell Company and University of Chicago MBA. It was there in the early 1980s when Banz, Blume, Keim, Reinganum, Ritter, Roll, Stambaugh, and other students at the most strongly efficient market-oriented U.S. finance department published small stock market anomalies papers in top finance journals and opened up the area. Miller, a strong efficient market academic but also savvy practical student of the markets used to tell Ziemba: "The half life of an anomaly is 3 years." Ziemba's experience since 1982, when he first traded the turn-of-the-year effect in the futures markets, is that when markets are regular (not too high volatility), the anomalies tend to work. However, each year or play usually is slightly different and may move around, so constant research and careful risk control is important in using these results in trading. The true test is whether you can use them to make excess risk-adjusted profits, and Ziemba believes this to be the case. This chapter also updates some of the results from Dzhabarov and Ziemba (2010) and various anomaly papers Ziemba has published.

Stock Trader's Almanac discusses some such anomalies in yearly updates; see Hirsch and Hirsch (2011).

Anomalies of the seasonal variety as discussed in this chapter and in Keim and Ziemba (2000) are not fully accepted nor believed by many strong efficient market theorists. Part of this dismissal is that the anomalies are too small to be bothered with as Ross (2005) argues. So, more or less, does Fama (1970, 1991). The well-known book *A Random Walk Down Wall Street* (Malkiel 2011) even states that strong effects like the January effect do not exist.

There also is the serious issue of data mining since many published results are in sample and do not include tests out of sample. Statistical verification of the actual existence of significant seasonal anomaly effects is studied by Sullivan, Timmerman, and White (1999) who analyze 9,452 calendar-based trading rules. See also Hansen, Lunde, and Nason (2005) who study 181 calendar effects and Lo and MacKinley (1990) who discuss data snooping biases. Also, t values tend not to show statistical significance in many cases where successful trades have been made because of high standard deviations.

To clarify the differing attitudes of academics and investors on this issue, Ziemba and Ziemba (2007) argue that there are 5 basic stock market camps. Each has a cut or version of certain sections of the market and makes its point for a certain subset of market participants, instruments, and strategies. There may be other classifications but these provide a useful framework for discussion.

The 5 groups are:

1. Efficient Markets (E)
2. Risk Premium (RP)
3. Genius (G)
4. Hog Wash (H)
5. Markets are beatable (A)

As these groups are described in more detail in the Preface to this book using direct quotes from Ziemba and Ziemba (2007) we will proceed in this chapter to review the world of seasonal anomalies assuming we are in category A and we are looking at the data, possible explanations, and some limited trading results. More extensive trading results using futures to exploit seasonal anomalies are shown on the web site associated with this book, http://wp.zacks.com.

January Effect

We refer to the January effect as the tendency of small cap stocks to out-perform large cap stocks in the month of January. Rozeff and Kinney (1976)

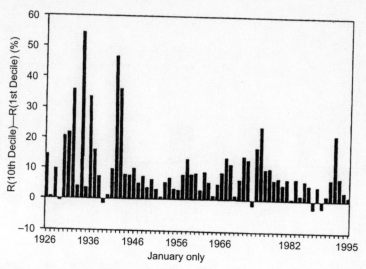

FIGURE 9.1 January Effect, 1926–1995. January size premium = *R*(10th)–*R*(1st).
Source: Booth and Keim 2000.

showed that equally weighted indices of all the stocks on the NYSE had significantly higher returns in January than in the other 11 months during 1904–1974. Keim (1983) documented the magnitude of the size effect by month using 1963–1979 data. He found that half the annual size premium was in January. Blume and Stambaugh (1983) showed that, after correcting for an upward bias in mean returns for small stocks that was common to earlier size effect studies, the size effect was only in January. Figure 9.1 shows the historical evidence from January 1926 to December 1995 of the difference in January between the lowest decile and the highest decile by market capitalization of the NYSE index plus AMEX and Nasdaq stocks of similar size. Only 5 years out of 70 did small caps underperform in January and in most years, the small cap outperformance is considerable. The R10th–R1st decile returns averaged 4.48% with a *t* = 2.83 from January 1982 to December 1995.

To update, we calculated the Russell 2000/S&P 500 futures spread by month from 1993 to 2010. As argued by Rendon and Ziemba (2007), the January turn-of-the-month effect still exists but has moved to December. Indeed, Figure 9.2 shows that the small cap/large cap spread is positive in December and negative in January.

The January monthly effect for small and large cap stocks measured by the Russell 2000 and S&P 500 futures has been negative during January 1993–December 2010 and January 2004–December 2010 as can be seen in Figures 9.3a and b and 9.4a and b. The results show the

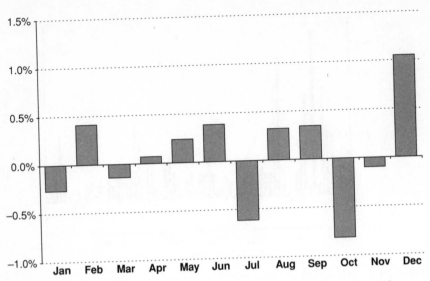

FIGURE 9.2 Russell 2000/S&P 500 Futures Spread Average Returns during the MOY, 1993–2010

historically expected very negative October in the recent S&P 500 data and in both sets of Russell 2000 data. Surprisingly, the historically strong months of November, January, and February were negative for both the small and large cap data. Although most of the other seasonality effects have still produced valuable reliable anomalies, the monthly effect does not seem to be of much use for traders and investors. However, sell in May and go away, discussed later, does add value.

Several subsequent analyses built on Keim's study considered the possibility that the January effect was diminishing based on the inclusion of later years of data, but Easterday, Sen, and Stephan (2008) also expanded their study to include years before Keim's analysis, which allowed them to better assess trends in the January effect's magnitude. They included the years from 1946–2007, performing a time series analysis according to the 3 subperiods in relation to Keim's 1963–1979 window: before, during, and after. Over this period, they studied NYSE and AMEX firms and, from 1971 onward, they also considered NASDAQ firms, which allowed them to consider more small cap stocks in their analysis.

Contrary to studies based on the Keim period and later years, Easterday et al. do not conclude that the January effect is declining. In other words, they do not find evidence that investors are acting on the arbitrage opportunity and internalizing it into higher prices.

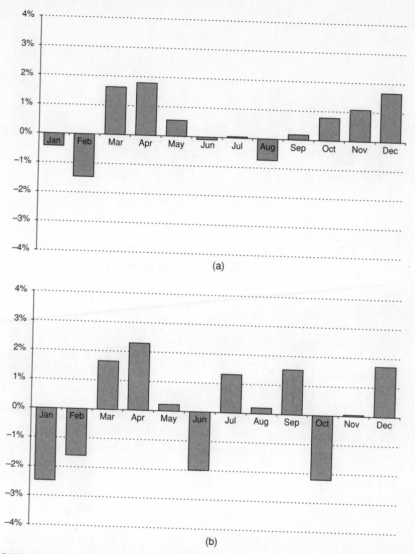

(a)

(b)

FIGURE 9.3(a) S&P 500 Futures Average Monthly Returns 1993–2010. **(b)** S&P 500 Futures Average Monthly Returns 2004–2010

Instead, they find that the January effect continues to be robust in small firms and that, in recent years, it has not so much diminished as returned to a level similar to the effect exhibited prior to 1963. Easterday et al. also considered trading volume in January, which should be higher if investors are actively arbitraging the January effect opportunity, but they did not find any evidence of higher trading volumes.

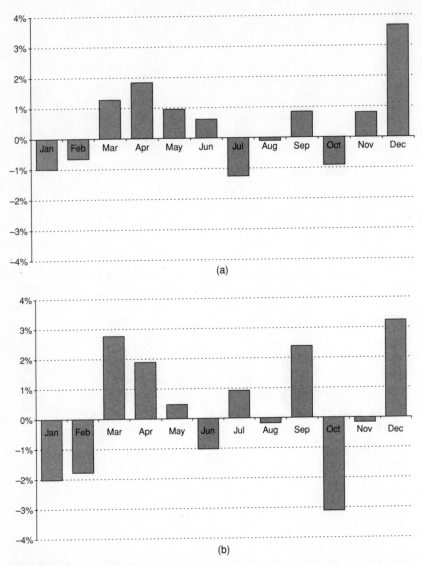

FIGURE 9.4(a) Russell 2000 Futures Average Monthly Returns 1993–2010.
(b) Russell 2000 Futures Average Monthly Returns 2004–2010

Haug and Hirschey (2006) also extensively analyzed the January effect, using both value-weighted and equally weighted equity returns. Their findings concur with Easterday and particularly note the consistency of the January effect in small capitalization stock returns across time. For instance, they find that the difference in average mean value-weighted portfolio return is 0.40% from 1802–2004, and that this number is even greater, 0.61%, from 1952–1986 (roughly the period Keim studied expanded twofold).

Haug and Hirschey explore potential explanations of the January effect phenomenon, ruling out biases that would more markedly affect large capitalization stocks, such as the timing considerations of institutional investors during portfolio rebalancing around official reporting periods. Statistical arguments brought up by Sullivan, Timmerman, and White (1999), among others, center around the inherent statistical problem of testing an empirical aspect of a data set using the same data set, which fundamentally calls into question the underlying statistical methods used in the analysis. Additionally, theories concerning relatively small investors concern end-of-year tax considerations or income events, such as year-end bonuses, which lead to new purchases in the new year. However, both of these potential explanations come into question when considering international indices under different tax regime timing and across changes in tax laws that should have an effect.

Among other measures, Haug and Hirschey use the Tax Reform Act of 1986 to test these and other behavioral hypotheses as potential explanations of the January effect, but they reach contradicting conclusions using different data, namely value-weighted and equal-weighted returns. They ultimately conclude that each of these explanations remain potential but unproven drivers of the still perplexing January effect phenomenon.

Trading the January Small Cap Effect in the Futures Markets

The evidence suggests that small stocks outperform large stocks at the turn of the year (TOY). Yet, transaction costs, particularly bid-ask spreads and price pressures, take away most, if not all, of the potential gains. See for example, Stoll and Whaley (1983) and Keim (1989) on these effects in January. However, transaction costs to trade index futures are a tenth or less of those for the corresponding basket of securities, and even more important, there is much less market impact. Hence, it may be profitable to buy long positions in small stock index futures and sell short positions in large stock index futures. This pair of positions is known as a spread trade. The strategy must anticipate the effect in the marketplace, in particular, the price impact of buying and selling futures contracts. Stock index futures began trading in the United States in May 1982. The Value Line minus S&P 500 and Russell 2000 minus S&P 500 spreads are two ways to measure and possibly capture any advantage small stocks may have over large cap stocks.

Clark and Ziemba (1987) describe doing this trade for the 1982/1983 TOY. At that time the Value Line, which had about 1,700 stocks, was geometrically weighted. Hence, by the geometric-arithmetic inequality this produced a downward drift of about 1% per month. After 1988, the index became price-weighted arithmetic. Clark and Ziemba used the following trading rule:

> *buy the spread on the first closing uptick, starting on December 15 and definitely by the 17th, and sell on January 15. Waiting (to enter) until (−1) now seems to be too late: possibly finance professors and their colleagues, as well as other students of the turn-of-the-year/January effect who are in on the strategy, move the VL index. There seems to be a bidding up of the March VL future price relative to the spot price.*
>
> —Clark and Ziemba 1987, p. 805

Their idea at that time was that the January small-firm effect existed and occurred during the first 2 weeks of January in the cash market (as argued by Ritter 1988; see also comments by Ziemba 1988), but that futures anticipation would move the effect in the futures markets into December. Hence, an entrance into the Value Line/S&P 500 futures spread trade in mid-December and an exit in mid-January should capture the effect if it actually existed. With data up to the 1985/1986 TOY, their trade rule was successful and profits were made each year. They concluded that small cap advantage was mainly in the first half of January, with some anticipation in the final days of December, and with a large cap advantage in the second half of January.

Ziemba continued trading this spread for the 14 TOYs from 1982/1983 to 1995/1996 and updated the results in Ziemba (1994) and Hensel and Ziemba (2000).

Hensel and Ziemba (2000) analyzed the January effect in the futures markets and concluded that for the 1980s and early 1990s there was a small cap advantage in the futures and cash markets. However, they show that from 1994 to 1998 there was no advantage in the cash market, and that anticipation built up in the last half of December in the futures markets. As a consequence, for the 4 TOYs during the 1994–1998 period, the January effect only existed in the last half of December, in the futures market. They analyzed small minus large spread trades between the Value Line and the S&P 500 futures contracts and concluded that the January effect was exploitable in the futures markets in this period.

Rendon and Ziemba (2007) updated Hensel and Ziemba (2000) to analyze the 7 TOYs from 1998/1999 to 2004/2005 for the Value Line minus S&P 500 spread trade, and provided additional evidence by analyzing a second spread trade involving the Russell 2000 and the S&P 500 futures contracts. From 1998 to 2005, their analysis shows that the January effect is still present in the futures markets in the Value Line minus S&P 500 spread trade, but that it has become increasingly risky to try to exploit it because of the marginal liquidity of the Value Line stock index futures contract. For the Russell 2000 minus S&P 500 spread trade, the January effect has been profitable.

For more details on this type of trading please see the Seasonal Anomaly page on the web site associated with this book, http://hema.zacks.com.

The January Barometer

Historically, returns in January have been a valuable signal for the returns in the following 11 months that year. If stocks have positive returns in January, then it is likely that the market as a whole will rise in that year. Hirsch (1986), who first mentioned this in 1972, has called this the January barometer. In the yearly updated Stock Trader's Almanac by Jeffrey A. Hirsch and Yale Hirsch (2011), they define it as the full year rather than the last 11 months. We look at this both ways, full year and last 11 months, for the U.S. S&P 500 in Figure 9.8. The supposition is that:

if the market rises in January, then it will rise for the year as a whole; but if it falls in January, then there will be a decline or a flat market that year.

Figure 9.5 updates Hensel and Ziemba (1995a) and Ziemba (1994), which had the results for the 54 years 1940–1993. There are 71 years in the total sample with a 17-year update to the end of December 2010.

For the 71 years, when the return in January was positive, the rest of the year (ROY) was up 86.4% of the time. This compares with 70.4% of all years that the whole year was up.

When the return in January was negative, which was 27 of the 71 years, the rest of the year was down 48.1% of the time. Thus, even in years when January is down, the whole year is about equally likely to be up or down. This 48.1% is significantly less than the 73.2% of all the years that the rest of the year went up. Figure 9.7 also shows the full year return for the 4 cases with arithmetic and geometric mean returns. We conclude that the January barometer does add value and is useful in various ways. Negative Januarys like 2008 had good predictive value, but the measure is not infallible. For example, 2010 had positive 11-month and 12-month returns despite a negative January. However, as in other cases of negative January but positive 11- and 12-month returns, those returns are, on average, small.

In the 17-year update (1994–2010), the results as seen in Figure 9.5 are similar with the January ROY up 80% (8 of 10) of the time.

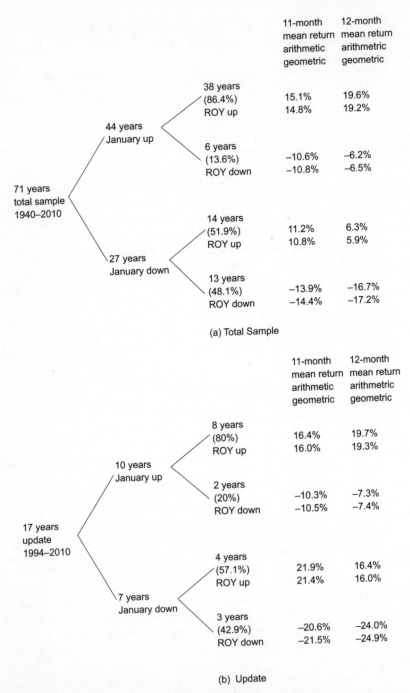

FIGURE 9.5 January Barometer Results, 1940–2010 and 1994–2010

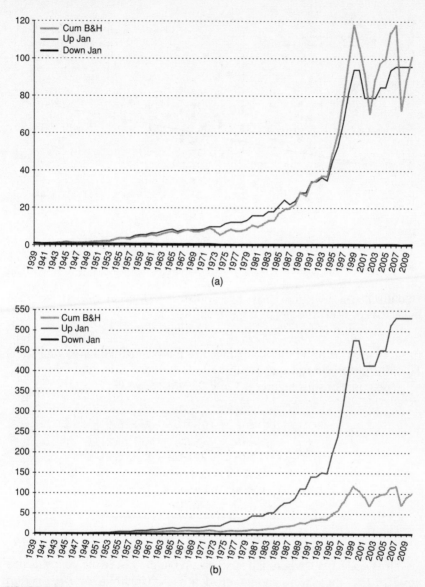

FIGURE 9.6(a) Positive and Negative January and B&H Cumulative Returns S&P 500 Index (Cash) 1940–2010, Rest of Year. **(b)** Positive and Negative January and B&H Cumulative Returns. S&P 500 Index (Cash) 1940–2010 Full Year

Figure 9.6a shows the cumulative rest of year returns for positive January, negative January, and buy and hold. Buy and hold beats positive January and has the highest final wealth with negative January producing almost no gains at all. Buy and hold had returns that were high except

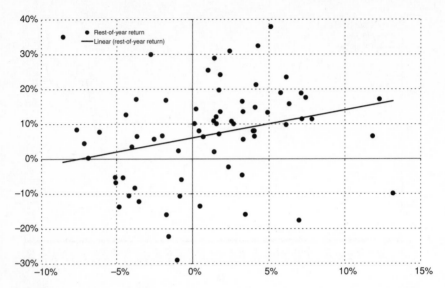

FIGURE 9.7 January Return (x-axis) versus Rest-of-Year Return (y-axis). S&P 500 Index (Cash), 1940–2010

the 2007–2009 drop in the S&P 500 led to the positive January dominating. Figure 9.6b has the full year results.

The equations for Figures 9.7 and 9.8 are:

$$
\begin{array}{llll}
\text{ROY} = & 0.0604 & +0.801\text{Jan} & R^2 = 6.7\% \\
 & (3.45) & (2.22) & \\
\text{ROY}+ = & 0.12665 & -0.2700\text{Jan}+ & R^2 = 0.5\% \\
 & (4.27) & (-0.46) & \\
\text{ROY}- = & -0.0840 & -1.91\text{Jan}- & R^2 = 7.2\% \\
 & (-1.36) & (-1.40) & \\
\end{array}
$$

Bronson (2011) reminds us that the January barometer has had 6 false positives since 1940, where January was up but the rest of the year was negative. In 1947 there were enough dividends and January returns to overturn this loss for the whole year. So that leaves the following 5 January positive net return of the year negative returns (not including dividends) as in Table 9.1.

There have also been 14 false negatives since 1940 where January was negative but the rest of the year is positive. We differ from Bronson by simply saying that if January is negative, the rest of the year is noise. So Bronson argues that the January barometer has failed to signal the direction

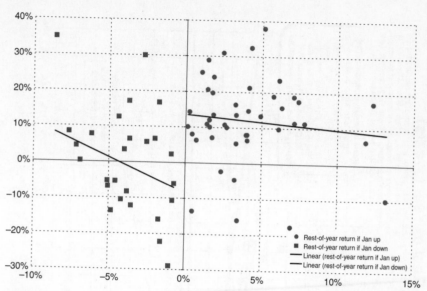

FIGURE 9.8 January Return (*x*-axis) (Up and Down Cases) versus Rest-of-Year Return (*y*-axis). S&P 500 Index (Cash), 1940–2010

of the stock market 19 of the past 71 years, some 27% of the time. Agreeing with us, the stock market was up 73% of the time (52 of 71 years).

However, Bronson argues that the barometer is getting less accurate recently. Indeed 12 of the 19 failures (60%) have occurred in the 32 years since 1978. Figure 9.9 shows Bronson's graph relating the rest of the year percent change as a function of January's percent change. His regression suggests that the rest of the year percent change equals 6% plus 80% of January's percent change. Compare this with our previous regression with a minuscule 0.5% R^2 and a rest of the year return of 12.6% minus 0.27 times

TABLE 9.1 Returns for Positive January, Negative Rest of Year, %

Year	January	ROY	Year
1946	7.0	−17.6	−11.9
1947	2.4	−2.3	0.0
1966	0.5	−13.5	−13.1
1987	13.2	−9.9	2.0
1994	3.3	−4.6	−1.5
2001	3.5	−16.0	−13.0

Source: Bronson (2011).

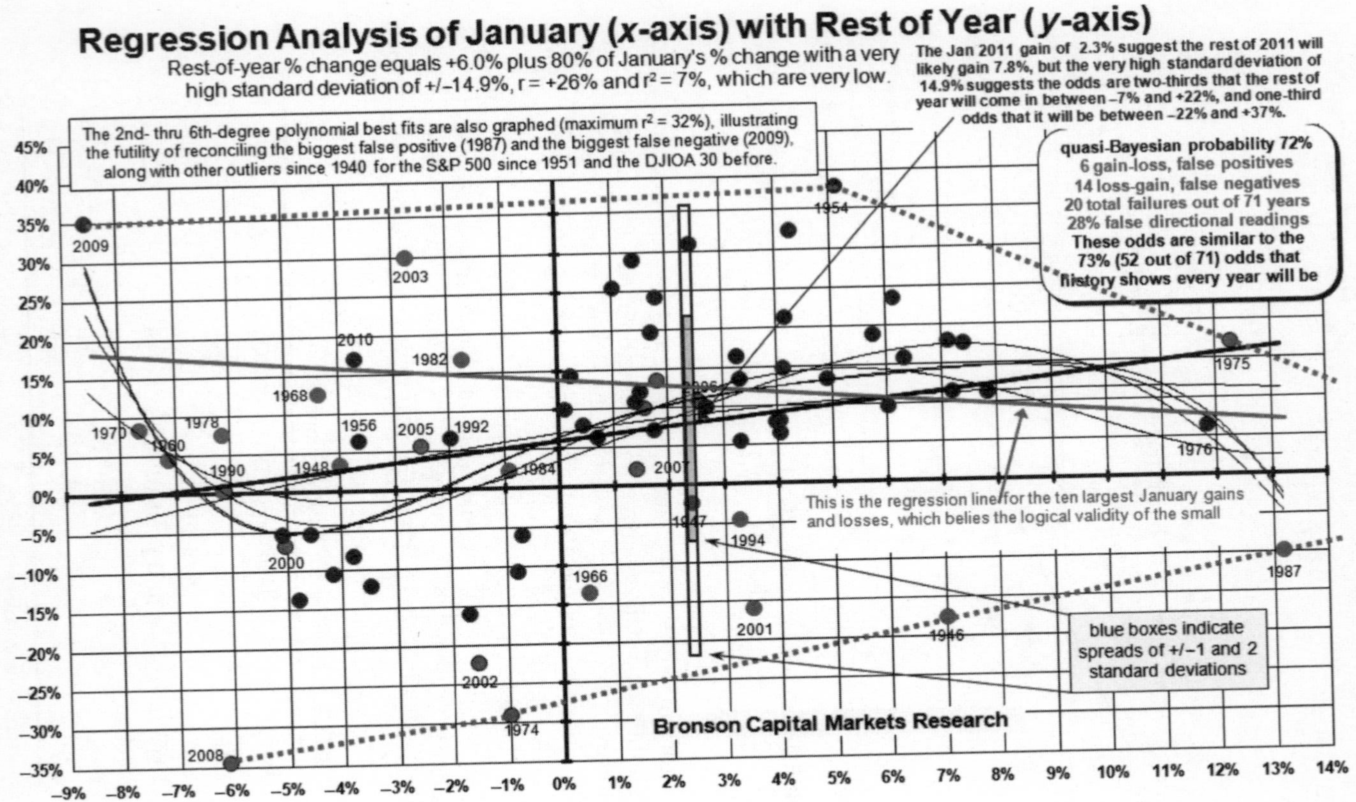
Regression Analysis of January (x-axis) with Rest of Year (y-axis)
Rest-of-year % change equals +6.0% plus 80% of January's % change with a very high standard deviation of +/–14.9%, r = +26% and r² = 7%, which are very low.
The Jan 2011 gain of 2.3% suggest the rest of 2011 will likely gain 7.8%, but the very high standard deviation of 14.9% suggests the odds are two-thirds that the rest of year will come in between –7% and +22%, and one-third odds that it will be between –22% and +37%.
The 2nd- thru 6th-degree polynomial best fits are also graphed (maximum r² = 32%), illustrating the futility of reconciling the biggest false positive (1987) and the biggest false negative (2009), along with other outliers since 1940 for the S&P 500 since 1951 and the DJIOA 30 before.
quasi-Bayesian probability 72%
6 gain-loss, false positives
14 loss-gain, false negatives
20 total failures out of 71 years
28% false directional readings
These odds are similar to the
73% (52 out of 71) odds that
history shows every year will be
This is the regression line for the ten largest January gains and losses, which belies the logical validity of the small
blue boxes indicate spreads of +/–1 and 2 standard deviations
Bronson Capital Markets Research
45%
40%
35%
30%
25%
20%
15%
10%
5%
0%
–5%
–10%
–15%
–20%
–25%
–30%
–35%
–9%
–8%
–7%
–6%
–5%
–4%
–3%
–2%
–1%
0%
1%
2%
3%
4%
5%
6%
7%
8%
9%
10%
11%
12%
13%
14%
2009
2003
2010
1982
1968
1970
1960
1978
1990
1948
1956
2005
1992
1984
2007
1954
1975
1976
1947
1994
2000
1966
2001
1946
1987
2002
1974
2008

FIGURE 9.9 Regression Analysis of January Return with Rest of Year.

Source: Bronson (2011).

January's return. His low 7% R^2 exceeds ours. He concludes that January 2011's gain of 2.3% yields a forecast of a rest of 2011 gain of 7.8%. This gain is quite close to those we hear from the TV forecasters.

Hirsch and Hirsch (2011) and Ziemba (2010) discuss this first 5-day-of-January predictor with data from 1950–2010. The last 37 positive first 5 days were followed by full year gains 32 times (86.5%) and a mean gain of 14.0% for the 37 years. The 23 negative first 5 days had 12 positive (52.2%) years and 11 negative years. The full month January barometer has been an even better predictor except 2009, so we have focused on that, but the 5 days are important to look at. To conclude, the 2008 signal was the strongest at –5.3%, the negative first 5 days were the worst ever, and the negative January led to the very devastating 2008 with a yearly loss of –38.5% for the S&P 500.

The results we have found are supplemented with other studies as follows.

Brown and Luo (2006) consider the performance of the January barometer (JanB) in the United States from 1941–2003 and find it has predictive ability. More recently, Stivers, Sun, and Sun (2009) find, using the simple spread approach, the power of the JanB in U.S. indexes has declined since it was published in the early 1970s but that it remains a useful market timing technique in the 1975–2006 period. Additionally, Sturm (2009) shows the JanB is particularly powerful in the first year of the presidential cycle.

Cooper, McConnell, and Ovtchinnikov (2006) focus on the 1940–2006 period and consider the robustness of results using NYSE data dating back to 1825. They call the effect the "other January effect" but we prefer January barometer. In addition to testing the JanB with the full market index, Cooper et al. also find it has predictive value for both small and large stocks and value and growth stocks. The effect persists after adjustment for business cycle and macroeconomic variables, investor sentiment, and the presidential cycle.

Cooper et al. found that over the previous 147 years, the spread between the 11-month return following positive versus negative Januarys was 7.76%, and other papers have reported spreads of 10%+. Though consensus exists around this conclusion that January returns have a predictive power, the consensus dissipates at the crucial point: can you profit from it?

How to Trade the January Barometer

The apparent predictive power of the JanB leads us to questions of if and how investors should trade to profit by it. The following strategies have been analyzed as ways to use the JanB to outperform a passive buy-and-hold strategy (see also Figure 9.6).

1. Standard JanB Strategy: Stay out of the market in January and go long or short for the remainder of the year depending on whether the January return is positive or negative.
2. JE + JanB Strategy: Go long in January based on the original January effect (because market returns in January are positive on average) and, for the remainder of the year, follow the standard JanB strategy.
3. JE + JanB T-bill Strategy: Go long in January based on the original January effect.

If the January return is positive, go long. If the January return is negative, invest in T-bills.

Regarding the standard JanB strategy, Marshall et al. and Cooper et al. came to a similar conclusion that a passive buy-and-hold strategy beats the standard JanB strategy. This result is unsurprising given that this strategy calls for staying out of the market in January to wait for the market signal before investing from February through December. By skipping January, the investor misses the excess returns experienced in January as documented as the original January effect.

Therefore, the 2 subsequent strategy alternatives both assume the investor goes long in January in order to benefit from the January effect.

The JE + JanB Strategy also underperforms a simple buy-and-hold strategy. Cooper et al. report that, although it was much lower than the return after a positive January, the average yearly return after negative Januarys was also positive at 5.71%, so a short strategy in these periods earns less than the T-bills or the buy-and-hold strategy. Cooper et al. also point out the substantial losses from tail risk in very good years occurring after negative Januarys, when shorting the market would have been disastrous for the investor.

Both Cooper et al. and Marshall et al. find the JE + JanB T-bill strategy to be the best of the 3 forementioned alternatives, but they disagree on whether this strategy is superior to the buy-and-hold baseline.

For example, during the period from 1940 to 2006, Cooper et al. report average annual buy-and-hold returns of 11.94% compared to a yearly average of 12.79% for the JE + JanB T-bill strategy. Cooper et al. conclude that following this strategy is of value to investors based on the past data.

Marshall et al. reach the opposite conclusion through the same data, finding that the JanB cannot be used by investors to outperform a passive long strategy. For the period from 1940 to 2007, they find average yearly buy-and-hold returns of 12.68% and JE + JanB T-bill strategy returns of 13.09%. Marshall et al. say the discrepancies between the two conclusions are based on dissimilar statistical significance and risk assessment calculations as well as differing opinions of the economic significance of <0.05% difference in annual returns, which excludes transaction costs and uses simple spreads that they find biased away from investors' trading realities.

The only way the JE + JanB T-bill strategy differs from the buy-and-hold strategy is that, following Januarys with negative returns, the investor opts for T-bills instead of equity. The former strategy does not outperform the buy-and-hold strategy because, following Januarys with negative returns, average 11-month T-bill returns are only marginally larger than average 11-month equity returns.

The International January Barometer

Hensel and Ziemba (1995b), Easton and Pinder (2007), and Stivers, Sun, and Sun (2009) address the performance of the JanB in international markets. Hensel and Ziemba find similar results in Switzerland and Europe and global as the United States. Namely, about 85% positive years and rest of years following positive Januarys and noise about 50-50 following negative Januarys. The mean returns have the same basic behavior, being more favorable for positive than for negative Januarys. So positive Januarys do seem to have positive predictive power.

Bohl and Salm (2010) study the predictive power of stock market returns in January for the rest of the year for 19 countries. They find that the barometer works well in the United States, as we know, and in Norway and Switzerland. However, it did not predict well in the other 16 countries, which included Japan, France, Spain, and Germany.

The data periods vary by country but are long, for example, Australia 1903–2007, Austria 1970–2007, Belgium 1951–2007, Canada 1936–2007, and France 1896–2007. In many cases it is the high sigma leading to too low Ts which caused the significant nonpredictability, but in some cases, the signal is actually going the wrong way in their regression model. Therefore, care is needed in these various countries to use the barometer for added value.

Sell-in-May-and-Go-Away

September and October have historically had low stock market returns with many serious declines or crashes occurring in October. Table 9.2 has results for 2993–2000. Also the months of November to February have historically had higher than average returns; see, for example, Gultekin and Gultekin (1983) and various papers in Keim and Ziemba (2000). This suggests the strategy to avoid the bad months and be in cash then, and only be long the stock market in the good months. Sell-in-May-and-go-away, which is sometimes called the Halloween effect, is 1 such strategy that is of 10 discussed in the financial press. Figures 9.10 and 9.11 show this

TABLE 9.2 S&P 500 Futures Average Returns, September and October, 1993–2010

	1993	1994	1995	1996	1997	1998	1999	2000	2001
Sep	−0.87%	−2.17%	4.48%	6.09%	5.51%	6.86%	−1.79%	−4.58%	−8.38
Oct	1.87%	2.59%	−0.77%	2.59%	−3.78%	7.38%	5.73%	−1.15%	1.46%
	2002	2003	2004	2005	2006	2007	2008	2009	2010
Sep	−11.31%	−1.43%	0.94%	1.03%	3.02%	4.07%	−9.79%	3.16%	8.31%
Oct	7.96%	5.51%	1.32%	−2.08%	2.79%	1.00%	−20.11%	−2.07%	3.74%

strategy using the rule sell on the first trading day in May and buy on the sixth trading day before the end of October, for the S&P 500 and Russell 2000 futures indexes for the years 1993–2010, respectively. This rule did indeed beat a buy-and-hold strategy. The tables which show the monthly returns, respectively, for those 17 years are displayed at the web site http://hema.zacks.com on the Seasonality page.

For the S&P 500 a buy-and-hold strategy turns $1 on February 4, 1993, into $1.96 on December 31, 2010, whereas, sell in May and move into cash, counting interest (Fed funds effective monthly rate for sell in May) and dividends for the buy and hold, had a final wealth of $3.73, some 90.7% higher. For the Russell 2000, the final wealth was $2.04 and $4.94, respectively, some 141.7% higher.

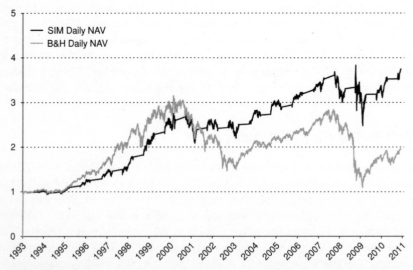

FIGURE 9.10 S&P 500 Futures Sell in May (SIM) and B&H Cumulative Returns Comparison 1993–2010. (Entry at Close on Sixth Trading Day before End of October. Exit First Trading Day of May.)

FIGURE 9.11 Russell 2000 Futures Sell in May (SIM) and B&H Cumulative Returns Comparison, 1993–2010. (Entry at Close on Sixth Trading Day before End of October. Exit First Trading Day of May)

Figure 9.11 shows the results of the strategy application to S&P 500 and Russell 2000 futures in the years 1993–2010. The funds are in T-bills when they are not in the market. In both cases, sell-in-May-and-go-away is superior to buy and hold.

Doeswijk (2005) offers a new hypotheses after reviewing two existing explanatory hypotheses. Bouman and Jacobsen (2002) confirm the empirical and historical basis of the maxim, finding that the sell-in-May effect holds in 36 of the 37 countries included in their analysis. They consider vacation timing as a potential cause of the sell-in-May effect, suggesting the timing of summer vacations may cause temporal variation in appetites for risk aversion. However, they find evidence of the sell-in-May effect in their subset of southern hemisphere countries, which, under their hypothesis, would be expected to have a different seasonal pattern.

Another hypothesized link between seasonality and stock returns is Seasonal Affective Disorder (SAD), which was studied in Kamstra, Kramer, and Levi (2003) and Garrett, Kamstra, and Kramer (2004). SAD is a disorder in which the shorter, relatively sunless days of fall and winter cause depression, which some recent research links to an unwillingness to take risk. Kamstra (2003) concludes that the SAD explanation does not lead to a profitable trading strategy because the risk premium varies with the seasonal effects. Like the vacation-timing hypothesis, Doeswijk finds the SAD hypothesis insufficient, because SAD is known to start as early as September. Therefore, the historically high November returns cannot be explained.

Doeswijk (2005) offers a new hypothesis to explain the sell-in-May effect. He posits that, in the fourth quarter of each year, investors are overly optimistic about the upcoming year. This excessive optimism leads to attractive initial returns followed by a renewed realism that readjusts expectations. Unlike the SAD hypothesis, which suggests a varying risk premium, the optimism cycle hypothesis reflects a constant risk premium but a varying perception of the economic outlook. In order to test this hypothesis, Doeswijk ran 3 analyses: (1) the global zero-investment seasonal sector-rotation strategy, (2) the seasonality of earnings growth revisions, and (3) the initial returns of IPOs as a proxy for investor optimism.

According to the optimism cycle, investors are overoptimistic at the end and beginning of the year. If this hypothesis is correct, a winning investment strategy is going long in cyclical stocks and short in defensive stocks during the winter period from November through April (winter) and following the opposite strategy from May through October (summer). (These stock groups are chosen for their relative exposure to the general economy, with cyclical stocks having a high exposure and defensive stocks a low exposure.) To test this strategy, Doeswijk uses the MSCI World index of global stock returns from 1970–2003 and tests the data as a whole, in two 17–year subperiods, using several variations on timing of the winter period and various sector definitions. The study runs regressions using monthly market capitalization-weighted price return indexes and their monthly log returns.

Doeswijk finds that, on average, during the study period, winter returns are a significant 7.6% higher than summer returns and the strategy works in 65% of the years. On a monthly basis, average performance of the global zero-investment strategy is 0.56%, which is significant at the 1% confidence level. Using further regression analysis techniques, Doeswijk also isolates the market timing effects from the seasonality and finds that seasonality alone accounts for approximately half of the excess returns.

Like the optimism-cycle strategy, both other analyses in the Doeswijk study support the optimism-cycle hypothesis. Doeswijk finds that expected earnings growth rates follow a seasonal cycle and that these changes have an effect on stock performance. The third analysis uses initial IPO returns, which show a remarkable seasonality, as a proxy for investor confidence. Using this investor confidence proxy as an independent variable, the regression result for remaining excess return is not statistically significant, which supports the optimism-cycle hypothesis.

Along with the 3 supporting analyses, Doeswijk explains a qualitative argument in favor of his optimism-cycle hypothesis. He argues that, since this phenomenon is one based on an aspect of human psychology, it tricks investors into repeating the same biases every year. Importantly, this cycle of optimism and pessimism is not generally accepted, which Doeswijk argues allows for investors who understand it to profit from it as a free lunch until it is more widely accepted and the arbitrage opportunity is absorbed into the market.

Same Month Next Year

Heston and Sadka (2007) review predictability models for average stock returns based on past returns, such as short-term and long-term momentum and reversal effects. Several studies confirm various predictability patterns, but several potential explanations of these patterns exist, including data snooping, risk compensation, or behavioral theories. By expanding the analysis outside the United States, Heston and Sadka reduced the potential bias of data snooping and uncovered new information about the relative applicability of predictability models in different countries. The paper analyzes 12 European countries plus Canada and Japan using a data set of monthly returns from 1985 to 2006.

Heston and Sadka analyze monthly stock returns using cross-sectional regressions. They begin their analysis by analyzing various lagging return variables to check for various existing temporal prediction patterns, such as short-term momentum effects and medium-term reversal effects. They confirm that the momentum effect holds in their international sample, with the exception of medium-term momentum effects not being present in Japan. They also uncover a new pattern, a 1-year lag with a reversal effect in the intervening months. Additionally, the study expands upon the positive return continuation of 1-year lags by checking on lags of every 12 months for up to 120 months. They find that the positive returns are present in these longer term yearly lag periods, though some results in longer time frames were not statistically significant due to insufficiently large sample sizes in some cases.

Heston and Sadka also analyze potential portfolio strategies to make use of this uncovered pattern. They use the decile-spread methodology of Jegadeesh and Titman (1993) to investigate various time horizons and sorting methods and additionally analyze calendar effects, such as the January effect. They analyze return patterns according to liquidity measures and by country and find that neither explains the temporal pattern. They also consider if the temporal pattern is a result of common international risk factors, finding that different countries are correlated in the short term but over longer time horizons the correlation is, though still positive, notably weaker and sometimes statistically insignificant. They conclude that international diversification around this strategy is beneficial and the reason that capital market segmentation may leave rewards for seasonal risks specific to different countries or that in different countries seasonal news may cause relatively predictable behavioral responses that are reflected in return movements.

Holiday Effects

There has been a very strong holiday effect in U.S. markets throughout the twentieth century. Ariel (1990), Zweig (1986), Lakonishok and Smidt (1988) have documented this. For example, for the 90 years from 1897 to 1986, Lakonishok and Smidt found that fully 51.5% of the nondividend returns on the Dow Jones industrials were made on the approximately 8 yearly preholidays. Ariel using data from 1963–1982 found a very strong effect with the average preholiday having returns that were about 23 times an average day for large capitalized stocks measured by a value weighted index of all NYSE stocks. Small capitalized stocks (equally weighted NYSE stocks) had returns 14 times larger but since this period was one of extremely high small stock returns, the actual returns exceeded the large capitalized securities. Lakonishok and Smidt also found that preholidays were associated with higher mean returns on all days of the week compared to average returns those days. Investigation of the holiday effect in Japan by Ziemba (1991) yielded very similar results. Using daily data on the Nikkei stock average from May 1949 when the market opened up after World War II to 1988, he found that the typical preholiday had returns of about 5 times the average nonpreholiday trading day, namely, 0.246% versus 0.0489%.

Holiday effects in other countries are discussed by Ziemba (1994) and in the survey by Cervera and Keim (2000) and other papers in the Keim and Ziemba (2000) volume.

Historically it was the preholiday that had the highest returns with the −3 day having the next highest returns, with the day after the holiday having negative returns.

A regression to separate out the effects on trading days −3 to +2 around a holiday using 0, 1 variables led to the daily return.

R =	0.0352 +	0.0799	0.0222	0.1894	0.0663	0.00114
		Day−3 +	Day−2 +	Day−1 −	Day+1 +	Day+2
	(3.745)	(1.491)	(0.424)	(3.709)	(−1.334)	(0.023)

Observe the high positive coefficient and t-value on the −1 day in the cash market. The evidence we have to update this to 2010 is from the futures markets from 1993–2010 and it is that the effect seems to have moved to the −3 day before the holiday and is much weaker than in the past. The preholiday is marginally positive for both the S&P 500 and Russell 2000. Labor day for the Russell 2000 is the most reliable with a mean gain of 0.88% with a $t = 4.81$ and 15 of 16 positive. President's day was also reliable 82.4% of the time with a $t = 2.11$. Since none of the holidays were highly significantly positive for the S&P 500 and, except for these two the Russell 2000 results were marginal, we conclude that the holiday effect exists to some extent on the −3 day but has diminished greatly in the 1990s

TABLE 9.3 Futures Holiday Average Returns by Day, 1993–2010

S&P 500

Count	4536	144	144	144	144	144	3704
St dev	0.0124	0.0123	0.0099	0.0105	0.0130	0.0141	0.0125
Average	0.02%	0.20%	−0.04%	0.05%	0.08%	0.09%	0.01%
Z	1.2404	1.8982	−0.5321	0.5366	0.7052	0.7306	0.6590
Positive	53.2%	55.6%	52.1%	50.0%	54.9%	59.0%	52.9%
	All days	Pre H −3	Pre H −2	Pre H −1	After H 1	After H 2	Others

Russell 2000

Count	4543	145	145	145	145	145	3705
St dev	0.0147	0.0153	0.0124	0.0124	0.0151	0.0184	0.0147
Average	0.03%	0.33%	0.01%	0.14%	0.04%	0.07%	0.01%
Z	1.2218	2.5715	0.1280	1.4005	0.2868	0.4506	0.2673
Positive	53.2%	63.4%	53.8%	52.4%	50.3%	56.6%	52.8%
	All days	Pre H −3	Pre H −2	Pre H −1	After H 1	After H 2	Others

Note: For some years Christmas 2 AH= New Year −3PH.

and 2000s. The mean gain for the S&P 500 was 0.19% ($t = 1.74$) and the Russell 2000 was 0.26% ($t = 2.14$).

Table 9.3 documents the overall results for these two indexes on days −3 to +2 plus other days and all the days.

Figure 9.12 shows the holiday average returns per day for the S&P 500 futures on the days −3 to +2 from 1993–2010. This shows the strong −3 day. Figure 9.13 has this by holiday. Figures 9.14 and 9.15 have the results for the Russell 2000.

The Sell on Rosh Hashanah

The Rosh Hashanah anomaly relates to the Jewish New Year. In 2009, that was close of September 18 to open on September 28 for the trading days. The origin of this practice seems to be the belief that many Jewish investors liquidate their portfolios during the holiday so that their attentions could be fully focused on their worship or—more likely in today's world—not on trade.

Could this really be true in our current markets?

Going back to 1915, the performance of the DJIA is −0.62% from the last close before Rosh Hashanah until 8 days later with the last close before Yom Kippur. From then to December 31 averaged a respectable 1.99%; see TheStreet.com and the Kirk Report.

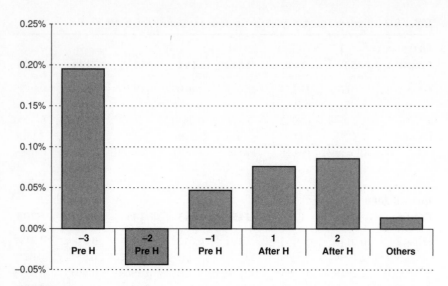

FIGURE 9.12   S&P 500 Futures Average Returns by Day (–3, –2, –1, 1, 2) by Day, 1993–2010

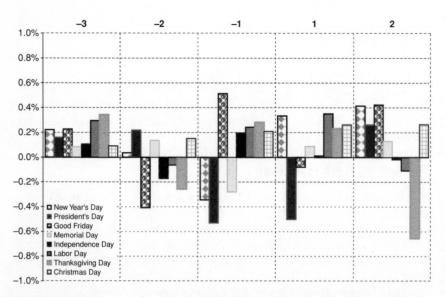

FIGURE 9.13   S&P 500 Futures Holiday Average Returns by Holiday, 1993–2010

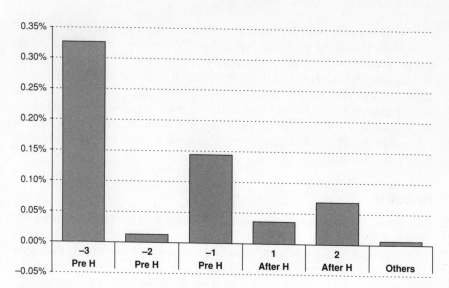

FIGURE 9.14 Russell 2000 Futures Average Returns by Day (−3, −2, −1, 1, 2) by Day, 1993–2010

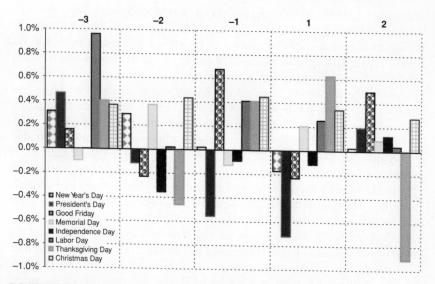

FIGURE 9.15 Russell 2000 Futures Holiday Average Returns by Holiday, 1993–2010

What happened in 2009 and 2010? In 2009, the close on September 18 was 1068.30 and the close on September 25 was 1044.38, so −2.24%. So the anomaly worked. Rosh Hashanah for Jewish Year 5771 began at sunset Wednesday, September 8, 2010, and ended at nightfall Friday, September 10, 2010, and Yom Kippur began on Friday, September 17, 2010. The close on September 8 was 1098.87 and the close on September 16 was 1124.66, for a gain of 2.35%. So the anomaly did not work in 2010. The close on December 31, 2010, was 1257.64 or a gain of 11.82% from the close on September 16, 2010.

Ramadan

Bialkowski, Etebari, and Wisniewski (2009) study stock returns during the Muslim holy period of Ramadan in 14 predominantly Muslim countries during the period from 1989–2007. They find that stock returns during Ramadan are almost 9 times higher (38.1% versus 4.3%) than during the rest of the year and that this conclusion persists after controlling for other known calendar anomalies like the January Effect, Halloween effect, and Turn-of-the-week effect. Their explanations for this phenomenon rely on recent behavioral theories that connect investor emotions with their decisions. Specifically, they suggest that these excess returns are a result of increased investor optimism experienced during Ramadan as a time of relative happiness, solidarity, and social identity for Muslims. They go as far as to suggest that Ramadan may cause mild states of euphoria, as suggested by Knerr and Pearl (2008). This upbeat or positive sentiment then causes relative overconfidence and an increased willingness to take risk, such that investors perceive investments as of relatively higher value. Bialkowski et al. also consider that, during this relatively healthy period, there may be a higher demand for equities, as documented by Rosen and Wu (2004). They, however, do not find any evidence of a higher trading volume during Ramadan.

In their study, Bialkowski et al. discuss Ramadan to shed light on its potential emotional effects, review the clinical effects of fasting, and review empirical evidence on the effects of Ramadan on equity prices in 14 Islamic countries. Their empirical results compare the average returns during the holy month and the rest of the year and find that 11 of 14 countries studied have higher returns during Ramadan; the countries that did not exhibit this anomaly are Bahrain, Saudi Arabia, and Indonesia. They mention the effects of relatively few observations in the case of Bahrain and Saudi Arabia and note the outlier of the Asian crisis in Indonesia affecting its equity prices during Ramadan.

They further test their results by 2 event studies, benchmarking returns against a constant-mean-return model as well as a predictive market model using a proxy of 23 industrialized countries that do not have Muslim majorities. In these tests, they calculated cumulative abnormal returns (CAR) as returns in excess of what an investor should expect in the absence of Ramadan, finding this CAR to fall between 2.5% and 3.1%, depending on the event study approach. Among other robustness tests, Bialkowski et al. analyze if this CAR may be compensation for increased risk during Ramadan by examining return volatility, but they do not find any supporting evidence. In fact, they find that, except for Turkey, all countries studied actually showed decreased volatility during Ramadan.

Bialkowski et al. also test their results for illiquidity effects, exchange rate considerations, and other accepted calendar effects, but they find that the Ramadan effect remains anomalous and can most likely be explained by temporal changes in investor psychology. They conclude that investors can profit in Muslim stock markets by buying shares at the beginning of Ramadan and selling them at its end, though they do not explicitly model this strategy nor do they estimate transaction costs.

Day-of-the-Week Effects

Historically in U.S. markets, there have been differences in the daily mean returns across the days of the week. A common finding is high Friday returns and low Monday returns. Early papers showing this are Cross (1973), French (1980), Gibbons and Hess (1981), Gultekin and Gultekin (1983), Lakonishok and Levi (1982), and Rogalski (1984). Lakonishok and Smidt (1988) relate the weekend effect to the turn-of-the-month effect (see that section of this chapter). Harris (1986) investigated time-of-day effects. Stocks advanced near the close in all days, including on the negative Mondays and positive Fridays. The Monday negative returns accrued over the weekend for large cap stocks but during the Monday trading session for small cap stocks. Stocks tend to advance in the first 45 minutes of trading on all days except Monday, when they fall. Wang, Li, and Erickson (1997) using 1962–1993 data show that the Monday declines are from last 2 Mondays of the month and that there is no monthly effect in the first 3 weeks. Kamara (1997) showed that the weekly effects declined in 1962–1993 because of increased institutional trading in large cap stocks. However, the small cap effect remains. Futures minus spot S&P returns are reversed as traders anticipate the effect. Chen and Sinal (2003) argue that short sellers close positions on Fridays, which increases prices, and the new Monday shorts lead to Monday losses. Chan, Leung, and Wang (2004) argue that the Monday decline effect is largely due to individual not institutional investors. The Monday decline is strongest in stocks with low institutional holdings. Moreover, the mean return on Monday is the same as on the other 4 days of the week for stocks with high institutional holdings.

International evidence was provided by Dubois and Louvet (1966), Jaffe and Westerfield (1985ab), and Jaffe, Westerfield, and Ma (1989). Steeley (2001) argued that the weekend effect in the United Kingdom disappeared in the 1990s. Moreover, the day-of-the-week effects are explained by news arrivals.

Kato (1990), Kato, Schwartz, and Ziemba (1989), Ziemba (1993) also study Japanese returns. Kato (1990) found negative Tuesdays, not Mondays, and positive Wednesday and Saturday returns. Ziemba (1993) investigated weeks ending on Friday with a full trading session in 2 parts with a break on Saturday with only the first session. He found that in the weeks with Friday endings, Fridays were positive and Mondays negative. However, in the weeks with Saturday trading, Saturdays were higher positive and the negative day was the Tuesday. Somehow the 2 days were needed for the fall. Choudhry (2000), using January 2000 to June 2005 data from Indonesia, Malaysia, the Philippines, South Korea, Taiwan, and Thailand showed the presence of the day-of-the-week effects in both stock returns and volatility and a possible spillover from the Japanese stock market.

Table 9.4 from Chukwuogor-Ndu (2006) shows the mean return from European stock markets from January 1997 to December 2004. Friday is positive in all 15 countries studied and Mondays are mixed, some positive, some negative. Tuesdays and Thursdays are also positive in most countries. Standard deviations are high so statistical significance is weak.

TABLE 9.4 Average Daily Returns of the EFM for the Period January 2, 1997–December 31, 2004

Country	Mon	Tue	Wed	Thur	Fri
Austria	0.0299	0.0233	0.0118	−0.0157	0.0037
Belgium	0.0036	−0.3000	0.0011	0.3270	0.0134
Czech Republic	0.0059	0.0154	0.0229	0.0242	0.0152
Denmark	0.0057	0.0185	0.0213	0.0153	0.0240
France	−0.0120	0.0178	−0.0094	0.0278	0.0139
Germany	0.0395	0.0253	−0.0196	0.0104	0.0125
Italy	−0.0137	0.0360	−0.0286	0.0280	0.0384
Netherlands	0.0540	0.0179	−0.0194	−0.0010	0.0252
Russia	0.0428	0.1280	−0.0903	0.0721	0.1125
Slovakia	−0.1101	0.0371	0.0480	0.0313	0.0035
Spain	−0.0303	−0.7170	−0.0532	0.7840	0.0220
Sweden	0.0551	0.0138	−0.0564	0.0177	0.0407
Turkey	−0.1730	−0.0329	0.0122	0.2069	0.2396
Switzerland	0.0070	0.0132	0.0121	0.0245	0.0357
United Kingdom	−0.0181	0.0200	0.0095	0.0141	0.031

Source: Chukwuogor-Ndu (2006).

French (1980), using data from 1953 to 1977 on the S&P composite, found that Friday returns had a positive mean as did Tuesday to Thursday, but Monday had negative returns. This refuted 2 hypotheses:

1. That returns occur continuously over time, so Monday should have 3 times the average day mean time
2. That all days have the same mean return since returns are generated during trading time, which are the same for all days.

Keim and Stambaugh (1984) extend the research back to 1928 that Mondays have negative mean returns for exchange-traded stocks of all firm sizes and for OTC stocks.

They also found that Friday to Monday correlations were higher than the other days. Abraham and Ikenberry (1994) find the same effect. When Friday is negative, Monday is negative 80% of the time with a –0.61% mean return. However, when Friday was positive Monday is positive on average returning +0.11%. The effect like most anomalies is strongest in small- and mid-cap companies.

Lakonishok and Maberly (1990) show that there was an increase in individual as opposed to institutional trading who sell more than buy on Mondays. Connolly (1989) showed that the strength of the day-of-the-week finding depends crucially on the estimation and testing methods used. Sullivan, Timmermann, and White (2001) provide a strong econometric argument regarding the care needed to get proper statistical conclusions. Using 100 years of daily data, they find anomalies like the day-of-the-week and weekend effects are significant, but, if you consider data mining, the anomalies are not statistically significant over the whole universe of data.

Summary: The cash evidence is strong that there was a weekend effect with positive Fridays and negative Mondays. However, the strength of the effect has diminished and it is hard to prove that it is not data snooping and out of sample. Moreover, the effect seems to reverse in the futures markets. The reasons for the effect are many and varied. The question of whether you can implement strategies based on these results remains. Arsad and Coutts (1997) argue that liquidity and other transactions costs might limit this possibility. We now look at the recent data in the futures markets.

To update, we compute the daily returns in the S&P 500 and Russell 2000 futures from 1993 to 2010. Recall that with anticipation the futures might reverse the cash effect. Figures 9.16a and b and Table 9.5 give the results. In the futures markets for the S&P 500 all days were positive with Thursday essentially zero. Monday has higher average returns than all the days. All the days have gains slightly more than 50% of the time. The Russell 2000 is very different with higher returns on all the days except for Mondays, which were negative. Still, all days were positive slightly more than 50% of the time. Finally, Table 9.6 and Figures 9.16a and b show the results by Days of the Week.

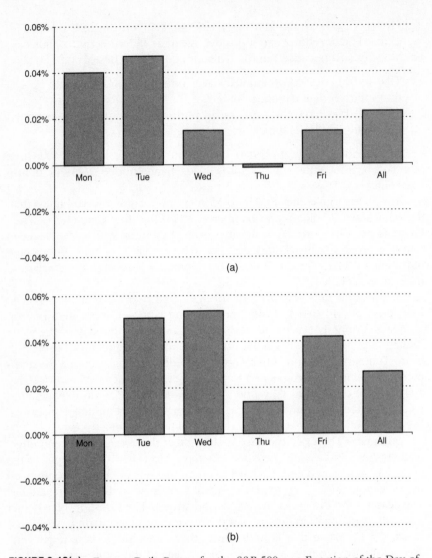

FIGURE 9.16(a) Futures Daily Return for the S&P 500 as a Function of the Day of the Week, 1993–2010. **(b)** Futures Daily Returns for the Russell 2000 Function of Day of the Week, 1993–2010

Seasonality Calendars

Ziemba and Schwartz (1991) made seasonality calendars for the first section of the Tokyo Stock Exchange (TSE) for the years 1988–1992. The days were ranked from –4, the worst, to +4, the best. A regression predicts the expected daily change of the index based on all the seasonal effects. Each

TABLE 9.5 Futures Daily Returns as Function of Day of the Week, 1993–2010

	Mon	Tue	Wed	Thu	Fri	All
S&P 500						
Count	872	928	926	911	905	4542
Mean	0.04%	0.05%	0.01%	0.00%	0.01%	0.02%
St Dev	0.0136	0.0129	0.0118	0.0122	0.0114	0.0124
t-stat	0.8661	1.1062	0.3787	−0.0344	0.3791	1.2405
Positive	55.30%	51.30%	54.10%	53.30%	52.20%	53.20
Russell 2000						
Count	877	927	926	916	906	4552
Mean	−0.03%	0.05%	0.05%	0.01%	0.04%	0.03%
St Dev	0.0157	0.0149	0.0145	0.0148	0.0134	0.0147
t-stat	−0.552	1.0306	1.1192	0.2821	0.9423	1.2218
Positive	51.80%	52.10%	55.30%	51.40%	54.90%	53.10

trading day has both a ranking and an expected performance. Of course, this ranking and performance does not consider the current economic environment and recent news so it could be off, but it gives one an idea of what to expect and what to look for.

Canestrelli and Ziemba (2000) investigated seasonal anomalies in the Italian stock market from 1973 to 1993. The results show that the effects have been found in the United States, Japan, and other markets such as the weekend, turn-of-the-year, monthly, holiday, and January barometer were present in Italy during that period. The data used were 7,668 days from January 3, 1973 to December 31, 1993 of which 5,238 were trading days. The highest daily return was +8.03% and the lowest −10.02%. The return distribution was fatter in the tails than Gaussian normal and there was autocorrelation in these returns. They did a careful analysis of these anomalies and readers may refer to their paper in Keim and Ziemba (2000). They also ranked the days into seasonality calendars using the following regression:

$$Rt = a1^D \text{Monday} + a2^D \text{Tuesday} + a3^D \text{Friday} + a4^D \text{1stDay} + a5^D \text{Easter}$$
$$+ a6^D \text{Christmas} + a7^D \text{1stNov} + a8^D \text{Jan} + a9^D \text{Day30} + a10^D \text{Day31} + ut$$

	Monday	Tuesday	Friday	1st Day	Easter	Xmas	1st Nov	Jan	Day 30	Day 31
Mean	−0.2221	−0.2082	0.0705	1.2667	0.6832	0.3048	0.6672	0.1419	0.3150	0.2386
(St Dev)	(0.0442)	(0.0431)	(0.0439)	(0.0809)	(0.2945)	(0.29801)	(0.2820)	(0.0653)	(0.1003)	(0.1355)
t-stat	−5.03**	−4.83**	1.61	15.66**	2.32*	1.09	2.37*	2.17*	3.14**	1.76

$Cost = 0.00 R_2 = 0.0582 R_{2adj} = 0.0566 D.W. = 1.58 F = 32.44$

**Referring to H_0: $a_1 = a_2 = a_3 = = a_{10} = 0$.

*indicates 5% confidence level

**indicates 1% confidence level

TABLE 9.6 Futures Daily Returns as Function of Day of the Week by Month, 1993–2010

	Mon	Tue	Wed	Thu	Fri
S&P 500					
January	0.18	−0.12	0.13	−0.10	−0.14
February	0.11	−0.13	−0.05	−0.11	−0.16
March	0.01	0.10	0.03	0.17	0.08
April	−0.06	0.30	0.00	0.31	−0.15
May	0.24	0.05	0.03	−0.14	−0.02
June	−0.09	−0.04	0.04	0.12	−0.04
July	0.00	0.00	0.09	0.00	−0.07
August	−0.01	−0.14	0.20	−0.16	−0.06
September	−0.14	0.15	−0.11	−0.14	0.27
October	0.14	0.17	−0.31	0.08	0.14
November	0.08	0.03	−0.01	0.06	0.12
December	0.05	0.18	0.13	−0.13	0.18
Russell 2000					
January	0.08	−0.10	0.12	−0.06	−0.25
February	0.10	−0.11	0.02	−0.10	−0.08
March	−0.11	0.10	0.07	0.27	−0.01
April	−0.34	0.32	0.13	0.42	−0.12
May	0.26	0.15	−0.12	−0.07	0.05
June	−0.19	−0.06	0.15	0.16	0.10
July	−0.10	0.00	0.01	−0.15	−0.06
August	−0.08	−0.14	0.33	−0.15	0.01
September	−0.10	0.27	−0.10	−0.10	0.23
October	0.09	−0.14	−0.30	0.04	0.15
November	0.08	0.00	0.07	−0.03	0.08
December	−0.01	0.33	0.27	−0.08	0.38

The results indicate the following ranking of the anomalies by importance of their effect on daily stock returns:

1. First day of the monthly account
2. Monday
3. Tuesday
4. Day 30 (calendar, not trading)
5. First November
6. Easter
7. January

8. Day 31 (calendar, not trading)
9. Friday
10. Christmas

Dzhabarov and Ziemba made similar calendars for the S&P 500 and Russell 2000 for 2010. Figure 9.17 shows the seasonality calendar and results for the S&P 500 and Russell 2000 futures for January 2010. The results of the exercise with January's S&P 500 = −3.72% and Russell 2000 = −3.79% are in Figure 9.19. When the authors created the calendar in 2009 they chose to use the coefficients from 2004 to 2009 rather than from 1993 to 2009 to employ the most current results. This way also offered better goodness of fit (higher R-squared).

Each box for a given trading day shows the model expected returns on the right and real returns added after January 2010 on the left for each of two index futures plus a ranking from −4 the worst to −3, −2, −1, 0, +1, +2, +3 and +4 the best (Russell 2000 first, S&P 500 second). Obviously, economic news may dominate a particular day, but the calendars add value. To compute the calendars, regressions were run on all the days around an anomaly concept and then a streamlined equation with only the best predictors was used to construct the expected values and calendar weightings. The authors also used turn-of-the-year variables, which consistently generated positive returns though they were not statistically significant. The variables that are working: for Russell 2000 third day before holiday (positive), turn-of-the-month good days (positive), turn-of-the-year good days (positive), third day before options expiry (positive), and for S&P 500 third day before holiday (positive), turn-of-the-month good days (positive), turn-of-the-year good days (positive), third day before options expiry (positive).

Political Effects

When Congress Is in Session

Ferguson and Witte (2006) find a strong correlation between Congressional activity and stock market returns such that returns are lower and volatility higher when Congress is in session. They use 4 data sets, including the Dow Jones Industrial Average since 1897, the S&P 500 index since 1957, and the CRSP value-weighted index and CRSP equal-weighted index since 1962. They compare mean daily stock returns and annualized returns when the U.S. Congress is in and out of session. Depending on the index tested, statistically significant differences in average daily returns range from 4–11 basis points per day. Annualized stock returns are 3.3–6.5% higher when Congress is out of session, and between 65 and 90% of capital gains have

January 2010 Calendar and Returns

Legend

RL code	RL day score
RL real r	RL expectedr
SP code	SP day score
SP real r	SP expectedr

Code: TOM = Turn of the month, RL = Russell 2000 future, SP = S&P500 future

Sunday	Monday	Tuesday	Wednesday	Thursday	Friday	Saturday
					1 New Year's Day	2
3	4 TOM 2.15% 0.15% 0 1.62% 0.12% 1	5 -0.20% 0.15% 0 0.31% 0.12% 1	6 -0.02% -0.12% 0 0.07% -0.10% 0	7 0.50% -0.12% 0 0.40% -0.10% 0	8 0.64% -0.12% 0 0.35% -0.10% 0	9
10	11 -0.50% -0.12% 0 0.09% -0.10% 0	12 -0.67% -0.12% 0 -0.74% -0.10% 0	13 0.82% -0.12% 0 0.66% -0.10% 0	14 0.76% -0.12% 0 0.33% -0.10% 0	15 -1.42% -0.12% – -1.14% -0.10% 0	16
17	18 ML King Day	19 1.54% -0.12% 0 1.19% -0.10% 0	20 -1.30% -0.12% 0 -1.03% -0.10% 0	21 -1.96% -0.12% 0 -2.03% -0.10% 0	22 -1.47% -0.12% 0 -1.80% -0.10% 0	23
24	25 TOM -0.08% 0.17% 1 0.14% 0.12% 1	26 TOM -0.81% 0.17% 1 -0.48% 0.12% 1	27 TOM 1.00% 0.17% 1 0.67% 0.12% 1	28 TOM -1.85% 0.17% 1 -1.39% 0.12% 1	29 TOM -0.74% 0.17% 1 -0.81% 0.12% 1	30
31			Jan 2010 RL return -3.79% Jan 2010 SP return -3.72%			

FIGURE 9.17 January 2010 Calendar and Results

occurred when Congress is not in session (which is notably greater than the proportionate number of days Congress is not in session).

Ferguson and Witte also test these results in several ways. First, they analyze if the Congressional effect is just a proxy for other known calendar effects, such as the day-of-the-week effect, January effect, and preholiday effect. They conclude that, after controlling for these anomalies, there is still a congressional effect of 3–6 basis points per day, which means that no more than half of the congressional effect is captured by controlling for other known anomalies. The study also tests for robustness and finds there is a low probability that these results are the effect of a spurious statistical relationship.

Next, they test if public opinion toward Congress accounts for the congressional effect by using public polling data as a proxy for general investors' attitudes toward Congress. They use 162 polls from 1939 to 2004, though 112 of these were conducted after 1989. They find that an active Congress does not itself lead to poor stock returns but rather that the public's opinion of that active Congress accounts for the depressed returns. They also find that each index exhibits volatility that is significantly lower when Congress is not in session and that this is also driven by public opinion.

Then Ferguson and Witte test the implications of this predictive capability on optimal investor asset allocation using the models of Kandel and Stambaugh (1996) and Britten-Jones (1999); they find that trading on the congressional effect would allow investors to better allocate between equities and cash and to achieve a higher Sharpe ratio.

Ferguson et al. consider 3 alternatives as possible explanations of the congressional effect, concluding that their findings may be explained by viewing public opinion of Congress as a proxy for investors' moods, regulatory uncertainty, or rent-seeking. The mood-based hypothesis follows other studies in behavioral finance that suggest depressed investors are relatively risk averse, which, in this case, would imply that negative public opinion of Congress was depressing investors and dampening returns. The regulatory uncertainty hypothesis follows from the implication that there is more uncertainty in the market when Congress is in session, such that risk and, therefore, returns are higher. The rent-seeking hypothesis is based on Rajan and Zingales (2003) and suggests that concentrated economic interests limit the efficiency of markets such that they are less efficient and biased toward powerful financial players when Congress is in session.

Election Cycles

Herbst and Slinkman (1984), using data from 1926 to 1977, found a 48-month political/economic cycle during which returns were higher than average. This cycle peaked in November of presidential election years. Riley and

Luksetich (1980) and Hobbs and Riley (1984) showed that, from 1900–1980, positive short-term effects followed Republican victories and negative returns followed Democratic wins. Huang (1985), using data from 1832–1979 and for various subperiods, found higher stock returns in the last 2 years of political terms than in the first 2. This finding is consistent with the hypothesis that political reelection campaigns create policies that stimulate the economy and are positive for stock returns. These studies concerned large cap stocks.

Hensel and Ziemba (1995c, 2000) investigated several questions concerning U.S. stock, bond, and cash returns from 1928 to 1997. They asked: Do small and large capitalization stock returns differ between Democratic and Republican administrations? Do corporate bond, intermediate- and long-term government bonds, and Treasury bill returns differ between the 2 administrations? Do the returns of various assets in the second half of each 4-year administration differ from those in the first half? Were Clinton's administrations analogous to past Democratic administrations? We also discuss here the terms of George W. Bush and Barack Obama to update to the end of 2010.

Their results indicate a significant smallcap effect during Democratic presidencies. Small cap stocks (the bottom 20% by capitalization) had higher returns during Democratic than Republican administrations. There has also been a small cap minus large cap S&P advantage outside the month of January for the Democrats. The higher returns with Democrats for small cap stocks are the result of gains rather than losses in the April–December period.

The turn-of-the-year small-firm effect, in which small cap stock returns significantly exceed those for large cap stocks in January, under both Republican and Democratic administrations, occurred during these 70 years. This advantage was slightly higher for Democrats, but the difference is not significant. Large cap stocks had statistically identical returns under both administrations. For both Democratic and Republican administrations, small and large cap stock returns were significantly higher during the last 2 years of the presidential term than during the first 2 years. Moreover, bond and cash returns were significantly higher during Republican compared with Democratic administrations. The results also confirm and extend previous findings that equity returns have been higher in the second half compared with the first half of presidential terms. This finding is documented for small and large cap stocks during both Democratic and Republican administrations. Finally, two simple investment strategies based on these findings yielded superior portfolio performance compared with common alternatives during the sample period. The results cast doubt on the long-run wisdom of the common 60/40 stock-bond strategy since all 100% equity strategies investigated had much higher wealth at the end of the sample period.

TABLE 9.7 Annual Average Equity Returns for Presidential Election Months and the Subsequent 13 Months, 1928–1997, Minus Annualized Monthly Averages

Return Period	1928–1997		1998–2010		1928–2010	
	Large	Small	Large	Small	Large	Small
Election + next 13 months	8.12	6.51	4.08	12.20	7.54	7.33
Annual average	10.12	12.02	5.19	8.22	9.34	11.42
Annual difference	−2.00	−5.51	−1.11	4.00	−1.79	−4.09

Monthly means were annualized by multiplying by 12.

Indeed the 1942–1997 returns were 24 times higher with the strategy small caps with Democrats and large caps with Republicans than the 60/40 mix, and the updated 1998–2010 returns shown in Table 9.9 show similar outperformance.

Table 9.7 shows that both small and large cap stocks had lower mean returns in the 13 months following an election. Figure 9.21 shows the specific months following the election for large (S&P 500) and small cap (bottom 20%) stocks.

The 1928–1997 period encompassed 18 presidential elections with an update to 2010 and 3 more elections. The end of 1997 included the first year of Clinton's second term. There were 33 years of Republican and 37 years of Democratic administrations during this period. The update to the end of 2010 covers the last 3 years of Clinton's second term plus 2 George W. Bush terms plus the first 2 years of Barack Obama's administration, namely, 1998 to 2010, a period in which small cap stocks outperformed large cap stocks. Tables 12 and 13 on the web site list and compare the first year, first 2 year, last 2 year, and whole-term mean returns under Democratic and Republican administrations from January 1929 to December 1997 and for January 1937 to December 1997, a period that excludes one term for each party during the 1929 crash, subsequent depression, and recovery period plus the update to 2010. Each term is considered separately, so 2-term presidents have double entries. The t-values shown in Table 12 on the web site test the hypothesis that, during the 1928–1997 period, returns did not differ between Democratic and Republican administrations.

From 1929 to 1997, the mean returns for small stocks were statistically higher during the Democratic presidential terms than during the Republican terms. The data confirm the advantage of small cap over large cap stocks under Democratic administrations. Small cap stocks returned, on average, 20.15% a year under Democrats compared with 1.94% under Republicans for the 1929–1997 period. This difference, 18.21%, was highly significant.

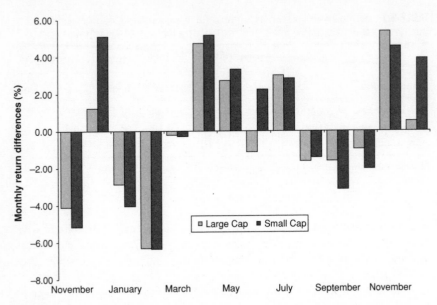

FIGURE 9.18 Stock Monthly Return Differences: Presidential Election Months and the Subsequent 13 Months Minus Monthly Averages

The first year return differences for this period were even higher, averaging 33.51%.

For a more extensive analysis of these relationships and the relationships over the last 2 years during Democratic and Republican administrations see the Seasonal Anomaly page on the web site associated with this book, http://hema.zacks.com.

U.S. Bond Returns after Presidential Elections

Investors can also benefit from the relationship between election cycles and fixed-income returns.

Figure 9.18 illustrates average return differences for bonds during election months and the subsequent 13 months (1929–1997) minus each month's 1928–1997 average return, using bond data from Ibbotson Associates consisting of monthly, continuously compounded total returns for long-term corporate bonds, long-term (20-year) government bonds, intermediate (5-year) government bonds, and cash (90-day T-bills). Figure 9.21(b) updates this to 2010. Corporate, long-term government, and intermediate government bond returns were all higher than the monthly average in the year following an election only in May, October, and November in the 1928–1997 period. The update only has 3 elections and the monthly pattern

TABLE 9.8 Annualized Average Monthly Return

Term	President	Party	Bonds	Cash	Bonds-Cash
1929–1932	Hoover	Republican	4.61	2.26	2.35
1933–1936	Roosevelt	Democratic	5.05	0.20	4.85
1937–1940	Roosevelt	Democratic	3.73	0.08	3.65
1941–1944	Roosevelt	Democratic	1.74	0.25	1.49
1945–1948	Roosevelt/Truman	Democratic	1.48	0.50	0.98
1949–1952	Truman	Democratic	1.24	1.35	−0.11
1953–1956	Eisenhower	Republican	1.19	1.66	−0.47
1957–1960	Eisenhower	Republican	4.24	2.54	1.70
1961–1964	Kennedy/Johnson	Democratic	3.21	2.84	0.37
1965–1968	Johnson	Democratic	2.76	4.43	−.67
1969–1972	Nixon	Republican	7.06	5.19	1.87
1973–1976	Nixon/Ford	Republican	7.42	6.25	1.17
1977–1980	Carter	Democratic	3.17	8.11	−4.94
1981–1984	Reagan	Republican	13.71	10.39	3.32
1985–1988	Reagan	Republican	10.35	6.22	4.13
1989–1992	Bush	Republican	10.77	6.11	4.66
1993–1996	Clinton	Democratic	5.74	4.30	1.44
1997–2000	Clinton	Democratic	5.77	5.07	0.69
2001–2004	Bush	Republican	3.69	1.84	1.85
2005–2008	Bush	Republican	4.00	3.40	0.61
2009–2010	Obama	Democratic	2.06	0.14	1.92

From 1998–2010 we used the 3-month T-bill secondary market rate discount basis for cash and market yield and U.S. Treasury securities at 5-year constant maturity, quoted on investment basis for bonds.
Source: Updated from Hensel and Ziemba (2000b).

is different than it was in the past. As Table 9.8 indicates, the performance of fixed-income investments differed significantly between Democratic and Republican administrations. All fixed-income and cash returns were significantly higher during Republican than during Democratic administrations during the two study periods. The high significance of the cash difference stems from the low standard deviation over terms. The performance of fixed-income investments differed very little between the first 2 years and the last 2 years of presidential terms.

The distribution of Democratic and Republican administrations during the 1929–1997 period played a part in the significance of the fixed-income and cash returns. As Table 9.8 indicates, the cash returns for the first 4 Democratic administrations in this period (1933–1948) were very low (0.20%, 0.08%, 0.25%, and 0.50% annually). This result largely explains why the term cash-return differences are so significant (t-value $= -12.31$ for 1929–1997). Democratic administrations were in power for 3 of the 4 terms during the 1941–1956 period, when government bonds had low returns. Bond returns in the 1961–1968 period (both Democratic terms) and 1977–1980 period (Democratic) were also low.

SOME SIMPLE PRESIDENTIAL INVESTMENT STRATEGIES Two presidential party-based investment strategies suggest themselves. The first is equity only and invests in small caps with Democrats and large caps with Republicans; the second, a simple alternating stock-bond investment strategy, invests in small cap stocks during Democratic administrations and intermediate government bonds during Republican administrations. The test period was January 1937 through December 1997 with an update from 1998 to 2010.

The common 60/40 (large cap/bonds) portfolio investment strategy provides a benchmark for comparison with the 2 strategies. Transaction costs were not included, but they would have a minor effect on the results because the higher return presidential strategies trade, at most, every 4 years. These investment strategies all lost money until the early 1940s; see Table 9.9, which shows the cumulative wealth.

The two presidential investment strategies performed well over the sample period. The strategy of investing in small cap stocks during Democratic administrations and large cap stocks during Republican administrations produced greater cumulative wealth than other investment strategies. The alternating stock-bond strategy of investing in small cap stocks under Democrats and intermediate bonds under Republicans produced the second-highest cumulative wealth. Both of these presidential-party-based strategies had higher standard deviations than large cap stocks alone during the 1937–1997 period. Clinton's first administration had returns for small and large cap stocks, bonds, and cash consistent with the past. However, in the first 14 months of his second administration, large cap stocks produced higher returns than small cap stocks.

TABLE 9.9 Value of $1 Initial Investment in 1997 and 2010

Date	Large Cap (S&P)	Small Cap	Presidential (SC/Int)	Presidential (SC/LC)	60/40 Benchmark
Jan 1937–Dec 1997	346.1	453.2	527.9	963.2	140.5
Jan 1942–Dec 1997	639.0	2044.1	2380.9	4343.8	180.9
Jan 1937–Dec 2010	565.2	959.5	1310.6	1407.9	242.4
Jan 1942–Dec 2010	1043.5	4327.6	5910.8	6349.5	312.1

Source: Hensel and Ziemba (2000); updated.

In the update in Table 9.9 we see that, for the 1942–2010 period, small cap stocks (Russell 2000 from 1998) produced about 4 times the gains of large cap S&P 500 stocks (4,327.6 versus 1,043.5). However, the small cap with Democrats and large cap with Republicans was even higher at 6,349.5. Meanwhile, the 60/40 portfolio was at 312.1, less than one-twentieth as much. Table 9.10 displays the mean returns and standard deviations for the various subperiods for the various strategies.

REMARKS An interesting finding of this study was the much higher small-stock returns during Democratic administrations as compared with Republican administrations. This finding is consistent with the hypothesis that Democrats devise economic policies that favor small companies and consequently, their stock prices. The 33.51% point difference between small stock performance in Democratic and Republican administrations in the first year in office and the 18.21% difference for the full 4-year term are very large. In 2011, during Obama's Democratic tenure the small cap Russell 2000 index has exceeded its 2007 high but the S&P 500 has not.

This political-party effect is different from the well-known January small-firm effect, which has been present for Republicans as well as Democrats. We found in addition a substantial small stock/large stock differential outside of January during Democratic rule, which is displayed on the web site http://wp.zacks.com. Large stock returns were statistically indistinguishable between Democrats and Republicans, but bond and cash returns were significantly higher during Republican than during Democratic administrations. We also confirmed and updated Huang's finding that large cap stocks have had higher returns in the last 2 years of presidential terms; this finding applies regardless of political party and for both small and large cap stocks.

A study of the differences in economic policies that lead to the divergence of investment results according to which political party is in office would be interesting. Clearly, candidates seeking reelection are likely to favor economic policies that are particularly attractive to the public; and those policies are consistent with higher stock prices. Cash returns did not differ significantly between the first and second 2-year periods of Democratic and Republican presidential terms.

Election Cycles: Other Literature

Stovall (1992) and Hensel and Ziemba (1995, 2000) documented the presidential-election-cycle effect, which showed that stock markets generally fell during the first 2 years after a U.S. presidential election and rose during the last 2 years. Other subsequent studies have documented the economically and statistically significant difference in equity returns during the first and second half of presidential terms for Republican and

TABLE 9.10 Average Returns and Standard Deviations for Different Investment Strategies for Different Investment Horizons.

Dates	# Years	Large Cap		Small Cap		Pres (SC/Int)		Strategies Pres (SC/LC)		60-40	
		Mean	StDev	Mean	StDev	Mean	StDev	Mean	StDev	Mean	StDev
Jan 1937–Dec 1997	61	10.9	15.8	13.3	24.5	12.6	20.7	14.1	22.8	8.6	10
Jan 1938–Dec 1997	60	11.8	15.5	14.9	23.7	14.3	19.8	15.8	22	9.2	9.8
Jan 1948–Dec 1997	50	12.3	14	13.9	19.2	13.1	12.7	14.9	16.5	9.7	9
Jan 1958–Dec 1997	40	11.6	14.2	14.7	20.2	14.6	13	15.6	17	9.7	9.3
Jan 1968–Dec 1997	30	11.4	15.1	12.7	21.5	14.3	12.4	14.3	17.5	10.1	9.9
Jan 1978–Dec 1997	20	15.4	14.7	16.3	19.5	15.9	13.8	17.2	17.9	12.9	9.9
Jan 1988–Dec 1997	10	16.6	11.9	15.2	14.9	13.7	9.9	16.2	13.2	13.2	8.2
Jan 1993–Dec 1997	5	18.4	10.6	17.7	13.3	17.7	13.3	17.7	13.3	13.5	7.4
Jan 1995–Dec 1997	3	27.1	11.2	22.1	15.1	22.1	15.1	22.1	15.1	19.7	7.6
Jan 1993–Dec 1997	3	19	9.4	19	9.4	19	9.4	19	9.4	10	4.3
Jan 1993–Dec 1993	1	9.5	6.1	11.1	9.8	11.1	9.8	11.1	9.8	4.3	6.5
Jan 1993–Dec 1994	2	5.4	8.5	22.9	14.2	22.9	14.2	22.9	14.2	19.3	5.9
Jan 1995–Dec 1996	2	26.3	8.4	20.5	17.6	20.5	17.6	20.5	17.6	20.5	10.5
Jan 1997–Dec 1997	1	28.8	15.8	12	23.5	11.9	20.1	12.5	22	7.9	11.7
Jan 1937–Dec 2010	74	8.9	16	13.3	22.8	13.2	19.3	13.9	21.2	8.4	11.6
Jan 1938–Dec 2010	73	9.6	15.7	12.3	18.7	12.1	13.7	12.8	16.5	8.7	11.5
Jan 1948–Dec 2010	63	9.7	14.6	15.5	19.5	16.1	14.1	16	16.9	10.4	12
Jan 1958–Dec 2010	43	10.7	14.9	14	20.3	16.3	14	14.9	17.3	11	12.7
Jan 1968–Dec 2010	33	10.2	15.6	17.7	18.5	18.5	15.1	17.7	17.4	13.9	13.4
Jan 1978–Dec 2010	23	13.2	15.5	17.8	16	18.9	14.5	17.3	15.4	14.9	14.3
Jan 1988–Dec 2010	13	12.4	15	12.4	20.5	9.7	13.3	9.3	17.4	5.9	9.1
Jan 2003–Dec 2010	8	7.7	15.2	6.2	21.9	8.3	15.7	4.9	19.7	4.7	10
Jan 2008–Dec 2010	3	-0.3	16.7								

Source: Hensel and Ziemba (2000) and update to 2010.

Democratic administrations. Some studies use more detailed models. Wong and McAleer (2008) examine the cyclical effect that presidential elections have on equity markets using a spectral analysis technique and an exponential generalized autoregressive conditional heteroskedastic (GARCH) intervention model to correct for time dependence and heteroskedasticity. They consider the period from January 1965 to December 2003 using weekly data with dummy variables to designate the year of the term and the president's party.

Wong and McAleer find a cyclical trend that mirrors the 4-year election cycle with a modified cycle of between 40 and 53 months. They find that stock prices generally fall until a low point during the second year of a presidency and then rise during the remainder, peaking in the third or fourth year. During the current Obama Democratic administration, the low was in March 2009 in his first year and the market has nearly doubled since then to the end of January 2011. Wong and McAleer also find this presidential-election-cycle effect to be notably more significant under Republican administrations, leading them to posit that the Republican Party may engage in policy manipulation in order to benefit during elections relatively more than their Democratic counterparts. For instance, the second-year and third-year effect estimates are not significant for Democratic administrations.

Wong and McAleer explain the presidential election cycle as follows. During the first year of a presidency, voters are on average optimistic, and presidents are likely to put their most divergent and expensive new policies in place, because they have the mandate of the voters and reelection time is furthest away. These early measures are relatively disadvantageous to business profits and stock prices because they usually involve higher taxes and spending and possibly new regulations. Then, during the second year of a term, presidents begin to alter their policies to ones that are less drastic and more voter-friendly.

The presidential-election-cycle effect persists when looked at by president and by party. For instance, the only two presidents who did not exhibit the cycle effect were Ronald Reagan and Bill Clinton during their second terms, during which they would not have reelection incentives like first-term presidents. Empirical results also find that Republicans who were subsequently reelected had a positive effect during the second-year of their term instead of the negative effect expected by the presidential-election-cycle hypothesis. This suggests these Republicans may have used government policies to their favor to win reelection and should be useful for incumbent presidents to consider in their electoral strategy. This last conclusion, however, does not follow from the conflicting observation that bull markets have tended to coincide with subperiods under Democratic administrations. Wong and McAleer conclude that this anomaly was present during most of the last 40 years and is likely still present in the market.

Turn-of-the-Month Effects

Historically there have been high returns for both large and small cap stocks around the turn of the month (TOM). Market advisors such as Merrill (1966), Fosback (1976), and Hisrch (1986) have argued that stocks advance at the TOM. Ariel (1987) documented this for the United States using equally and value weighted indices of all NYSE stocks from 1963–1981; see Figures 9.19a and b.

The 5 days –1 to +4 historically were the TOM and had a large amount of the monthly gains. Indeed that period and the second week actually had all the monthly gains. Ariel (1987) found the following portfolio gains:

	Equally weighted	Value weighted
First half of trading month	2,552.40%	565.40%
Last half of trading month	−0.25%	−33.80%
Nineteen years	2545.90%	339.90%

Lakonishok and Smidt (1988) found that during the 90-year period, 1897–1986, the large capitalized Dow Jones industrials rose 0.475% during the 4-day period –1 to +3 each month, whereas the average gain for a 4-day period was 0.061% with an increase in prices over 56% of the time. The average gain per month over these 90 years was 0.349%. Hence, aside from these 4 days at the TOM, the DJIA actually fell.

The effect has continued in recent years even in the presence of index futures contracts which began trading in the United States in 1982. Hensel, Sick, and Ziemba (1994) found for the period May 1982 to April 1992 using the S&P 500 large cap and Value Line small cap indexes, consistent with the previous evidence that about two-thirds of the months, gains occur on trading days –1 to +4, the TOM, and the rest of the months, gains occur on trading days +5 to +9 so that all or more than all of the gains occur in the first half of the month. The second half was, at best, noise. The effect was monthly dependent with the largest gains in January and size dependent with the small capitalized value line index of about 1,650 stocks having higher means and lower standard deviations than the large capitalized S&P 500 index. There was partial anticipation in the futures market as shown in Figure 9.20. For the small capitalized value line index, the cash effect on day –1 was partially anticipated on days –4 to –2. Then the effect in the cash market on days +2 and +3 was partially anticipated on day +1. Hence, the cash market effect on days –1 to +4 was as Ariel found for the 1963 to 1981 data with small gains on days –4 to –2. For the large capitalized S&P 500 index, the results were similar except that there are higher returns in the

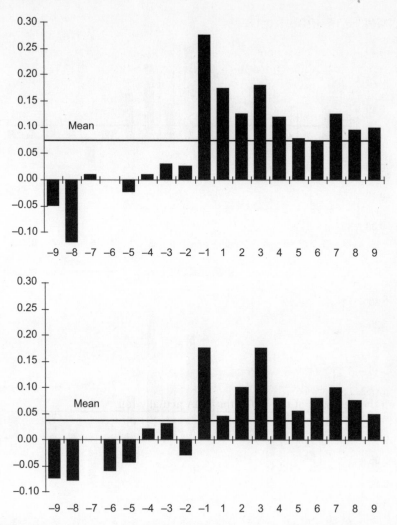

FIGURE 9.19 The United States Turn-of-the-Month Effect, Mean Daily Percent Returns on Trading Days –9 to +9, 1963–1981.
Source: Ariel 1987.

cash market in the anticipation period (–4 to –2) and lower returns in the –1 to +4 period.

The reasons for the TOM effect are several but they are largely cash-flow and institutionally based. See Hensel, Sick, and Ziemba (1996) and Gonzalez (2006) who discusses that paper. The U.S. economy uses a system in which much money is paid on the –1 day, such as salaries and bills and debt

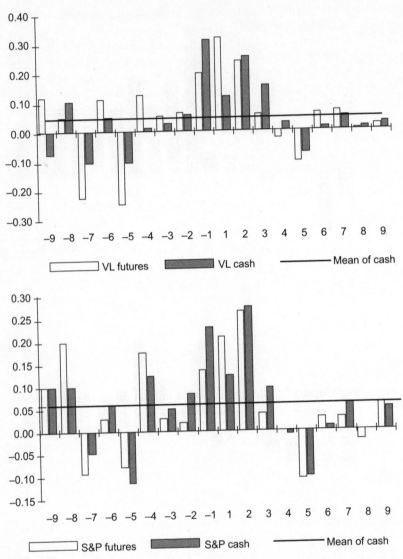

FIGURE 9.20 Mean Percentage Daily Returns in the Cash and Futures Market for Small and Large Capitalized Stocks by Trading Day of the Month, May 1982–April 1992

Source: Hensel, Sick, and Ziemba 1994.

payments. In addition to some of this money being invested in the stock market, there are institutional corporate and pension-fund purchases at that time. These cash flows vary by month and lead to higher average returns in January, which has the highest cash inflow. Ogden (1990) presents some empirical support of this hypothesis and related monetary actions for U.S. markets. Another factor in this effect seems to be behavioral. One manifestation is that bad news, such as that relating to earnings announcements is delayed and announced late in the month, whereas good news is released at the beginning of the month; see Penman (1987). Bouges, Jain, and Puri (2009) show a TOM effect in the S&P ADR.

The turn of the month was similar in Japan, except that the dates change with the turn being days −5 to + 2, with +3 to +7 being the rest of the first half of the month. Ziemba (1989, 1991) investigated this. The reasons for the effect in Japan seem to be:

- Most salaries were paid during the period of the twentieth to the twenty-fifth day of the month, with the twenty-fifth being especially popular.
- There was portfolio window dressing on day −1.
- Security firms could invest for their own accounts on amounts based on their capitalization. Since their capitalization usually rises each month and is computed at the end of the month, there is buying on day −3 to account for this. Buying was done as soon as possible.
- Large brokerage firms had a sales push that on day −3, and it lasted 7 to 10 days.
- Employment stock holding plans and mutual funds received money in this period to invest, starting around day −3.
- Individual investors bought mutual funds with their pay, which they received on calendar days 15 to 25 of the month; the funds then invested in stocks with a lag, so most of the buying occurred on days −5 to +2.
- For low liquidity stocks, buying occurred over several days by dealing in accounts to minimize price pressure effects.

Using data on the NSA from 1949 to 1988 Ziemba (1991) found that all of the days −5 to +2 had significantly positive returns. As in the United States, all the gains occurred in the first half of the month and the second half had zero or negative returns.

Ziemba (1989) investigated the futures market trading outside Japan on the Simex in Singapore on the TOM and other anomalous effects in Japanese security markets during the period September 1986 to September 1988 before there was futures trading on the Nikkei Stock Average (NSA) or Topix in Japan. He found that the spot effect was consistent with past data so the futures market did not alter the effect. However, the futures market in Singapore totally anticipated the effect on days −8 to −5 with a total average

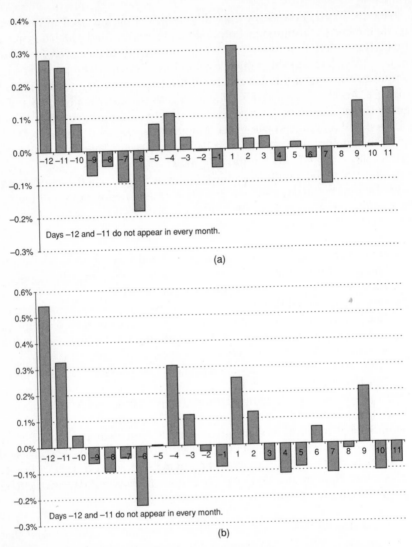

FIGURE 9.21(a) S&P 500 Futures Average Daily Returns in Respect to TOM, 1993–2010. **(b)** S&P 500 Futures Average Daily Returns in Respect to TOM, 2004–2010

rise on 2.8%. Then when the effect occurred on days –5 to +2 and the spot market gained 1.7%, the futures market was flat.

In our update for the U.S. markets using S&P 500 and Russell 2000 futures data from 1993–2010 and 2004–2010, we found that the TOM effect still exists with a bit of anticipation. Figures 9.21a and b and 9.22a and b and document the results. Tables showing more detailed results are displayed at

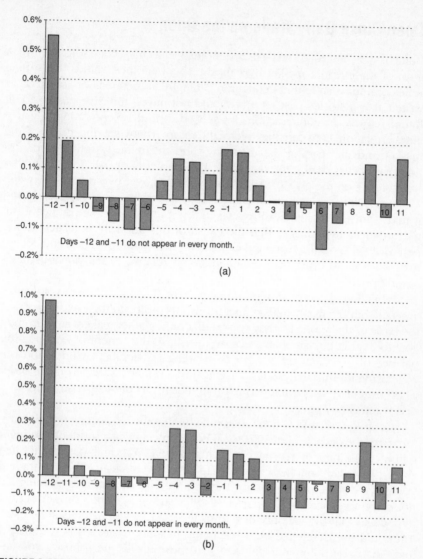

FIGURE 9.22(a) Russell 2000 Futures Average Daily Returns in Respect to TOM, 1993–2010. **(b)** Russell 2000 Futures Average Daily Returns in Respect to TOM 2004–2010

the web site **hema.zacks.com**. For example, for the S&P 500, for the longer sample and also for the shorter more recent data, the days -5 to +2 all have positive returns except –1 and –2 (which have small mean losses). For the Russell 2000, the same days all have positive mean returns for the longer sample and for the more recent data with –2 having a slightly negative mean.

Open/Close Daily Trade on the Open

Branch and Ma (2006) analyze an anomaly that may contradict the weak form of the efficient market hypothesis. This hypothesis holds that a time series of returns should not contain meaningful autocorrelation, or, in other words, that a stock's past returns should not have predictive power about future returns. In contradiction, Branch et al. find a very strong negative autocorrelation between the overnight return (between the close of the market and its opening the next day) and the intraday return (the portion that occurs during the day while the market is open). The study analyzes stocks on the NYSE, AMEX, and NASDAQ over two periods between 1994 and 2005, as well as breaking them down into size categories, and it finds statistically significant results across each subsample. Branch et al. go further to hypothesize that the cause of this anomaly is related to the behavior of specialists or market makers and their strategies and incentives on how to open their assigned stocks relative to the previous day's closing price.

Branch et al. also consider whether there is a strategy that exploits this anomaly but offer only initial conclusions. According to their explanation of the basis of the anomaly, they reason that only market makers are currently able to exploit this anomaly because they have the benefit of knowing the balance of overnight orders. For the trading public, their main actionable conclusion for this analysis is advice against a public trader placing an order to be executed at opening, which they equate to putting in an order at a disadvantageous price.

Cooper, Cliff, and Gulen (2008) exhibit that the U.S. equity premium return over the decade from 1993 to 2006 has solely been a result of overnight returns, with intraday returns being close to zero. Although past studies had shown that daily market closures had a relatively clear effect on trading volume and stock price volatility, the implications as far as return timing did not carry a consensus. Cooper et al. offer strong evidence supporting the hypothesis that the majority of returns are made when markets are closed. They find the difference between night and day returns is between 2.61 and 7.61 basis points per day and that these results are robust across asset types, subperiods, and markets (including NYSE, AMEX, NASDAQ, and Chicago Mercantile Exchange). The study finds that typical explanations such as risk, earnings surprises, and illiquidity do not substantially explain this pattern and instead imply that there is an inefficiency in market opening and closing mechanisms. Particularly they suggest this may carry tradable implications for portfolio managers, particularly those with low marginal trading costs.

Weather: Sun, Rain, Snow, Moon, and the Stars

Hirschleifer and Shumway (2003) point out that psychologists have documented correlation between sunshine and behavior for decades. Sunshine has been linked to tipping (Rind 1996) and lack of sunshine to depression (Eagles 1994) and suicide (Tietjen and Kripke 1994). People feel good when the sun shines, and when they feel good, they are more optimistic and may be more inclined to buy stocks thus leading to higher stock prices.

Roll (1992) argues that:

> *weather is a genuinely exogenous economic factor ... it was a favorite example of an exogenous identifying variable in the early econometrics literature ... because weather is both exogenous and unambiguously observable ... weather data should be useful in assessing the information processing ability of financial markets.*

See also Trombley (1997), Kramer and Runde (1997), and Loughran and Schulz (2004). Hirshleifer and Shumway (2003), following the earlier paper by Saunders (1993), examine the relation between morning sunshine at a country's leading stock exchange and market index stock returns that day at 26 stock exchanges internationally from 1982–1997. They find that sunshine is strongly positively correlated with daily stock returns. After controlling for sunshine, other weather conditions such as rain and snow are unrelated to returns. Keef and Roush (2007), using data on 26 international stock exchanges show the not surprising result that the sunshine effect is monotone stronger the further one is from the equator and the per capita GDP. There is no effect at the equator and a big effect on northern stock exchanges. An interesting question for future research, which we are working on for a forthcoming paper, is whether the sunshine effect has anything to do with sell-in-May-and-go-away, which suggests being out of the stock market in the sunniest time of the year.

Yuan, Zheng, and Zhu (2006) investigate the relationship between lunar phases and stock market returns in 48 countries. Stock returns are lower on the days around a full moon compared to the days around a new moon. The return difference is 3–5% per year based on equal and value weighted global portfolios. The result is not due to changes in stock market volatility or trading volumes. Also the lunar effect is not explained by announcements of macroeconomic factors or major global shocks, and is independent of calendar anomalies such as January, day-of-the-week, calendar month, or holiday effects.

Conclusions and Final Remarks

In the main, the anomalies are still there with some moving around. In the past, some of the anomalies such as the TOM and January effect had very high prediction accuracy. Currently, the January barometer and sell-in-May-and-go-away, which deal with longer-range predictions, have similar reliability. Other anomalies such as the January and holiday effects still exist and add value. The monthly effect has become noise and has no predictive value.

For more details on seasonal anomaly-based strategies that are managed by Ziemba, see the web site associated with this book http://hema .zacks.com.

References

Abraham, A., and D. L. Ikenberry. 1994. The individual investor and the weekend effect. *Journal of Financial and Quantitative Analysis* 29 (2): 263–277.

Ariel, R. A. 1987. A monthly effect in stock returns. *Journal of Financial Economics* 18: 161–174.

Ariel, R. A. 1990. High stock returns before holidays: existence and evidence on possible causes. *Journal of Finance* 45: 1611–1626.

Arsad, Z., and J. A. Coutts 1997. Security price anomalies in the London International Stock Exchange: A 60 year perspective. *Applied Financial Economics* 7: 455–464.

Banz, R. 1981. The relationship between return and market value of common stock. *Journal of Financial Economics* 9: 3–18.

Bialkowski, J. P., A. Etebari, and T. P. Wisniewski. 2009. Piety and profits: Stock market anomaly during the Muslim Holy Month. Finance and Corporate Governance Conference 2010 Paper. Available at SSRN.

Blume, M. E., and R. R. Stambaugh. 1983. Biases in computed returns: an application to the size effect. *Journal of Financial Economics* 12, 387–404.

Bohl, M. T., and C. A. Salm. 2010. The other January effect: International evidence. *European Journal of Finance* 16: 173–182.

Booth, D. G., and D. Keim. 2000. Is there still a January effect? In *Security market imperfections in world wide equity markets*, edited by D. B. Keim and W. T. Ziemba, 169–178. Cambridge, UK: Cambridge University Press.

Bouges, J. C., R. Jain, and Y. R. Puri. 2009. American depository receipts and calendar anomalies. *Applied Financial Economics* 19 (1): 17–25.

Bouman, S., and B. Jacobsen. 2002. The Halloween indicator, sell in May and go away: Another puzzle. *American Economic Review* 92 (5): 618–1635.

Branch, B. S., and A. Ma. 2006. The overnight return, one more anomaly. SSRN.

Bronson, R. E. 2011. Bronson Capital Market Research "What January Effect?" www.ritholtz.com/blog/2011/02/what-January effect-2/.

Brown, L. D., and L. Luo. 2006. The January barometer: further evidence. *Journal of Investing* 15 (1): 25–31.

Cadsby, C. B., and M. Ratner. 1992. Turn-of-the-month and pre-holiday effects on stock returns: Some international evidence. *Journal of Banking and Finance* 16: 497–509.

Canestrelli, E., and W. T. Ziemba. 2000. Calendar anomalies in the Italian stock market, 1973–1993. In *Security market imperfections in world wide equity markets*, edited by D. B. Keim and W. T. Ziemba, 337–363. Cambridge, UK: Cambridge University Press.

Cervera, A., and D. B. Keim. 2000. High stock returns before holidays: international evidence and additional tests. In *Security market imperfections in world wide equity markets*, edited by D. B. Keim and W. T. Ziemba, 512–531. Cambridge, UK: Cambridge University Press.

Chan, S. H., W.-K. Leung, and K. Wang. 2004. The impact of institutional investors on the Monday seasonal. *Journal of Business* 77 (4): 967–986.

Chen, H., and V. Singal. 2003. Role of speculative short sales in price formation: The case of the weekend effect. *Journal of Finance* 58 (2): 685–706.

Chopra, V., and W. T. Ziemba. 1993. The effect of errors in mean and co-variance estimates on optimal portfolio choice. *Journal of Portfolio Management* (Winter): 6–11.

Choudhry, T. 2000. Day of the week effect in emerging Asian stock markets: Evidence from the GARCH model. *Applied Financial Economics* 10 (3): 235–242.

Chukwuogor-Ndu, C., Stock market returns analysis, day-of-the-week effect, volatility of returns evidence from European financial markets 1997–2004. *International Research Journal of Finance and Economics* 1: 112–124.

Clark, R., and W. T. Ziemba. 1987. Playing the turn-of-the-year effect with index futures. *Operations Research* XXXV: 799–813.

Connolly, R. A. 1989. An examination of the robustness of the Weekend Effect. *Journal of Financial and Quantitative Analysis* 24 (2): 133–169.

Cooper, M. J., M. T. Cliff, and H. Gulen. 2008. Return differences between trading and non-trading hours: Like night and day. SSRN.

Cooper, M. S., J. J. McConnell, and A. V. Ovtchinnikov. 2006. The other January effect. *Journal of Financial Economics* 82 (2): 315–341.

Cross, F. 1973. The behavior of stock price on Fridays and Mondays. *Financial Analyst Journal* 29: 67–69.

Dimson, E. (ed.). 1988. *Stock market anomalies*. Cambridge, UK: Cambridge University Press.

Dimson, E., and P. Marsh. 1999. Murphy's Law and market anomalies. *Journal of Portfolio Management* 25: 53–69.

Doeswijk, R. 2005. The optimism cycle: Sell in May. *De Economist* 156 (2): 175–200.

Dubois, M., and P. Louvet. 1996. The day-of-the-week effect: The international evidence. *Journal of Banking and Finance* 20: 1463–1484.

Dzhabarov, C., and W. T. Ziemba. 2009. Do seasonal anomalies still work? Longer working paper, UBC.

Dzhabarov, C., and W. T. Ziemba. 2010. Do seasonal anomalies still work? *Journal of Portfolio Management* 36 (3): 93–104.

Eagles, J. M. 1994. The relationship between mood and daily hours of sunlight in rapid cycling bipolar illness. *Biological Psychiatry* 36: 422–424.

Easterday, K. E., P. K. Sen, and J. Stephan. 2008. The persistence of the small firm/January effect: Is it consistent with investors' learning and arbitrage efforts? *The Quarterly Review of Economics and Finance* 49 (3): 1172–1193.

Easton, S. A., and S. M. Pinder. 2007. A refutation of the existence of the other January effect. *International Review of Finance* 3–4 (7): 89–104.

Fama, E. F. 1970. Efficient capital markets: A review of theory and empirical work. *Journal of Finance* 25: 383–417.

Fama, E. F. 1991. Efficient capital markets II. *Journal of Finance* 46 (5): 1575–1617.

Fama, E. F. (1998). Market efficiency, long-term returns and behavioral finance. *Journal of Financial Economics* 25: 383–417.

Fama, E. F., and R. French. 1992. The cross-section of expected stock returns. *Journal of Finance* 47: 427–65.

Ferguson, M. F., and H. D. Witte. 2006. Congress and the stock market. SSRN.

Fosback, N. G. 1976. *Stock market logic*. Fort Lauderdale, FL: The Institute for Economic Research.

French, K. 1980. Stock returns and the week-end effect. *Journal of Financial Economics* 8: 55–70.

Fung, W., D. A. Hsieh, N. Y. Naik, and T. Ramadorai. 2006. Hedge funds: Performance, risk and capital formation. Technical report, London Business School.

Garrett, I., M. Kamstra, and L. A. Kramer. 2004. Winter blues and time variation in the price of risk. *Journal of Empirical Finance* 12 (2): 291–316.

Ghosh, S., G. Bhalla, and W. T. Ziemba. 2007. The January barometer, 1926–2005. Technical Report, Sauder School of Business.

Gibbons, R. S., and P. Hess. 1981. Day of the week effects and asset return. *Journal of Business* 54: 579–96.

Gonzalez, M. 2006. Buying stock? Consider turn-of-the-month effects. *Wall Street Journal.*

Gorenstein, P. 2010. A "Super Boom" in stocks? Dow 38k by 2025, says the Stock Traders Almanac. *Investing/Yahoo Finance.*

Gultekin, M., and N. B. Gultekin. 1983. Stock market seasonality: International evidence. *Journal of Financial Economics* 12: 469–481.

Hansen, P. R., A. Lunde, and J. M. Nason. 2005. Testing the significance of calendar effects. Federal Reserve Bank of Atlanta Working Paper No. 2005-02.

Harris, L. 1986. A transaction data study of weekly and intra daily patterns in stock returns. *Journal of Financial Economics* 16: 99–117.

Haug, M., and M. Hirschey. 2006. The January effect. *Financial Analysts Journal* 62 (5): 78–88.

Hensel, C., G. Sick, and W. T. Ziemba. 1994. The turn of the month effect in the S&P 500, 1926–1992. *Review of Futures Markets* 13 (3): 827–856.

Hensel, C., G. A. Sick, and W. T. Ziemba. 1996. Investment results from exploiting turn-of-the-month-effects. *Journal of Portfolio Management* (Spring): 17–23.

Hensel, C., and W. T. Ziemba. 1995a. The January barometer. *Journal of Investing* 4 (2): 67–70.

Hensel, C., and W. T. Ziemba. 1995b. The January Barometer: Swiss, European and global results. *Finanzmarket and Portfolio Management,* 9 (2): 187–196.

Hensel, C., and W. T. Ziemba. 1995c. United States investment returns during Democratic and Republican administrations, 1928–1993. *Financial Analysts Journal* (March/April): 61–69.

Hensel, C. R., and W. T. Ziemba. 2000a. Anticipation in the January effect in the US futures markets. In *Security market imperfections in world wide equity markets,* edited by D. B. Keim and Ziemba, 179–202. Cambridge, UK: Cambridge University Press.

Hensel, C. R., and W. T. Ziemba. 2000b. How does Clinton stand up to history? US investment returns and presidential party affiliations. In *Security market imperfections in world wide equity markets,* edited by D. B. Keim and W. T. Ziemba, 179–202. Cambridge, UK: Cambridge University Press.

Herbst, A. F., and C. W. Slinkman. 1984. Political-economic cycles in the US stock market. *Financial Analysts Journal* 40 (2): 38–44.

Hirsch, J. A., and Y. Hirsch. 2011. *Stock traders almanac: Wiley yearly updates.* Hoboken, NJ: John Wiley & Sons.

Hirsch, Y. 1986. Don't sell stocks on Monday. New York: Facts on File Publications.

Hirshleifer, D., and T. Shumway. 2003. Good day sunshine: Stock returns and the weather. *Journal of Finance* 58 (3): 1009–1032.

Hobbs, G. R., and W. B. Riley. 1984. Profiting from a presidential election. *Financial Analysts Journal* 40 (2): 46–52.

Hou, K., and D. T. Robinson. 2006. Industry concentration and average stock returns. *Journal of Finance* 6 (4): 1927–1956.

Huang, R. D. 1985. Common stock returns and presidential elections. *Financial Analysts Journal* 41 (2): 58–65.

Hudson, R., K. Keasey, and K. Littler. 2002. Why investors should be cautious of the academic approach to testing for stock market anomalies. *Applied Financial Economics* 12, 681–686.

Jacobs, B. I., and K. N. Levy. 1988a. Calendar anomalies: Abnormal returns at calendar turning points. *Financial Analysts Journal* 44, 28–39.

Jacobs, B. I., and K. N. Levy. 1988b. Disentangling equity return regularities: New insights and investment opportunities. *Financial Analysts Journal* 44, 18–43.

Jacobs, B. I., and K. N. Levy. 1988c. On the value of value. *Financial Analysts Journal* 44: 47–62.

Jacobsen, B., A. Mamun, and N. Visaltanachoti. 2005. Seasonal, size and value anomalies. SSRN.

Jaffe, J., and R. Westerfield. 1985a. Patterns in Japanese common stock returns: day of the week and turn of the year effect. *Journal of Financial Quantitative Analysis* 20: 261–272.

Jaffe, J., and R. Westerfield. 1985b. The week-end effect in common stock return: The international evidence. *Journal of Finance* 40: 433–454.

Jaffe, J., R. L. Westerfield, and C. Ma. 1989. A twist on the Monday effect in stock prices: Evidence from the U.S. and foreign stock markets. *Journal of Banking and Finance* 13: 641–650.

Jagannathan, R., A. Malakhov, and D. Novikov. 2006. Do hot hands persist among hedge fund managers? An empirical evaluation. Technical Report, Northwestern University.

Jegadeesh, N., and S. Titman. 1993. Returns to buying winners and selling losers: Implications for stock market efficiency. *Journal of Finance* 48: 65–91.

Kamara, A. 1997. New evidence on the Monday seasonal in stock returns. *Journal of Business* 70 (1): 63–84.

Kamstra, M. J., L. A. Kramer, and M. D. Levi. 2000. Losing sleep at the market: The daylight-savings anomaly. *American Economic Review* 90: 1005–1011.

Kamstra, M. J., L. A. Kramer, and M. D. Levi. 2003. Winter blues: A SAD stock market cycle. Federal Reserve Bank of Atlanta Working Paper No. 2002-13a.

Kato, K. 1990. Weekly patterns in Japanese stock returns. *Management Science* 36: 1031–1043.

Kato, K., S. L. Schwartz, and W. T. Ziemba. 1989. Day of the week effects in Japanese stocks. In *Japanese capital markets*, edited by E. J. Elton and M. J. Gruber, 249–281. Cambridge, UK: Ballinger.

Keel, S. P., and M. L. Roush. 2007. A metaanalysis of the international evidence of cloud cover on stock returns. *Review of Accounting and Finance* 6 (3): 324–338.

Keim, D. B. 1983. Size related anomalies and stock return seasonality: Further empirical evidence. *Journal of Financial Economics* 12: 3–32.

Keim, D. B. 1989. Trading patterns, bid-ask spreads, and estimated security returns: The case of common stock returns at the turn of the year. *Journal of Financial Economics* 25: 7598.

Keim, D. B., and R. F. Stambaugh. 1984. A further investigation of the Weekend Effect in stock returns. *Journal of Finance* 39 (3): 819–835.

Keim, D. B., and W. T. Ziemba (eds.) 2000. *Security market imperfections in world wide equity markets*. Cambridge, UK: Cambridge University Press.

Kramer, W., and R. Runde. 1997. Stocks and the weather: an exercise in data mining or yet another capital market anomaly. *Empirical Economics* 22: 637–641.

Lakonishok, J., and M. Levi. 1982. Week-end effects on stock returns: A note. *Journal of Finance* 37: 883–89.

Lakonishok, J., and E. Maberly. 1990. The Weekend Effect: Trading patterns of individual and institutional investors. *Journal of Finance* 45 (1): 231–243.

Lakonishok, J., and S. Smidt. 1988. Are seasonal anomalies real? A ninety-year perspective. *Review of Financial Studies* 1: 403–425.

Lo, A. W., and A. C. MacKinlay. 1990. Data-snooping biases in tests of financial asset pricing models. *Review of Financial Studies* 3 (3): 431–467.

Loughran, T., and P. Schultz. 2004. Weather, stock returns and the impact of localized trading behavior. *Journal of Financial and Quantitative Analysis* 39 (2): 343–364.

Lucey, B. M., and A. Pardo. 2005. Why investors should not be cautious about the academic approach to testing for stock market anomalies. *Applied Financial Economics* 15: 165–171.

MacLean, L. C., E. O. Thorp, Y. Zhao, and W. T. Ziemba. 2011. How does the Fortune's Formula-Kelly capital growth model perform? *Journal of Portfolio Management* (forthcoming Summer).

MacLean, L. C., E. O. Thorp, and W. T. Ziemba (eds.). 2011. *The Kelly investment criterion: Theory and practice*. Singapore: World Scientific.

Malkiel, B. 2011. *A random walk down Wall Street* (11 ed.). New York: W. W. Norton.

Marquering, W., J. Nisser, and T. Valla. 2006. Disappearing anomalies: a dynamic analysis of the persistence of anomalies. *Applied Financial Economics* 16: 291–302.

Martikainen, T., J. Perttunen, and W. T. Ziemba. 1994. The turn-of-the-month effect in the world's stock markets, January 1988–January 1990. *Finanzmarket and Portfolio Management* 8 (1): 41–49.

Merrill, A. A. 1966. *Behavior of prices on Wall Street*. New York: The Analysis Press.

Patterson, S. 2010. *The Quants: how a new breed of math whizzes conquered Wall Street and nearly destroyed it*. New York: Crown Business.

Penman, S. H. 1987. The distribution of earnings news over time and seasonalities in aggregate stock returns. *Journal of Financial Economics* 18: 199–228.

Reinganum, M. 1981. A misspecification of capital asset pricing: Empirical anomalies based on earnings yields and market values. *Journal of Financial Economics* 9: 19–46.

Rendon, J., and W. T. Ziemba. 2007. Is the January effect still alive in the futures markets? *Finanzmarket and Portfolio Management* 21: 381–396.

Riley, W. B., Jr., and W. A. Luksetich. 1980. The market prefers Republicans: Myth or reality? *Journal of Financial and Quantitative Analysis* 15 (3): 541–559.

Rind, B. 1996. Effects of beliefs about weather conditions on tipping. *Journal of Applied Social Psychology* 26: 137–147.

Ritter, J. 1988. The buying and selling behavior of individual investors at the turn of the year. *Journal of Finance* 43: 701–717.

Rogalski, R. 1984. New findings regarding day of the week returns over trading and nontrading period. *Journal of Finance* 39: 1603–1614.

Roll, R. 1983. Vas ist das? The turn-of-the-year effect and the return premia of small firms. *Journal of Portfolio Management* 9 (Winter): 18–28.

Roll, R. 1992. *Weather*. In *The new Palgrave dictionary of money and finance*, edited by P. Newman, M. Milgate, and J. Eatwell. London: Macmillan Press.

Roll, R. 1994. What every CFO should know about scientific progress in financial economics: what is known and what remains to be resolved. *Financial Management* (Summer): 69–75.

Rosenberg, B., K. Reid, and R. Lanstein. 1985. Persuasive evidence of market inefficiency. *Journal of Portfolio Management* 11: 9–16.

Ross, S. A. 2005. *Neoclassical finance*. Princeton, NJ: Princeton University Press.

Rozeff, M. S., and W. R. Kinney, Jr. 1976. Capital market seasonality: The case of stock returns. *Journal of Financial Economics* 3: 379–402.

Saunders, E. M., Jr. 1993. Stock prices and Wall Street weather. *American Economic Review* 83: 1337–1345.

Schwartz, S. K. 2010. The best of times for stocks may be ahead. CNBC.com, Tuesday, Oct. 26.

Schwartz, S. L., and W. T. Ziemba. 2000. Predicting Returns on the Tokyo Stock Exchange. In *Security market imperfections in world wide equity market*, edited by D. B. Keim and W. T. Ziemba. Cambridge, UK: Cambridge University Press, 492–511.

Stoll, H. R., and R. E. Whaley. 1983. Trading costs and the small firm effect. *Journal of Financial Economics* 12: 5779.

Stone, D., and W. T. Ziemba. 1993. Land and stock prices in Japan. *Journal of Economic Perspectives* (Summer): 149–165.

Stovall, R. 1992. Forecasting stock market performance via the presidential cycle. *Financial Analysts Journal* 48 (3): 5–8.

Sturm, R. 2009. The "other" January effect and the presidential election cycle. *Applied Financial Economics* 19: 1–9.

Sullivan, R., A. Timmerman, and H. White. 2001. Dangers of data mining: The case of calendar effects in stock returns. *Journal of Econometrics* 105 (1): 249–286.

Thaler, R. H. 1992. *The winners curse*. New York: The Free Press.

Tietjen, G. H., and D. R. Kripke. 1994. Suicides in California (1968–1977)— Absence of seasonality in Los Angeles and Sacramento counties. *Psychiatric Research* 53: 161–172.

Trombley, M. A. 1997. Stock prices and Wall Street weather: Additional evidence. *Quarterly Journal of Business and Economics* 36: 11–21.

Wachtel, S. 1942. Certain observations on seasonal movements in stock prices. *Journal of Business* (April): 184–193.

Wang, K., Y. Li, and J. Erickson (1997). A new look at the Monday effect. *Journal of Finance* 52, 2171–2186.

Yuan, K., L. Zheng, and Q. Zhu (2006). Are investors moonstruck? Lunar phases and stock returns. *Journal of Empirical Finance* 13, 1–23.

Ziemba, R. E. S., and W. T. Ziemba. 2007. *Scenarios for risk management and global investment strategies*. Hoboken, NJ: John Wiley & Sons.

Ziemba, W. T. 1988a. Discussion of "The buying and selling behavior of individual investors at the turn of the year" by Jay R. Ritter. *Journal of Finance* XLIII: 717–719.

Ziemba, W. T. 1988b. Synopsis of "Playing the turn of the year effect with index futures." *OR/MS Today* XV: 37–38.

Ziemba, W. T. 1989. Seasonality effects in Japanese futures markets? In *Research on pacific basin security markets*, edited by Rhee and Chang. Amsterdam: North Holland.

Ziemba, W. T. 1991a. Fundamental factors in Japanese stock returns, 1979 to 1989. *Investing* (Winter): 73–79.

Ziemba, W. T. 1991b. Japanese security market regularities: monthly, turn of the month and year, holiday and Golden Week effects. *Japan and the World Economy* 3, 119–146.

Ziemba, W. T. 1993. Comment on "Why a Weekend Effect?" *Journal of Portfolio Management* (Winter): 93–99.

Ziemba, W. T. 1994a. Investing in the turn-of-the-year effect in the futures markets. *Interfaces* (May–June).

Ziemba, W. T. 1994b. Worldwide security market regularities. *European Journal of Operational Research* 74: 198–229.

Ziemba, W. T. 2005. The symmetric downside risk Sharpe ratio and the evaluation of great investors and speculators. *Journal of Portfolio Management* (Fall): 108–122.

Ziemba, W. T. 2010. Bubbles, Belichick and the One that Got Away. Wilmott, London, January.

Ziemba, W. T. 2011. A tale of 5 investors: Response to private letters from Professor Paul A. Samuelson. Working Paper.

Ziemba, W. T., W. Bailey, and Y. Hamao (eds.) 1991. *Japanese financial market research*. Amsterdam: North Holland.

Ziemba, W. T., and C. Hensel. 1994. Worldwide security market anomalies. In *Philosophical Transactions of the Royal Society*, Series B, Number April, edited by S. Howison, F. Kelly, and P. Wilmott, 495–509.

Ziemba, W. T., and S. L. Schwartz. 1991a. The growth in the Japanese stock market, 1949-90 and prospects for the future. *Managerial and Decision Economics* 12: 183–195.

Ziemba, W. T., and S. L. Schwartz. 1991b. *Invest Japan*. Chicago: Probus Publishing.

Zweig, M. 1986. *Winning on Wall Street*. New York: Warner Books.

Go to http://hema.zacks.com for abstracts and links to papers.

CHAPTER 10

Size and Value Anomalies

Oleg A. Rytchkov

In this chapter, we consider the size and value anomalies. We first provide a brief overview of both anomalies and summarize the initial evidence for them. In particular, we describe how they contributed to the development of the Fama-French three-factor model, one of the most recognized risk models. There is still no consensus in the literature about whether the value premium represents a compensation for some risk or should be attributed to mispricing, and we present the main arguments in this continuing debate. Next, we discuss the cross-sectional and time-series variation in the magnitude of the value premium. A better understanding of such variations may cast new light on the origin of the value anomaly as well as improve the performance of investment strategies that seek to exploit the anomaly. We continue this chapter with a special section devoted to the size anomaly. There we review major stylized facts about the anomaly and present several explanations for it. We conclude this review by summarizing international evidence on the value and size anomalies and by discussing value strategies implemented within and between various asset classes.

The Early Days

Since its development by Sharpe (1964), Lintner (1965), and Mossin (1966), the Capital Asset Pricing Model (CAPM) has been accepted as the main model describing the risk-return relation in financial markets. According to the CAPM, the riskiness of each stock is solely determined by its beta, which, in turn, characterizes the correlation between returns on the stock and the market portfolio. Thus, the CAPM predicts that the excess expected returns, required by investors who hold stocks, are proportional to betas. However, empirical tests conducted in the late 1970s and early 1980s revealed patterns in expected stock returns that cannot be explained by the CAPM. Such violations of the CAPM are known as asset pricing anomalies, and the most prominent of them are the size and value anomalies.

The size anomaly is an empirical finding that small companies earn higher risk-adjusted returns than their larger counterparts. It was first documented by Banz (1981) who showed that the smallest 20% of firms earn an annual return that is almost 5% higher than the return on other firms. Reinganum (1981) confirms the existence of the size anomaly by using a broader sample and decile portfolios.

The value anomaly is a tendency of value stocks (stocks with low prices relative to their fundamentals) to outperform growth stocks (stocks with high prices relative to their fundamentals). Common measures of value are the earnings-to-price, book-to-market, and cash flow-to-price ratios (E/P, BE/ME, and CF/P, respectively). The idea that value stocks have higher returns than growth stocks goes back to Benjamin Graham and David Dodd, who put it forward in their famous book, *Security Analysis*. Formal statistical tests of the value anomaly were performed by Stattman (1980) and Rosenberg (1985), who used the book-to-market ratio as a value indicator. Basu (1977) discovered an alternative version of the value anomaly using the E/P ratio. Jointly, the size and value anomalies were considered by Fama and French (1992) who argued that the cross-sectional variation in stock returns is completely captured by size and BE/ME, but not by market beta, leverage, or the E/P ratio.

Fama-French Three-Factor Model

The Fama-French risk model was developed as an extension of the CAPM that can explain the value and size anomalies. In a seminal paper, Fama and French (1993) suggest two new risk factors: the difference in returns on portfolios with high book-to-market and low book-to-market ratios (HML) and the difference in returns on portfolios with small stocks and large stocks (SMB). They show that the size premium and the value premium can be considered as a compensation for risk related to these new factors. In this sense, the Fama-French model provides a risk-based explanation for the anomalies and claims that the abnormal returns for small and value stocks are associated with high betas of these stocks with respect to the HML and SMB factors.

Value Anomaly: Risk or Mispricing?

The interpretation of HML and SMB as risk factors has stimulated an active discussion whether higher returns on value stocks and small stocks indeed represent a compensation for risk (i.e., are related to stock betas) or should be attributed to mispricing caused by various investors' behavioral biases (i.e., are associated with the stock characteristics).

There are a number of possible psychological reasons why investors might overvalue growth stocks and undervalue value stocks. First, investors may give too much weight to past performance; in general, growth stocks have high historical growth. It is possible that investors project past performance too far into the future, overvaluing growth stocks and undervaluing value stocks. Second, it is possible that investors choose to invest in good companies regardless of whether those companies are fairly priced, that is, they overpay for growth. Third, it is possible that greater media or analyst coverage of growth stocks convinces investors that they are better investments.

In particular, Lakonishok, Shleifer, and Vishny (1994) argue that market participants irrationally extrapolate recent sales growth into the future and become overly optimistic about firms that grew fast in the past and overly pessimistic about firms that had a lackluster performance. As a consequence, investors overvalue growth firms and undervalue value firms. Moreover, Lakonishok, Shleifer, and Vishny (1994) find no evidence that value stocks underperform growth stocks in bad states of the world, understood as recessions. Hence, the value premium is not justified as a compensation for risk. Daniel and Titman (1997) identify stocks that have low book-to-market ratio and high exposure to the HML factor as well as stocks with high book-to-market ratio and low exposure to the HML factor, and they conclude that stock characteristics (book-to-market ratios) but not factor betas determine stock returns. Using a longer sample period from 1929 to 1997, Davis, Fama, and French (2000) reexamine their evidence and demonstrate that the sample used by Daniel and Titman (1997) is quite special and that results reverse in a longer sample, indicating that betas but not characteristics are priced. In a recent paper, Hoberg and Welch (2009) develop a new approach to constructing test portfolios, arguing that the efficiency of the asset pricing tests performed by Daniel and Titman (1997) and Davis, Fama, and French (2000) can be substantially improved. Hoberg and Welch (2009) demonstrate that the Fama-French factors cannot price the optimized test portfolios and their abnormal returns are economically meaningful and robust.

Even though the Fama-French factors can at least partially explain the value premium, Fama and French (1993) provide no clear economic interpretation to risks associated with the HML and SMB factors. One of the first economic explanations suggested for the value premium is based on the idea that high book-to-market firms have a higher risk of corporate distress, and that the value premium is a compensation required by investors for holding such stocks. Consistent with this explanation, Fama and French (1995) find that high BE/ME signals persistent poor earnings and low BE/ME signals strong earnings. The relation between BE/ME and firm distress was further tested by Vassalou and Xing (2004) who measure the probability of distress using a default likelihood indicator (DLI) constructed for individual firms using equity data. These authors claim that high-default-risk firms earn higher returns than low-default-risk firms only to the extent that they have high BE/ME. If these firm characteristics are not met, firms do not earn higher returns, even if their risk of default is actually very high. Vassalou and Xing (2004) conclude that default risk is intimately related to the book-to-market and the BE/ME effects should be viewed as default effects.

This conclusion is not fully supported by other studies that use different measures of default risk. Dichev (1998) uses Altman's Z-score model and finds that the bankruptcy risk is not rewarded by higher returns. He concludes that the value premium is unlikely to proxy for a distress factor related to bankruptcy. A similar result is obtained by Griffin and Lemmon (2002), who use Olson's model for predicting bankruptcy and who argue that the value anomaly must be due to mispricing.

Zhang (2005) offers an alternative explanation for the value premium that is based on costly reversibility of investments and countercyclical price of risk. Costly reversibility implies that firms face higher costs in cutting than in expanding capital. For example, consider two stocks. The first is a growth stock, a fast-growing alternative energy company with a low book-to-market ratio. The second is a value stock, a large automobile manufacturer with a high book-to-market ratio. In good times, the automobile manufacturer is not very risky. However, when the state of the economy worsens, it has a tough time disinvesting, and there is no way for such a company to avoid costly dismantling of its existing equipment. This inflexibility leads to a higher risk for investors and, hence, higher required returns. By contrast, when tough economic times hit the fast-growing alternative energy company, it can simply postpone or cancel new investments. This flexibility in exercising growth options results in lower risk of growth firms and lower returns.

One of the main challenges of the empirical research on the value anomaly is that the rational and behavioral explanations are difficult to disentangle. Even if the book-to-market ratio, but not the HML beta is associated with higher returns, we cannot claim that there is no risk-based explanation for the value anomaly. As Fama (1991) points out, every asset pricing test is a joint test of market rationality and the particular asset pricing model used to describe risk factors. In other words, whenever we observe abnormal returns, we cannot judge whether market participants behave irrationally or whether our theoretical model—and, hence, our understanding of risks priced by the market—is incorrect.

The problem of distinguishing the contributions of characteristics and betas into stock returns is exacerbated by possible nonlinearities in the relation between betas and characteristics. As demonstrated by Gomes, Kogan, and Zhang (2003), even if stock returns are completely characterized by a conditional CAPM, the cross-sectional association between firm characteristics and stock returns can be detected even after controlling for empirical estimates of betas. Furthermore, as emphasized by Brav and Heaton (2002), the predictions of both behavioral and rational theories are often very similar and do not contradict each other. As a result, it may be difficult to distinguish them empirically.

Alternative Value Indicators

Although the value/growth classification is usually based on the book-to-market ratio BE/ME, alternative value indicators are often used by practitioners. All such indicators scale the stock price by fundamental characteristics. The most popular of them is the price-to-earnings ratio (P/E) and its reciprocal, the E/P ratio. In this form, the value anomaly was initially discovered by Basu (1977), who finds that, in contradiction to the CAPM, stocks with low P/E ratios (value stocks) had higher risk-adjusted returns than stocks with high P/E ratios (growth stocks).

In particular, Basu (1977) documents that from April 1957 to March 1971 the difference in annual raw returns between the top and bottom quintile portfolios based on P/E was 6.75%. After adjusting for market beta, the corresponding difference was 7.32%. These results are weaker if differential tax effects are taken into account—the low P/E portfolio would presumably have a higher dividend yield and, hence, higher taxes per unit of return than the high P/E portfolio. Assuming tax rates of 25% and 50% for capital gains and dividends, respectively, the difference between top and bottom P/E-based portfolios shrinks to 4.86%, implying that the tax effects alone cannot explain the value anomaly.

Although the P/E ratio is a natural value indicator, it is less popular in academic literature than BE/ME. This may be attributed to the findings of Fama and French (1992), who show that BE/ME absorbs the role of E/P in explaining the cross-section of stock returns and claim that the relation between E/P and average returns is due to the positive correlation between E/P and BE/ME.

Some of the alternative value indicators suggested in the literature represent individual components of the book-to-market ratio. For example,

Penman, Richardson, and Tuna (2007) consider a decomposition of the BE/ME ratio into operating and financing components. The operating component is represented by the enterprise book-to-market ratio, defined as a ratio of net operating assets (the sum of the book value of common equity and net debt) and the market value of net operating assets (the difference between financial liabilities and financial assets plus the market value of common equity). It pertains to operations and potentially reflects operating risk, whereas the leverage component of BE/ME reflects the financing risk. Penman, Richardson, and Tuna (2007) demonstrate that the enterprise BE/ME is positively related to stock returns, whereas the relation between the leverage component and returns is negative. Moreover, they find that from 1962 to 2001, the difference in size-adjusted annual returns on the top 5% and bottom 5% of stocks ranked by the enterprise BE/ME was 15.9%, suggesting that the enterprise BE/ME is also a discriminator between value and growth.

Another value indicator is the enterprise multiple (EM), defined as the enterprise value (the value of common stock, preferred stock, and debt, minus cash) divided by operating income before depreciation (EBITDA). Low EM companies should be considered value firms, and high EM firms are growth firms. Loughran and Wellman (2010) demonstrate that BE/ME and EM have similar abilities to explain the cross-section of stock returns during the 1963–2009 time period. The average monthly return difference between low and high EM deciles is 0.82% for equally weighted returns and 0.64% when the returns are value-weighted. Moreover, the explanatory power of EM survives even after controlling for BE/ME.

Time Variation in the Value Premium

Although the value anomaly is a robust phenomenon, the magnitude of the value premium is not constant and the value strategy can produce periods of poor performance. Figure 10.1 presents the difference in annual value-weighted returns on top and bottom value quintiles of all NYSE, AMEX, and NASDAQ stocks (realized value premium) over the period 1927–2010. Despite positive average value premium, growth stocks outperformed value stocks in 35 out of 84 years (42% of the time) and annual losses in several years exceeded 20%.

To illustrate the impact of the variation in the value premium on portfolio performance, we present a path of hypothetical wealth accumulation produced by the value strategy. Assuming that an investor allocated $1 to the strategy in 1926, we computed the value of this investment in each of the subsequent years and plot it in Figure 10.2. Again, we observe that

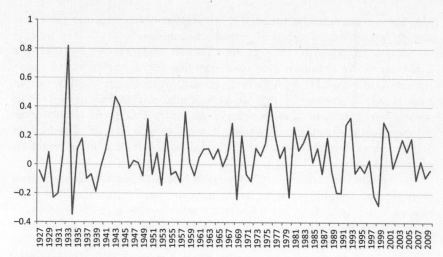

FIGURE 10.1 The Value Premium in U.S. Equity Returns in 1927–2010

Data source: Kenneth R. French Data Library (http://mba.tuck.dartmouth.edu/pages/faculty/ken.french/data_library.html).

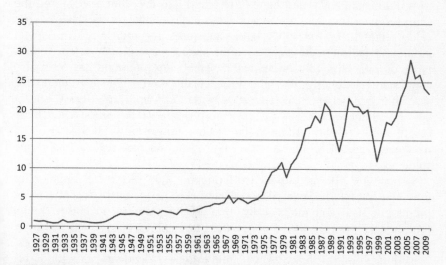

FIGURE 10.2 Hypothetical Wealth Accumulation Produced by the Value Strategy in 1927–2010

Data source: Kenneth R. French Data Library (http://mba.tuck.dartmouth.edu/pages/faculty/ken.french/data_library.html).

although on average the value of the investment increases, the growth is not stable and there are several periods of steep losses.

The variability of the value premium illustrated by Figures 10.1 and 10.2 underscores the importance of understanding the dynamics of the value premium. In particular, being able to predict the value premium, investors may pursue a strategy known as style timing, which prescribes to shift wealth between value and growth stocks based on signals about future relative style performance. However, it is not easy to find good predictors for the value premium, and substantial effort has been made in the literature to construct them.

Sorensen and Lazzara (1995) suggest forecasting the value premium using innovations in industrial production. Kao and Shumaker (1999) cite several macroeconomic factors such as term premium, real bond yield, and earnings yield gap (the difference between the earnings-to-price ratio of the S&P 500 index and the long-term bond yield) as good proxies for future value premium. Asness, Friedman, Krail, and Liew (2000) suggest using the value spread and the earnings growth spread as predictors of the value premium. They define the value spread as a difference between fundamental ratios (BE/ME, E/P) of growth and value portfolios, and the earnings growth spread as a difference in their forecasted earnings growth rates. Asness, Friedman, Krail, and Liew (2000) find that the value spread and the earnings growth spread are indeed statistically significant predictors of the value premium in 1982–1999, and when used together they can explain around 30% of the total variation in the annual value premium. The importance of value spread as a predictor of the value premium has been also confirmed by Cohen, Polk, and Vuolteenaho (2003) who document that the difference between BE/ME ratios of the low- and high-BE/ME portfolios is a significant predictor of the return on the HML portfolio. Rytchkov (2010) shows how the Kalman filter technique can be used for extracting information about future value premium from all past realizations of the value spread.

There are several papers exploring the business cycle variation of the value premium. Petkova and Zhang (2005) document that the value premium varies countercyclically, that is, the premium increases during recessionary periods. This conclusion was confirmed by Chen, Petkova, and Zhang (2008), who estimate the expected value premium using expected rates of dividend growth and expected dividend-price ratios for value and growth portfolios. Gulen, Xing, and Zhang (2010) arrive at a similar conclusion, using a two-state Markov switching model. Overall, the countercyclical behavior of the expected value premium supports the risk-based explanations of the value anomaly suggested in Zhang (2005).

Cross-Sectional Variation in the Value Premium

The strength of the value anomaly varies not only over time, but also across stocks. There are several studies showing that the value premium is high for some groups of stocks and undetectable for others.

Pontiff (2006) argues that the idiosyncratic volatility can be thought of as a proxy for costs of arbitrage, which prevent sophisticated investors from exploiting asset pricing anomalies and eliminating abnormal returns. As a result, anomalies may be much stronger on stocks with high idiosyncratic volatility. This intuition has been confirmed by Ali, Hwang, and Trombley (2003) who show that the value premium is higher for stocks with higher idiosyncratic volatility. Moreover, it appears to be more pronounced for stocks with higher transaction costs and lower investor sophistication. Ali, Hwang, and Trombley (2003) interpret these findings as evidence that the value premium is caused by mispricing and the arbitrage risk is an important factor of its existence.

A similar logic indicates that if the value premium is caused by mispricing, it should be stronger for stocks with low institutional ownership. Indeed, institutions are better informed than individual investors and on average should arbitrage anomalies away more effectively. Nagel (2005) confirms this prediction demonstrating that, even after controlling for size, low BE/ME stocks underperform high BE/ME stocks within the lowest institutional ownership quintile by 1.47% per month over the sample period 1980–2003. For comparison, in the quintile with the highest institutional ownership the value premium is only 0.47%.

Motivated by the same intuition, Shu (2010) explores the relation between the trader composition and the strength of the value anomaly across stocks. He calculates the fraction of institutional trading volume (FIT) for each stock-quarter and shows that the value premium is decreasing in the FIT measure. In particular, the difference in monthly stock returns between the highest and lowest book-to-market decile portfolios is 1.25% per month in the lowest FIT tercile but only 0.28% in the highest FIT tercile. The difference of 0.97% per month is highly statistically significant. A natural interpretation of these results is that individual investors, who are the primary traders of low FIT stocks, are more susceptible to behavioral biases than institutional investors, and these biases are the main source of the value anomaly.

The idea that institutional investors mitigate the value anomaly was challenged by Jiang (2010) who finds that institutional trading is associated with a widening of the value premium. Jiang (2010) argues that the herding behavior among portfolio managers leads to price destabilization. Portfolio managers take less reputational risk if they go along with consensus stock picks; they can share the blame with other portfolio managers if they make bad calls. If portfolio managers herd, that is, if they buy and sell portfolio stocks in the same direction as the consensus, overpriced stocks tend to become more overpriced and underpriced stocks tend to become more underpriced.

Daniel and Titman (2006) find that intangible returns, that is, stock returns that are not explained by accounting measures, are negatively related to future returns. If institutions trade in the same direction based on intangible information, it would support the herding hypothesis. Jiang (2010) tests this hypothesis and documents that institutional trading is indeed consistent with the herding behavior.

Because herding would tend to destabilize prices, the value premium should be largest when herding behavior is aligned, that is, when institutions herd strongly toward purchases of growth stocks or toward sale of value stocks. To test this hypothesis, Jiang (2010) performed a subportfolio analysis using NYSE, AMEX, and NASDAQ stocks from 1981–2004. First, the stocks were sorted into BE/ME terciles. Next, the high and low BE/ME terciles were each divided into deciles by the LSV herding measure, which was developed by Lakonishok, Shleifer, and Vishny (1994) to measure the strength of herding behavior. The average monthly value premium for the (value, large sell) minus (growth, large buy) portfolio was 1.22% (15.66% annualized), compared to 0.26% (3.17% annualized) for the (value, large buy) minus (growth, large sell) portfolio. Portfolios constructed using different measures of institutional trading (change in institutional holdings and change in the number of institutions with holdings) produced directionally similar value premium differences.

The contradiction between Shu's and Jiang's findings may be due to the difference in their measures of institutional trading. Shu's measure is based on trading volume, while Jiang's measures consider the net increase or decrease in institutional holdings. Based on the evidence presented by these two authors, it seems that institutional trading may enhance the value premium when institutions buy and hold stocks, and decrease the value premium if the volume of trading is large relative to the change in institutional holdings. This notion is consistent with the idea that some institutional players operate with a buy-and-hold mind-set, whereas others take advantage of short-term mispricing.

Another cross-sectional difference in the strength of the value anomaly was documented by Griffin and Lemmon (2002) who compare the magnitude of the value premium across portfolios with different probability of distress and find that the value premium is stronger among firms with greater distress risk. For each year from 1965–1996, NYSE, NASDAQ, and AMEX firms were independently sorted into quintile portfolios by the level of financial distress proxied by Ohlson's O-score and tercile portfolios by

BE/ME. The average annual return of the value–growth portfolio in the high-distress quintile was 14.44%, compared to 3.87% in the low-distress quintile. This difference is predominantly produced by low returns on the low BE/ME firms in the high O-score group. Vassalou and Xing (2004) who use a completely different measure of distress arrive at a similar conclusion. They find that the value premium exists only in the 2 quintiles with the highest default risk. Within the highest default risk quintile, the annual return difference between value and growth stocks is around 30%, and it goes down to 12.7% for the stocks in the second-highest default risk quintile. There is no BE/ME effect in the remaining stocks on the market.

Anatomy of the Size Anomaly

Although the size anomaly and the value anomaly played equally important roles in the developing of the Fama-French 3-factor model, now they have a different status in the literature. The value anomaly is shown to be a robust phenomenon, which admits several theoretical explanations. On the contrary, the existence of the size anomaly in the last 20 years has been questioned in the literature. Moreover, it is not obvious whether it is a separate phenomenon requiring a theoretical explanation or a manifestation of other known anomalies.

There is abundant evidence that the size effect in the United States is produced to a large extent by extraordinary performance of small stocks in January.[1] This pattern was first documented by Keim (1983) and Brown, Kleidon, and Marsh (1983). In particular, Keim (1983) finds that almost 50% of the size effect is due to January abnormal returns. Later, a strong relation between the size anomaly and the January effect was confirmed by Daniel and Titman (1997).

Another possible explanation for the size premium is that it actually represents a compensation for illiquidity. Stoll and Whaley (1983) show that for the NYSE stocks the size anomaly disappears (and in certain cases even reverses) when the bid-ask spread is taken into account. However, their results were challenged by Schultz (1983) who argues that when the NYSE and AMEX stocks are considered together, the size anomaly does not disappear even after adjusting for transaction costs.

There is some evidence in the academic literature suggesting that the strength of the size anomaly varies across different time periods. Horowitz, Loughran, and Savin (2000) show that there is no consistent relationship between size and realized returns in the period 1980–1996. Schwert (2003) observes that in the years 1982–2002 the size premium has been much

---

[1]Chapter 9 of this Handbook provides an extensive discussion of the January effect.

smaller than in 1926–1982. He attributes this decline to the impact of the publications of the papers that discovered the anomaly. In a recent study, Hou and Dijk (2010) confirm that for 1984–2005 the annual size premium is less than 1%, which is statistically and economically insignificant. These authors attribute the disappearance of the size anomaly to profitability shocks. They argue that before 1984 profitability shocks were close to zero for all size deciles. However, after 1984 small firms experienced, on average, negative profitability shocks, whereas big firms experienced positive shocks. As a result, the realized returns on small firms/big firms are lower/higher than the expected returns and the realized size premium underestimates the actual size premium.

Figure 10.3 depicts the realized size premium, which is defined as the difference in annual value-weighted returns on top and bottom size quintiles of all NYSE, AMEX, and NASDAQ stocks, over the period 1927–2010. In particular, Figure 10.3 shows that in the period prior to its discovery in 1983 the size anomaly had several years of superior performance. However, right after 1983 a long period of negative returns starts, which culminates in 1998 when the realized size premium was −40%. It is not surprising that, after such poor performance, the existence of the size anomaly was questioned. However, in 1999 the size anomaly came back and in several subsequent years small stocks substantially outperformed big stocks. As in the case of the value premium, we also illustrate the volatility of the realized size premium tracking a hypothetical $1 investment in the size strategy made in 1926. The accumulated value is depicted in Figure 10.4. Again, we observe

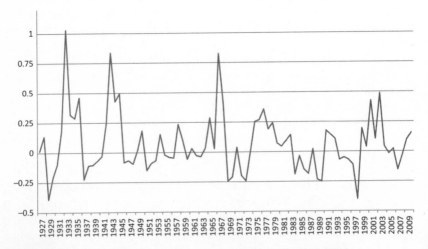

FIGURE 10.3   The Size Premium in U.S. Equity Returns in 1927–2010

Data source: Kenneth R. French Data Library (http://mba.tuck.dartmouth.edu/pages/faculty/ken.french/data_library.html).

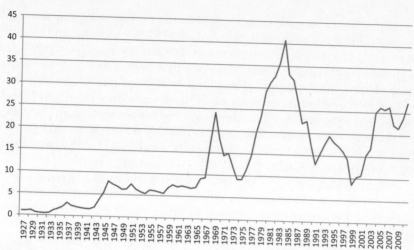

FIGURE 10.4 Hypothetical Wealth Accumulation Produced by the Size Strategy in 1927–2010

Data source: Kenneth R. French Data Library (http://mba.tuck.dartmouth.edu/pages/faculty/ken.french/data_library.html).

that there was a huge spike in the profitability in the late 1970s and early 1980s followed by a pronounced decline during which the hypothetical portfolio lost almost 75%.

The strength of the size anomaly also varies across stocks. Fama and French (2008) demonstrate that the size anomaly owes much of its power to very small stocks. In particular, they allocate NYSE, AMEX, and NASDAQ stocks into three size groups—microcaps, small stocks, and big stocks. The breakpoints are chosen to be the twentieth and fiftieth percentiles of the market capitalization for NYSE stocks. Microcaps represent almost 60% of all sample stocks, but account for only 3% of total market capitalization. Fama and French (2008) document that, within the microcap group, tinier stocks have higher average returns. In particular, the average slope in the regression of returns on market capitalization for microcaps is −0.46 with the t statistic of −6.95. It is almost 6 times larger than the corresponding slope for all but microcap stocks, which is −0.08 with the t statistic of −1.92.

Demirtas and Guner (2008) find that the bulk of the size effect is attributable to firms with poor past earnings relative to expectations. They sort NYSE, AMEX, and NASDAQ stocks into 10 portfolios using the sample of NYSE stocks for determining the decile cutoffs. The same stocks were then independently sorted into 2 categories: leaders, which had higher than expected profitability in the prior year, and laggards, which had lower than expected profitability in the prior year. Expected profitability was calculated using the fitted value for each stock obtained by regressing the Earnings/ Book Assets of all stocks on Tobin's Q, Dividend/Book Equity, and log Market Equity. Deviations from expected profitability are negatively correlated with future profitability; firms with poor past profitability tend to experience better future profitability, and firms with good past profitability tend to experience worse future profitability, as described by Fama and French (2000). The intersection of the size deciles and the leader/laggard categories results in 20 subportfolios. The average monthly returns from 1971 to 2001 for a hedge portfolio of small – big laggards was 1,25% (16.08% annualized) vs. 0.68% (8.47% annualized) for small – big leaders.

These findings support the behavioral hypothesis that investors overreact to bad news by overselling stocks with poor past performance. The authors also tested whether earnings surprises drove these excess returns, which, if true, would provide additional evidence to support the behavioral hypothesis. If small, beaten down stocks are systematically undervalued by investors, then future earnings announcements should result in upside surprises. Conversely, risk-based explanations for the size premium don't explain why beaten-down stocks should generate unusually large earnings surprises.

Demirtas and Guner (2008) demonstrate that the small – big laggard portfolio returned an average of 0.84% for the three-day window (−1, +1) around quarterly earnings announcements from 1971–2001. These 12 days (annualized by multiplying by 4) produced a return of 3.36% each year, accounting for 22.4% of the portfolio's total annual returns. Thus, investor overreaction to bad news may be partially responsible for the size premium.

The overreaction hypothesis does not seem to work in the opposite direction, however. If investors overreact to prior good earnings news, it would stand to reason that leaders would be subject to negative earnings surprises. The returns on the 3-day earnings announcement window for leaders were positive, suggesting that this is not the case. Therefore, if investors overreact, they appear to overreact only to bad news.

In summary, the size effect seems to be alive, but there are serious questions about the source of this anomaly, its consistency, and its likely persistence in the future. Given the large year-to-year variation in the size effect, investors should be cautious about using a size-based strategy when investing over a short time horizon.

International Evidence

The presence of the size and value anomalies in international markets provides additional evidence that these anomalies are real phenomena, not the result of data mining.

In particular, the size effect has been detected in several international markets. Heston, Rouwenhorst, and Wessels (1999) examine the size anomaly in 12 European countries and find that size is negatively related to average returns in 11 of them, and the relation is statistically significant in 5 countries. Herrera and Lockwood (1994) document a negative relation between returns and firm size for the Mexican stock market and Elfakhani, Lockwood, and Zaher (1998) find a similar result in the Canadian stock market. Rouwenhorst (1999) examine 20 emerging stock markets. Although it is difficult to detect size premium at the level of individual countries when the number of stocks is small and the history of observations is limited, the paper demonstrates that an internationally diversified portfolio of small stocks has significantly outperformed a portfolio of large stocks by approximately 70 basis points per month when countries are equally weighted.

The value anomaly is also a quite robust phenomenon, whose presence has been documented for various foreign markets. Chan, Hamao, and Lakonishok (1991) study the Japanese stock market and find high abnormal returns on the value strategy. Fama and French (1998) show that the value premium is pervasive. They examine 12 major EAFE (Europe, Australasia, and Far East) countries and demonstrate that in 11 of them (Italy is an exception) value stocks outperform growth stocks. Remarkably, the results are not sensitive to the choice of the ratio used for measuring value. Although for some countries the difference in returns on value and growth stocks is not statistically significant at the conventional level, the diversified global value portfolio formed on BE/ME outperforms the global growth portfolio by 7.68% per year and this value premium is more than three standard errors from zero.

Many subsequent studies confirmed the conclusions of Fama and French (1998) and extended their results. For example, Lam (2002) finds that BE/ME and E/P can explain the cross-section of returns in the Hong Kong stock market, but the market beta does not have any explanatory power. Gharghori (2009) reports evidence on the E/P and BE/ME effects in the Australian market. From 1993–2005 the large – small BE/ME hedge portfolio had average monthly returns of 1.28% (16.49% annualized) and the large – small E/P hedge portfolio had average monthly returns of 0.61% (7.57% annualized).

Value Premium: Evidence from Alternative Asset Classes

The value anomaly is not limited to equity. Asness, Moskowitz, and Pedersen (2009) find that the value premium is ubiquitous across asset classes including stocks, country equity indexes, bonds, currencies, and commodities. Furthermore, the returns to the value strategy are positively correlated across these asset classes, and negatively correlated with returns on momentum strategies. Because the value and momentum strategies both earn positive returns, the strategies combining them offer significantly better risk/return profiles than either strategy alone.

Although, for individual stocks, the definition of value is conventional and is based on the book-to-market ratio, for other asset classes it requires some modification. For country stock indexes, Asness, Moskowitz, and Pedersen (2009) aggregate individual stock BE/ME ratios by computing the average value-weighted book-to-market ratio for the index constituents. For commodities, the value measure is defined as the spot price 5 years ago divided by the most recent spot price (effectively, it is an inverse of the return over the last five years). For currencies, the value measure is the negative of the 5-year return on the exchange rate, taking into account the interest earned, which is measured using local 3-month LIBOR rates. For country bond indexes, the authors define the value measure as the real bond yield (the yield on the MSCI 10-year government bond index minus forecasted inflation for the next 12 months).

Within each asset class, Asness, Moskowitz, and Pedersen (2009) sort individual securities into 3 portfolios (high, medium, and low) based on the value metric. For individual stocks, the constructed portfolios are value weighted, whereas for other asset classes portfolios are equally weighted.

The returns on the value strategy implemented within various asset classes suggest that the value premium is ubiquitous. The returns on the value strategy appear to be very similar across the United States, United Kingdom, and Europe (the value premium is around 3.5% per year) and about two-and-a-half times stronger in Japan (10.6% per year). For currencies, the value premium was 3.8% in 1975–2008, and for commodities it was 5.8% in the same period. Asness, Moskowitz, and Pedersen (2009) show that these premia cannot be explained by the global CAPM.

Although usually the value strategy is implemented within a given asset class, its analog can also be defined for asset classes themselves. Blitz and Vliet (2008) ranked 12 asset classes using a certain value metric to obtain 4 monthly rebalanced portfolios, each containing 3 asset classes. For equity assets, the E/P ratio is used as a value indicator, whereas the standard yield-to-maturity is used for bond assets. To make the value indicators comparable across asset classes, Blitz and Vliet (2008) also make several asset-specific adjustments to correct for the slope of the yield curve, default risk, and structural difference between equity markets.

Blitz and Vliet (2008) document that, in the period from February 1986 to September 2007, the difference in annual returns on the top and bottom value portfolios formed from the asset classes was, on average, 7.9%. The strategy's alpha with respect to the Fama-French-Carhart four-factor model was 11.2%, and conservatively adjusted for transaction costs, the strategy yielded an average annual return of 5.6%.

References

Ali, Ashiq, Lee-Seok Hwang, and Mark A. Trombley. 2003. Arbitrage risk and the book-to-market anomaly. *Journal of Financial Economics* 69: 355–373.

Asness, Clifford S., Jacques A. Friedman, Robert J. Krail, and John M. Liew. 2000. Style timing: value versus growth. *Journal of Portfolio Management* 26: 50–60.

Asness, Clifford S., Tobias J. Moskowitz, and Lasse Heje Pedersen. 2009. Value and momentum everywhere. AFA 2010 Atlanta Meetings Paper.

Banz, Rolf W. 1981. The relationship between return and market value of common stocks. *Journal of Financial Economics* 9: 3–18.

Basu, S. 1977. The investment performance of common stocks in relation to their price–earnings ratios: A test of the efficient markets hypothesis. *Journal of Finance* 32: 663–682.

Blitz, David, and Pim Van Vliet. 2008. Global tactical cross-asset allocation: Applying value and momentum across asset classes. *Journal of Portfolio Management* 35: 23–38.

Brav, Alon, and J. B. Heaton. 2002. Competing theories of financial anomalies. *Review of Financial Studies* 15: 575–606.

Brown, Philip, Allan W. Kleidon, and Terry A. Marsh. 1983. New evidence on the nature of size-related anomalies in stock prices. *Journal of Financial Economics* 12: 33–56.

Chan, Louis K. C., Yasushi Hamao, and Josef Lakonishok. 1991. Fundamentals and stock returns in Japan. *Journal of Finance* 46: 1739–1764.

Chen, Long, Ralitsa Petkova, and Lu Zhang. 2008. The expected value premium. *Journal of Financial Economics* 87: 269–280.

Cohen, Randolph B., Christopher Polk, and Tuomo Vuolteenaho. 2003. The value spread. *Journal of Finance* 58: 609–641.

Daniel, Kent D., and Sheridan Titman. 1997. Evidence on the characteristics of cross-sectional variation in stock returns. *Journal of Finance* 52: 1–33.

Daniel, Kent D., and Sheridan Titman. 2006. Market reactions to tangible and intangible information. *Journal of Finance* 61: 1605–1643.

Davis, James L., Eugene F. Fama, and Kenneth R. French. 2000. Characteristics, covariances, and average returns: 1929 to 1997. *Journal of Finance* 55: 389–406.

Demirtas, K. Ozgur, and A. Burak Guner. 2008. Can overreaction explain part of the size premium? *International Journal of Revenue Management* 2: 234–253.

Dichev, Ilia D. 1998. Is the risk of bankruptcy a systematic risk? *Journal of Finance* 53: 1131–1148.

Elfakhani, Said, Larry J. Lockwood, and Tarek S. Zaher. 1998. Small firm and value effects in the Canadian stock market. *Journal of Financial Research* 21: 277–291.

Fama, Eugene F. 1991. Efficient capital markets: II. *Journal of Finance* 46: 1575–1617.

Fama, Eugene F., and Kenneth R. French. 1992. The cross-section of expected stock returns. *Journal of Finance* 47: 427–465.

Fama, Eugene F., and Kenneth R. French. 1993. Common risk factors in the returns on stocks and bonds. *Journal of Financial Economics* 33: 3–56.

Fama, Eugene F., and Kenneth R. French. 1995. Size and book-to-market factors in earnings and returns. *Journal of Finance* 50: 131–155.

Fama, Eugene F., and Kenneth R. French. 1998. Value versus growth: The international evidence. *Journal of Finance* 53: 1975–1999.

Fama, Eugene F., and Kenneth R. French. 2000. Forecasting profitability and earnings. *Journal of Business* 73: 61–175.

Fama, Eugene F., and Kenneth R. French. 2008. Dissecting anomalies. *Journal of Finance* 63: 1653–1678.

Gharghori, Philip, Ronald Lee, and Madhu Veeraraghavan. 2009. Anomalies and stock returns: Australian evidence. *Accounting and Finance* 49: 555–576.

Gomes, Joao, Leonid Kogan, and Lu Zhang. 2003. Equilibrium cross-section of returns. *Journal of Political Economy* 111: 693–732.

Graham, Benjamin, and David Dodd. 1934. *Security analysis.* Whittlesey House, McGraw-Hill Book Company, New York.

Griffin, John, and Michael L. Lemmon. 2002. Book-to-market equity, distress risk, and stock returns. *Journal of Finance* 57: 2317–2336.

Gulen, Huseyin, Yuhang Xing, and Lu Zhang. 2011. Value versus growth: Time-varying expected stock returns. *Financial Management*, forthcoming.

Herrera, Martin J. and Larry J., Lockwood. 1994. The size effect in the Mexican stock market. *Journal of Banking and Finance* 18: 621–632.

Heston, Steven L., K. Geert Rouwenhorst, and Roberto E. Wessels. 1999. The role of beta and size in the cross-section of european stock returns. *European Financial Management* 5: 9–27.

Hoberg, Gerard, and Ivo Welch. 2009. Optimized vs. sort-based portfolios. AFA 2010 Atlanta Meetings Paper.

Horowitz, Joel L., Tim Loughran, and N. E. Savin. 2000. Three analyses of the firm size premium. *Journal of Empirical Finance* 7: 143–153.

Hou, Kewei, and Mathijs A. van Dijk. 2010. Profitability shocks and the size effect in the cross-section of expected stock returns. Fisher College of Business Working Paper 2010–03–001.

Jiang, Hao. 2010. Institutional investors, intangible information, and the book-to-market effect. *Journal of Financial Economics* 96: 98–126.

Kao, Duen-Li, and Robert D. Shumaker. 1999. Equity style timing. *Financial Analyst Journal* 55: 37–48.

Keim, Donald B. 1983. Size-related anomalies and stock return seasonality. *Journal of Financial Economics* 12: 13–32.

Lakonishok, Josef, Andrei Shleifer, and Robert W. Vishny. 1994. Contrarian investment, extrapolation, and risk. *Journal of Finance* 49: 1541–1578.

Lam, Keith S. K. 2002. The relationship between size, book-to-market equity ratio, earnings–price ratio, and return for the Hong Kong stock market. *Global Finance Journal* 13: 163–179.

Lintner, John. 1965. The valuation of risk assets and selection of risky investments in stock portfolios and capital budgets. *Review of Economics and Statistics* 47: 13–37.

Loughran, Tim, and Jay W. Wellman. 2010. New evidence on the relation between the enterprise multiple and average stock returns. *Journal of Financial and Quantitative Analysis*, forthcoming.

Mossin, Jan. 1966. Equilibrium in a capital asset market. *Econometrica* 34: 768–783.

Nagel, Stefan. 2005. Short sales, institutional investors and the cross-section of stock returns. *Journal of Financial Economics* 78: 277–309.

Penman, Stephen H., Scott A. Richardson, and Irem Tuna. 2007. The book-to-price effect in stock returns: Accounting for leverage. *Journal of Accounting Research* 45: 427–467.

Petkova, Ralitsa, and Lu Zhang. 2005. Is value riskier than growth? *Journal of Financial Economics* 78: 187–202.

Pontiff, Jeffrey. 2006. Costly arbitrage and the myth of idiosyncratic risk. *Journal of Accounting and Economics* 42: 35–52.

Reinganum, Marc R. 1981. Misspecification of capital asset pricing: Empirical anomalies based on earnings' yields and market values. *Journal of Financial Economics* 9: 19–46.

Rosenberg, Barr, Kenneth Reid, and Ronald Lanstein. 1985. Persuasive evidence of market inefficiency. *Journal of Portfolio Management* 11: 9–17.

Rouwenhorst, K. Geert. 1999. Local return factors and turnover in emerging stock markets. *Journal of Finance* 54: 1439–1464.

Rytchkov, Oleg. 2010. Expected returns on value, growth, and HML. *Journal of Empirical Finance* 17: 552–565.

Schultz, Paul. 1983. Transaction costs and the small firm effect. *Journal of Financial Economics* 12: 81–88.

Schwert, William G. 2003. Anomalies and market efficiency. In *Handbook of the economics and finance*, edited by G. M. Constantinides, M. Harris, and R. M. Stultz. Amsterdam: North Holland.

Sharpe, William F. 1964. Capital asset prices: A theory of market equilibrium under conditions of risk. *Journal of Finance* 19: 425–442.

Shu, Tao. 2010. Trader composition and the cross-section of stock returns, Working Paper, University of Georgia.

Sorensen, E., and C. Lazzara. 1995. Equity style management: The case of growth and value. In *Equity style management*, edited by R. Klein and J. Lederman. Chicago: Irwin.

Stattman, Dennis. 1980. Book values and stock returns. *The Chicago MBA: A Journal of Selected Papers* 4: 25–45.

Stoll, Hans R., and Robert E. Whaley. 1983. Transaction costs and the small firm effect. *Journal of Financial Economics* 12: 57–79.

Vassalou, Maria, and Yuhang Xing. 2004. Default risk in equity returns. *Journal of Finance* 59: 831–868.

Zhang, Lu. 2005. The value premium. *Journal of Finance* 60: 67–103.

Go to http://hema.zacks.com for abstracts and links to papers.

CHAPTER 11

Anomaly-Based Processes for the Individual Investor

Leonard Zacks

A s discussed in the Preface of this book, professional investors use the results of anomaly research to create multifactor models to manage market neutral and long portfolios. Market neutral portfolios are designed to generate a consistently positive return whereas long portfolios are designed to outperform an index. Although both the market neutral[1] portfolios and the long portfolios[2] are available to individual investors as mutual funds, a growing number of individual investors have begun managing their own portfolios using these quant techniques. The objective of this chapter is to provide some guidance to investors who want to implement an anomaly-based multifactor market neutral or long quant process.

Many of these self-directed quant investors are individuals with a quant bent who have been deeply disappointed with the returns generated by a broker or financial advisor and have decided that they can do it better themselves without paying the 1–2% fee charged by most advisors. Others are day traders and technical traders who have begun to realize that they are running their own anomaly-based process but are using only the momentum anomaly and would like to improve performance by adding some of the other anomalies to their processes. A third group are investors nearing retirement, many of whom have worked in the investment industry, who

---

[1]See footnote 6 of the Appendix to this book for list of market neutral mutual funds.
[2]See Table A.2 in the Appendix to this book for list of long quant based mutual funds.

find that managing their own customized quant portfolios is a fascinating and profitable new pastime that can outperform their 401(k).

To help these self-directed quant investors, this chapter first explains how market neutral is able to increase expected returns at any level of risk when added to a portfolio and then outlines how one can use ETFs to create a market neutral portfolio. We then turn to long portfolios and describe how individual investors can outperform an index by using academic and commercial anomaly-based stock scoring systems. We conclude this chapter with a discussion of some of the issues faced by investors who would like to run their own anomaly-based quant processes.

Increasing Returns Using Market Neutral

By creating a market neutral asset class within an account, most individual investors can increase their expected return without increasing their risk.

The Asset Allocation Process

To appreciate this unique characteristic of the market neutral asset class we need to first review the asset allocation process. Although each investor may use a slightly different set of asset classes, a typical asset allocation might be something like the one listed in Table 11.1.

For the last half century the most logical way to make this type of asset allocation has been to use the Markowitz mean-variance methodology taught in introductory MBA finance classes. Most professional investors use the Markowitz process to create their asset allocations and, although they may not realize it, the allocations of many individual investors were also set using the Markowitz process.

TABLE 11.1 Typical Asset Allocation

Asset Class	% of Portfolio
U.S. equity large cap growth	15
U.S. equity large cap value	25
U.S. equity small cap growth	5
U.S. equity small cap value	5
International equity	5
Fixed income	45
Total	100%

Virtually all the software used by financial advisors to make asset allocation decisions for their clients is based on the Markowitz process, and the model portfolios created by brokerage firms and recommended by their advisors are frequently created by quant departments at the brokerage firms using the Markowitz process. So we can safely say that the current asset allocations of many individual investors were probably developed based on Markowitz mean-variance techniques.

Forecasts of Asset Class Returns

The starting point of the Markowitz allocation is a set of forecasts for the future returns of each of the asset classes. These return forecasts are used by the software together with the historical variance and correlation relationships among the asset class returns to create the efficient frontier, which consists, at each level of risk, of the portfolio that provides the highest expected average return.

From an asset allocation perspective, the most interesting results of the anomaly research are that long/short portfolios can be created with average returns that range from 5% to 15% per year, that these returns have low standard deviations compared to other asset classes, and that they have very low or even negative correlations with the returns of other asset classes. These unique statistical properties have led some professional investors to classify these long/short portfolios as a new asset class, called equity market neutral.[3]

These statistical properties of the market neutral returns are so attractive when compared to other asset classes, such as large cap value, that an advisor making an asset allocation decision may find it hard to conclude that his client should own anything other than a market neutral portfolio.

Readers can see this intuitively by comparing the market neutral return of 5% to 15% per year, which would be realized in both up and down markets, to the returns over the last few years of their own portfolios.

The attractiveness of market neutral portfolios becomes even more compelling if we look at asset allocations using the Markowitz process.

The first step in the Markowitz allocation is to specify the time horizon over which the investor will maintain his allocation and to forecast the returns over that horizon. The investor using the Markowitz process assumes that the returns of an asset class are uncertain[4] and specifies the mean and

---

[3]Although the term *market neutral* includes other processes such risk arbitrage, we will use the term *market neutral* for only equity market neutral.

[4]Technically the return is a random variable and the advisor using the Markowitz process forecasts the mean and standard deviation of this random variable. Buried in the Markowitz formulation is also the assumption that the random variable has a normal distribution and/or the investor has a quadratic utility function.

TABLE 11.2   Annual Asset Class Returns and Standard Deviations over the Past
15 Years

	Average Return %	Standard Deviation %
1 Large cap growth	8.32	18.51
2 Large cap value	9.77	15.52
3 Small cap growth	7.58	24.66
4 Small cap value	10.74	17.58
5 International	6.54	16.67
6 Fixed income	5.86	6.82
7 Market neutral	10.14	2.99

Note: The average return and standard deviation of the asset classes are the returns and
standard deviations of the following indexes: large cap growth (Russell 1000 Growth), large
cap value (Russell 1000 Value), small cap growth (Russell 2000 Growth), small cap value
(Russell 2000 Value), international (MSCI EAFE), fixed income (Merrill Lynch U.S. Corp
5–10 year, AAA Index), market neutral (Dow Jones Credit Suisse Hedge Fund–Equity Market
Neutral Index).

the standard deviation of the returns of each asset class while the correlations
among the returns of the asset classes are taken to be their historical values.

To understand how market neutral impacts the asset allocation, we first
create the efficient frontier with 6 traditional asset classes and then add
market neutral as the seventh asset class to show how the efficient frontier
dramatically changes. We use each asset class' average return and standard
deviation over the past 15 years as our estimate of the mean and the standard
deviation of the future returns of the asset class.

For the return of the market neutral asset class we use the actual returns
of professionally managed market neutral portfolios which are tracked by
Dow Jones/Credit Suisse.

You can see in Table 11.2 that over the past 15 years the return of the
market neutral index (10.14%) was the second highest of the 7 asset classes,
just slightly below small cap value (10.74%) while the standard deviation
of the market neutral index (2.99%) was much less than that of any of the
other asset classes.

Using the forecasts for the first 6 asset classes from Table 11.2, we first
create the efficient frontier, shown in Figure 11.1.

The portfolios on this line, which are the set of efficient portfolios that
can be created using the first 6 asset classes in Table 11.2, have expected
returns on the Y axis from 6% to 11% with standard deviations on the X
axis from about 6% to 18%. Because of the returns and standard deviations
from Table 11.2 the portfolios on the frontier, such as A, B, and C, consist

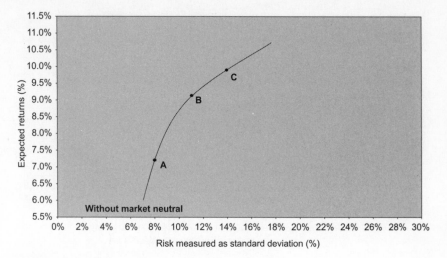

FIGURE 11.1   Efficient Frontier without Market Neutral

TABLE 11.3   Asset Allocation of Portfolios on Efficient Frontier

	A	B	C
Large cap value	15%	18%	21%
Small cap value	31%	50%	67%
Fixed income	54%	32%	12%
Total	100%	100%	100%

of allocations to three of the six asset classes – large and small cap value and to fixed income (see Table 11.3).

If we then add asset 7, market neutral, the efficient frontier changes dramatically to become the upper line in Figure 11.2.

The expected returns of the portfolios on this new frontier range from 9.5 to 11% with standard deviations from 3% to 18% and as shown in Table 11.4, fixed income and large cap value are no longer in the portfolios on this efficient frontier.

But more importantly, if you compare Portfolios A, B, and C on the 6 asset frontier in Figure 11.2 with Portfolios A', B', and C', which can be created if we include market neutral as an asset, you see clearly that A', B', and C' have the same risk as A, B, and C, but each has a higher expected return and would be preferred by investors.

Therefore, if a rational investor agrees with the return forecasts in Table 11.1, the inescapable conclusion is that the investor should include market neutral assets as a large component of his/her asset allocation.

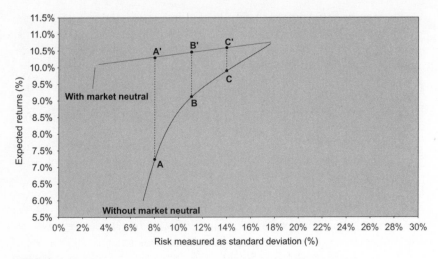

FIGURE 11.2   Efficient Frontier with and without Market Neutral

TABLE 11.4   Asset Allocation of Portfolios on Efficient Frontier Using Market Neutral

	A'	B'	C'
Small cap value	50%	68%	85%
Market neutral	50%	32%	15%
Total	100%	100%	100%

When Not to Include Market Neutral

However, over a short investment horizon the expected asset class returns will certainly deviate from their historical 15-year averages, and if one can accurately forecast these deviations, market neutral may not be an attractive asset class.

For example, if an investor expects that the return of large cap growth stocks over an investment horizon will be greater than 10% per year, the market neutral asset class,whose average returns are around 10% per year may disappear from the Markowitz allocation.

Alternatively if an investor takes a longer-term perspective and looks back at the average returns of asset classes over the past 30 years, rather than the past 15 years, they will find that the returns of many of the equity asset classes averaged 10% to 12% per year. Since these are higher than the 10% market neutral returns, an asset allocation based on these higher forecasts would include allocations to the traditional equity style box asset classes—large, mid, and small cap divided into value and growth. In summary, if investors believe that long equity returns will average less than 10% per year over their investment horizons they should allocate a significant portion of their portfolios to market neutral.

Using ETFs to Add a Market Neutral Asset to a Portfolio

Self-directed investors can incorporate the market neutral asset class into their portfolios by directly implementing the value or the size anomaly using index funds and ETFs. If an investor believes that value will outperform growth over the next time period, it is very easy to create a hedge return by buying an ETF that duplicates the value index and shorting an ETF that matches the growth index.[5]

The most direct spread is to go long the IShares Russell 3000 Value ETF (IWW) and short the IShares Russell 3000 Growth ETF (IWZ). An investor can also generate returns from the value growth spread in the large cap universe by going long the IShares Russell 1000 Value ETF (IWD) and short the Russell 1000 Growth ETF (IWF) or they can buy the Vanguard S&P 500 Value ETF (VOOV) and short the Vanguard S&P 500 Growth ETF (VOOG) if they believe that the value anomaly will be stronger within the S&P 500 companies.

Although this would not be advised by the author of Chapter 10, who believes that size is not an anomaly, it is also easy to add a market neutral asset based on the size anomaly to a portfolio by buying an index fund or ETF that duplicates a small cap stock index and shorting an ETF that duplicates a large cap index. There are a number of small or micro cap ETFs and Mutual Funds one can choose for the long side of the hedge, and ETFs one can use for the short side.[6]

How Long to Hold a Market Neutral Position?

Once an investor has made the decision to use one of these long/short spreads to add market neutral to a portfolio, they should plan to maintain these holdings for at least 5 years because, as discussed in Chapter 10, the value/growth spread and the small/large spread are long-term relationships that may reverse in any 1- or 2-year period.

---

[5]You cannot short a mutual fund, so you cannot use a mutual fund for the short side of your hedge.
[6]Small and microcap ETFs include the IWM, VTWO, EWRS, VIOO, IJR, VB, EES, SLY, SCHA, PJM, PZI, and the FDM. The three most liquid large cap ETFs to use for the short side are the IShares Russell 1000 ETF (IWB), the Vanguard Large Cap ETF (VV), and the IShares S&P 100 ETF (OEF).

An investor who looks at the changing signs of the value/growth spread or the large/small spread over time and considers predicting if value or growth or large or small will be the best performing asset class over the next quarter, they may want to reconsider. Although there are a few investment organizations that attempt to predict these style-box returns using a technique called tactical asset allocation,[7] their success has been very limited and has not been supported by academic research. Most academics would say that one cannot predict style-box returns and should rely on the value and the size anomaly because these are risk factors that are inherent in the equity markets.

Using Stock Scoring Systems to Outperform Indexes

If one's objective is to outperform a specific index the simple decision is to buy a mutual fund designed to outperform the index.

However, if an investor is self-directed and would like to avoid the fees of mutual funds or would like to change the weights of the stocks in an existing portfolio to improve performance, using one of the anomaly-based stock scoring models documented in the academic literature or provided by commercial firms may be attractive.

Academic Stock Scoring Systems for Value and Growth

There are two academically developed stock scoring systems that have begun to be used by self-directed individual investors, one designed to enhance returns for value portfolios and one for growth portfolios.

The research described in Chapter 5 carried out by Piotroski provides a scoring system that may enhance returns to a value portfolio. Although institutional investors have an edge over individual investors when using the Piotroski score, individual investors who have an allocation to large cap value, mid cap value, or small cap value can directly apply the published Piotroski score to their portfolios.

Since 2000 the Piotroski scoring system for value stocks has become well known and widely publicized with articles such as Lipton (2009) appearing in *Forbes*, *BusinessWeek*, and other publications. A number of web sites, including Zacks.com, Graham Investor.com, OldSchoolValue.com, and magicdilligance.com provide the Piotroski score for use by individual investors.

---

[7]Tactical asset allocation was a hot investment process among institutional investors from 1985 to 1995, but performance was not good and very few investment firms are still using this process.

Although not as well known as Piotroski, another academic stock scoring system, created by Mohanram and also described in Chapter 5, applies to growth stocks and can provide direction to investors who want to enhance the return to growth stocks.

Commercial Stock Scoring Systems

Twenty-five years ago, before the advent of the personal computer, investors used 3 commercial stock scoring systems to select stocks, each of which was based on multiple anomalies. They were: the Valueline Rank, CANSLIM, and the Zacks Rank.

VALUE LINE The granddaddy of stock rankings is the Value Line Rank which debuted in 1965 and is based on the momentum anomaly (Chapter 8) and the surprise anomaly (Chapter 4).

Value Line uses a proprietary methodology involving the 10-year trend of relative earnings and prices, recent earnings and price changes, and earnings surprises versus the Value Line analyst estimates. Initially limited to the 1,700 stocks followed by the Value Line analysts, the VL Timeliness Rank was designed to predict returns for the next 6 to 12 months.

Value Line's seemingly outrageous claims such as "grows by 20,000%" eventually attracted the attention of academics and in a seminal paper, which some believe was the first crack in the efficient market paradigm, the Nobel prizewinner Fisher Black said "Value Line Rank works" (Black 1973). This was confirmed again 10 years later by Stickel (1985) and is still being tested 20 years after Stickel by Nayar, Singh, and Yu (2008) who analyzed the relationship between changes in the Value Line Rank, EPS surprises and price momentum prior to the earnings announcement and concluded that the drift following Value Line's timeliness upgrades cannot be explained as a mere manifestation of the post-earnings announcement drift.

CANSLIM In the 1980s, Bill O'Neil, the publisher of *Investor's Business Daily*, developed an investment philosophy termed CANSLIM that utilizes fundamental anomalies (Chapter 5), and the momentum anomaly (Chapter 8) as well as human judgment. The CANSLIM philosophy was first explained to the public in O'Neil (1988) as a trading philosophy, rather than as a total ranking system, and consists of the following 7 elements:

1. **C** refers to quarterly earnings growth, which, to be attractive, should be at least 25% and should be accelerating in recent quarters.
2. **A** refers to annual earnings growth, which should also be above 25%.
3. **N** refers to new products, which should power the earnings growth.

4. **S** refers to supply and demand, which can be reflected in the trading volume particularly during price increases.
5. **L** refers to leader or laggard because O'Neil recommends buying the "leading stock in a leading industry." The relative price strength rating (RPSR) was designed by O'Neil to identify leaders and laggards.
6. **I** refers to institutional sponsorship, which is a gauge of the buying and selling of the stock by mutual funds and other institutional investors.
7. **M** refers to the market indexes because CANSLIM prefers buying when the indexes are going up.

Using the CANSLIM philosophy *Investor's Business Daily* provides a number of ranks of stocks including relative strength, accumulation, SMR, and then creates a composite rank. The 100 stocks with the best composite ranks are listed in the *Investor's Business Daily* newspaper. In 2003, *Investor's Business Daily* began publishing indexes of these stocks, the IBD 100 and the IBD 85-85.

ZACKS RANK   The third widely used stock scoring system, the Zacks Stock Rank, with values 1, 2, 3, 4, and 5, is based on the estimate revision anomaly (Chapter 3) and the surprise anomaly (Chapter 4).

Although the essence of the Zacks Rank can be found in Zacks (1979), the Rank was not created until 1982 when Zacks Investment Research became the first firm to collect individual sell-side estimates of quarterly earnings, to use these to calculate a consensus estimate of quarterly EPS, and to calculate the quarterly EPS surprises based on the consensus of analyst estimates. Building on this work and patterns in estimate revisions, Zacks first provided the Zacks Stock Rank in 1982 to institutional investors and in 1992 began also providing it to individual investors. The Rank is available weekly and daily and is based on 4 factors:

1. Agreement: This is the extent to which all brokerage analysts are revising their earnings estimates in the same direction. The greater the percentage of analysts who are revising their estimates upward, the better the score for this component.
2. Magnitude: This is a weighted average of the recent percent changes in the consensus estimates for the current and the next fiscal years.
3. Upside: This is the difference between the Zacks calculated most accurate estimate and the consensus estimate. A large difference suggests that the consensus will soon be changing and moving towards the most accurate estimate.
4. Surprise: This is based on the last few quarters' surprises.

Each of these components is given a raw score nightly and the raw scores are then combined to create the Zacks Rank.

Do These Scoring Systems Work?

Although the amount of return enhancement depends on the specific investment universe to which an investor applies these stock scoring systems, the marketing material of the 3 services reports annual average returns, over the past 20 years, that are in the range of 10–30% per year for the top portfolio in various universes.[8]

These returns are based on hypothetical portfolios consisting of the top-rated stocks from these systems, rebalanced monthly, with no transaction costs.

These returns are quite spectacular, as 20% per year for 20 years would increase an initial investment of $10,000 to $380,333 and 25% per year would place you among the world's top three investors—Buffett, Simons, and Thorp as identified by Ziemba (2007), so the first question often asked by individuals considering using these stock scoring systems is, "Has anyone been able to generate such amazing returns using these ranking systems?"

In general, the answer is no, because an actual portfolio would incur transaction costs, which, as we will see later in this chapter, can be quite high and depend on the number of stocks in the portfolio, the bid-ask spreads of the stocks, and the price impact of the portfolio trading. To determine the realistic returns one can expect using these commercial stock scoring systems an investor needs to run backtests using realistic transaction costs, which we are discussed on page 302.

Institutional investors use these rankings by purchasing data files containing the rankings from the three vendors and use their own systems to integrate the rankings into their investment processes while individual investors use web-based or client-server screening systems provided by the vendors.

For example, if investors want to use the Value Line Rank to enhance the returns of large cap growth, they would use the tools provided at the Value Line web site. Investors can create a portfolio consisting of the Value Line number-1 stocks that are large cap growth and rebalance the portfolio monthly or weekly to ensure that it always contains Value Line number-1 stocks that are large cap growth.

---

[8]The actual performance claims of these services can be found at the web sites www.zacks.com, www.valueline.com, and www.investors.com.

To serve individual investors who believe in the scoring systems but do not want to use the scores directly, each of these firms also offers investment management services though an affiliated investment advisor.

Implementation of Anomaly-Based Quant Processes

For readers interested in developing their own quant investment processes we first discuss backtesting and which anomalies to use in your quant model. We then suggest how to interpret anomaly research within the framework of an investor's mean variance based asset allocation decision, discuss transaction costs, high turnover strategies with smaller accounts and end this chapter with a review of data traps in backtesting.

What Is Backtesting?

Most investors building a quant process would like to know how their process would have worked in the past before applying it to their current portfolio. They can learn this by using a backtesting system. Backtesting systems consist of software and associated databases and are used to test the performance of proposed quant investment processes in the past. One can easily specify buy and sell rules or stock screens, apply these screens to specified universes of stocks as of various historical dates, create the portfolios of the stocks that passed the screens, and track the performance of such portfolios. Backtesting systems generally include realistic transaction cost modules so that an investor can estimate the after-transaction cost returns that would have been realized in the past had any specific process been implemented. The same backtesting systems are then used to implement the quant strategy going forward.

Almost all professional equity investment organizations employ an individual quant analyst or a full quant department that uses backtesting systems to test various investment processes.

There are also a growing number of individual investors who have begun to use backtesting systems to develop and trade their own quant anomaly-based portfolios. Although backtesting was originally developed for professional investors and the systems used by individuals have far fewer features than the systems used by professional investors, there are a number of backtesting systems suitable for use by individual investors.

The development of backtesting systems designed for individual investors began with the PC-based technical trading systems such as MetaStock and Worden Brothers.

With the creation of the Internet, other technical trading systems were developed such as NinjaTrader, Trading Blox, SmartQuant, RightEdge,

TradersStudio, QuotesPlus, and Amibroker. Some of these PC- and internet-based systems added the ability to backtest technical trading strategies and a few included some key fundamental ratios such as PE.

Over time, 4 systems—Tradestation; Research Wizard; Portfolio 123; and MetaStock, expanded their capabilites and now provide both technical and fundamental backtesting, which are the functions required to build and implement anomaly-based trading systems. In addition to there four systems two discount brokers, Fidelity and Ameritrade, offer limited backtesting to their active trader clients.

Which Anomalies to Consider?

Obviously the most important question that needs to be answered by any investor considering an anomaly-based quant process is "Will the anomaly exist in the future?" As discussed earlier in this book, one group of academics believes that, if they can improve their risk models, the anomalies will disappear using the improved risk adjusted returns, whereas another group believes that the anomalies are permanent because behavioral finance shows that the anomalies are endemic to human nature and will continue to exist under all risk models.

Bob Jones, one of the most experienced professional investors using anomalies and the manager of the Goldman Sachs Asset Management Quant Investing team has considered this issue in depth in Jones (2010), where he reports that many of his colleagues believe that "anomalies are based on human behavioral biases" and will continue long into the future.

Holding periods are the second most important factor to consider when selecting the anomalies to use in a quant process. The anomalies discussed in prior chapters have approximately the following holding periods:

Accruals	one year
Analyst related	days, a quarter
Surprise	days, a quarter
Momentum	days, weeks, months
Net stock	1–3 years
Seasonal	can only be implemented at specific times
Fundamental	quarter or year
Insider	weeks
Value/size	decades

Professional and individual investors use all of these anomalies in their quant processes, although net stock is used less frequently than the others because of the long holding period over which the excess returns are realized.

When seasonal anomalies are used, the process implemented is much more of a trading strategy than a quant investment process so very few large active equity investment organizations include seasonal anomalies in their processes.[9]

Value and size, although they have the longest time frame over which they are realized, are the most widely used by professional quants. During the 1980s there was an 8-year period when large cap outperformed small cap, so investors who were using the size anomaly during this period, and their clients, were quite unhappy. Today many professionally managed quantitative long active equity portfolios have a value tilt and a small size tilt.

Individual investors selecting an anomaly also need to consider the amount of time they are willing to devote to managing their portfolio. Anomalies such as insider trading or recommendation changes require daily attention to the process and tight control of transaction costs so that managing a quant portfolio using these anomalies can become a full-time activity. Low turnover anomalies such as accruals are attractive because they require only a few days per quarter and also have low transaction costs.

Reading and Understanding the Anomaly Literature

The anomaly returns reported in the academic research are almost always presented as risk adjusted returns relative to a specific risk model. Consequently to decide if the results of a specific article can be of value a new quant investor needs to understand the concept of a risk model.

WHAT IS A RISK MODEL?   A risk model is in most cases a linear relationship that expresses the expected average return of a stock in terms of a constant, called alpha, and the sensitivity of the stock to a number of risk factors. The simplest risk model is called the Market Model, where the average return of any stock is alpha plus the sensitivity of the stock to the market and this sensitivity is called beta. The appendix of Chapter 1 provides a comprehensive review of the types of risk models that have been created. Under the assumption of market equilibrium each risk model defines its own efficient frontier on the investor's risk return chart. For example the frontier created by the Market Model is a straight line from the market portfolio to the risk free rate on the Y axis while the frontier created by the Fama French 3 factor model or any other linear risk model is a hyperbola whose exact shape depends on the covariance among the risk factors. This

---

[9]The author of Chapter 9, Dr. William T. Ziemba, is one of the few well-respected academics who is also a professional seasonal anomaly trader.

frontier, created by a risk model, describes the expected return that an investor should be able to realize at any level of standard deviation, if the risk model is "true."

HOW ARE RISK MODELS USED IN ANOMALY RESEARCH? Risk models are used in anomaly research to determine if the return of a portfolio is appropriate given the risk of the portfolio. To determine the risk of a portfolio the risks of the individual stocks in the portfolio are aggregated. The portfolio return is then compared to the return predicted by the risk model for an asset with the same risk as the portfolio's aggregated risk. If the predicted return differs from the actual return, the portfolio return is termed an anomaly. For example, if we are using the Market Model as the risk model and a stock or a portfolio has a beta of 0.5 and the expected return of the market is 8%, the expected return of the stock or portfolio would be 4%. If a portfolio were found that had an aggregate beta of 0.5 but whose return was 6%, its risk adjusted return would be 2% (6%–4%) and it would be reported as an anomaly.

RISK ADJUSTED RETURNS AND YOUR EFFICIENT FRONTIER From the perspective of an individual investor using the Markowitz asset allocation process discussed earlier in this chapter the important information provided by an anomaly article is not the risk adjusted return but rather the mean and standard deviation of the anomaly portfolio. Within this Markowitz framework, a rational investor would determine if an anomaly should be considered for use in his portfolio by first deciding if the risk model used in the paper is a good approximation to reality. If so, the investor would plot the efficient frontier defined by the risk model and anomaly point, which will be above the model's efficient frontier, on a risk return chart (see Figure 11.1), and make his asset allocation decision using the resulting chart.

IF I DO NOT ACCEPT THE RISK MODEL HOW SHOULD I RESPOND TO AN ANOMALY ARTICLE? If you are a skeptic, as am I, and do not believe that any of the risk models are "good" approximations to reality you can still find significant value in an anomaly article that reports a positive risk adjusted return. To do this you first need to obtain two numbers from the article, the raw mean return (i.e., the return before the risk adjustments) and the standard deviation of the return of the anomaly portfolio. You should then plot this point on your risk/return chart, and see if this new point is above your own personal efficient frontier. If so, then the anomaly portfolio should be included in your asset allocation.

WHAT IF THE RISK ADJUSTED ANOMALY RETURN IS ZERO? If an academic article reports a zero risk adjusted anomaly return, you have no real reason to consider implementing the portfolio because you can create an asset with the same raw return and standard deviation by directly using the risk factors. For example, if the risk model was CAPM, you could duplicate the raw anomaly return and standard deviation by using the market portfolio; whereas if the risk model was the Fama-French model, you could duplicate the anomaly return by creating a portfolio consisting of Growth, Value, Large, Small, and Market ETFs.

Number of Stocks in a Quant Portfolio

There are two effects that need to be considered when deciding the number of stocks to be included in an anomaly-based quant portfolio. The first, which applies to all portfolios, is that transaction costs, as a percent of portfolio value, are much higher when a portfolio contains more stocks. The other is that, to achieve the anomaly returns reported in the literature, a portfolio may need to include 100 or more stocks on both sides of the hedge.

This issue was addressed by Lev and Nissim (2007) who showed that, as the number of stocks in the portfolio increases, the probability increases of generating returns that are due to the anomaly and not due to the many other random events that impact stock prices.

Figure 11.3, adapted from this paper, shows how the probability of outperforming varies with the number of stocks in the portfolio using the accrual anomaly. As the number of stocks in an accrual-based hedge portfolio increases from 10 to 160, the probability of the hedge portfolio returns being positive in the next year increases from 60% to 75%.

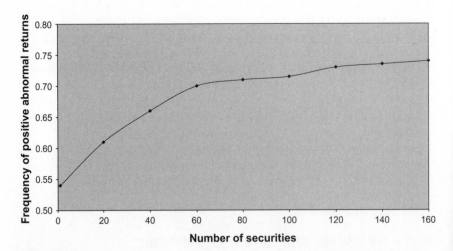

FIGURE 11.3 Frequency of Positive Abnormal Returns from Trading on Accruals Information as a Function of Portfolio Size

This type of analysis, which can be done by some of the backtesting systems helps the quant investor make the trade-off between the number of stocks in the portfolio and the expected returns of anomaly-based strategies.

Trading Costs

An extensive academic literature has evolved, termed "limits of arbitrage" that attempts to determine if the returns to anomaly-based portfolios exceed trading costs. Although we have not summarized these papers in this book in an organized fashion, the general conclusion seems to be that anomalies do exist, that many are stronger in the smaller less liquid stocks, but that the trading costs in these illiquid stocks is so high that institutional investors cannot generate positive returns after transaction costs.

This conclusion may hold for large multibillion-dollar portfolios but it is not necessarily true for portfolios traded by individual investors. In fact it may turn out that the real beneficiaries of the anomaly research are the individual investors who are able to trade small amounts of illiquid stocks using anomaly strategies. There are 3 components of transaction costs that will impact returns that a quant investor needs to consider.

BID-ASK SPREAD   In general, the bid-ask spread equally impacts institutional and individual investors.[10] The bid-ask spread exists because stocks are bought at the ask price and sold at the bid price. Since backtesting systems use closing prices, when doing a backtest one should deduct a percentage from the returns for the bid-ask spread. The bid-ask spread for a typical large cap company is 0.1% of the price, whereas the bid-ask spread for a small cap can be 0.5% of the price.[11] This can have a meaningful impact on returns. For example, if a process has a turnover of 50% per month, and the average bid-ask spread in the investment universe is 0.5%, an investor will incur 0.5% less return for each buy/sell pair, so the bid-ask related transaction cost would be 0.25 per month, or about 3% per year.

MARKET IMPACT   The least important component of transaction costs for most individual investors but the one that makes anomaly trading difficult for large institutional investors, is the market impact of their trading. For most individual quant investors who are trading mid to large cap companies, the market impact is insignificant and one can ignore this component of

---

[10]This is not totally true as the trading by institutional investors can actually have an impact on the bid-ask spread during the period when the trades are taking place.

[11]The NYSE reported in 2001 average bid-ask spreads of 0.14% to 0.39% in "Comparing Bid-Ask Spreads on NYSE and Nasdaq Immediately Following Decimalization," NYSE Research Dept., July 26, 2001.

transaction costs when doing backtests. However, if an individual investor is trading mcirocap stocks or has a large portfolio, the market impact of trading can be important.

A good rule of thumb is that if a trade represents less than 5% of the average daily volume in a stock, the trade will have little impact on the stock price if it is executed during one day, but as institutional investors know all too well, if a position in a stock represents a few days' volume, the investor needs to closely manage the trades over time to minimize the market impact of the trading.

BROKERAGE COMMISSIONS Over the last few years the commission costs paid by institutional investors have dropped to perhaps $1/2$ to 1 cent per share, whereas the cost paid by individual investors using discount brokers has settled at about $10 per trade plus a percentage of the market value for large trades.

Because of these economics, most observers immediately conclude that individual investors cannot trade high turnover anomaly-based strategies, which require large numbers of stocks in the portfolio.

Figure 11.4 shows the annual commission costs, as a percentage of total portfolio value for portfolios with various market values and numbers of stocks assuming a cost of $10 per trade and a turnover of 50% each month.

It is clear that, with any size portfolio with a 50% turnover, the more companies the higher the commission cost will be as a percentage of the market value. For example if an investor has a $100,000 portfolio with 10 stocks, each month there would be 5 buys and 5 sells at $10 per trade so that the commission cost would be $100 or 0.1% per month or 1.2% per year,

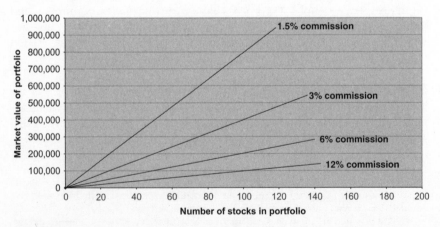

FIGURE 11.4 Commission Dependence on Number of Stocks and Market Value (assuming 50% turnover and $10 per trade)

whereas if the same portfolio had 100 stocks, the commission cost would be 1% per month or 12% per year. If the return of the anomaly strategy is 10% per year, the strategy would not be viable if the commission cost was 12% per year. This was the case until the year 2000.

High Turnover Strategies with Smaller Accounts

Fortunately for individual investors interested in managing quant portfolios a brokerage firm, Folio FN, was founded in 2000 by former SEC commissioner Steve Wallman, to enable investors to run high turnover strategies with a portfolio of less than $10,000.

Folio FN does not charge a per-trade fee, such as $10 per trade, but rather charges a fixed fee which as of June 2011 was about $300 per year per account. For this fee, a client is entitled to unlimited trading. The wrinkle is that the investor does not control his own trades and cannot place limit orders or stop loss orders without paying additional fees. At Folio FN, an individual can create a portfolio of 100, 200, or even 300 stocks, and rebalance weekly, with 100% turnover, and the total commission cost for the year will only be $300. As Folio FN clients enter their trades into the Folio system, the potential trades remain in a pending trade list until a specific time during the day when Folio executes in one batch all the trades of all its customers at the market price.

This system is not very appealing to the active trader who wants to capture the extra one-fourth or one-eighth on his trade or decompose a larger trade into smaller trades or execute a trade based on level 2 NASDAQ time and sales information, but it is ideal for the individual investor who wants to implement an anomaly-based portfolio. Using the preceding example with a $100,000 portfolio, with 100 stocks and 50% turnover per month, the commission costs at Folio FN would be $300 per year, or less than one-third of 1%, rather than the $12,000 or 12% per year costs at a discount broker.

Data Traps in Backtesting

Institutional and individual investors who have developed custom quant processes have invariably found that it is easier to identify a quant strategy that has amazing backtest performance than it is to develop a process that will work in the future.

Many of the problems that plague quant strategies can be avoided if the quant investor carefully considers out of sample performance and the 3 biases that creep into backtested quant strategies.

IN-SAMPLE VERSUS OUT-OF-SAMPLE PERFORMANCE If an investor backtests 50 carefully formulated anomaly-based strategies, using data from the

10 years ending 2010, one of these strategies will deliver the best backtest performance. If the investor then decides to use that process going forward, he would be accused of data mining, and many professional investors would have little confidence that the backtested process would continue to work in the future.

However, if the investor were to do the backtests over the 5 years ending 2005 and then test the same processes over the 5 years ending 2010 and the same 2 or 3 processes were near the top in both time periods, professional investors would say that the process has worked out of sample and would have much more confidence that it would continue into the future.[12]

So as new quant investors explore processes, they should always select a time period to be used as a hold-out sample during which they can test the process and see that it continues to perform out of sample.

LOOK AHEAD: SURVIVOR AND RESTATEMENT BIAS IN BACKTESTING   When doing a backtest, the data is perhaps more important than the software because of 3 data-related problems that can distort the backtest results and cause an investor to implement a process that will not generate future returns. The 3 data-related problems are look-ahead, survivor, and restatement bias.

Look-ahead bias occurs when the data used in the backtest was not available on the date that appears in the database. For example, if quarterly EPS is dated in the database as of 6/30/2006 but was not reported until a month after that date, a quant ranking created on 6/30/2006 would not have been able to have used the EPS value on 6/30/2006.

Survivor bias occurs when the database used in the backtest only in-cludes companies that currently exist. For example, if one is testing the bankruptcy anomaly from Chapter 5 and the database does not include the companies that were delisted, the results of the quant model will be misleading.

Restatement bias occurs when companies restate prior financial results and the database used in the backtest includes the restated numbers but not the original values. For example, if revenue for company ABC for the year ending 2004 was $1 billion and was then restated as of June 2005 to be $500 million, the value that should be used by the quant backtest as of end of the year 2004 should be the original $1 billion, not the restated value of $500 million.[13]

---

[12]Hold out samples do not need to be sequential years.
[13]The Compustat quarterly database suffered from this problem for many years, but it was corrected with the offering of the point-in-time data. The Zacks fundamental database has never suffered from this problem.

By asking your backtest provider about survivor, restatement, and look-ahead bias in the databases that accompany the software, you should be able to avoid these data traps found in backtesting.

In conclusion, my advice to the new quant investor is to give it a try and be persistent if your first model does not produce the returns you expect. Use the techniques of backtesting to understand where your model did not work and find ways to improve it. I am confident that you will be rewarded for your efforts.

End of the Tour

We hope this tour through the world of investment anomalies has given you some bit of information that you may be able to use to improve the performance of your own portfolio. The authors of this book welcome your comments and suggestions, which can be posted to our web site associated with the book at http://hema.zacks.com.

References

Black, F. 1973. Yes, Virginia, there is hope: Tests of the value line ranking system. *Financial Analysts Journal* (September 1973) pg. 10–14.

Lipton, J. 2009. Piotroski Profits, Forbes On Line, 02.23.09, www.forbes.com.

Jones, R. C. 2010. Maybe it really is different this time. *Journal of Portfolio Management* 36 (2): 60–72.

Lev, B., and Nissim, D. 2006. The persistence of the accruals anomaly. *Contemporary Accounting Research*, vol 23, Numb 1, pg. 193–226.

Nayar, N., Singh, A., and Yu W. 2008. Unraveling a puzzle: The case of value line timeliness rank upgrades. papers.ssrn.com

O'Neil. 1988. *How to Make Money in Stocks: A Winning System in Good Times and Bad.* McGraw Hill, New York.

Stickle, S. 1983. The effect of value line investment survey rank changes on common stock prices. *Journal of Financial Economics* 14 (1): 121–143.

Zacks, L. 1979. EPS forecasts: Accuracy is not enough. *Financial Analysts Journal* March/April, 53–55.

Ziemba, R. E. S., and Ziemba, W. T. 2007. *Scenarios for Risk Management and Global Investment Strategies* Hoboken, NJ: John Wiley & Sons.

Go to http://hema.zacks.com for abstracts and links to papers.

APPENDIX

Use of Anomaly Research by Professional Investors

This appendix first outlines how the results of anomaly research are used in 3 areas of professional quant investing—statistical arbitrage, high frequency trading, and equity multifactor models. Because the primary use of the anomaly results is in multi-factor models we then estimate the size of the assets managed in hedge funds, institutional separate accounts, and mutual funds using multifactor models.

From Academia to Wall Street

For nearly 50 years hundreds of professors have published literally thousands of articles related to the efficient market and anomalies. This research has changed the nature of equity investing.

The anomaly research can be separated into two broad phases. The first from 1960 to 1975 created and supported the concept of an efficient market, whereas the second phase, much of which is summarized in this book, began in the late 1970s and documented anomalies that were inconsistent with the efficient market paradigm.

Both phases had a dramatic impact on equity investing: The result of the first phase was the development of index funds. As a direct consequence of the early academic research, in 1973 Wells Fargo Investment Advisors working with Bill Sharpe of Stanford, and American National bank working with students of Eugene Fama from the University of Chicago created and offered the first index funds to their institutional clients. A year later Vanguard launched the first mutual fund designed to match an index, and index funds as we know them came into existence. According to Strategic

Insight, a mutual fund data provider, over \$2 trillion is managed in index funds and index matching ETFs over all asset classes.

The second phase of anomaly research led to the development of active quant equity investing. Beginning in the mid-1970s, large investment organizations incorporated the anomaly research into their investment processes by hiring MBAs and PhDs as quantitative analysts or portfolio managers and by employing professors who produced this research as consultants. In parallel with this hiring, some of the academics who pioneered the anomaly research formed their own investment management firms to manage equity portfolios using anomaly-based processes.[1]

This diffusion of anomaly research from academia to Wall Street over the last few decades gave rise to 3 types of equity quant processes—multifactor processes, statistical arbitrage, and high-frequency trading, which are now used extensively by investment management firms and hedge funds.

Statistical Arbitrage

Statistical arbitrage, or stat arb as it's often called, as explained in Durbin (2010) may have begun in 1978 on the Morgan Stanley trading desk, with a trade consisting of going long GM and short F. This quickly expanded to general pairs trading and then over the 1990s expanded again to include long and short market neutral portfolios consisting of groups of securities selected from among 6,000 U.S. stocks and ETFs, and 300,000 options, index futures, and options on index futures. Even this, however, does not cover the full scope of statistical arbitrage today, which can involve U.S. and non-U.S. securities, fixed income, commodities, and derivatives. An elementary overview of stat arb can be found in Pole (2007) while a sample of the mathematics used in stat arb can be found in Avellaneda (2010).

Examples of specific stat arb strategies documented in the academic literature include cross-listed stocks (Hansda 2003, Koumkwa 2008, Gagnon 2010), futures and stock indexes (Monoyios 2002), foreign currency (Liu 1992), pairs of stocks (Lin 2006), portfolios of stocks (Dunis 2005), and groups of foreign currencies (Baillie 1989, and Kroner 1993).

Although statistical arbitrage has been a very successful quant strategy,[2] the firms that manage portfolios using statistical arbitrage are not primarily relying on the results of the anomaly research summarized in this book. They have carried out their own research to identify price- and volume-related

---

[1]Some examples of these firms are Jacobs Levy Equity Management, LSV Asset Management, Roll and Ross Asset Management, and Rosenberg Capital Management.
[2]Peterson (2010) provides ample documentation of the massive returns, profits, and related compensation associated with use of statistical arbitrage by hedge funds and brokerage firm proprietary trading departments.

anomalies not known to their academic colleagues, which, although similar to the momentum anomaly in Chapter 8, are decidedly more sophisticated. Although one can speculate that many of the stat arb firms incorporate the anomaly research into their processes in some fashion, there is virtually nothing published on this subject. Most of the academic literature related to statistical arbitrage deals with the underlying mathematics and does not discuss the details of the processes used to create real world portfolios.[3]

High-Frequency Trading

High-frequency trading emerged from stat arb when performance of the stat arb strategies began to decay during 2000 to 2002 and the hedge funds doing stat arb realized that if they could execute thousands of trades before their competitors they could make a small profit on each trade. Peterson (2010) describes how this evolution took place at Citadel and Renaissance. In its current form, the success of high-frequency trading has little to do with anomalies and much to do with exploiting quirks in the regulations and policies governing POSIT and other direct access trading systems provided by the exchanges and related ECNs.

Multifactor Models

The primary use of anomaly research by professional quant investors is to create multifactor models to manage equity portfolios. Jones (2010) discusses the difficulties of tracking the total assets managed using multifactor models and estimates that the total assets have grown by a factor of 5 over the last 10 years.

Multifactor processes use one or more of the anomalies discussed in the chapters of this book to create an alpha model whose objective is to rank a universe of stocks based on the probability of outperforming a given benchmark. The alpha model is then used within an optimization framework or is provided to a portfolio manager who subjectively incorporates the ranking into his portfolio. The general methodology for creating multifactor models is well known and described in Chincarini (2008) and Fabozzi (2010) and specific techniques for the U.S. market can be found in Jacobs and Levy (1998) and for the Japanese market in Schwartz and Ziemba (2000).

The multifactor anomaly-based models are used in two types of active quant equity investment processes—market neutral and long. The market neutral processes rely on both the long and the short sides of the anomalies

---

[3]Two books are Vidyamurthy (2004) and Kestner, (2003). For interesting examples of stat arb published in some physics journals see Bertram (2010) and Wissner-Gross (2010).

to create portfolios whose objectives are absolute performance while the long processes use only the long side of the anomalies and create long portfolios whose objectives are to outperform various equity indexes.

Assets in Market Neutral Portfolios

As you read the research summarized in the chapters of this book you will quickly see that a core concept of anomaly strategies is the creation of a hedge portfolio that is both long and short based on the same anomaly. The returns of these types of portfolios, which seem to average about 10% per year, are termed market neutral, since in theory they should not depend on the direction of the broad market.

Investment organizations today offer market neutral processes as hedge funds, as separately managed institutional accounts and as mutual funds.

Hedge Funds

The objective of the equity market neutral[4] hedge funds is to produce a consistent stream of monthly returns that can be leveraged. For example if an equity market neutral process has a 10% annual return,[5] the return of the same process leveraged 3 to 1 will be over 25% per year after all costs.

According to the hedge fund data service Hedge Fund.net there are about 300 hedge funds with total assets of $42.8 billion that are classified as equity market neutral. These hedge funds are located in the United States and off shore and use both U.S. and non-U.S. equities to generate the market neutral returns. During 2010, the assets in the equity market neutral hedge funds increased by 13% due to net flows.

Separate Institutional Accounts

The objective of the separately managed equity market neutral account is to deliver an annual return equal to T Bills + 2% to 8% and a correlation of zero with other asset classes. Portfolios at the lower end of the 2–8% range may be dollar, sector, and beta neutral and are used as an alternative to cash whereas portfolios with the 8% target returns may be added to an institutional portfolio to improve the risk return characteristics of the total

---

[4]Equity market neutral is only one of a number of types of market neutral hedge funds; others use convertible bonds, merger arbitrage, and derivatives to produce market neutral returns.
[5]The Dow Jones Credit Suisse Hedge Fund Index of equity market neutral hedge funds has, in fact, generated an average return of 10% per year over the past 15 years.

portfolio. According to eVestment Alliance, which tracks the performance of separate accounts, there are 36 investment organizations that offer the equity market neutral process as separate institutional accounts, with total assets of $10.8 billion.

Mutual Funds

One might expect based on the assets in the equity market neutral hedge funds and separate accounts, that market neutral mutual funds would be quite common. However, this is not the case. Only a small percent of the 3500 equity mutual funds are market neutral.[6] As of the end of 2010, data from Strategic Insights, shows that in aggregate the market neutral mutual funds had only $2.9 billion in total assets under management, which represented less than one-tenth of 1% of the total $5,721 billion in active equity mutual fund assets.

Assets in Long Portfolios

Although the idea of a market neutral asset class may be the most interesting new concept to come out of the anomaly research, by far the largest impact of anomaly research on investing has been the creation of a large number of quant portfolios run using multifactor anomaly-based models that are designed to outperform various indexes.

These long multifactor processes are offered to institutional investors in separately managed long accounts and to individual investors in long mutual funds.

Long Separate Accounts

Table A.1, compiled by LSV Asset Management from the eVestment Alliance database of separately managed institutional investment products, shows that for some key asset classes, 20–30% of the products identify their primary

---

[6]Of the 24 mutual funds classified as market neutral by Lipper, only the following 7 seem to use multifactor processes: DWS Disciplined Market Neutral A, Vanguard Market Neutral, American Century Equity Market Neutral A, J P Morgan Market Neutral, Virtus Market Neutral A, JPM Highbridge Stat Mkt Neutral A, JPMorgan Multi-Cap Mkt Neutral A, and James Advantage Market Neutral As an example of the confusion surrounding market neutral, the mutual fund with "Market Neutral" in its name that added the most assets in 2010, the TFSMX, is not market neutral but has a significant long bias.

TABLE A.1 Number of Investment Products

Asset Class	Quant	Fundamental	% Quant
U.S. large cap value	48	150	24
U.S. large cap core	50	104	32
U.S. large cap growth	36	166	17
U.S. large cap enhanced index	47	7	84
EAFE	37	115	24

investment process as Quant,[7] whereas 80% of the enhanced index funds are quant processes.

Although this table only covers 5 of the perhaps 40 asset classes into which equity portfolios are classified, a reasonable conclusion is that 25% of all of the equity accounts managed for institutional investors employ an anomaly-based multifactor alpha model.

However, the number of investment organizations that are managing these accounts is relatively small because when an investment organization manages quant portfolios they generally manage such a portfolio in each of many asset classes. Therefore, in total there may be no more than 50 investment organizations managing long quant portfolios using multifactor models

Long Mutual Funds

The number of mutual funds using a multifactor process is not as easy to determine as the number of separate accounts because the mutual fund databases from Morningstar or ValueLine do not indicate if a mutual fund is using a quant investment process. Consequently, to identify those funds that are using a pure quant process requires one to read the text in the prospectuses. Zao (2006) did this by using software to process the prospectus text of all equity mutual funds and found that in 1993 there were 54 U.S. equity mutual funds that used a quant process and they represented 2.7% of U.S. equity mutual fund assets. By 2003 the number of quant funds had increased to 160, which was 10% of the active equity funds and 5.5% of total active equity assets.

Although we cannot easily determine the number of mutual funds that use multifactor models or the total AUM in these funds, they clearly do exist in many asset classes as shown in Table A.2.

---

[7]Funds tracked by eVestment self-identify their primary and secondary investment styles as quant or fundamental or combined.

TABLE A.2 Selected Long Mutual Funds Using Multifactor Models

Name of Fund	Ticker Symbol
Large Cap	
Blackrock Large Cap Core	MDLRX
Columbia Large Cap Core Quantitative	AQEAX
DWS Growth and Income	SUWAX
Fidelity Disciplined Equity	FDEQX
JP Morgan Intrepid America	JIAAX
Schwab Core Equity	SWANX
Vanguard Growth and Income	VQNPX
Mid Cap	
Hennessy Cornerstone Growth	HFCGX
JP Morgan Intrepid Mid Cap	PECAX
Vanguard Strategic Equity	VSEQX
Bridgeway Aggressive Investor	BRAGX
Small Cap	
American Century Small Company	ASQAX
Stratton Small Cap	STSCX
Large Cap Growth	
Blackrock LCG	MDLHX
Clavest LC Growth	CLCIX
Goldman Sachs Structured Large Cap Growth	GCVAX
Intech Risk Managed Growth	JDRAX
JP Morgan Intrepid Growth Select	JPGSX
Large Cap Value	
Blackrock LCV	MDLVX
LSV Value Equity	LSVEX
Small Growth	
Bridgeway Small Growth	BRSGX
T. Rowe Price Diversified Small Cap Growth	PRDSX
Small Value	
Bridgeway Small Value	BRSVX
Northern Small Cap Value	NOSGX

United States versus International

The foregoing brief outline of the use of multifactor models by professional investors only covers the use in the U.S. market. As can be seen from the other chapters in this book, over the last 10 years anomaly research has been published in perhaps 25 non-U.S. markets where the accounting infrastructure is extensive enough for anomalies to exist. This research has been carried out primarily by academics employed at the non-U.S. universities, many of whom were trained in the United States. In parallel with this growth of anomaly research in non-U.S. universities we can assume that multifactor investment processes have been implemented by local investment organizations active in many of these markets although no solid estimates of the size of this activity are easily available.

References

Ahmed, P., and S. Nanda. 2005. Performance of enhanced index and quantitative equity funds. *Financial Review* 40: 459–479.

Avellaneda, Marco, and J. H. Lee. 2008. Statistical arbitrage in US equity markets, *Quantitative Finance.*

Berk, J., and R. Green. 2004. Mutual funds flow and performance in rational markets. *Journal of Political Economics* 112: 1269–1295.

Bertram, W. K. 2010. Analytic solutions for optimal statistical arbitrage trading. In *Physica A: Statistical mechanics and its applications.* New York: Elsevier.

Bessembinder, Hendrick. 1998. Market efficiency and the returns to technical analysis. *Financial Management* 27 (5).

Baillie, R. T., and T. Bollerslev. 1989. Common stochastic trends in a system of exchange rates. *Journal of Finance* 44 (167).

Carhart, M. 1997. On persistence in mutual fund performance. *Journal of Finance* 52: 57–82.

Celeghin, D. (November 2005). The geeks shall inherit the Earth? *CQA Research Insight* 1 (4).

Chincarini, Ludwig B. 2006. *Quantitative equity portfolio management: An active approach to portfolio construction and management.* New York: McGraw-Hill.

Chang, E., and W. G. Lewellen. 1985. An arbitrage pricing approach to evaluating mutual fund performance. *Journal of Financial Research* 8: 15–30.

Chen, H., N. Jagadeesh, and R. Wermers. 2000. The value of active mutual fund management: An examination of the stock holdings and trades of fund managers. *Journal of Financial and Quantitative Analysis* 35: 343–368.

Daniel, K., M. Grinblatt, S. Titman, and R. Wermers. 1997. Measuring mutual fund performance with characteristic-based benchmarks. *Journal of Finance* 52: 1035–1058.

Dunis, C. L., and R. Ho. 2005. Co-integration portfolios of European equities for index tracking and market neutral strategies. *Journal of Asset Management* 6: 33.

Durbin, Michael. 2010. *All about high frequency trading.* New York: McGraw Hill.

Elliott, R. J., J. van der Hoek, and W. P. Malcolm. 2005. Pairs trading. *Quantitative Finance* 5: 271.

Ehrman, K. R. 2005. *The handbook of pairs trading: Strategies using equities, options and futures.* Hoboken, NJ: John Wiley & Sons.

Elton, E., M. Gruber, S. Das, and M. Hlavka. 1993. Efficiency with costly information: A reinterpretation of evidence for managed portfolios. *Review of Financial Studies* 6: 1–22.

Engle, R. F., and C. W. J. Granger. 1987. Co-integration and error correction representation, estimation and testing. *Econometrica* 55: 251.

Fabozzi, Frank J. (2008). Challenges in Quantitative Equity Management, CFA Institute

Fabozzi, Frank, Focardi S, and Kolm P. 2010. *Quantitative Equity Investing,* John Wiley, New York.

Fodor, A., D. T. Lawson, and D. R. Peterson. 2009. Do hedge funds arbitrage market anomalies? Available at SSRN: http://ssrn.com/abstract=1081943.

Gagnon, L., and G. A. Karolyi. 2010. Multi market trading and arbitrage. *Journal of Financial Economics* 97: 53.

Grinblatt, M., and S. Titman. 1989. Mutual fund performance: An analysis of quarterly portfolio holdings. *Journal of Business* 62: 393–416.

Grinblatt, M., and S. Titman. 1992. The persistence of mutual fund performance. *Journal of Finance* 47: 1977–1984.

Granger, C J. J. 1981. Some properties of time series data and their use in econometric model specification. *Econometrics* 12: 121.

Hansda, S. K., and P. Ray. 2003. Stock market integration and dually listed stocks. *Economic and Political Weekly* 38: 741.

Hendricks, D., J. Patel, and R. Zeckhauser. 1993. Hot hands in mutual funds: Short-run persistence of relative performance, 1974–1988. *Journal of Finance* 48: 93–130.

Ippolito, R. 1989. Efficiency with costly information: A study of mutual fund performance, 1965–1984. *Quarterly Journal of Economics* 104: 1–23.

Jacobs Levy. 1998. Disentangling equity returns. *Financial Analyst Journal* 44. 3 May–June 1968.

Jensen, M. C. 1968. The performance of mutual funds in the period 1945–1964. *Journal of Finance* 23: 389–416.

Jones, R. C. 2010. Maybe it really is different this time. *Journal of Portfolio Management* (Winter 2011), 36 (2): 60–72.

Kestner, L. 2003. *Quantitative trading strategies.* New York: McGraw Hill.

Kothari, S., and J. Warner. 2001. Evaluating mutual fund performance. *Journal of Finance* 56: 1985–2010.

Kroner, K. F., and J. Sultan. 1993. Time varying distributions and dynamic hedging with foreign currency futures. *Journal of Financial and Quantitative Analysis* 28: 535.

Koumkwa, S., and R. Susmel. 2008. Arbitrage and convergence, evidence from Mexican ADRs. *Journal of Applied Economics* XI: 399.

Lin, Y., M. McCrae, and C. Gulati. 2006. Loss protection in pairs trading through minimum profit bounds, a co-integration approach. *Journal of Applied Mathematical Decision Science* 2006: 1.

Liu, P. C., and G. S. Maddala. 1992. Rationality of survey data and tests for market efficiency in the foreign exchange markets. *Journal International Money and Finance* 11: 366.

Malkiel, B. 1995. Returns from investing in equity mutual funds, 1971 to 1991. *Journal of Finance* 50: 549–572.

Monoyios, M., and L. Sarno. 2002. Mean reversion in stock futures markets: A nonlinear analysis *Journal of Futures Market* 22: 285.

Peterson, S. 2010. *The Quants.* New York: Crown Business.

Pole, Andrew. 2007. *Statistical arbitrage: Algorithmic trading insights and techniques.* Hoboken, NJ: John Wiley & Sons.

Gregory-Allen, Russell B., Hany A. Shawky, and Jeffrey Stangl. 2009. Quantitative vs. fundamental analysis in institutional money management: Where's the beef. *Journal of Investing* (Winter) 18 (4): 42–52.

Schwartz, S. L, Ziemba, W. T. (2000). "Predicting Returns on the Tokyo Stock Exchange." In *Security Market Imperfections in World Wide Equity Markets*, edited by D. B. Keim and W. T. Ziemba, 492–511. Cambridge University Press.

Vidyamurthy, G. 2004. *Pairs trading: Quantitative methods and analysis.* Hoboken, NJ: John Wiley & Sons.

Wermers, R. 2000. Mutual fund performance: An empirical decomposition into stock-picking talent, style, transaction costs, and expenses. *Journal of Finance* 55: 1655–1695.

Wermers, R., T. Yao and J. Zhao. 2007. The investment value of mutual fund portfolio. AD Wissner-Gross disclosure. Working Paper, University of Maryland.

Wissner-Gross, A. D. 2010. Relativistic statistical arbitrage. *Physical Review E*, pre.aps.org.

Zhao, J. 2006. Quant jocks and tire kickers: Does the stock selection process matter? Available at: http://finance.eller.arizona.edu/documents/doctoral/JZhao.JobMarketPaper.pdf.

About the Contributors

Daniel Cohen, PhD

Daniel Cohen is an associate professor of accounting at the School of Management at the University of Texas at Dallas. He holds a PhD in accounting from the Kellogg School of Management at Northwestern University. Throughout his academic career, Daniel has been on the faculty at the University of Southern California (Marshall School of Business), New York University (Stern School of Business), and University of Pennsylvania (Wharton School of Business). Cohen's research focuses on issues related to capital markets, financial reporting and disclosures, discretionary accounting choices, corporate governance, federal and state regulation, and analyst earnings forecasts. Cohen has published numerous articles in leading academic journals such as *Journal of Accounting and Economics, Journal of Accounting, Auditing and Finance, Review of Accounting Studies,* and the *Accounting Review.* Cohen is also an associate editor at the *Journal of Accounting and Economics* and serves on the editorial boards of *Contemporary Accounting Research, The International Journal of Accounting,* and *The Accounting Review.*

Patricia M. Dechow, PhD

Patricia M. Dechow is the Donald H. and Ruth F. Seiler Professor of Public Accounting at the Haas School of Business, University of California, Berkeley. She has held faculty positions at the University of Michigan and the Wharton School at the University of Pennsylvania. She has a PhD in Accounting and Finance from the University of Rochester and a Bachelor of Commerce (First Class Honors) from the University of Western Australia. Her research interests focus on the nature and purpose of accounting accruals, evaluating the quality of earnings, the use of accounting information by investors, and the effect of analysts' forecasts on investor perceptions. Her research has been published in *The Accounting Review, Journal of*

317

Accounting and Economics, Journal of Accounting Research, Journal of Financial Economics, Review of Accounting Studies, and *Contemporary Accounting Research.* She has been an Editor for *The Accounting Review,* and is currently an Associate Editor for the *Review of Accounting Studies* and *Management Science.*

Ian Dogan, PhD

Ian Dogan has a PhD in financial economics with a specialization in insider trading. Dogan has provided consulting services to institutional investors and hedge funds, and managed a $200+ million fund using a strategy he developed utilizing insider transactions. He is also the founder of InsiderMonkey.com, a financial web site that provides free real-time insider-trading data and daily commentaries about corporate insiders and prominent hedge fund managers. Insider Monkey serves the outcome of the methodologies developed by Dogan to ordinary investors who don't have access to academic quality research and tools to shape their investments

Lee M. Dunham, PhD, CFA

Lee Dunham is currently an assistant professor of finance at Creighton University. Dunham earned his PhD in Finance from the University of Nebraska–Lincoln. Prior to his PhD training at the University of Nebraska–Lincoln, Dunham earned a Master's of Science in Financial Economics from the University of New Orleans (2005) and a Master's of Business Administration from the University of Missouri–St. Louis (2002). Dunham also holds a Bachelor's of Science in Business Administration from the University of Missouri–St. Louis (1999). In addition, Dunham has also earned the CFA designation. Prior to working in academia, Dunham worked for Commerce Trust Company in St. Louis, where he co-managed the trust company's portfolio of all closely held securities held in trust.

Dunham's research interests include dividend theory, asset price volatility, behavioral finance, and mutual fund performance. Dunham currently teaches advanced corporate finance at the undergraduate level as well as fixed income and derivative courses in the Master's of Security Analysis and Portfolio Management program at Creighton University. His work has been published in a number of journals, including the *Journal of Banking and Finance,* the *Journal of Economics and Finance,* and the *Journal of Index Investing.*

Constantine Dzhabarov

Constantine S. Dzhabarov is a research analyst at Alpha Lake Financial Analytics Corp in Vancouver, BC, Canada. His MBA with honors is from Atkinson Graduate School of Management, Salem, Oregon. He has more than 10 years experience in theoretical development and practical testing of intermarket financial trading models. He has traded futures and options for private and institutional accounts since 2001. His research is in security market imperfections and he published in the *Journal of Portfolio Management* in 2010 an update on stock market anomalies and a survey of U.S. and worldwide seasonal anomalies with Professor William T. Ziemba. Together they run private accounts based on seasonal anomalies.

Ian Gow, PhD

Ian Gow is an assistant professor of business administration at the Harvard Business School. His primary research interests relate to the use of accounting information in markets and contracts, valuation, regulation of capital markets, and corporate governance.

Prior to joining the Harvard faculty, Ian was an Assistant Professor of Accounting and Management at Kellogg School of Management, at Northwestern University and prior to that he worked in the Global Valuation and Accounting Team at Morgan Stanley and with consulting firm Stern Stewart, where he advised companies on the use of economic value-added (EVA) in performance measurement, valuation, and incentive compensation. He has also worked in the General Motors Treasurer's office in New York and with Andersen Consulting in Sydney. He received a PhD in Business Administration from Stanford University, an MBA with distinction from Harvard Business School, and a degree in commerce and a law degree from the University of New South Wales (Australia).

Mozaffar Khan, PhD

Mozaffar Khan is an assistant professor at the Carlson School of Management, University of Minnesota. From 2005–2010, he was an assistant professor at the MIT Sloan School of Management. Khan is a financial economist with expertise in asset pricing and investments, corporate financing policy, the recent financial crisis, and financial reform and regulation, corporate financial reporting, cost accounting, strategic cost management, and performance measurement. He is an associate editor of the *Journal of Accounting and Economics* and the *Asia-Pacific Journal of Accounting and Economics*, and holds a PhD from the University of Toronto.

Natalya V. Khimich

Natalya V. Khimich is a PhD student at the Haas School of Business, University of California, Berkeley. She has a Master of Science in Physics and Applied Mathematics from the Nizhny Novgorod State University, Russia and a Master of Science in Accounting from the University of Central Florida. Her research interests focus on the role of accounting information in stock price formation, the forecasting of earnings using financial statement analysis, and accounting for innovation and intangible assets.

Oleg Rytchkov, PhD

Oleg Rytchkov is an assistant professor at the Fox School of Business and Management at Temple University. He earned a doctorate degree in financial economics from the Sloan School of Management, MIT (2007) and a doctorate degree in physics from the Steklov Mathematical Institute (2001). Prior to joining the Fox School in 2009, Rytchkov was on faculty at the McCombs School of Business, University of Texas at Austin. At Temple University, Rytchkov teaches classes in investment management and business econometrics for MBA and doctoral students. He is an active researcher with interests in theoretical and empirical asset pricing, functioning of capital markets, and financial econometrics. Rytchkov has presented at various seminars and top academic conferences including the Western Finance Association meetings, European Finance Association meetings, and Financial Management Association meetings, and published his research in peer-refereed journals. Rytchkov is a member of the Financial Management Association and European Finance Association.

George Serafeim, PhD

George Serafeim is an assistant professor of business administration at the Harvard Business School. Serafeim's research interests are international, focusing on capital markets and on the social, environmental, and governance performance of firms. His work has been published in prestigious academic journals such as the *Review of Accounting Studies*, *Journal of Accounting Research*, *Best Paper Proceedings of the Academy of Management* and *Financial Analysts Journal*. Serafeim earned his doctorate in business administration at Harvard Business School, and his master's degree in accounting and finance from the London School of Economics and Political Science.

Richard G. Sloan, PhD

Richard G. Sloan is the L. H. Penney Professor of Accounting at the University of California, Berkeley's Haas School of Business. From 2006 to 2008, Sloan was Managing Director of Equity Research at Barclays Global Investors. Previously, Sloan was the Victor L. Bernard PricewaterhouseCoopers Collegiate Professor of Accounting, Professor of Finance, and Director of the Tozzi Electronic Finance Center at the University of Michigan's Ross School of Business. He also served for five years on the faculty of the University of Pennsylvania's Wharton School. Professor Sloan's research focuses on the role of accounting information in investment decisions and is published in leading accounting, finance, and economics journals. He is widely recognized and has received numerous awards for his research on earnings quality. He currently serves as managing editor for the *Review of Accounting Studies* and is the author (with Russell Lundholm) of the textbook *Equity Valuation and Analysis*. He holds a PhD from the University of Rochester and a BCom from the University of Western Australia.

Daniel Taylor, PhD

Daniel Taylor is an assistant professor at The Wharton School of the University of Pennsylvania. His research focuses on the effect of financial reporting on capital markets, corporate governance, and managerial incentives. His research appears in leading academic journals including *The Accounting Review, Journal of Accounting and Economics, Journal of Accounting Research, Journal of Financial Economics*, and *Marketing Science*. He regularly attends and presents at professional meetings and was previously awarded a Deloitte Foundation Fellowship. He holds a bachelor's degree in Economics from the University of Delaware, a master's degree in Economics from Duke University, and a PhD in Business from Stanford University.

Tzachi Zach, PhD

Tzachi Zach is an assistant professor of accounting at the Fisher College of Business at Ohio State University. He has a PhD in business administration (accounting) from the Simon School of Business at the University of Rochester. He obtained his BA and MA from Tel Aviv University. Tzachi's research has been published in the *The Accounting Review, Review of*

Financial Studies, Review of Accounting Studies, Journal of Accounting, Auditing, and Finance, and *Journal of Accounting & Economics.* He has served as an ad-hoc reviewer for the *The Journal of Accounting and Economics, The Accounting Review, Journal of Accounting Research, Contemporary Accounting research, Review of Accounting Studies, Review of Finance,* and the *Journal of Finance.*

Leonard Zacks, PhD

Leonard Zacks has been CEO of Zacks Investment Research since 1978. Prior to co-founding Zacks, Len was a quant equity analyst at A.G. Becker & Co. in Chicago and an analyst at the Rand Corporation in Los Angeles. He received a PhD in operations research (1969), an MS in physics (1967), and a BS in mathematics (1965) all from MIT. Zacks Investment Research, whose original mission was to create more accurate consensus estimates, now provides a wide range of investment information and backtesting software services to individual and professional investors. Its investment management subsidiary, Zacks Investment Management, manages $1.9 billion for individuals and institutions using multifactor models based, in part, on anomaly research.

William T. Ziemba, PhD

William Ziemba is the Alumni Professor (Emeritus) of Financial Modeling and Stochastic Optimization in the Sauder School of Business, University of British Columbia where he taught from 1968 to 2006. His PhD is from the University of California, Berkeley. He has been a visiting professor at Cambridge, Oxford, London School of Economics, University of Reading (ICMA Centre), and Warwick in the U.K., at Stanford, UCLA, Berkeley, MIT, University of Washington, and University of Chicago in the United States, Universities of Bergamo, Venice, and Luiss in Italy, University of Zurich, University of Tsukuba in Japan, and the National University of Singapore. He has been a consultant to a number of leading financial institutions including the Frank Russell Company, Morgan Stanley, Buchanan Partners, RAB Hedge Funds, Gordon Capital and Private International Wealth Management. His research is in asset-liability management, portfolio theory and practice, security market imperfections, Japanese and Asian financial markets, sports and lottery investments, and applied stochastic programming. He has written 8 books and over 100 articles on quantitative finance, the latest book being *The Kelly Capital Growth Investment Criterion* with legendary hedge-fund trader Edward Thorp and Leonard MacLean.

Index

328   Index